D1446622

Russian Dramatic Theory from Pushkin to the Symbolists

University of Texas Press Slavic Series, No. 5

General Editor: Michael Holquist
Advisory Board: Robert L. Belknap
John Bowlt
Edward J. Brown
Victor Erlich
Robert L. Jackson
Hugh McLean
Sidney Monas
I. R. Titunik
Edward Wasiolek
René Wellek

The Dan Danciger Publication Series

Russian Dramatic Theory from Pushkin to the Symbolists

An Anthology

Translated and edited by Laurence Senelick

University of Texas Press, Austin

Requests for permission to reproduce material from this work
should be sent to Permissions, University of Texas Press,
Box 7819, Austin, Texas 78712.

Library of Congress Cataloging in Publication Data
Main entry under title:
Russian dramatic theory from Pushkin to the Symbolists.
   (University of Texas Press Slavic series; no. 5)
   Bibliography: p.
   Includes index.
   1. Dramatic criticism—Soviet Union—Addresses,
essays, lectures.   2. Theater—Soviet Union—History—
19th century—Sources.   I. Senelick, Laurence.   II. Series.
PN1707.R8   891.72'009   81-1718
ISBN 0-292-77025-1   AACR2

For Yuly Iosifovich Kagarlitsky, scholar and enthusiast

Contents

x   *Contents*

Foreword

The Russian drama, though officially little more than two hundred and fifty years old, not only has distinguished itself as one of the most vital and influential in world literature, with a theatrical tradition equally imaginative and impressive, but has developed around it a stimulating critical literature. From the first, the theater in Russia bore the responsibility of educating the people and instilling civic virtues, ideas of nationality and progressive opinions; on a less teleological plane, it was an arena where the latest aesthetic ideas were popularized. Russian dramatists and dramatic critics felt obliged to keep the theater aware of its duties; their commentary bristles with admonitions, injunctions, advice and mockery meant to direct the drama into the proper channels. At the end of the nineteenth century, during the so-called "Crisis of the Theater," serious thinkers attempted to provide a new theoretical basis that would allow Russian drama and theater successfully to confront the problems of a world in turmoil and to surmount old conventions and habits so that they might be the art forms of a new Jerusalem.

The concept for this volume arose from my graduate seminars in Russian drama and the frustrations encountered in finding a convenient compendium of major critical statements in English. (No anthology of dramatic criticism exists in Russian, and some of the items included here are hard to find in the original, so the bringing together of many diffuse pieces may interest the Russian specialist as well.) In the American anthologies of dramatic criticism most readily accessible, Russian culture before the Soviet period is represented only by snippets from Chekhov's letters and excerpts from Tolstoy's well-known *What Is Art?* Since Chekhov's epistolary remarks were very much *ad hominem* and as criticism relate to specific instances, and since Tolstoy's fulminations were in their own time thought bizarre and retrograde, they constitute an uncharacteristic sampling of Russian writing on the drama.

The selections included here range from abstruse speculations on the nature of art and reality to evaluations of specific performers, but each has been chosen because it involves broad questions of style, genre, the nature of the theater and dramatic viability. Little theatrical "reviewing" is included because my emphasis is literary rather than historical, and even Pushkin's and Chekhov's articles on the stage of their time extend to wider issues of national art. However, in many of these pieces, the theater is taken to be an organic adjunct of literary drama, and the "Crisis of the Theater" essayists find it necessary to establish a *raison d'être* for the theater's existence before prescribing a proper repertory. This collection, then, is intended as a conspectus of Russian thought on drama and theater over the course of the nineteenth and early twentieth centuries, covering major writers and several genres of critical writing: the discursive essay, the lyrical effusion, the taxonomic analysis, the polemic, the retrospective and the critique in dialogue. Certain themes indicated in the Introduction recur with an almost fugal regularity and variation.

I have also chosen these items with an eye toward the Russian repertory, which explains the omission of much interesting criticism of Shakespeare and European tragedy. (Obviously Vyacheslav Ivanov's essay on Greek tragedy is an exception to the rule, but it is such a central statement of Ivanov's influential ideas on Dionysian drama that its presence may help explain his followers' speculations on the mysterium.) As the references to Ibsen and Maeterlinck begin to proliferate, the growing importance of avant-garde Western drama can be seen.

I begin with Pushkin because it is with his writings that Russian drama enters the mainstream of European literature; although his fragmentary comments do not bulk large in the canon of his works, they are important addenda to the romantic debate on tragedy and historical drama. There follows a nearly contemporary running commentary on the Russian drama by its masters: Pushkin on his predecessors; Gogol on himself (typically); Belinsky on Pushkin, Gogol and Griboedov; Bely and Andreev on Chekhov; Annensky on Gorky; and the symbolists on one another. I have ended before the Revolution, for although a great deal of interesting criticism emerges from the Marxist and formalist schools after 1917, these approaches have already been better served in translation than have the symbolists. Postrevolutionary criticism which takes off from new premises deserves a volume to itself.

No anthologist can avoid omissions. In this particular case, the original selection had to be drastically pruned to meet the exigencies of space and economics. Spatial limitations compelled the exclusion of important long articles already available in translation, such as Dobrolyubov's pieces on Ostrovsky and Meyerhold's "On Theater: Toward a History and Technique." Ostrovsky himself wrote prolifically on the theater, but his writings deal mainly with administrative problems of organizing dramatic schools and developing an audience. Other pieces by Bely, Evreinov, Blok and Annensky might be preferred to those that appear here, and other interesting thinkers like Chulkov and Remizov would under other circumstances deserve a place. It is hoped that the Introduction will serve to fill in the gaps.

En revanche, each piece included appears in its entirety, for in speculative writing, it is of prime importance that the author's train of thought, choice of examples and even digressions can be followed exactly. Many of these pieces are translated complete for the first time, and the translations are intended to be faithful. When an author, like Sologub, is willfully obscure and allusive, the editor hopes the notes and glosses will clarify matters.

To this end the annotation is ample in providing context, and in most cases I have sought to avoid the laconic "So-and-so-vich (1800–1849), a writer" as unhelpful and pointless. Because I expect any reader of this collection to be somewhat grounded in either dramatic literature or Russian literature, I have not glossed such commonly known names as Molière, Dostoevsky or Euripides or provided identification for such familiar characters as Macbeth and Anna Karenina.

The system of transliteration is addressed not to Slavic scholars but to the ordinary student who is more at home with Chekhov and Meyerhold than with Čexov and Mejerxol'd. However, I have steered clear of old-fashioned French and German spellings, and so refer to Chaikovsky and Shalyapin, rather than Tschaikowski and Chaliapine. For Slavicists, a more formal method of transliteration is used in the bibliography.

I gratefully acknowledge the enthusiasm and encouragement offered this project from its inception by Professors Donald Fanger and Jurij Striedter of the Department of Slavic Languages and Literature of Harvard University; the keen critical faculties of Professor Simon Karlinsky of the Department of Slavic Languages and Literature of the University of California at Berkeley, and his valuable suggestions on lexical choices; the loan of a rare copy of Evreinov's "Vvedenie v monodramu" by Alma Law of the Russian Institute of Columbia University; the warm welcome given the project by Iris Tillman Hill, former humanities editor of the University of Texas

Press, and the even warmer aid and abetment of her successor, Suzanne Comer, whose support has been unflagging; the yeomanly labors of Michael McDowell, Jeffrey Starr and Patricia Fina, who typed and duplicated several stages of manuscript; and the patient indulgence of seven years' worth of Tufts University graduate students on whom the early drafts of these translations were first inflicted.

Introduction

I

If one stretches a point, the first Russian writer on the drama may be reckoned Avraamy, bishop of Suzdal, who left circumstantial accounts of the mystery plays of the Annunciation and the Ascension which he beheld at a synod in Florence in 1439. His narrative described the performance and its trappings, quoted from the script, outlined the plot and in short provided a reasonable equivalent of a sound newspaper review. Awed and delighted by the unaccustomed spectacle (the bulk of his remarks is devoted to the pulley system by which the angels were hoisted and lowered), the bishop failed to be critical. He concluded his account with the feckless apology, "I have described this to the best of my ability, but one cannot do it justice, for it was so wondrous and ineffable. Amen."[1] This indiscriminate receptivity characterizes Russian writing on the theater well into the eighteenth century, for the objects of scrutiny were few; there was no Russian drama outside of folk plays (beneath criticism), church tropes (above criticism) and court spectacles (beyond criticism). Even after the foundation of the first professional acting company in 1756 and the beginnings of an indigenous repertory, criticism remained tentative. Court gazettes and budgets of news reported but did not appraise, and one can find perspicacious commentary only in the more private agencies of letters and diaries, and in works such as satires and the prefaces of printed plays, aimed at connoisseurs of literature; in the prefaces the playwrights strove, as they invariably do, to justify their techniques, precondition their audiences, apostrophize their posterity and denigrate their rivals.

As a latecomer, indigenous Russian drama was hampered by its legacies from the West. Peter the Great had favored German culture, Anna Ioannovna Italian and Catherine the Great the French of the Enlightenment; outmoded aesthetic fashions were worn as the latest style in literature and art. At a time when Lessing was directing his compatriots from Racine toward Shakespeare, and Diderot was proposing a *genre sérieux* in prose to replace the turgid pomposities of verse drama, the Russian theater was still encumbered by faulty translations and patchy adaptations of neoclassic tragedy and Molièrean comedy. Theater had begun as an exotic import, and the run-of-the-mill writer could see no connection between it and ordinary Russian life; foreign imprimatur was sought as a guarantee of quality. It is significant that the first Russian periodical devoted wholly to the theater was published in German as *Russische Theatralien* (1789). Thus, with a polite literature just a-borning, criticism had either to concentrate on foreign works or to use them as a standard of comparison by which to measure the native productions. This helps to explain the medley of attraction and indignation whenever criticism had to deal with anything in the slightest degree original or out of the common.

Attempts were made to Russify the stage. Despite his utter reliance on the codices of Boileau (his "Epistle on the Art of Poetry" is a patent imitation of *L'Art poétique*), Aleksandr Sumarokov (1717–1777) tried in his tragedies to clap neoclassic armor and periwigs onto heroes of medieval Russian history. Somewhat defensively, he justified his imitations by declaring that, when he began writing in the 1730s,

> we had no poets yet, nor was there anyone from whom to learn. I traversed unguided what seemed a dense forest, which hid the haunt of the Muses from my sight, and though I owe a great deal to Racine, I took him into account only after I had emerged from the forest and the mount of Parnassus had hoved into view. But Racine was French and could not instruct me in the Russian language. So far as the Russian language, purity of style, poetry and prose are concerned, I am obliged wholly to myself.[2]

Sumarokov and his fellow dramatist Mikhail Kheraskov had begun writing plays as a leisure activity as students in the Noble Cadet Corps, thereby foreshadowing the great increase in dramatic and theatrical activity that occurred after 1762, when Catherine released the nobility from many of its responsibilities to the state. These aristocratic origins and recreational associations of the literary drama removed it from the immediate concerns of Russian society, a situation which later criticism felt called upon to redress; at the same time the drama was freed, like the nobility, from court duties, and under the proper circumstances, it could learn to speak with an individual voice.

An incipient rebellion against foreign fashion could be sensed in stage comedy, where the foibles of Russian life were depicted and Francophilia flayed. The leading foe of European drama was P. A. Plavilshchikov (1760–1812), an actor and playwright whose essay "The Theater," which appeared in the *Spectator* (*Zritel'*) in 1792, was a manifesto for a national drama.

> What boots it to a Russian to know that some Tatar Genghis Khan conquered China and performed many noble exploits there? It is far more sensible for children to see that their father is great, rather than someone else. . . . What care we about the irreconcilable feud presented in *The Tombs of Verona*? We must first learn about what happened in our own country. Kozma Minin the tradesman is a character most deserving of stage celebrity. . . . we have our own manners, our own nature, and consequently, we ought to have our own tastes.[3]

Not content with pointing up the futility of neo-Aristotelian unities and translations at third hand, Plavilshchikov prescribed Russian history as the most suitable theme for tragedy and the life of the merchant and peasant classes as ideal subject matter for comedy. He himself composed some plays set in these milieux to serve as examples.

Plavilshchikov's polemical refusal to appreciate any foreign work was not immediately seconded by theatrical journalists. They remained for the most part hacks, who hoped to curry favor with the theater administration, influential litterateurs or pretty actresses. But his aggressive insularity and insistence on "buying Russian" became a keynote of the Slavophile writers of the Nikolaean era and reached a crescendo in the debate about Ostrovsky. Without using the term, Plavilshchikov had opened the discussion of *narodnost'*, or national quality, to which all serious Russian writing about drama addresses itself in one way or another throughout the nineteenth century, whether it be Pushkin seeking a means to dramatize his country's history, Gogol trying to use local manners as a basis for comedy, Grigoriev extolling the "popular" aspect of Ostrovsky or Chekhov poking fun at the outlandish style of Sarah Bernhardt. Prince Pyotr Vyazemsky's inceptive definition of *narodnost'* as an "expression of a people's character and opinions" was sufficiently vague to embrace both descriptions of the peasantry (*narod* as common people) and expressions of chauvinist sentiment (*narod* as nation). How could either be served by stage conventions and types that had been evolved in other, often inimical cultures? The eighteenth century had crammed Russian characters, language and history into the tight lacing of stock dramatic types, alexandrine couplets and stereotypic idioms, ready-made plots, rigid act and scene structure and decorous stage behavior. Breaking the old rules might best be accomplished after new guidelines had been laid down and new critical principles established: hence the urgent need for dramatic theory and manifestos by the end of Catherine's reign.

But a major impediment to the development of lively and outspoken dramatic criticism was the special censorship directed at the theater. All performers of the imperial state theaters were designated as personal chattels of the emperor and consequently held inviolable by public rebuke, although they might be subject to abuse and even corporal punishment within the organization. A government ukase of 1815 declared, "Opinions concerning the imperial theater and the actors in His Majesty's service are taken to be inappropriate in any periodical."[4] The result was the bland and noncommital notices of theatrical activity during the reign of Alexander I. The code of censorship endorsed by his successor Nicholas I after the Decembrist uprising of 1825 was ultra-strict, and its punctilio spelled ruin for a great many literary journals in the 1830s. The *Moscow Telegraph* (*Moskovskiy telegraf*), for example, was banned in 1834 for its dispraise of Nestor Kukolnik's fulsomely patriotic melodrama *The Hand of the Most High Has Saved the Fatherland,* the emperor's favorite play. And just as the censorship banished from the boards original works like *Boris Godunov* and *Woe from Wit,* it likewise prevented criticism that might have nurtured such works.

However, in the same year that the Nikolaean code was instigated, the governmentally favored journalist Faddey Bulgarin (1798–1859) argued that printed criticism was the only means by which good performers might receive their just deserts; critiques, he insisted in an appeal to the authorities, were therefore well intentioned, and any true critic would avoid "offensive dealing in personalities."[5] His daily newspaper the *Northern Bee* (*Severnaya pchyola*) received permission to publish theatrical reviews on the days following performances, and other journals followed suit. Bulgarin's intimacy with the government led him to apportion praise and blame, if not by personality, at least in accordance with his view of the political reliability of authors, a critical tenet which, unhappily, has remained a constant in Russian letters. Like Gwendolen in *The*

Importance of Being Earnest, he and his fellows found that the injunction to speak one's mind was as much a pleasure as a moral duty.

II

Vissarion Belinsky's statement in 1834 that *"we have no literature"*[6] might as easily read "we have no criticism," and certainly no dramatic criticism worthy of the name. It might be argued that the lack of any profound or perspicacious criticism was in fact a boon; it failed to prevent the emergence of three masterpieces—*Woe from Wit, Boris Godunov* and *The Inspector*—whose authors were free to develop their own ideas of dramatic structure and characterization, unhindered by a universally accepted canon of taste. However much these plays diverge from the standards of European drama, they are less a rebellion against conventional norms than unhampered expressions of the playwrights' personally evolved ideas. Griboedov, Pushkin and Gogol had weighed and found wanting contemporary modes of drama; what they had to say could not be said within the formulaic confines of traditional genres, and so they ignored them. The resultant plays were themselves more effective in demolishing outworn forms than any theory, no matter how carefully constructed and boldly enunciated, could have been.

From his early youth, Aleksandr Pushkin (1799–1837) had been an ardent fan of the theater, but his angle of vision shifted from that of spectator to practitioner after his detention at his estate Mikhailovskoe (1824–1826). There he took a pragmatic interest in the theory of tragedy and popular drama as he began work on *Boris Godunov.* Pushkin's plays are the only works which bore the impress of his critical opinions during his lifetime; although often intended for publication, his critical writings never saw print but remained in manuscript (hence the fragmentary nature of so many pieces), occasionally read by intimates, and unpublished until the second half of the nineteenth century, by which time the stage had already been influenced by Gogol and Ostrovsky.

The Pushkin of "My Remarks on the Russian Theater" is still the knowing man-about-town of his first years in Petersburg, but some important critical issues are concealed beneath what looks like a casual record of current performances. Although purporting to be a *catalogue raisonné* of actors (and especially actresses) on the Petersburg stage, it begins with an inquiry into the nature of the audience. The drama, as the only form of literature which an illiterate can apprehend immediately, was of considerable importance in educating a backward people; Gogol's later insistence that the theater be a rostrum or pulpit became a rallying cry for progressive reformers, and the Moscow Maly Theater was known by the middle of the century as the "other Moscow University." Pushkin's perspective is different: how can an actor—and by extension, a dramatist—be inspired by the frivolous, unresponsive audience of dandies and bureaucrats who fill the first rows of the stalls? Only a discerning, receptive audience can judge quality and assist in the development of a truly valuable theater.

By lauding Semyonova as the best Russian tragedienne, Pushkin was raking through the embers of a fiery debate that had raged in 1808/9, when the French actress Mlle. George had toured Russia. Battle lines were drawn between critics who valued George for her affecting classicism and scorned Semyonova as a pale copy and those who showed off their patriotism by decrying George's Gallic singsong and praising Semyonova's native gifts. Vasily Zhukovsky (1783–1852), forerunner of the romantic movement, sedulously analyzed George's acting in a series of notices in the *Messenger of Europe* (*Vestnik Evropy*, 1809), concluding that her inner coldness vitiated her technique by failing to arouse in the spectator an emotion equal to the drama's meaning. Declamation was not enough. This became the central issue of critical debate on Russian acting for almost a century. Petersburg was taken to be the home of highly technical, polished but essentially unimpassioned actors like Karatygin and Sosnitsky, Moscow as the home of impetuous, moving but uneven actors like Mochalov and Shchepkin. When Rachel, the last great paragon of neoclassic declamation, arrived on tour in 1853/4, the debate flared up again; but by that time, a more natural Russian acting style was the order of the day, and she seemed to the connoisseurs to be a throwback of genius rather than a model for emulation.[7] Pushkin, although hardly a declared romantic in 1820, nonetheless came down squarely on the side of Semyonova and of sensibility over artificiality, of impulse over calculation.

These early notes also articulate Pushkin's dissatisfaction with the Russian repertory; like so many of his contemporaries, he turned to Shakespeare for inspiration. Vladimir Nabokov was at great pains in his notes to *Evgeny Onegin* to prove that Pushkin knew little English, and certainly it is unlikely that the poet was master enough of the language to read Shakespeare in the original. He was first acquainted with Shakespeare's plays in Letourneur's French version and knew thoroughly François Guizot's critical preface with its characterization of Shakespeare as variegated, rich in detail, nonconsecutive but versatile, his dramas founded on "unity of impression." As late as 1825, while at work on *Godunov*, Pushkin complained of his own lack of expertise in English. At the same time, he was steeped in A. W. Schlegel's *Lectures on Dramatic Art and Literature*; Schlegel's emphasis on inherent national peculiarities that must be fostered by the literary treatment of history obviously was reflected in Pushkin's remarks on popular drama. Pushkin also seems to have adopted Schlegel's view of Shakespeare as incomparable at portraying the diversity of feelings within a dramatic character, and as a psychologist who realized that personality was not something fixed and homogeneous but an organism fluctuating with circumstances and harboring sharp contradictions. Certainly Schlegel's enthusiasm prompted Pushkin's remark in a letter: "(Je n'ai pas lu Calderon ni Vega) mais quel homme que ce Schakespeare [sic]! j'en reviens pas. Comme Byron le tragique est mesquin devant lui!"[8] It led him further to assert in the rough draft of a preface to *Godunov* that Shakespeare's drama presents a better model for the Russian theater than do Racine's courtly tragedies.

But what keeps Pushkin's remarks on popular drama from being a mere paraphrase of Schlegel or a Russian recension of Lessing's *Hamburg Dramaturgy* and Stendhal's *Racine et Shakespeare* is the emphasis on *narodnost'*. Drama's origins in the public square mean that, Antaeus-like, it must come back to its earthy beginnings to take strength. Even so, mere content will not suffice. Alluding to works which had defined *narodnost'* as the exploitation of national themes and heroes, Pushkin had animadverted, unconsciously echoing Plavilshchikov,

> *What is "narodny" in the Petriad or Rossiad except the names?* . . . What is "narodny" in Kseniya, discoursing . . . in iambic hexameter with a confidante in the middle of Dimitry's camp? . . . Climate, type of government, religion lend each people a particular physiognomy, which is more or less *reflected* in the glass of poesy. There is a pattern of ideas and feelings, a myriad of habits, beliefs and customs appertaining exclusively to a given people.[9]

Turning to Pogodin's manuscript tragedy based on Karamzin's history of the Russian state, Pushkin applauded the material treated. The situation of Martha the Seneschal's Wife is rich in dramatic contradictions: Russia undeniably benefited from consolidation by

Ioann III, but the independence of Novgorod perished in the process. Just such a complication of values provides the tragic quotient that enables a history play to be more than mere chronicle. Martha is right in defending her city's autonomy, Ioann is right in demanding subservience to a bigger idea of the Russian nation. Not only does the clash of two such principles provide high drama and even tragedy in the Hegelian sense; it can promote an understanding of the forces that created modern Russia. But the next step is to find the form that best contains this struggle, and here Shakespeare's example is useful and no more. Imitation Shakespeare cannot substitute for a wholly indigenous form. Pushkin's own *Boris Godunov* yields nothing to critics who seek in it a kind of failed *Macbeth*, for the poet's wrestling with blank verse and a loose Elizabethan alternation of scenes are less vital than his view of the Russian people as the central hero and of a national destiny worked out through the fates of Boris and the false Dmitry.

Hence, Pushkin's objection to neoclassic drama was not so much formal as substantive. If alexandrines and confidants bespeak the French civilization of the *grand siècle*, well and good; but the Russian stage has to incarnate the Russian temperament.

III

"To my mind," Pushkin wrote in his diary (7 April 1835), "Gogol began the history of Russian criticism." He was referring specifically to the article "On the Progress of Periodical Literature," but Nikolay Gogol (1809–1852) had no doctrinaire program to advance at this early stage of his career. Of the three camps into which literary criticism of the 1830s and 1840s might be divided, Gogol was closest in sympathy to that headed by his friend S. P. Shevyryov, the patrician ideologue of the *Muscovite* (*Moskvityanin*), who regarded Europe as decadent and therefore a bad example for Russian artists. The second camp, the more folk-oriented Slavophiles—led by S. T. Aksakov, another of Gogol's intimates—agreed that Western art was misleading, but they disagreed with Shevyryov on the matter of blind loyalty to government measures; their touchstone in art was idealism. The materialistic critics, of whom Belinsky—a zealous champion of Gogol's writing—was foremost, opposed both Slavophile coteries as reactionary. But for all his associations, Gogol steered clear of membership in any camp and followed an idiosyncratic path. His critical *aperçus* are emotionally charged, highly personal responses, often couched in rhapsodical or comical rhetoric.

Much of his criticism is special pleading, intended to clear the way for his own works. And nowhere is this more the case than in his comments on the theater.

In "Petersburg Notes for 1836," as Dr. Johnson said of metaphysical poetry, "the most heterogenous ideas are linked by violence together." Some of this is due to the patchwork construction of the essay. The first part, written in 1835, is a classic characterization of Moscow as a slipshod homebody and Petersburg as a buttoned-up gadabout; the second, on the theatrical scene—begun in 1836—was wholly reworked while Gogol was abroad, stitched onto part I and published in 1837. Some of the consequent jumble is pure Gogolian free association, beginning with images of flight, ending with an apostrophe to escape and punctuated throughout with vignettes of rapid motion. But the piece is held together well enough by its recurrent use of contrasts: Moscow vs. Petersburg, private lives vs. popular amusements, Carnival vs. Lent; and when Gogol insists that he is interested primarily in those entertainments accessible to all classes, and focuses on the theater, he points up a contrast between the existing repertory and an ideal and, of course, *narodny* one.

Except for a brief respite during the Napoleonic wars when it was thought unpatriotic to support French culture, a fresh wave of foreign influences had swamped the youthful Russian drama, even as classicism ebbed. The German Kotzebue's lachrymose, agonized plays of domestic tribulation were favorites in the early 1800s; they were bitterly assailed as *Kotsebyatina*, but Kotzebue was director of the German theater in Petersburg, so they were eventually imitated with success, as in Ozerov's heroic and tear-drenched tragedies. The public, nourished on this and Walter Scott, next supp'd full with horrors furnished by romantic *mélodrame*. Melodrama and the Gothic mode were to receive serious attention from the formalist critics of the 1920s,[10] but in their own time they were condemned by serious thinkers. Pushkin, after a flirtation with the Byronic hero, had eventually repudiated him as one-dimensional and superficial; and Gogol, though not so averse to Byronism, was irked by melodrama's sensationalism, its appeal to the nerves rather than the heart. But Gogol's chief indictment was that melodrama dwells on the unusual and the bizarre, whereas his own chosen *modus operandi* was to take the banal and ordinary in life and render them strange, dilating the overlooked and the trivial until their profiles become monstrous. Cups of cold poison and unsheathed daggers were irrelevant to a dramatist like Gogol, whose most outrageous stage action is to have a bridegroom jump out a window (in *Getting Married*). But although an indigenous melodrama did not evolve, melodramatic devices and *coups de théâtre* infested Russian social and historical plays of the mid-century and lingered until Chekhov's day.

An even more infectious invader was the *vaudeville*, a light comedy of modern life interspersed with verses set to well-known tunes; unknown in Russia in 1812, by 1823 it was crowned with bays in Prince Shakhovskoy's *News on Parnassus or The Muses' Triumph*. Shakhovskoy, an archfoe of the romantics, was himself responsible for the first true Russian vaudeville, *The Versifying Cossack*; and even Pushkin was requested, unsuccessfully, to try his hand at the genre. In the 1830s, when Gogol was firing invective at such a hybrid misfit as a Russian vaudeville, it was still primarily musical and lightweight. But in the next decades, as if to contradict Gogol, the vaudeville was naturalized and fostered a school of comic playwrights, led by Dmitry Lensky, whose works constitute a valuable record of Russian middle-class life as well as a roster of eminently stageworthy farces. Again Gogol's objections were personally prompted: the vaudeville of his day was too stereotypical and remote from reality to serve his high-minded view of comedy as a panacea for Russia's ills.

Sumarokov in his *Epistles* had decreed that "the nature of comedy is to emend manners by scorn. To make people laugh and to reform are its main principles." This neatly if tritely summed up most philosophical attitudes toward comedy since Aristotle: it was to castigate minor private vices and abnormal, antisocial behavior; amuse in the process; and, through laughter, exercise a therapeutic function. Characteristically, Gogol, a comic writer, expanded this definition by claiming for comedy in the modern world the role that tragedy had once filled. His comic masterpiece *The Inspector* had been performed in St. Petersburg in 1836 at the special behest of the emperor; its reception was enthusiastic in the main, although those rows of stalls that Pushkin had deplored, the bureaucrats and fashionables, greeted it coldly, and the hack journalists, headed by Bulgarin, dismissed it with contempt. Still, it played to packed houses and won glowing tributes from the better authorities on literature. But Gogol preferred to consider the performance a disaster; his letters are full of such remarks as "a prophet is without honor in his own country," "the author concerned with honor must live elsewhere" and "all classes are against me." This *Schadenfreude* comes not so much from wounded vanity as from Gogol's insistence on making the comic author into a field preacher with a mandate to correct not private faults but the abuses of an entire society.

His first salvo in this holy war was the playlet *A Theater Lets Out after the Performance of a New Comedy*. Like Molière's *Critique de l'École des Femmes*, it is a polemical defense *pro domo* in dialogue, intended to appeal to the same audience that had witnessed the play under discussion, in other words to appeal to a jury that had already reached its verdict. If the form was traditional in European drama, it was unique in Russian letters, "something only a Gogol is capable of," claimed an admiring Belinsky. The censorship forbade its performance, finding that "opinions are to be met with therein which, albeit well-intentioned, are audacious in respect to civil servants, the government and the Russian people," and it was not until 1902 that it received a stage production. Gogol may have begun writing it the very day after *The Inspector* opened, and there can be no doubt that many of its lines are attributable to specific critics; but, reworking the piece in Rome in 1842, Gogol hoped to generalize it in such a way that it would become an abstract theoretical statement. "It must be made somewhat idealized," he wrote to his editor, "so that it may have application to every play that stings social abuses, and therefore I ask you not to hint or disclose that it was written on the occasion of *The Inspector*."[11]

Gogol was replying not only to his foes but to his friends (in his usual extravagant way), excluding *The Inspector* from any interpretation but his own. The play was to be read as more than a funny comedy that "heals many grievances and drives away much spleen," as the reviewer for the *Russian Disabled Veteran (Russkiy invalid)* had put it. Similarly, although Gogol recites a litany of lip-service to the notion of the government as a benign Argus, he was eager to contradict Prince Vyazemsky's suggestion in the *Contemporary* that the one "honorable and right-thinking character is the government, which, striking abuses with the force of the law, leaves them to be corrected by the weapon of mockery." The government may appear vicariously at the end of *The Inspector* to the consternation of the characters, but it is not seen to strike (as it is in Fonvizin's *The Minor*). Gogol promoted Laughter as the one honorable character, the end not the means of correction; the laughter is aroused by the inventions of the comic writer, who becomes a demiurge, more far-seeing and effective than any government agency.

Gogol also sought to refute the sympathetic charge that he was simply copying from life, putting down the ugly facts of Russian malpractices; in his "Primer of Literature" (1844/5) he argued that "the significance of dramatic or narrative poetry diminishes proportionately as the author loses sight of the significant and forceful idea that impels him to create and is a mere describer of the scenes that pass before him, without arranging them in proof of something that must be said to the world."[12] Stendhal's mirror moving along a highway would not suffice as Gogol's ideal of art; for him, a writer implied a missionary. At the same time he denied copying his characters and incidents, protesting, "I never *sketched* a portrait, in the sense of a plain copy. I *created* a portrait but created it out of consideration [*soobrazhenie*] and not imagination [*voobrazhenie*]. The more things I took into consideration, the more accurate was my finished creation."[13] It may sound peculiar for a writer to denigrate his imagination in this way. But Gogol was anxious to certify his fictional products as something more than mere imaginings; he seems to regard *voobrazhenie* as what Coleridge termed "fancy," which "must receive all its materials ready made from the law of association," and *soobrazhenie* as the Coleridgean imagination which "dissolves, diffuses, dissipates . . . struggles to idealize and to unify" (*Biographia Literaria*, ch. 13). Certainly, Coleridge's view that imagination is a vital force which vivifies essentially fixed, dead objects would be congenial to Gogol, whose universe of "dead souls" is brought to life precisely by the power of his structure-providing, recreative mind. The squalid vices and villains of provincial Russia—whom so many characters in *A Theater Lets Out* refuse to contemplate or believe in—are indeed, as Gogol insists, hoisted to another level by the writer's *soobrazhenie*, the act of contemplating them. Gogol's ability to establish a self-sustained Gogolian world (in drama as elsewhere) chimes in with Coleridge's conception of Shakespeare as a genius working from meditation, whose material is less important than the mental process he puts it through. But Gogol never succeeded in conciliating the intense idiosyncrasy of his "considerational" reconstructions of reality—his comic vision—with his sense of moral purpose.

Gogol never ceased to elucidate, annotate, gloss and revise *The Inspector*. Ancillary material includes a so-called "letter to a literary man" deploring the deficiencies of the first performance, a set of instructions to those who would stage the play properly and two versions of a "Denouement" in which actors of the Moscow Maly Theater expound Gogol's new concept of the play as an allegorical morality. With each of these appendices, the play is seen less and less as a comedy: the plight of the characters is called "tragic" and the situation terrifying. Eventually, in the last phase of Gogol's life, in the throes of religious mania, he confused his comic and his salvational notions of drama and propounded a theatrical utopia that was nothing of the sort.

"On the Theater, on a One-sided View of the Theater and on One-sidedness in General" (1845) in his *Selected Excerpts from Correspondence with Friends* reiterates the theater's identity as a pulpit and the need to segregate it from "those capering ballets, vaudevilles, melodramas and gorgeously gaudy performances which pander to depraved tastes and hearts." [14] Properly staged, the great drama of the past will attract audiences with its noble messages. But, in keeping with his respect for authority and the deeply reactionary tenor of his religious convictions, Gogol laid the charge for such a staging on one man: a first-class actor who would instill in lesser actors his understanding of a play and would control the artistic unity of the finished production. Again, this idea is drawn from Gogol's experiences with *The Inspector*, when he tried in vain to have the Moscow opening directed not by the theater's manager but by the brilliant comic actor Mikhail Shchepkin. But whatever the actual antecedents, the idea strikingly foreshadows the call for a unified style in drama made by the symbolists at the end of the century. Gogol fancied the control of a work of art by one authoritarian, a source of certainty, almost a longed-for *alter ego* to contrast with his own insecurity and vacillation in the face of public opinion; but the principle is akin to Evreinov's argument for a single point of view in monodrama, Sologub's insistence on the dramatist as be-all and end-all and Meyerhold's advancement of the director as ultimate "author of the spectacle."

In another essay in the same work, "On the Essence of Russian Poetry and Its Originality" (1846), Gogol reduced drama to an adjunct of satire, with *The Minor* and *Woe from Wit* as his prize specimens. To label them, he came up with what he believed to be a new phrase, "true social comedies," for "our comic authors have been moved by social rather than personal motives, and stood up not against an individual but against a whole mass of abuses, against a society's divagation from the right road." [15] As always, the claim could fit his own plays, especially when he defends the truth-to-Russian-nature of Fonvizin's and Griboedov's characters and their plays' lack of conventional form. But his broader pretensions for comedy as an instrument of public correction were avidly adopted by the so-called civic critics of the following generation.

IV

"Lyric poetry, epic, drama: do you award one or another of them a definite preference or love all equally? A hard decision, isn't it? And

yet I love drama for choice and this seems to be the common taste."
So wrote Vissarion Belinsky (1811–1848) at the start of his career,[16]
and although by its end the novel had elbowed its way among the
contestants, he remained faithful to his chosen love. Much of his
journalistic responsibility involved regular reviewing of the theaters
in Moscow and Petersburg; his collected works teem with conscientious notices of dozens of footling vaudevilles, melodramas and
chauvinistic extravaganzas. Even at their best (as in the lengthy article on Mochalov's Hamlet) these pieces lack flair; Belinsky was no
Hazlitt, and there are few passages that blaze forth with a memorable portrait of a performance, few phrases that brand the mind in-
delibly with an actor's quality. But there is a good deal of careful
evaluation, withering sarcasm and an underlying conviction that
the theater has an important task to fulfill. For the drama, in Belinsky's view, uses individuals to exhibit all humanity and is therefore the art form closest to its audience; as we the public become
more engrossed in the emotions and fate of other human beings on
stage, our egoism evaporates and we become better persons and better citizens. This is essentially an eighteenth-century outlook.

Belinsky's essay on dramatic poesy was part of a young man's
ambitious scheme to compose a work defining all the types of literature once and for all; it was never completed. But as an early work, it
is more attractive than many of Belinsky's later compositions in its
enthusiasms and sympathies. And although it exemplifies his life-
long obsession with content, it has, by way of definitions, a few astute things to say about form. Belinsky adjudged classical art to be
a harmonious equipoise of form and idea and romantic art an im-
balance of idea over form: only the Greeks and Romans are classics,
only minstrels and troubadours romantics. Modern art (and this includes Shakespeare) reconciles classic and romantic. Drama itself is
but another reconciliation, a synthesis of subjective lyric poetry and
objective epic.

As a dogged follower of Hegel, Belinsky believed tragedy to be
the sublimest form of drama and the sublimest of tragedies to be
Sophocles' *Antigone*, because it best realizes the notion of ethical
tension between two characters who treat their partial goods as if
they were absolutes. The conflict between Creon and Antigone is
reconciled, for Hegel, in the mind of the spectator who realizes how
the mistake in perception precipitated the catastrophe and who understands that the conflict was part of a dialectical struggle toward a
higher synthesis. For all his bandying about of Hegelian terminology, Belinsky's recurrent use of the concept of "reconciliation" was a

useful tool in understanding his contemporaries. Hegel allowed him to discard the old polarization of tragedy and comedy, so that he could deem the latter "a drama in exactly the same sense as what is usually called tragedy is."[17] For Hegel, as for Nietzsche later on, the growth of comedy spelled the ruination of Greek tragic poetry; but Belinsky faced a modern literature rather short on tragedy and strongest in its comic authors. If Gogol was to get the credit due him, comedy had to be rehabilitated as a major literary genre. So, in Belinsky's interpretation, comedy is the reverse or photographic negative of a tragic situation; comic protagonists, unlike their tragic counterparts, must struggle not with the necessary and intrinsic, but with the fortuitous and extrinsic. The fundamental spiritual purpose of life is constantly at odds with the phenomenal world, and the result is the common comic contradiction between the protagonists' will and their achievements. Thus, as he would later elaborate in his essay on *Woe from Wit*, Belinsky ranks Griboedov's play below Gogol's *Inspector*, because the former merely paints a lurid picture of a society, whereas the latter genuinely creates a "negative reality," the play's hectic action covering up a spiritual void that reverberates in the life outside the theater. Belinsky's Hegelianism also exonerates Russian playwrights from the accusation that they leave their dramas open-ended; since reconciliation takes place in the mind of the spectator, matters need not be settled at the fall of the curtain. The audience will extrapolate the ideal synthesis inherent in the totality of the "negative reality" from the stage to the given situation and will leave the theater with a sense of life as it should be.

Belinsky's ideological heirs Nikolay Chernyshevsky (1828–1889) and Nikolay Dobrolyubov (1836–1861), less sensitive than he to aesthetic nuance, propagated the notion of literature as a tool of social progress; in a backward culture literature had a responsibility to be encyclopedic in its interests, and drama, as the most immediate of forms, with a wide popular appeal, played a leading part in this. To take one example of strained exegesis, Chernyshevsky's essay on Aristotle's *Poetics* makes a bizarre effort to prove that fate as a motive force in tragedy does not have Aristotle's authority but derives from German philosophy, for Chernyshevsky associated fate with a limitation of human life that might discourage progress. Real tragedy must forego the supernatural and the superhuman alike; fate must remain an auxiliary force, and the residual impression of a play should be inspiring or encouraging. So reductive a view—too purblind to recognize tragic catharsis as more than boosterism—was widely accepted by his followers, and goes far to explain why tragedy in the classical or Shakespearean style was never widely imitated in Russia. The conflict of individuals with their destinies could provide fewer lessons for the body politic than would the conflict of individuals with society.

Grist for these dogmatizing mills was supplied by Aleksandr Ostrovsky (1823–1886). Ostrovsky can hardly be said to have burst onto the Russian stage, for his works—like those of so many before and after him—first became known, owing to the rigors of the theatrical censorship, on the printed page or at private readings. But the freshness of his plays and their portrayal of the merchant milieu, along with his prolific output, made him the rock around which critical debate churned and boiled. As usual, sides were taken on paraliterary grounds. Ostrovsky had from the outset been adopted by the Slavophile party, and his first full-length play (*The Bankrupt*) was published in their organ, the *Muscovite* (*Moskvityanin*), in 1850; consequently, partisans of folk culture and Russian national characteristics extolled the ethnographic and folksy facets of his writing. This, in turn, provoked a hostile reaction from the Westernizers, who disparaged his plays as formless satires and the world he depicted as a figment of his fancy. The position was delicate for Ostrovsky himself, since he was by no means a stalwart Slavophile and looked on much of old Russian tradition with disfavor; but he could hardly afford to alienate his original supporters. Yet, by 1857, he had become a contributor to the Westernizers' *Contemporary*, which regularly published his latest plays, and when its editorial staff moved to *Fatherland Notes* (*Otechestvennye zapiski*), he loyally followed its lead. To one of its editors, the poet Nikolay Nekrasov, he wrote in 1869, "We two alone know the people and how to love it, and can sense its needs in our heart without armchair Westernizing or puerile Slavophilia."[18]

Ostrovsky's refusal to be categorized made him a bugbear to critics long after he had been accepted by actors and audiences. The diversity of opinion stirred up by his first plays culminated in Dobrolyubov's authoritative article "The Kingdom of Darkness," which appeared in the *Contemporary* (no. 7, 1859).[19] With his insistence on art as propaganda for progressive ideas and his proneness to judge literary characters as if they were creatures of flesh and blood, Dobrolyubov had only scorn for those critics who defined Ostrovsky's quality, his "new word," as *narodnost'*. Slowly working his way through the plots of all of Ostrovsky's plays to date, he found that the characters could be roughly divided into two groups: the agents of *samodurstvo* (Ostrovsky's coinage, a pun meaning both "home-grown tyranny" and "self-made stupidity") who perpetrated the "kingdom of darkness" by their selfishness, hypocrisy, ignorance, greed, narrow-mindedness and cruelty; and those who offered a pro-test, usually futile, against this kingdom. As Russian society is pres-ently constituted, Dobrolyubov opined, goodness of heart and virtue make few dents in the solid mass of *samodurstvo*. By this schema-tization, which hinted that all contemporary Russia *was* the king-dom of darkness, he simplified Ostrovsky's dramas into protest plays and thus provided them with a passport into the good graces of the Westernizers.

However, the Slavophiles were not willing to yield to the enemy someone they considered their own discovery, and Dobrolyubov's essay was met by "After Ostrovsky's *The Storm*," an impassioned and somewhat breathless rejoinder from Apollon Grigoriev (1822–1864) in the form of two open letters to the novelist Turgenev.[20] Of the major critics of the period, Grigoriev was the most abused in his time and the most neglected after it. His collected writings have yet to be canonized in impressive Academy of Science editions as those of his contemporaries were long ago, and scholars have yet to iden-tify all the pieces he was compelled to publish anonymously or pseudonymously because of the opprobrium with which he was cov-ered by fellow journalists. It was they who pilloried him when he characterized Ostrovsky as a "new word in literature"; the phrase became a pretext for gibes, epigrams and burlesques. Grigoriev in turn disdained his fellow journalists, qualifying them either as "the-orists," by which he meant tendentious moralizers like Chernyshev-sky and Dobrolyubov, or "aesthetes" neglectful of wider social ques-tions, like Pavel Druzhinin and Pavel Annenkov.[21] Grigoriev's own critical method began with a record of his intuitive response to an artistic stimulus which he then tried to verify quasi-scientifically. This system hoped to combine the best of both worlds, for it strove to be objective, precise and unprejudiced, even as it preserved the in-tensity and vibrancy of a personal reaction. This had the benefit of segregating a literary work from extraneous social or political ques-tions of the day and regarding it as an integral portion of a literary tradition. At the same time, Grigoriev's "organic criticism," as it has come to be known, sought out those peculiarly national characteris-tics that defined the work under examination.

This lack of *parti pris* distinguished Grigoriev's scrutiny of Ostrovsky from that of Dobrolyubov. Instead of selecting a conve-nient pigeonhole in which to thrust a not-fully-understood body of work, Grigoriev was careful to denote differences among the plays; and even when he did use a catch-phrase—which, not surprisingly, is *narodnost'*—to define Ostrovsky's quality, he went to some lengths to define the term exactly and to clarify the way in which different "populist" writers may or may not embody it. His awareness of predecessors and epigones permitted him to place Ostrovsky within a living tradition, most notably as a divergent offshoot of Gogol, whereas other critics could see the new author only as a *lusus naturae*.

Dobrolyubov's reaction to Grigoriev and to *The Storm* appeared in "A Ray of Light in the Kingdom of Darkness," published in the *Contemporary* (no. 10, 1860), dutifully reprinted in Soviet anthologies but a grotesque misreading of the play. Dismissing other interpretations out of hand, he argued that "the function [of criticism] is to note and point out facts . . . and to judge on the basis of facts," a duty which might reveal a critic's own shortcomings: "if a critic reproaches Ostrovsky for having presented Katerina in *The Storm* as a loathsome and immoral woman, he does not inspire remarkable confidence in the purity of his own moral sentiments."[22] In other words, *honi soit qui mal y pense*. Stoutly maintaining that the new play supported his original thesis, he went on to the startling conclusion that this drama about an inhibited adulteress, whose fears and superstitions push her to suicide to escape her stifling environment, was in fact a refreshing paean to the best elements in the Russian spirit and that Katerina was an exemplary rebel against *samodurstvo*.

Although Grigoriev made no move to contest this weird (but widely accepted) notion, it was savaged from a more unexpected quarter by the ultra-utilitarian critic Dmitry Pisarev (1840–1868). In a ferociously chaotic article, "Motifs of Russian Drama," in the *Russian Word* (*Russkoe slovo*, no. 3, 1864) he lambasted what he called Dobrolyubov's "subjectivity" in analysis (so much for following facts!) and called for an objective, rationalistic evaluation of the incidents in *The Storm*. So far as Pisarev was concerned, Katerina acted like a fool. This anti-idealistic polemic then devolved into snide allusions to Ostrovsky's other plays, suggesting, for instance, that the somber drama *Hard Times* should be refashioned into a vaudeville.

The critical furore surrounding Ostrovsky did not abate even as the repertory swelled with his dramas and audiences grew accustomed to his style. The regular reviewers carried on the customary tactic of deploring each new drama as a falling-off from his former work and then, a few years later, using the same drama as a stick to beat its most recent successor. But by the late 1880s he had become an establishment figure, artistic director of the Moscow Imperial Dramatic Theater, and his works had assumed an almost classical aura.

To some extent, Vasily Sleptsov (1836–1878) subscribed to the critical bromides of his age; his fugitive writings on the theater insist on its value as a contributor to social progress and on Ostrovsky's skill at exposing the evils of Russian life. But he was unwilling to sacrifice art to tendentiousness, and his article "A Type of the Current Drama" is aimed precisely at the crudeness of effect used by dramatic authors to convey their edifying message. The genre under attack is that variety of *pièce bien faite* known as the "problem play," in which the solidly carpentered mechanism of the plot is put to the service of some social question. Aleksandr Herzen, in discussing the "woman question," had noted its ubiquity:

> From ballads and legends the protest grows into the novel and the drama. In the drama it becomes a force. In the theatre outraged love and the gloomy secrets of family injustice found their tribunal, their public hearing. Their case has shaken thousands of hearts, wringing tears and cries of indignation against the serfdom of marriage and the fetters of the family rivetted on by force. The jury of the stalls and the boxes have over and over again pronounced the acquittal of individuals and the guilt of institutions.[23]

Despite the paradox that social questions do not admit of the facile solutions dictated by the neat structure of the well-made play, an illusion was conveyed that such drama was worthy because of its serious intent. Ostrovsky, as noted, was valued by some critics primarily for his supposed exposure of social abuses, much as Ibsen's *Ghosts* was often taken in his lifetime as a tract against congenital syphilis and bad marriages. Ostrovsky's imitators and competitors, especially Dyachenko and Potekhin, invariably spun their plots so that at least some reference was made to a current problem. Dyachenko, heavily dependent on French masters, specialized in drawing-room dramas of divorce, adultery and an amoral high society, while Potekhin delved into the plight of the peasantry and the malpractices of provincial gentry and bureaucracy.

Sleptsov's critique, written in the typically flippant and face-tious tone of the Victorian columnist, can therefore be applied to a good deal of nineteenth-century drama within and without Russia. That its main target happens to be the only play Nikolay Leskov ever wrote adds to its interest; and if *The Profligate* is not quite the incompetent piece of balderdash Sleptsov makes it out to be (it is, in fact, one of the earliest plays to deal with factory workers and was revived with moderate success by the Second Moscow Art Theater in 1924), its shortcomings are endemic to the whole genre. However, Sleptsov's animosity may stem from the fact that Leskov had satirized him unmercifully in his novel *No Way Out* (1864), though more for his radicalism than for his dramatic opinions.

The turbulent critical activity of the 1850s and 1860s ended abruptly with the untimely removal of its leading exponents: Chernyshevsky was imprisoned in 1862, Dobrolyubov died in 1861, Druzhinin and Grigoriev in 1864, Pisarev in 1868. No new playwright of Ostrovsky's stature came to the fore, and, with the abolition of the state monopoly on theaters in 1882, European boulevard drama and its counterfeits predominated. The only interesting ripple in the turgid waters of dramatic theory between the Ostrovsky debate and the end of the century was the appearance of Dmitry Averkiev's (1836–1905) *On Drama*, the first Russian work devoted wholly to the theory of drama as a separate art form. (It had appeared in installments in the *Russian Messenger* [*Russkiy vestnik*] for 1877/8 and was reprinted in 1893 with two new supplements.) The author was not an aesthetician or a philosopher but a practicing dramatist and journalist; unfortunately, the low intellectual calibre is not compensated by a lively style or astute pragmatism. Averkiev showed himself to be an arch-conservative who swore fealty to Aristotle the tutelary genius, with Lessing as angelic choir. The dramatic laws laid down by Aristotle are taken to be eternal and immutable, and therefore all who transgress them, including the neoclassicists, the romantics, the well-made playmakers and Ostrovsky, are rejected out of hand for ignoring the clear-cut line between comedy and tragedy. The only motive for drama is the human struggle against the force of circumstance, and therefore "the dramatic artist errs against his art when he bends all his strength to delineate with special precision how one character's will conflicts with another's."²⁴ Amidst all this retrograde clutter, Averkiev did manage to say something interesting about comedy. The high point of tragedy is the suffering of the protagonist, an honorable person; therefore the high point of comedy must also be the protagonist's suffering. But in comedy, the main character is the only one who conceives himself or herself to be suffering, while the audience perceives the error. Applied to the plays of Molière, this is a viable criterion, and it is to be regretted that the rest of the work did not match it.

V

In the 1880s, when Anton Chekhov (1860–1904) began his writing career as a humorous journalist, his duties entailed much theatergoing, for he wrote what amounted to a behind-the-scenes gossip column punctuated by occasional reviews. This activity led to an acquaintance with actors and managers, and his correspondence began to be studded with tidbits of greenroom scandal and pithy allusions to the latest productions. As his friendship with professionals deepened and he himself became an active dramatist, his commentary on the theater grew more caustic and exasperated. "I implore you," he wrote to the playwright Ivan Shcheglov, "please fall out of love with the stage."

> True, there is a lot of good in it. The good is overstated to the skies, and the vileness is masked. . . . The modern theater is a rash, an urban disease. The disease must be swept away, and loving it is unhealthy. You start arguing with me, repeating the old phrase, the theater is a school, it educates and so forth. . . . But I am telling you what I see: the modern theater is not superior to the crowd; on the contrary, the life of the crowd is more elevated and intelligent than the theater. . . . The theater is a snake sucking your blood. Until the literary man in you triumphs over the dramatist, I will give you hell and see your plays damned.[25]

His often quoted remarks about actresses being cows who fancy themselves goddesses, about actors steeped in conceit and ignorant of life outside the poolroom, date from this period. But in the early 1880s, high spirits and glancing malice were more his style, the tone of one who loves the theater and is embarrassed to be loving something unworthy.

"More about Sarah Bernhardt" (1881) is a sequel to Chekhov's mock-biography of the touring star supposedly based on her press releases ("It's incredible, my friends! No sooner does one start writing about Sarah Bernhardt than one has the urge to tell a few lies."), in which he stoutly refused to be impressed by a reputation. "More," written after he had at least seen her perform, starts on the same jeering note but moves toward an earnest restatement of the theme of French know-how versus Russian sincerity, familiar since the days of Mlle. George and Rachel. Despite the know-it-all style that "Antosha Chekhonte" practiced in those medical student days, the aesthetic concerns that underlie it reflect a connoisseur's interest in acting and strike a chord that continues throughout Chekhov's later work—the importance of integrity and industry in the artist's profession. He was to prefer Eleonora Duse's simplicity and honesty and later distilled the *prima donnas* of the Bernhardt school into Arkadina in *The Seagull*.[26] Bernhardt went on touring, however, and a few years later Valery Bryusov was to react to her Cleopatra much as Chekhov had to her Adrienne Lecouvreur.

Recoiling from the banality of the contemporary theater and its overindulgence in cheap morality and flashy effects, Chekhov was among the first Russian writers to be attracted to symbolist drama. Although (as both Stanislavsky and Olga Knipper-Chekhova attest) he regarded Ibsen as neither lifelike nor stageworthy, "complicated, involved and cerebral," he was, like many others, strangely attracted to Maurice Maeterlinck's "odd wonderful plays [which] make an enormous impression."[27] What impressed him seems to have been the theatrical imagination revealed in the plays; mystical doctrines mattered less than that a play should work on stage. In his letters to would-be dramatists, Chekhov continually repeated the need to see and understand how plays worked in the theater. He was reluctantly compelled to reject Björnstjerne Björnson's metaphysical drama *Over Ævne*, which he found moving and intelligent, because "it won't do for the stage, because it can't be played, there's no action, no living characters, no dramatic interest."[28] (Incidentally, this is the same argument Nina advances against Treplyov's play in *The Seagull*.) But no cohesive theory of drama is to be cobbled together from Chekhov's voluminous correspondence. When scrutinized closely, his criticism turns out to be hints on craft: "avoid clichés," "be compact," "use realistic dialogue," "vary the characters," "put your climax in the third act but be sure the fourth is not anticlimactic." His eminently practical comments on Gorky's plays, for example, have to do with their effect on an audience and how "points" are to be made. Even his references to his own plays are meant to clarify particulars for the performers or react to specific performances. His well-known statement that "on stage people eat, drink, play cards and meanwhile their lives are being destroyed" is indeed a telegraphic synopsis of an aesthetic, but it is a symbolist aesthetic: beyond the commonplace surface of existing lurks the real life of the characters.

This aspect of Chekhov's mature dramas infuriated Lyov Tolstoy (1828–1910). "Where's the drama?!" he asked of *Uncle Vanya.* "Where is it hiding? The play is just marking time." "After that," a friend wrote to Chekhov, "Tolstoy declared that Astrov and Uncle Vanya are trashy people, loafers who avoid work and the country, which should be a means to salvation. . . . He also said that 'Astrov should marry Sonya, and Uncle Vanya the old nurse, and hanging around the professor's wife is wrong and immoral. . . .'"[29] Tolstoy's homiletic and simpleminded attitude toward Chekhov was altogether consistent with the animadversions on drama to be found in *What Is Art?* (1898). Russian criticism for years had heard similar denunciations of art for art's sake, similar appeals for a literature that spoke to the people and propagated virtue, the same Puritanism, in short. What it had not heard was the uncompromising abuse and repudiation of what was commonly accepted as great art. Tolstoy's hostility to Shakespeare was of long standing; possibly in his early years it was a pose to confound mindless praise of the bard, but, like all poses, with time it hardened into an irremovable mask. Yet Tolstoy could praise Shakespeare for his active characters and his dramatic quintessence when he wanted to damn Chekhov and modern drama.[30] Many of his objections to drama relate directly to the nature of the theater; the immediate response of an audience to a play places a greater burden of responsibility on the playwright, and the very crudeness of dramatic effect obscures and vitiates whatever moral might be intended. Instead of being instilled with Christian feeling, an audience is titillated or terrified, amused or excited. Much of Tolstoy's dissatisfaction with plays then—whether Shakespeare's, Chekhov's or Hauptmann's—seems an embarrassment at being an audience member, a refusal to admit to the playwright's manipulations. Tolstoy is unwilling to suspend his disbelief. Inept productions annoy him by not bodying forth the greatness of great drama; ingenious productions irritate him by camouflaging bad drama. The theater, after all, demands an acceptance of convention, of the simulated and the seductive, and Tolstoy's life was a denial of that demand in any sphere.

VI

The rejection of artifice in *What Is Art?* seemed all the more brutal because in 1898 it was totally out of step with its time. That same year the newly founded Moscow Art Theater earned its first successes with the greatest of artifices, a painstaking reproduction of the surface of life. Its co-founder Konstantin Stanislavsky hoped that audiences would forget that they were in a theater. But for all the ambitious claims of its progenitors, naturalism was never an objective technique. In France, where the school was perhaps purest, the emphasis on the sordid and seamy was in itself an indication of bias. In Russia, naturalist writers were not content merely to record the squalor of life but felt obliged to point out a means of overcoming it; the "civic" frame of mind of the 1850s and 1860s was slow to vanish. The repressive reign of Alexander III had limited the expression of these sentiments, and the result was a torpid inertia among the intelligentsia familiar to all readers of Chekhov. The same torpor, as we have noted, infected the theater of the 1880s. By the 1890s, Russia like the rest of Europe faced the new century with mingled presentiments of hope and dread; the intimation of a new era close at hand was both stimulating and unnerving. As older forms of art were considered outmoded and infirm, experiments, sometimes sophisticated, sometimes rudimentary, were made with new ones. Naturalism's effect on the theater had been seen in a greater attention to physical details, but no sooner did a rival appear in the guise of symbolism than the theater clamored for fresh methods and approaches in order to body forth a nonmaterial vision. European influences were as potent as ever; and such innovators as Wagner, Ibsen, Isadora Duncan, Max Reinhardt and Gordon Craig were quoted and emulated, adapted and absorbed. But unquestionably the two strongest influences on the Russian drama and its theorists at this time were Friedrich Nietzsche and Maurice Maeterlinck.

Nietzsche's reinterpretation of the ancient Greeks came as an inspiring jolt to Russian literary theory, for classical antiquity, at least since the time of Zhukovsky, had seemed irrelevant.

> Extravagance, wildness and Asiatic tendencies lie at the root of the Greeks. Their courage consists in their struggle with their Asiatic nature; they were not given beauty any more than they were given logic and moral naturalness; in them these things are victories, they are willed and fought for. . . .

Nietzsche had written in *The Will to Power*.[31] Change "Greeks" to "Russians" in this passage and the shock of recognition experienced by the Russian literati becomes clear. Westernizers could justify their endeavors as attempts to impose Apollonian form on the Dionysian *aziatchina* of the Russian spirit; Slavophiles could point to the artistic myth that resulted when modern form (Apollo) reshaped folklore (Dionysos). And no matter how hopeless Russian illiteracy and ignorance might appear, the force of will might still develop a high culture, as it did for the Greeks. Even more important for *fin de siècle* writers was Nietzsche's image of the tragic hero playing out his heroics in the face of certain annihilation: tragic catharsis not as a soothing purge of emotion but as a confrontation of the audience with the dark, hidden truths of human existence. This interpretation of tragedy had immediate appeal and significance to writers like Merezhkovsky, Ivanov, Bely and Sologub on the eve of war and revolution.

The weaker points in Nietzsche's *The Birth of Tragedy*—the failure to prove the Apollonian-Dionysian nexus as historical fact, the identification of Dionysos as Anti-Christ and the overemphasis on a synthesis in music-drama—allowed Vyacheslav Ivanov (1866–1949) so confidently to contrive his own version of the theory. His Greek scholarship was impressive, far better than Nietzsche's (which had been attacked by Wilamowitz-Möllendorf and other German philologists for shoddy research), and his studies of Hellenic religion more profound. In 1904/5 he published a number of articles concerning the myth of Dionysos in *New Path* (*Novy put'*) and *Questions of Life* (*Voprosy zhizni*), which had an immense influence. Like Nietzsche later in his life, Ivanov rejected the Hegelian synthesis of Apollo and Dionysos, and singled out the latter as the true fount of tragic inspiration. The Apollonian trappings of art were seen as a necessary evil, a dilution of the pure vision, useful only for noncommunicants. But the artist's task requires more than the initial ascent to the realm of Platonic Ideas through immersion in the Dionysian vision; it embraces a return to earth, the descent to convey the Ideas to lesser mortals. A symbolist poem or drama created by such a visionary will convey the soul of the reader or spectator *a realibus ad realiora*, from the real to the more real.

Ivanov gave much thought to the theatrical side of this procedure. An adherent of Vladimir Solovyov, whose mystical Christianity taught that the congregational and the individual religious spirits must be mediated by an artist-hierophant, Ivanov regarded the dramatist as the ideal keeper of the flame, bringing the audience of nonartists in touch with the higher realm. His articles expatiate on the Dionysian festivals of ancient Greece and the ritual origins of the theater, suggesting that modern drama would do well to recover the religious function it had lost. By revealing myth to humanity, the theater enables it to come in contact with the absolute, to intuit through art a reality greater than itself. Moreover, by reverting to its ritual beginnings, the theater will resume the choric or dithyrambic involvement of its audience, which will be a participant rather than an observer, a communicant with the higher truth. Ivanov also made much of the feminine component in tragedy, with woman as the true servant and exponent of Dionysos, who becomes equated with Christ. Of all his tenets, this was the least heeded, although the Hedda Gablers and Miss Julies of "decadent" drama might bear out Ivanov's thesis, and mysterious, neurasthenic women abound in Russian symbolist plays.[32]

Ivanov's ideas were expounded in his characteristically oracular and abstruse style, but they can be found scattered through the dramatic theories of almost every Russian writer of the time. The inspiriting concept of communion in the theater, of a sodality of performer and spectator, of the dramatist as priest of a new cult, was contagious. It turns up even in such improbable figures as the socialist ideologue Lunacharsky, dreaming of a time when "a free, artistic, ever-creative cult will turn temples into theaters and theaters into temples" and the designer Aleksandr Benois, calling for "liturgicality" in the ballet. Ivanov's own plays were modeled on those of Aeschylus but were far too consciously literary and antiquarian to increase the Dionysian quotient in the contemporary theater. Still, the rudiments of his theories were endlessly recycled.

The impact of Maeterlinck was equally vigorous, although it was not immediately felt in the theater. His vague, repetitive, almost submarine dramas were read with wonder and admiration (Chekhov even advised his friend Suvorin to make Maeterlinck the staple dramatist of his new theater), and his theoretical writings became the basis of much speculation on the nature of a modernist drama. In particular, the essay "The Tragical in Everyday Life," which posits a static drama proceeding within the mind of the protagonist, was quoted and requoted: "I have come to believe that an old man, sitting in his easy chair, patiently waiting, his lamp beside him, unconsciously hearkening to all the eternal laws that reign about his house . . . yet lives in reality, a more profound, more human, and more universal life than does the lover strangling his mistress, the captain conquering in battle or the husband 'avenging his honor.'"[33] For some decades the Russian stage had been dominated by melodramatic *coups de théâtre*, and by the 1890s the popular commercial playwrights Viktor Krylov and Yuzhin-Sumbatov were successfully carrying forward the tradition. To the serious-minded, Maeterlinck's alternative was alluring. Those who sought a fresh direction for the theater could turn to the late dramas of Ibsen with their portentous symbols; to the oneirism and pathology of Strindberg and Przybyszewski; or to Maeterlinck with his emphasis on the importance of stillness and waiting, the denial of external conflict and the characters as an emblematic ensemble. Chekhov found a means of reconciling Maeterlinck with realism; others adopted his style outright. Critics were compelled to come to terms with an obscure dramaturgy that few of them approved, which explains the abundant references to Maeterlinck, if only as a presence to be exorcised, throughout Russian dramatic writing in the first years of the new century.

It took a full decade for the cultural seepage to occur. Maeterlinck's early abstract one-acts *L'Intruse* and *Les Aveugles* were published in 1890, and *Le Trésor des humbles* appeared in book form in 1896. A Russian translation of his play *Intérieur* came out in 1894, and it was staged in St. Petersburg under the sensational title *Secrets of the Soul* in 1899, the first Maeterlinck play to receive a Russian production. But not until Meyerhold's experiments at the Moscow Art Theater Studio (which was closed to the public) and at Vera Kommissarzhevskaya's theater (1905/6) was a theatrical style found for them. The first Russian symbolist drama is often said to be Nikolay Minsky's febrile *Alma* (1900), but I would suggest that the play Konstantin Treplyov mounts in act 1 of *The Seagull* (1896) is Chekhov's cautious experiment with a Maeterlinckian format.

The plays of Chekhov have so often and so casually been relegated to the category of realism (though with the qualifier "poetic" attached) that it must be recalled that many of his contemporaries strove to link them to the symbolists. One of the first to try it was S. Sergeev (under the pseudonym "Glagol") in 1900 ("Glimmers of a New Trend in Art and the Moscow Theater," *Life* [*Zhizn'*], no. 19). Starting with the modish term "mood" (*nastroenie*) commonly applied to the Moscow Art productions of Chekhov, he noted that in a play like *Uncle Vanya* "the center of gravity is transferred to the mood"; if the play grips us and yet is devoid of regular stage action, it must conceal an inner action more significant than that which is palpable. In other words, symbolism. Interpretations along these lines increased after Chekhov's death in 1904, a year when Yuly Aikhenvald grandiosely wrote of the Chekhovian pause that it was the characters' souls calling to one another as unheard words sped homeward on airy wings (*Russian Thought* [*Russkaya mysl'*], no. 2).

Andrey Bely (Boris Bugaev, 1880–1934), another follower of Vladimir Solovyov, returned to the question several times. His obituary of Chekhov in the symbolist journal the *Balances* (*Vesy*, 1904) defined Chekhov as Turgenev and Tolstoy synthesized with Maeterlinck and Hamsun, because Chekhov deals in symbols as exponents of experience, the sole reality. Bely's earlier brief piece on *The Cherry Orchard* (included in the present collection) contains the provocative image of life as a skein of lace whose elaborate fabric must be penetrated before one can see through a single loop into the genuine reality beyond. The meaningless warp and woof of everyday life in a Chekhovian drama is riddled with interstices—pauses in dialogue, eruptions of flurried action—which expose the terrifying absolute that lies behind them. If Bely and Samuel Beckett had been contemporaries, the Russian might have quoted the Irishman's essay on Proust, to speak of "the perilous zones in the life of the individual, dangerous, precarious, painful, mysterious and fertile, when for a moment the boredom of living is replaced by the suffering of being."[34] Three years later, Bely's fullest statement on Chekhov in the *World of Art (Mir iskusstva*, nos. 11–12, 1907) compared him to Valery Bryusov. Bryusov, the true symbolist, sees the world as already formed symbols and transposes his artistic vision by communicating them as they are, whereas Chekhov begins with a realistic image which is then transformed into a symbol. The time scheme in Chekhov, as Bely propounds it, sounds Bergsonian in its interlacing of individual moments into the weft of duration.

The director Vsevolod Meyerhold (1874–?1943) was another who believed that the positivist approach to Chekhov was wrongheaded, as he wrote to the writer himself about *The Cherry Orchard* (8 May 1904): "the play is abstract like a symphony by Chaikovsky. . . . In [the third] act [the ball, which Bely also was to note as crucial] there is something Maeterlinckian, terrifying."[35] He amplified these remarks in his essay "The Naturalistic Theater and the Theater of Mood" (1908), claiming that the two were reconciled by the Moscow Art Theater in its productions of Chekhov, and had that theater followed the Chekhovian clues of rhythm and musicality, it would have succeeded better in realizing the nonrealistic modes of Maeterlinckian drama.

It takes little straining to see Chekhov as a symbolist; more effort is needed to apply the label to Gorky, but Innokenty Annensky (1856–1909) dared it. Annensky spent all of his life in the arid ruts of the tsarist educational system, as teacher, headmaster and school inspector, and simultaneously produced a body of brilliant symbolist poetry; he also translated all of Euripides into Russian, and the style of Greek tragedy powerfully influenced his own plays. In Annensky's view, tragedy is an eternal search for beauty, which is the only force that can redeem humanity, and therefore tragedy is the most universal form of artistic creation. His literary criticism was, in his opinion, permeated with this problem of creation and the justification of life; he referred to his critical essays as "reflections," a term which implied a proprietary attitude to the works he chose to examine. He preferred to deal only with those authors whose works and personalities were consonant with his own and had been absorbed into himself. The result is a criticism more impressionistic and recreative than objective, as insightful as it is capricious. This is especially true of his rhapsody on Chekhov's *The Three Sisters*, "A Drama of Mood," an evocative if exasperating recapitulation of the play, full of details not to be found in the original.

Annensky's only other endeavor in the criticism of modern drama was a troika of essays, harnessed under the title "Three Social Dramas" and devoted to Pisemsky's *A Hard Lot*, Tolstoy's *The Power of Darkness* and Gorky's *The Lower Depths*. (I have included the last, since Gorky's play is the most familiar to non-Russian readers and since Annensky's approach to it is refreshingly different from Soviet sociological studies.) Annensky was a remarkably auditory critic: he heard Chekhov's characters as "phonographic" replicas of life, imagined Pisemsky to have conceived his drama as sounds and tried to prove that Tolstoy's tragedy is unmusical because earthbound. But this feature interests him not at all in "Drama at *The Lower Depths*."[36] Instead, he begins with the outrageous statement that Gorky is a symbolist of the school of Dostoevsky, and the guiding force in the play is not economic conditions but Destiny, as in Greek tragedy. The difference is that for the modern age the protagonist is no longer single but collective. This point might as readily be made about a purely naturalistic play like Hauptmann's *The Weavers*, but it is especially valid within the tradition of Russian criticism. Inextricably bound to the human community, as the Russian viewpoint sees it, persons cannot confront their fates on a one-to-one level. But by the end of his essay, Annensky has quarreled with Gorky's anthropocentrism for being myopic and limiting. If the eternal search for beauty is the source of redemption, humans must aspire beyond themselves in order to be saved.

VII

Salvation, redemption, communion—the vocabulary makes it manifest that the old "civic" goals of public enlightenment and the expression of *narodnost'* had faded into the past. But the function of the drama as more than entertainment was still uppermost in the minds of the theorists. At first symbolism had been read as a cutting-loose from the old social responsibilities of literature and as the untrammeled manifestation of a private vision. So Valery Bryusov heralded it in his earliest pronunciamentos. But this aloofness from public concerns sat ill with Russian writers, so long indoctrinated by ideals of uplift and conscience; however attractive an ivory tower position might be, it seemed criminally frivolous in an age of political upheaval. The dilemma was skirted by concentrating on symbolism's mystical side; a religious attitude might be other-worldly, but it commented, if only by contrast, on affairs of this world. The artist, as we have seen with Ivanov, began to be interpreted as the creator of a new life and the savior of a dying humanity; the passkey to the new life was to be found in art. This pseudofunctionalism of symbolist literature received greater stress after the failed revolution of 1905, when idealistic dreams of communal love and the power of the Beautiful evaporated in a rude awakening. The ideal and the real conflicted more than the poets had hoped, and so they were compelled to doff the priestly robes and to avow the existential nullity of their symbols, myths and transcendental fantasies. Drama was exempted from its hieratic assignment, and the theater was free to be neither a temple nor a rostrum but a theater. Dramatists and critics turned from the Greek ritual and the medieval trope to the *commedia dell'arte* and the Elizabethan stage for patterns of "theatricality," illusion at its most candid and cynical.

One of those who had suffered the trauma of 1905 was the poet Aleksandr Blok (1880–1921), most of whose work in and around the theater is contained in the period 1906 to 1908. His early poetry, imbued with Solovyovian mysticism, had eulogized Beauty and eternal Sophia; but after 1905 his writing took on a bitter, ironic tinge, bemused by the contradictions between harsh reality and intellectual abstractions. "On Drama," Blok's conspectus of the Russian stage of his time, was composed the same year that his first play, *The Little Showbooth*, was staged by Meyerhold at Kommissarzhevskaya's theater. Since the chorus of that play is a panel of pedantic mystics puzzling out a symbolic meaning for the action transpiring before it, he had evidently recovered from his earlier illusions about art's relation to life. The only claim he made for his own "lyrical dramas" was that they were plays "in which the experiences of an individual soul . . . merely happen to be presented in dramatic form."[37]

For Blok the art of the theater was an indicator of the level of modern civilization, a mirror of the contradictions, vileness and veniality of contemporary life; the drama as a public forum hinders poets from escaping into the narrow circle of their more subtle personal feelings, and they find themselves tongue-tied or too loquacious in the presence of the all-powerful director and the hopelessly opaque spectators. In "On Drama," Blok shows weary contempt for Gorky and the post-Chekhovian naturalists, because a dependency on everyday life is bad for the theater. But he also condemns verbose dilettantes who toy with symbolism, for that saps the theater's red blood and vitality; indeed, *The Little Showbooth* has been held by some to be a parody of two contemporaneous mystery plays, Bely's *He That Is Come* and Bryusov's *Earth*. Still, it is surprising that Blok neglects to mention Sologub and Remizov, whose works for the stage have much in common with his own. Instead, he chooses to extol Mikhail Kuzmin and Leonid Andreev, whom many of his colleagues would have deemed poseurs. Dismissing Maeterlinck as meaningless to a pure Russian art ready to face the future, Blok paradoxically is at pains to establish the Russianness of Kuzmin, who was popularly branded as a cosmopolitan (a term journalists took to mean *pederast* much as the Stalinists later took it to mean *Jew*), and to confirm the optimism of Andreev, who was commonly viewed as a morbid skeptic.

To belittle the importance of foreign influences on Russian drama, Blok emphasized the lack of technique in Russian playwriting and maintained that such masters as Griboedov and Chekhov were phenomena *sui generis*. It is instructive to compare his panorama of the Russian scene with that of Meyerhold, four years later, for Meyerhold is both more schematic and more all-encompassing. Writing to instruct the English journalist George Calderon, Meyerhold developed a Darwinian descent of dramatists, sprung from a trinity of Pushkin, Gogol and (unexpectedly) Lermontov, whose reputation Meyerhold was eager to enhance. (He managed to achieve this a few years later in his production of *Masquerade*.) He shared Blok's opinion that Chekhov had no real posterity and also believed that Ostrovsky's progeny had many sins to atone for; but he was ultimately less sanguine even than Blok in identifying masterpieces. Reciting the roll call of new dramatists, many of whom Meyerhold had directed and commissioned, he merely remarked on their debts to past theater, without singling out any for special praise. By this time he was persuaded that the future of the drama was out of the hands of the dramatists.

Meyerhold had himself begun as an actor in the first seasons of the Moscow Art Theater before he repudiated its aesthetic. The international fame achieved by that company and its subsequent sanctification by the Soviet government have left an impression on foreigners that the Russian theater before the Revolution was an exclusive nursery of naturalism. The Art Theater's first successes resulted from copying the Meiningen style: historical authenticity in costume and setting, carefully grouped crowd scenes, attention to detail. But Stanislavsky put his emphasis on psychological truth, seeking the "inner experience" (*perezhivanie*) that motivates the action and the subtle nuances that are the cryptograms of human behavior; in this, he was drawing close to symbolist stasis and internalization (though without accepting a symbolist metaphysics). Pressured by outside critics and its own sense that it was neglecting its contemporaries, the Art Theater, too, tried to reconcile its psychological preoccupations with nonnaturalistic plays. The results were rarely successful, and eventually Maeterlinck, Hamsun, Blok and Andreev were dropped out of the repertory permanently. But the inability of the MAT to become a theater of "new forms" was due not to want of trying but to a lack of sympathy with, or rather understanding of, the meaning of symbolism. For all his good intentions, Stanislavsky, who had very Victorian ideas of art, sought truth in what Ivanov would have called *realia*, accessible to all; for the symbolists it inhered in *realiora*, the Platonic Ideas which can be perceived only by the true artist.

Outside pressure to open a Theater Studio in 1905 was put on Stanislavsky by Valery Bryusov (1873–1924), who became its literary advisor. As the leading spokesman, indeed publicist, for symbolism, Bryusov had used the Art Theater as his stalking horse in an all-out attack on theatrical naturalism in his article "Unnecessary Truth" (*World of Art* [*Mir iskusstval*], no. 4, 1902). The article began with a theoretical discussion of form and content in art, which deduced that form, like the materials out of which a work of art is made, does not affect the essential truth of the content, which issues from the artist's soul. Therefore, reproduction of externals, as in naturalism, is less important than the communication of the artist's own internal world; the theater should attempt to present not the phenomenal, but the noumenal. It logically follows that the theater cannot and should not pretend to reproduce real life, but should create conventional settings which conduce to and do not distract from the inner meaning of the drama. To this end, Bryusov held up the ancient theater as a model, not in the sense of Ivanov's return to religious origins, but as a conventional form that enabled its actors to minimize the physical in favor of the spiritual. For Bryusov, the theater was less a place of décor and spectacle than of acting; he insisted on the actor's primacy as the theater's *raison d'être*.

Bryusov identified the actor as a creator (read *poet*) in the theater, whose raw material consists of voice, pantomime, gesture and physical being as well as the words, action, characters and ideas in the drama performed. The dramatist must serve the actors, and therefore a literary play is only a pretext for the content that subsists in the performer's individuality. Symbolism freed the poet from the form and logic of the natural world; the theater must free the actor from the "unnecessary truth" of material objects and cluttered stages. The Stanislavsky approach suggested that environment defined psychology and human relationships; Bryusov thought it obscured the spiritual side of the life on stage, the performer's creative emotion. "The sole objective of the theater is to help the actor reveal his soul to the spectator," he concluded.

Ironically, the result of symbolism on the stage was to diminish the actor's independence and promote the dominance of the director, a development deplored by both Bryusov and Bely. Stanislavsky closed down the Theater Studio after Meyerhold's dress rehearsal of *The Death of Tintagiles*, ostensibly because the acting failed to meet the stylistic demands of the director; and Meyerhold's subsequent experiments with conventionalizing the actor at Kommissarzhevskaya's theater led to his controversial dismissal in 1908. It was clear that the demand for a unified vision in staging symbolist drama was creating a dictatorship of the director and reducing the actor to the kind of Über-Marionette Gordon Craig had called for in his dialogues. Working for Kommissarzhevskaya, translating *Pélléas et Mélisande*, Bryusov looked for a way out of the impasse. In his lecture "Drama of the Future" (May 1907), he developed the notion of the philologist A. A. Potebnya that art is a cognitive process analogous to scientific speculation. Drama and theater are a means of knowing the world through the phenomenon of action, and, as Bryusov pointed out, Aristotle had defined tragedy as the imitation of an action. Only acts of will constitute the subjects of drama, not as allegory or symbol of something else but as action in itself; hence, the mood-producing director is less vital than the acting performer. Both Maeterlinck's work and plays of everyday life (presumably including Chekhov's, which Bryusov held in low esteem) would drop out of the repertory of the future. Only *realistic* plays of action (Shakespeare, Calderón, Goethe and Pushkin of the classics;

Wedekind, Wilde, Hamsun and Verhaeren of the moderns) are suitable. And in fact many of these authors were produced by Kommissarzhevskaya in 1907/8.

Bryusov returned to the problem in his essay "Realism and Convention on the Stage" (1908), where he admitted that actors were by their three-dimensionality out of harmony with a conventionalized production. The only means of overcoming the actors' irrepressible quality of "liveness" would be to replace them with puppets. But since the theater is, by his own definition, a theater of acting and action, suppressing actors entails the abolition of the theater. Rather than go so far, Bryusov evoked the compromise of the Shakespearean stage, allowing certain simplified three-dimensional components of reality which would harmonize with and not detract from the actors, in other words, a synthesis between the actors' reality and the formalistic setting. This compromise, being pragmatic, opened up the theater's possibilities once more; and although most twentieth-century "simplified staging" looks back to Adolphe Appia as its originator, it might also acknowledge Bryusov's contribution.

Bryusov's sweet reasonableness and practicality were uncharacteristic of his fellows. The basic proposal of Fyodor Sologub's "Theater of a Single Will" (1908) is to make actor and director subservient to the playwright, "the single will," who is to read the play aloud, including the stage directions, as mannequin-performers go through the motions. Sologub's dramatic theory is not entirely novel (Goethe had recommended listening to a reading of Shakespeare with one's eyes closed to taste his true greatness), but it is a natural extension of his solipsistic philosophy. Human life is a form of nonexistence, except during childhood: therefore the theater should strive to return to the games of infancy. Humanity is prey to chance: therefore, no one loses anything by becoming a puppet. Black magic is an effective *modus operandi* in our fallen world as in art: therefore the theater must become incantatory and thaumaturgic, the drama a spell woven by the poet-warlock. God and life are mutually denying, and our mundane sphere is ruled by the Devil: therefore we must lose ourselves in the hectic rhythms of a dervish dance. The performance style (and here Sologub was indebted both to Maeterlinck, whose work he had translated, and to Meyerhold, who had directed his play *The Triumph of Death*) was to be cold and measured, the minor characters reduced to motivations for the central figure.

But there is a crucial contradiction in Sologub's scheme: these hieratic poses and carefully subordinated performers are supposed to co-exist with the free expression of childhood's make-believe, so that the spectators can merge with the spectacle as they did in their youthful sports. It is difficult to reconcile this playfulness—which sounds much like Evreinov's and Andreev's concept of theater in life—with the frigid and constrained behavior of mannequins. Another difficulty is Sologub's mythopoeic private language, in which *realia* (the world of appearances) are identified with the Sun-Dragon and Aisa, goddess of fortuity and chaos, "the prodigal sower of incidents," and *realiora* (the immutable truths) with Necessity and Death.

Like Ivanov, Sologub foresaw a union between audience and actor in which the rite becomes a frenzied, ecstatic dithyramb, when concealment will vanish and the Ideas will become manifest. "You'd be better off dancing with a sweet young thing," was Andrey Bely's caustic reply. Bely's impatience with the notion of the theater as a temple and drama as ritual is not a quarrel with Ivanov but with his popularizers; but the embittered tone he takes toward the mystery play is an abrupt about-face for one who before 1905 had enthusiastically subscribed to the Nietzschean doctrine of music-drama and to Ivanov's Dionysian rites as the theater of the future. His essay "On the Forms of Art" (*The World of Art* [*Mir iskusstva*], no. 12, 1902) applauded Ibsen for achieving a *millefeuille* texture of mood and musicality that combines with the dramatic action to produce an authentic many-layered symbolism. This quality pursued to its logical end would result in a true mysterium, itself the precursor or preceptor of the mystery into which our life-to-come will be transformed. Bely began work on his own eschatological mystery play, *The Anti-Christ*, but abandoned it, probably because he became aware of its pointlessness; certainly the apocalyptic vision of the world's end found in its two published fragments has more in common with Treplyov's "decadent" playlet in *The Seagull* than with the soul-rejoicing bond of all humanity envisaged by his colleagues.[38] The disappointments of the failed revolution and its aftermath dashed expectations of life-as-mystery, and Bely, who continued to regard Ibsen as the forerunner of the coming drama, had to revise his concept of the lessons a play might teach.

His next essay on the subject, "The Crisis of Consciousness and Henrik Ibsen," proclaims at the outset, "We are passing through a crisis."

Never before have the fundamental contradictions of the human consciousness collided so violently within the soul;

never before have the dualities of consciousness and feeling, of contemplation and will, of individuality and society, of science and religion, of morality and beauty, been so graphically expressed.[39]

The only way out of these contradictions is to seek the freedom that art provides when it is practiced religiously; but human beings, ever obsessed by the idea of fate, are too pessimistic to accept that solution. Here Ibsen is characterized as the prophet of a new religious awareness; the stuffy Norwegian drawing rooms he depicts are disturbed by an impulsive call to a life beyond this one, and the heroes of his late plays aspire, often with death as their reward, to answer the call. Sooner or later, the dead will awaken.

"Theater and Modern Drama" (1908) was Bely's most thorough development of his new attitude. With an odd glance backward at the civic critics, he insisted on the theater as a means to an end, a signpost to a freer future. Losing oneself in the Dionysian rites of the theater-temple is a perverse mistake, first, because the theater is not a temple and should not in any case be an end in itself; second, because communal delirium is an abnegation of the will, which is the chief human weapon against fate; and third, because individuals must seek their own road. Art is an explosive to be hurled against fate's prison walls; the dynamite imagery (which Bryusov also used on occasion) seems to reflect the political instability of the times. To accomplish all this, the theater must encapsulize those transitional moments when being turns into becoming and when the actual moment on stage opens up into the potentialities of the future. No longer a hybrid of music and drama, the theater is a way station between two separate dimensions, the fettered life of the present and the liberated life-to-be.

VIII

The pieces by Bely, Bryusov and Sologub that appear in this anthology were first published in a collection entitled *Theater: A Book about the New Theater* (1908) which also included essays by Lunacharsky, Benois, Meyerhold[40] and others (chiefly members of Vyacheslav Ivanov's Wednesday salon) and which, curiously, considering the antipositivist matter of many of the contributions, was dedicated to Stanislavsky. The more radical of its manifestos met with a storm of controversy, and it was countered in the same year by another anthology, *The Crisis in the Theater*, whose somewhat less illustrious contributors (Yury Steklov, V. Bazarov, V. Friche et al.) summed up their grievances in the querulous titles, "Theater or Puppet Show?" and "Real Life or Mystery Play?" The Ukrainian belletrist N. I. Nikolaev warned that *Theater* was the proclamation of a theatrical revolution, despite the diversity of opinion represented (he astutely caught Bryusov's "strategic mistake" in allowing the actor more importance than did Meyerhold). Boris Glagolin devoted an article to explaining how Bryusov, Bely and Meyerhold had copied their ideas from his own prior publications. But the overwhelming impression gleaned from the book was that, whatever solutions were offered, the theater was heading for the rocks.

The defeatist conclusion of Bely's essay—voiced by one who might have been thought an active proponent of symbolism on stage—that the cinema or the puppet show would take over the theater's function in future was symptomatic of a discouragement and ennui infecting the critics. This malaise was fostered by dissatisfaction with the many attempts made to stage nonnaturalistic drama in "avant-garde" ways. Bryusov's suggestion that in time the theater might become superfluous for imaginative persons was taken up and expanded by such influential pundits as Leonid Andreev (1871–1919) and Yuly Aikhenvald (1872–1928).

Himself a playwright who veered between Gorkian realism and a hysterical brand of decadence, and whose plays had been produced by both Meyerhold and the Moscow Art Theater, Andreev was unwilling to jettison the theater entirely. *Letters on the Theater* (1911–1914) is one of his more attractive works; it lacks the pretentious phrase-making and the portentous face-making that disfigure so much of his fiction and drama, and it breathes a genuine fondness for the phenomenon it analyzes. It was written at a time when Andreev's own pseudo-symbolist plays (*The Life of Man, Black Masks* and *Anathema*) had already bemused or thrilled audiences in Moscow and Petersburg, and he was turning to a more psychological, less "fashionable" style of playwriting, hoping—as Evreinov did in his lecture on monodrama—to integrate the spectator into the show. Using the Art Theater as his case in point, he traced its development from surface realism to the discovery of Chekhov, and his anatomy of Chekhov's dramatic technique, which injects psychology into every element in his plays, is particularly intriguing. The Art Theater then, complained Andreev, made the mistake of applying the Chekhovian method to every dramatist, no matter how inappropriate, and painted itself into a corner. Now, by adapting the novels of Dostoevsky, availing itself of a narrator much like Solo-

gub's "single will," it was tentatively striking out in a new and fruitful direction. But perhaps the most original aspect of Andreev's *Letters* is the consideration of the cinema as a medium capable of
assuming the theater's onerous need for spectacle and action, thus
leaving the theater free to concentrate on "inner experience" and
what Andreev calls "panpsychism." Liberated from its burden, the
theater could develop a new repertory, no longer reliant on great
novels but capable of generating its own forms to embody subtle
cogitation and modulated emotion. Andreev was too much a man of
the theater to forecast its utter annihilation, and so predicted an im-
proved rebirth.

Aikhenvald had no such compunction. As theater reviewer for
Russian Thought (*Russkaya mysl'*) and a literary critic well known
for demolishing inflated reputations, he observed the theater from
the stalls, not the side-scenes, and what he saw moved him to con-
temptuous derision. The theater, in his eyes, was woefully behind
the times, a crude survival of the past, and any attempts to salvage it
by "stylization," "conventionality" or "psychologism" were doomed
to failure, since they were contrary to the nature of the theater. Its
very concreteness makes it impervious to intellectual or poetic ex-
pansion. Reform implied ultimate rejection. He denied the theater's
independence as a valid art form, because of its reliance on literature, and he articulated an argument that may still be heard on the
lips of academics who disdain to look at Shakespeare on the stage: a
reader in the study can better realize the literary density and richness of a great play and bring the intelligent reader closer to the
author's thought. The author's rights in this matter, complained
Aikhenvald, are too often violated by actors and directors. In short,
he developed to a logical conclusion, almost *ad absurdum*, those
hints in Sologub and Bryusov that owned up to the theater's dilemma.

"Rejecting the Theater" (first published as "The End of Theater") became Aikhenvald's party piece; he printed it several times,
read it from the stage in a public debate and provoked a volume, *Debating the Theater* (1912), in which his denunciation was rebutted
by the directors Nemirovich-Danchenko and Fyodor Kommissarzhevsky, the critic Ovsyaniko-Kulikovsky, the playwright and actor
Yuzhin-Sumbatov and other luminaries. The gist of their attack was
that the actor fulfilled a far more potent role and staging entailed a
good deal more in the realization of a play than Aikhenvald granted.
But, remarked the critic A. S. Kugel, not one of these champions
said "a single word in defense of *passion*, that which excites, dis-
turbs, rejoices a man, and which no art can provide in so full a mea-

sure as does that of the theater."[41] In a certain sense, however, Aikhenvald's extreme position, if taken on its own terms, was unassailable; once one accepts the basic premise that the theater has more in common with life than with art, one can only see it as diminution of literary drama. "Rejecting the Theater," if overblown and rather precious in its rhetoric,[42] was a natural sequel to the schisms within literary circles and the crisis in the repertory.

One who did not accept Aikhenvald's premise at all was Nikolay Evreinov (1879–1953), whom Aikhenvald had patronized and teased in his lecture. Evreinov has never received his due as an original thinker. His many theoretical writings, larded with scholarship and leavened with mischievous wit, do not have the philosophical authority of an Ivanov or a Bely, and because his literary output was entirely dramatic, it has resisted study more than have the poems of Bryusov and Blok. Unlike Meyerhold, who could engineer a tenuous collaboration with the Soviet regime and practice his experiments in a working theater, Evreinov—once he had emigrated—was a man without a company, unable to test his surmises in the laboratory of the rehearsal room. None of his books has been reprinted, except for a rather cranky history of the Russian theater, and none is translated into English in its entirety. So he is known, if at all, through paraphrases and *précis* that fail to convey his erudition and mercuriality.

When Evreinov delivered his lecture on monodrama in 1908, he had already acted, directed and published a volume of plays, his most important venture being the Theater of Yore (*Starinnyy Teatr*) which specialized in authentic revivals of ancient and medieval drama, plays from periods before "theatricality" had been adulterated by realism. Theatricality was Evreinov's central thesis; garnering evidence from zoology, ethnography, behaviorism and virtually every field of knowledge, he stoutly maintained that all aspects of creation are permeated with an instinct for performance and the human race is under the sway of "theatrocracy." The playfulness of this principle might seem at odds with the earnestness of symbolism, but Evreinov's notion of monodrama pursued the same aim as Ivanov's Dionysian revel—the integration of the audience into the performance—but without the sacerdotal trimmings. Although the concept of a unified vision was not an uncommon one at the time (the so-called first German expressionist play, Oskar Kokoschka's *Murderer the Women's Hope*, had appeared the year before Evreinov's lecture), Evreinov's prime concern was to give the spectators the illusion that they are acting, not so that they can commune with a higher truth but so that theatergoing will have meaning for them.

Contemporary critics noted that Evreinov's illustrations were those of a stage director and not a dramatist, and with the exception of a few short plays by B. F. Geier and Evreinov's own *The Performance of Love* and the parody *Backstage at the Soul* (all produced at the revue theater the Crooked Mirror in St. Petersburg), the mono-dramatic technique was not adopted by playwrights. The best example of the monodramatic principle on the Russian stage was probably Gordon Craig's *Hamlet* at the Moscow Art Theater (1912): Craig had envisaged the play as seen through Hamlet's mind's eye, the rest of the characters portrayed only as perceived by the prince, who was accompanied by a phantasmal figure of Death. Stanislavsky's concentration on psychology and an imperfect realization of the stage design vitiated Craig's concept, but enough remained to suggest the pregnancy of Evreinov's ideas.[43]

Evreinov, therefore, was a polar opposite to Aikhenvald, and his rejoinder to "Rejecting the Theater" was not so much reasoned as energetic. He argued with some justice, that the best answer to Aikhenvald would be a slapstick *commedia* spoof of his pedantry, a show to inspire in the spectators the *passion* that Kugel demanded. Yet even Evreinov's apostrophe to the theater to repudiate moralizing and mysticism and return to mummery concluded with a threnody on the death of the old theater and a prophecy of the new.[44]

One month before the October Revolution, writing about the government's responsibility to support theaters, Aleksandr Blok iterated the theater's need to return to its wellsprings:

> The theater is that realm of art of which above all others it may be said: here art and life conjoin, here they meet face to face; here the eternal scrutiny of art and scrutiny of life occur; here these eternal enemies, who must never become friends, wrest the most precious victories from one another; the footlights are a firing-line; the strong and sympathetic spectator, finding himself in this battle array, is tempered in the ordeal by fire. The weak spectator becomes depraved and perishes. Art, like life, is at odds with the weak.
>
> Before the theater can actually become so, it must enter onto a retrograde path; it must, with a sharp movement, rise above all the various tendencies and crying evils of the day; it must break with prejudices; perhaps with the greatest prejudices of whole decades; it must resist the obstruction of dramaturgy and the stage by any values whatsoever—philosophical, journalistic, any except the theatrical; it must draw from

the always inexhaustible treasury, the treasury of *classical art,* i.e., the art over which time has no power.[45]

The course of events made this appeal seem all the more wistful and inappropriate. In the first flush of revolutionary socialism, there was an upsurge of theatrical energies that bore out many of the more improbable manifestos. Meyerhold put his constructivist theories in the service of communist enlightenment (or so he claimed), and Evreinov achieved a gargantuan fusion of spectator and spectacle with his mass recreation of the Storming of the Winter Palace. Other experiments, like the conventionalized eclecticism of the Second Moscow Art Theater under Mikhail Chekhov or Aleksandr Tairov's musical neoclassicism, seemed throwbacks to various symbolist tenets. The cinema began to fulfill the expectations of Bely and Andreev. And the new playwrights—Mayakovsky, Erdman, Olesha—parodied the symbolists (as in *Mystery Bouffe*) even as they effected a new kind of fantasy grounded in earthy reality. The formalist critics of the early 1920s sifted through the masterpieces of the past in their own process of disassemblage and reconstruction, rehabilitating devalued forms like melodrama and farce, assaying and assigning new values to old authors. But the prejudices Blok feared—the dictates of social purpose, state service and public enlightenment—regrouped with renewed strength and under the banner of "Socialist Realism" penned the Russian drama and its criticism into the limitations of shallow optimism, an arid style and a simplistic world view. In criticism, the sententious pedagogy of Belinsky became fused with the enthusiastic reportage of Bishop Avraamy of Suzdal.

Russian Dramatic Theory from Pushkin to the Symbolists

My Remarks on the Russian Theater
by Aleksandr Pushkin

Should one begin by talking about oneself, if one means to talk about others? Does the anonymous critic of Karamzin's *History*[1] need the moldy mask of a Luzhniki hermit? Should one take cover in a Finnish village in order to compare the German wench Lenore with the Scots wench Lyudmila and the Chuvash wench Olga?[2] Finally, is it really necessary for a lover of French acting and hater of Russian theater to pretend to be a one-eyed, armless veteran, as if a missing eyeball and a lopped-off limb granted full rights both to make cockeyed judgments and to be incapable of writing Russian?[3] I do not think so, and therefore I do not here affix my own service record or my birth certificate or a list of my friends and acquaintances or a personal apologia. The reader—who, in my opinion, cares naught for me—will not take the least offense at this, and if he has nothing else to do, he may peruse my *remarks on the Russian theater*, untroubled by my reasons for writing and publishing them.

It is the public that shapes dramatic talents. What is our public like?

Before an opera, a tragedy or a ballet begins, some young fellow saunters through all ten rows in the stalls, steps on everyone's feet and chats both with those he knows and those he does not.

"Where have you been?"—"With Semyonova, Sosnitskaya, Kolosova, Istomina."[4]—"Aren't you the lucky boy!"—"She's singing today—she's acting, she's dancing—we'll give her a round of applause—we'll call her before the curtain! She's so charming! Such eyes! Such a dainty foot! Such talent! . . ." The curtain goes up. The young fellow and his friends, moving from seat to seat, get carried

---

It is believed that this essay was begun sometime between January and May 1820, with the intention of publishing it in *Son of the Fatherland* (*Syn otechestva*), but was interrupted by Pushkin's exile from Petersburg. It was not published until 1895. The present translation is based on the text in A. S. Pushkin, *Polnoe sobranie sochineniy v desyati tomakh*, 3rd ed. (Moscow, 1964), VII.

away and burst into applause. I have no wish to chide perfervid, boisterous youth, I know that it craves indulgence. But can we rely on the opinion of such judges?

Often a singer of either sex, deserving of our audience's affection, goes off-key in an aria by Boïeldieu or della Maria.[5] The connoisseurs register it, the devotees intuit it, but they keep silent out of respect for talent. *The others* applaud on trust and shout "encore" for decorum's sake.

A tragic actor starts to rant more loudly or more vehemently than is his wont; the deafened "gods" go into transports, the theater rocks with applause.

An actress . . . But suffice it to say that our actors' talents cannot possibly be measured by the clamorous approbation of our audiences.

Another remark. A considerable portion of our parterre (i.e., the stalls) is too concerned with the fate of Europe and the nation, too careworn with work, too sober-minded, too grand, too cautious in expressing emotional reactions, to have anything to do with the quality of dramatic art (least of all the Russian kind). And if at half past six the same old faces do arrive from the barracks and council chamber to occupy the first rows of subscription seats, they regard this more as conventional etiquette than enjoyable relaxation. No matter what happens, it is impossible to expect from their chilly abstraction of mind any sensible notions or judgment, let alone the honest expression of any sort of feeling. Consequently, they serve only as a respectable embellishment of the Bolshoy Kamennyy Theater,[6] but definitely do not belong either in the crowd of devotees or among the enlightened or partisan judges.

One more remark. The high-and-mighty of our age, who bear on their faces the monotonous stamp of boredom, arrogance, fretfulness and stupidity—qualities inseparable from their type of occupation—these spectators who habitually fill the first rows, who glower at comedies, yawn at tragedies, doze at operas and pay attention perhaps only at ballets, what can they do perforce but cool the acting of the most zealous of our performers and inspire indolence and languor in their souls, if nature has endowed them with a soul?

But let us see whether Russian actors are worthy of such killing indifference. We shall separately analyze tragedy, comedy, opera and ballet, and try to be indulgent and strict, but above all impartial.

To speak of Russian tragedy is to speak of Semyonova and possibly no one else. Graced with talent, beauty, genuine and vivacious feeling, she owes her cultivation solely to herself. Semyonova never modeled herself on anyone. The soul-starved French actress George and the eternally enraptured poet Gnedich[7] may merely have given her hints about the secrets of art, which she grasped with the intuition of a candid soul. Acting that is always free, always clear, nobility of animated gestures, a resonant voice, evenly modulated, pleasant and frequent gusts of true inspiration, all these are her own appurtenances and are not borrowed from anyone. She ornamented the imperfect works of hapless Ozerov[8] and created the roles of Antigone and Moina;[9] she animated the measured lines of Lobanov;[10] on her lips we came to appreciate the Slavic verses of Katenin,[11] full of force and fire, though wanting in taste and harmony. In the motley translations[12]—patched together by several hands—which have now, regrettably, become the norm, we heard only Semyonova, and on stage the actress's genius sustained all those dismal compositions by poets in committee, which have been repudiated by each of their progenitors in turn. Semyonova is unrivaled. Biased rumors and offerings of the moment, news purveyed by word-of-mouth, came to an end; she has remained the sovereign queen of the tragic stage. There was a time when they tried to compare her with the splendid comic actress Valberkhova,[13] whose Dido was vividly reminiscent of simpering Célimène (just as in *The Jealous Wife** she even now reminds us of the Carthaginian queen). But true adherents of her talent have forgotten that they ever saw her in a crown and mantle, which she has very sensibly exchanged for a gown with a train and a plumed hat.

In the humble garb of Antigone, to the plaudits of a full house, young, sweet, shy Kolosova[14] appeared not long ago in the service of Melpomene. Her seventeen years, beautiful eyes, lovely teeth (consequently a frequent and charming smile), a charming lisp enchanted the judges of tragic talent. An almost unanimous verdict pronounced Sashenka Kolosova to be the heiress apparent to Semyonova. Throughout the play her acting never ceased to be interrupted by applause. At the tragedy's end, she was called forth with shouts of rapture, and when Mrs. Kolosova Senior

Filiae pulchrae mater pulchrior[15]

appeared in the subsequent ballet in Russian national costume and beaming with maternal pride, there was no end of roaring and shouting. The happy mother wept and silently thanked the ecstatic throng. An incident unique in the history of our theater. I relate it baldly,

---

*Some consider Miss Valberkhova's best role to be *The Jealous Wife*. That is absolutely wrong. Haven't they seen her in *The Misanthrope*, *The Accidental Wager*, *Mr. and Mrs. Emptyhouse*, etc.?

making no comment. Three times running Kolosova played three different roles with equal success. What was the upshot of it all? The delight in her talent and beauty gradually cooled down, the praise grew more moderate, the applause died away, and they stopped comparing her to the incomparable Semyonova; soon she began to appear before empty houses. Finally, on her benefit night, when she played the role of Zaïre, everyone fell asleep and woke up only when the Christian maid Zaïre, who died in the fifth act of the tragedy, reappeared at the end of a rather tedious vaudeville in a crimson sarafan and gold fillet and set about dancing a Russian folk-dance with great charm, to the tune of "In the orchard or the garden."

If Kolosova were less concerned with His Imperial Majesty's ADCs, and more with her roles; if she emended her monotonous crooning, harsh shrieking and Parisian pronunciation of the letter *R* (very pleasant in the drawing room but inappropriate on the tragic stage); if her gestures were to become more natural and not so affected; if she were not just to imitate the expression on Semyonova's face, but strove to adopt her profound conception of her roles as well: then we might hope to have in time a truly fine actress—not only splendid in person, but beautiful in mind, art and undeniable gifts. Beauty fades but talent is long a-withering. Who talks of Karatygina[16] these days, she who, by her own admission, could never understand the meaning of a single word in her role if it was written in verse? There was a time when a dazzled public raved about the amazing talent of Yakovlev's gorgeous mistress; now she is on a par with his lawful widow, and no one ventures to decide which of them is the more unintelligible and disagreeable. Modest, overlooked Yablochkina,[17] with a perfect understanding of the utter insignificance of the role of tragic confidante, is preferable to both of them with her simple, unconcerned verse reading, which at least does not steal focus from the leading lady's performance.

For quite a while Semyonova appeared before us partnered by the wild but passionate Yakovlev, who, sober, reminded us of Talma drunk. In those days we had two tragic actors! . . . Yakovlev died; Bryansky[18] took his place, but did not replace him. Bryansky is perhaps more decorous, generally has more stage dignity, more respect for his audience, memorizes his roles more thoroughly and does not hold up the performance with his "sudden indispositions"; but, on the other hand, what frigidity! What monotonous, ponderous crooning!

You'd make better sense, I think,
If you'd only take to drink.[19]

Yakovlev often emitted dazzling flashes of genius, occasionally flashes of a tuppence-colored Talma. Bryansky is ever and everywhere the same. Ever smiling Fingal, Thésée, Orosman, Jason, Dmitry—equally uninspired, bombastic, forced, tiresome. In vain you appeal to him: rouse yourself, my good sir! Let yourself go, blow your top, up and at 'em! Awkward, measured, inhibited in every gesture, he is unable to control either his voice or his body. Bryansky in tragedy has never stirred anyone and in comedy has never made anyone laugh. Nevertheless, as a comic actor he has the advantage and even true quality.

I leave to the mercies of the pit-boxes Shchenikov, Glukharev, Kamenogorsky, Tolchenov,[20] etc. All of them, welcomed with delight at first and, later, having sunk to be scorned by the very "gods," *perished without a sound.* But from the number of these outcasts we except Boretsky.[21] A love for his art, which some think is unrequited, lured him to the tragic stage. He has none of Yakovlev's majestic bearing or even Bryansky's passably pleasant demeanor, and he croons even more monotonously and tiresomely and, as a rule, is a worse actor than he. *Certes! c'est beaucoup dire*—even so, I prefer Boretsky to Bryansky. Boretsky has feeling; we have heard paroxysms of his soul in the roles of Oedipus and old Horace. We do not entirely despair of him. An eradication of all his bad habits, a total alteration in his methods, a new form of expression may turn Boretsky, who is gifted with emotional and physical capabilities, into an actor of great worth.

But let us leave the thankless field of tragedy and proceed to an analysis of comic talents.

On National-Popular Drama and the Play *Martha the Seneschal's Wife*

by Aleksandr Pushkin

[ROUGH DRAFT FOR THE ARTICLE]
Dramatic art originated in the public square—for the diversion of the common people. What does the common people like, what affects it? What language does it understand?

From the public square and fairs (the license of mystery plays). Racine transfers it to court. How did it make its appearance?

(Corneille, a Spanish poet.)[1]

Sumarokov, Ozerov—(Katenin).

Shakespeare, Goethe—his influence on current French theater, on us. The blissful ignorance of critics. Mocked by Vyazemsky,[2] they paid lip service, they accepted romanticism, but in fact not only fail to adhere to it, but childishly attack it.

What evolves in a tragedy? What is its aim? Man and the common people. Human fate, the common people's fate. That's why Racine is great, despite the constricted form of his tragedy. That's why Shakespeare is great, despite the unevenness, shoddiness, inelegance of finish.

What does a dramatist need? Some philosophy, impassivity, an historian's political ideas, intuition, a vivid imagination, no prejudice, no pet idea. *Freedom.*

An erroneous understanding of poetry in general and dramatic art in particular. What is the aim of drama?

This essay was written in the autumn of 1830, many of the specific comments on Pogodin's play *Martha the Seneschal's Wife* already having appeared in Pushkin's correspondence with its author. It was first published posthumously in 1841/2. The text is from A. S. Pushkin, *Polnoe sobranie sochineniy v desyati tomakh*, 3rd ed. (Moscow, 1964), VII. I have used the awkward "national-popular" to translate *narodny* in the title, because Pushkin means both drama which originates among the people and drama which is imbued with nationalistic traits.

What is drama?
How it took shape.
Ioann. His influence, his politics.
Shakespeare. *The common people.* Women.
The Seneschal's Wife. How Karamzin interpreted her in history.[3]
Kseniya.
Action (style).

[FINAL VERSION]
Even though aesthetics has developed so lucidly and extensively since the days of Kant and Lessing, we still cleave to the concepts of that ponderous pedant Gottsched,[1] we still go on repeating that the *beautiful* is an imitation of refined nature, and that the primary virtue of art is *utility.* Why then do painted statues please us less than do those purely of marble and bronze? Why does a poet prefer to couch his ideas in verse? And what kind of utility is there in a Titian Venus or the Apollo Belvedere?

Verisimilitude is still presumed to be the primary condition and basis of dramatic art. What if it were demonstrated that the very essence of dramatic art distinctly precludes verisimilitude? Reading an epic or a novel, we may often lose ourselves and assume that the incident depicted is not fiction but truth. In an ode or elegy, we may think that the poet was portraying his authentic feelings in authentic circumstances. But where is the verisimilitude of a building divided into two parts, one of which is filled with spectators who have agreed, etc.?

If we are to assume that verisimilitude consists of a strict observance of [unity] in costuming, local color, time and place, we shall straightway see that the greatest dramatists have failed to obey this rule. In Shakespeare, Roman lictors retain the manners of London aldermen. In Calderón, doughty Coriolano challenges a consul to a duel and flings a gauntlet at him. In Racine, the half-Scythian Hippolyte speaks the language of a well-bred young marquis. The Romans of Corneille are either Spanish cavaliers or Gascon barons, and Corneille's Clytemnestre is escorted by Swiss guards.[2] For all that, Calderón, Shakespeare and Racine stand on an unscalable summit, and their works comprise a perennial object of our studies and raptures.

Just what sort of verisimilitude, then, are we to require of a dramatic poet? To resolve this question, let us first consider what drama is and what its aim.

Drama originated in a public square and constituted a popular entertainment. The common people, like children, require amusement, action. The drama confronts them with a strange and unusual incident. The common people require violent sensations; even a public execution is for them a show.

Laughter, pity and terror are the three chords of our imagination, vibrated by dramatic enchantment. But laughter soon palls, and a complete dramatic action cannot possibly be founded on it alone. The ancient tragic poets disregarded this mainspring. Popular satire took exclusive possession of it and acquired a dramatic form closer to parody. In this way comedy arose which, over time, was perfected. Let us note that high comedy is grounded not only on laughter, but on character development, and not infrequently it approximates tragedy.

For the most part, tragedy depicted heinous crimes, supernatural ordeals, even physical suffering (e.g., Philoctetes, Oedipus, Lear). But habit blunts sensation—the imagination becomes accustomed to murders and executions, begins to regard them with indifference, whereas the depiction of the passions and effusions of the human soul is always a novelty, always engrossing, elevated and instructive. The drama began to control passions and the human soul.

Authenticity of passions and verisimilitude in emotions under given conditions arc what our intellect demands of dramatic poets.

Drama left the public square and betook itself to stately halls at the behest of a cultured, elite society. The poet migrated to the court. Nevertheless the drama remains faithful to its original intent—to act on the multitude, to engage its curiosity.

What captures the attention of a cultured, enlightened spectator if not the portrayal of important events in the state? Hence history—both peoples and kings—was transferred to the stage, brought before us by the dramatic poet.

In stately halls the drama changed, it lowered its voice. It no longer had any need to shout. It doffed the mask of exaggeration, indispensable in the public square but unneeded in a chamber; it appeared as more simple, more natural. More refined sensibilities no longer required a violent shock. Drama ceased to portray repulsive suffering, weaned itself of horrors and gradually grew decorous and grandiose. But there drama shed its universally comprehensible language and assumed a fashionable, select and refined idiom.

Hence the important difference between Shakespearean popular tragedy and Racinian court drama. The creator of popular tragedy was better educated than his spectators: he knew it and bestowed on them his free-spirited works, confident of his own higher status and of public recognition, felt unquestioningly by all. At court, on the contrary, the poet felt inferior to his public. The spectators were better educated than he, at least he thought so and so did they. He did not give free, bold rein to his fancies. He strove to intuit what was demanded by the refined taste of persons alien to him in status. He was afraid of dishonoring some high dignitary, offending some of his haughty spectators—hence the timorous prissiness, the ludicrous bombast that became proverbial (*un héros, un roi de comédie*), the habit of regarding persons of high station with a certain servility and endowing them with a strange, inhuman turn of phrase. In Racine (for instance) Nero does not simply say, *Je serai caché dans ce cabinet*—but, *Caché près de ces lieux je vous verrai, madame.* Agamemnon wakes his confidant and says to him grandiloquently, *Oui, c'est Agamemnon . . .*[3]

We have grown accustomed to this and feel that that's the way it ought to be. But one has to admit that if the heroes of Shakespeare's tragedies express themselves like stableboys, it does not strike us as strange, for we feel that even the exalted should express simple concepts as simple folk do.

I neither purpose nor dare to define the advantages and disadvantages of this or that tragedy—to trace the fundamental differences in the systems of Racine and Shakespeare, Calderón and Goethe. I hasten to survey the history of dramatic art in Russia.

With us, drama has never been a requisite of the common people. The bishop of Rostov's mystery plays, the tragedies of Princess Sophia Alexeevna[4] were presented at the tsar's court and in the apartments of the boyars closest to the throne—and were extraordinary merrymakings, not regular diversions. The first acting companies to appear in Russia did not attract the common people, who had no understanding of dramatic art and were unused to its conventions. Sumarokov[5] emerged, the most hapless of epigones. His tragedies, full of meaningless fustian, written in a barbarously effete language, pleased the court of Elizabeth as novelties, imitations of Parisian diversions. These flaccid, frigid works could have no influence on popular taste. The theater remained alien to our way of life. Ozerov realized this. He endeavored to give us national tragedy—and assumed that to do so one need only select a subject from national history, forgetting that the French poet took all the subjects for his tragedies from Roman, Greek and Jewish history, and that

Shakespeare's most popular tragedies were borrowed by him from Italian novellas.

After *Dmitry of the Don*, after *Pozharsky*,[6] the work of an immature talent, we still had no tragedy. Katenin's *Andromache*[7] (perhaps the best creation of our Melpomene in its power of true feeling and genuinely tragic spirit) certainly did not, however, rouse the stage, left empty following Semyonova's departure, from its torpor.

The idealized *Ermak*,[8] the lyrical work of an ardent young imagination, is not a dramatic work. Everything in it is alien to our manners and spirit, everything, including the fascinating charm of the poetry itself.

Comedy was more fortunate. We have two dramatic satires.[9]

Why then do we have no national-popular tragedy? First we had better determine whether one is possible. We have seen that popular tragedy originated in the public square, took shape and only then was summoned to aristocratic society. With us the process would have to be reversed. We would want to abase courtly, Sumarokovian tragedy to the level of the public square—but what obstacles are in the way!

Can our tragedy, bred up to the example of Racinian tragedy, break itself of its aristocratic habits? How can it shift from its measured, pompous and decorous dialogue to the vulgar frankness of popular passion, to the public square's freedom of opinion—how can it suddenly relinquish its servility, how can it do without the rules to which it has grown accustomed and without the forcible adaptation of everything Russian to everything European; where, from whom, is it to learn an idiom the common people can comprehend? What are the common people's passions, what are its heartstrings, where will it find its consonance—in a word, where are the spectators, where is the audience?

Instead of a public audience, it will encounter the selfsame narrow bounded circle—and will offend its haughty (*dédaigneux*) traditions; instead of consonance, response and applause, it will hear picayune, niggling criticism. Insurmountable obstacles will rise up in its path—before it can erect its trestle stage, it will have to transform and overthrow the customs, mores and precepts of whole centuries . . .

Before *us*, however, lies one essay at a popular tragedy.

Before we begin to evaluate *Martha the Seneschal's Wife*, let us thank the anonymous author[10] for the conscientiousness of his labor, an earnest of his genuine talent. He wrote his tragedy not out of vanity, avid for momentary success, nor to oblige the common ruck of readers who are not only unprepared for romantic drama, but even downright inimical to it.* He wrote his tragedy as the result of a powerful inner conviction, having devoted himself entirely to independent inspiration, isolating himself in his labor. In the present state of our literature, without such self-denial, nothing truly worthy of attention can be produced.

The author of *Martha the Seneschal's Wife* had as his aim the unfolding of a major historical event, the fall of Novgorod, which decided the issue of supreme sovereignty in Russia. History had already presented him with two great characters. First, Ioann [Ivan the Great], already delineated by Karamzin in all his awesome and glacial grandeur; second, Novgorod, whose characteristics had to be divined.

The dramatic poet—as impartial as fate—had to portray—as candidly as a profound, conscientious investigation of the truth and the vivacity of a youthful, ardent imagination would allow—the rebuff to expiring freedom as a profoundly deliberated blow which established Russia on its vast foundation. He was not to dodge the matter and incline to one side, to the disadvantage of the other. Not he nor his political opinions nor his covert or overt partiality was to find utterance in this tragedy—nothing but the people of bygone days, their minds, their prejudices. It was not his concern to vindicate and indict, to prompt the speeches. It was his concern to resurrect a bygone age in all its veracity. Did the author of *Martha the Seneschal's Wife* fulfill these primary and imperative conditions? We reply, he did—and if not throughout, then he was betrayed not by his desire or conviction or conscience, but by human nature, ever imperfect.

Ioann fills the tragedy. His thought sets in motion the whole ponderous mass, all the passions, all the mainsprings. In the first scene, Novgorod learns of his power-seeking pretensions and the unlooked-for campaign against it. The indignation, horror, differences of opinion, confusion produced by this news provide us with

*Not to mention the magazines whose verdicts have a decisive influence not only on the public but even on writers, who—although they contemn them—steer clear of sneers and abuse in print.

an advance understanding of his might. He has not yet appeared, but even at this point we, like Martha, sense his presence. The poet removes us to the Muscovite camp amid the disaffected princes, boyars and voivodes. Here too a consciousness of Ioann prevails and governs all thoughts, all passions. Here we see the might of his sovereignty, the subdued recalcitrance of the apanaged princes, the fear instilled in them by Ioann, the blind faith in his omnipotence. The princes freely and clearly understand what his action means, they project and propound lofty schemes, the emissaries from Novgorod await him. Ioann appears. His speech to the emissaries does not diminish the notion of him which the poet has succeeded in implanting. Cold, firm resolve, prepotent accusations, sham magnanimity, a cunning enumeration of grievances. We actually hear Ioann, we recognize his mighty concept of governance, we hear the spirit of his age. Novgorod replies to him in the person of its emissaries. What a scene! What historical accuracy! How he divines the diplomacy of a franchised Russian town! Ioann does not care whether they are right or wrong. He lays down his ultimatums, while he prepares for a decisive battle. But not with arms alone does cautious Ioann act. Treachery abets power. The scene between Ioann and the fictitious Boretsky seems to us out of keeping. The poet did not quite care to denigrate the betrayer of Novgorod—hence the arrogance of his speeches and the undramatic (i.e., implausible) leniency of Ioann. People may say, "He puts up with it, because he needs Boretsky"— true. But Boretsky would not have dared forget himself to Ioann's face, nor would the turncoat go on speaking with the free speech of a Novgoroder. On the other hand, how copiously, how calmly does Ioann unfold his ideas of governance!—and let us remark, such candor is a sovereign's highest form of flattery and uniquely worthy of him. Ioann's last speech—

> Russian boyars,
> Chieftains, princes, etc.

does not seem to us to correspond to the spirit of Ioann's reign. He has no need to inflame their zeal, he would not expatiate to them on the reasons for his actions. It would be enough for him to say to them, "Tomorrow's the battle, be prepared."

We leave Ioann, having learned his intent, his thoughts, his mighty will—and we next see him when he silently rides as conqueror through a Novgorod betrayed to him. His orders, transmitted to us by history, are also preserved in the tragedy, without fictional addenda or explanations. Martha predicts dynastic misfortunes for him and the extinction of his line. He replies:

> Whatsoe'er pleaseth the Lord—may it come to pass!
> I am at peace, having accomplished my task.

Such is the portrayal of Ioann, a portrayal which accords with history and is sustained at almost every point. In it the tragic poet is not inferior to his subject. He understands it clearly, accurately, he knows it intimately—and presents it to us without theatrical over-statement, without meaningless fustian, without hokum.

Petersburg Notes for 1836
by Nikolay Gogol

I

. . . Now really, look where the capital of Russia turned out to be! At the world's very brink! We Russians are a peculiar people: we had a capital in Kiev, but it was too warm there, not cold enough; so the Russian capital transferred to Moscow—no, not cold enough there either: God grant us Petersburg! It will be quite a stunt if the Russian capital snuggles up to the polar ice cap. I say this because its mouth is watering to get a close look at the polar bears. "Running away from Mother Moscow more than four hundred and fifty miles! That's what I call footloose!" say the Muscovites, squinting at the Finnish shore. But, to make up for it, what a wilderness 'twixt Mummy and Sonnyboy! What sights these be, what natural surroundings! The air is laced with fog; on the pale, gray-green earth stand charred stumps, pine trees, stands of fir, hillocks . . . It's a lucky thing that the roadway, darting like an arrow, and the singing, jingling Russian troikas speed by it in a twinkling. But the difference, oh the difference between the two! Mother Moscow is still today a Russian beardling, while Petersburg is already a fastidious German. How old Moscow has sprawled and spread! How unkempt she is! How the dandy Petersburg has spruced himself up and stood to attention! He is confronted on all sides by looking glasses: here the Neva, there the Gulf of Finland. Plenty of opportunity to look himself over. No sooner does he spot a bit of fluff or lint on him than, that very instant, off he flicks it. Moscow is an old homebody,

The first part of this article was written in 1835 and originally entitled "Moscow and Petersburg"; the second was begun in 1836 and entitled "The Petersburg Stage in 1835/6." The conflation, reworked by Gogol in Rome, was published over the signature *** in the *Contemporary* (*Sovremennik*, no. 6, 1837). The present translation is based on the text in N. V. Gogol, *Sobranie sochineniy v semi tomakh*, ed. S. I. Mashinsky, N. L. Stepanov and M. B. Khrapchenko (Moscow, 1967), VI.

who fries pancakes, stares at things from a distance and, without rising from her easy-chair, lends an ear to accounts of what goes on in the world. Petersburg is a hail-fellow-well-met who never stays at home, is always fully dressed and saunters up and down the escarpment's coping-stones, showing off for Europe, which sees but does not hear.

Petersburg bestirs himself, from cellars to garret; at midnight he begins baking French bread which will all be eaten the next day by the German folk, and all night long first one of his eyes gleams, and then the other. Moscow sleeps at night, and on the morrow, after crossing herself and bowing low in all directions, she rides to market with home-baked rolls. Moscow is feminine, Petersburg masculine. Everyone in Moscow is a bride, everyone in Petersburg a groom. Petersburg observes more propriety in his dressing, is not fond of garish colors or any startling or daring deviation from fashion; on the other hand, if something has already come into fashion, Moscow demands that it be fashion to the nth degree: if waists are worn long, let them be ever so long; if the lapels on swallowtail coats are wide, then hers are like barn doors. Petersburg is a prissy sort, a German through and through, who scrutinizes everything cannily and, before even considering enjoying himself, peers in his pocket. Moscow is old Russian nobility, and if she is having a good time, goes on having it until she drops and cares not whether she's already squandered more than her pocket holds: she hates half measures. In Moscow all magazines, no matter how scholarly, always append a fashion plate at the end of the issue. Petersburghers seldom include plates; when they do, the inexperienced reader coming upon one may be alarmed. Muscovite magazines talk about Kant, Schelling and so forth and so on; Petersburg magazines talk only about the public and benevolent intentions . . . In Moscow the magazines are in step with the times, but they are always late in coming out; in Petersburg the magazines are behind the times, but they come out punctually, on the designated date. In Moscow, writers barely keep alive, in Petersburg they get rich and thrive. Moscow is always riding somewhere, muffled up in a bearskin coat, most often to dinner; Petersburg, in a coarse woolen frockcoat, both hands thrust in his pockets, flies at full speed to the stock exchange or "the office." Moscow is on the town till four o'clock in the morning and does not get out of bed the next day before one; Petersburg is also on the town till four o'clock, but the next day, as if nothing at all had happened, scurries to work in his coarse woolen frockcoat. Russia with money to burn toddles along to Moscow and returns home empty-handed;

penniless Russia goes to Petersburg and then disperses to the four corners of the earth with a tolerable fortune. Russia crawls along to Moscow in winter tip-carts, along winter potholes, to buy and sell; the Russian folk go to Petersburg on foot in the summertime to build and work. Moscow is a storehouse, she piles up bales and bundles and looks down her nose at a retailer; Petersburg has wasted all his substance in dribs and drabs, parceled himself out and scattered into little shops and stores, and he angles for the retail shoppers. Moscow says, "If a customer needs it, he'll find it"; Petersburg pokes a sign under your very nose, excavates a wine cellar beneath your floor and sets up a hackney stand on your very threshold. Moscow pays no attention to her own inhabitants, but sends wares throughout all Russia; Petersburg sells cravats and gloves to its own civil servants. Moscow is a great bazaar; Petersburg is a well-lit department store. Russia needs Moscow; Petersburg needs Russia. In Moscow you seldom come across a button with an official stamp on a tailcoat; in Petersburg there is no tailcoat without official buttons. Petersburg loves to rally Moscow for her crudeness, clumsiness and want of taste; Moscow jabs at Petersburg for being mercenary and not knowing how to speak Russian. In Petersburg, at two o'clock, the people who stroll along Nevsky Prospect look as if they have emerged from the fashion plates bound into magazines and displayed in windows, even the old dames have such tiny, narrow waists it makes you laugh; when strolling in Moscow, even in the very heart of a fashionable crowd, you can always run into some biddy with a kerchief on her head and without the hint of a waist. Something more might be said, but in short—

A distance vast lies 'twixt the twain! . . .

[Griboedov, *Woe from Wit*]

II

It is difficult to take in the general aspect of Petersburg. It somewhat resembles a European-American colony: just as few native nationals and just as many assorted foreigners, not yet blended into a compact mass. It contains as many diverse nations as diverse strata of society. These societies are entirely distinct from one another: aristocrats, bureaucrats in the civil service, tradesmen, Englishmen, Germans, merchants—each constitutes entirely distinct circles which seldom mingle with one another, but for the most part live and enjoy themselves, invisible to one another.

And each of these classes, if one were to scrutinize them more closely, would be seen to consist of a multitude of other smaller circles, which do not intermingle either. Take, for instance, the civil servants. Junior assistants to head clerks make up their own circle, to which no department head would descend for anything in the world. The head clerk, for his part, holds his quiff a little higher in the presence of a bureaucrat from the chancellery. German workmen and German civil servants also constitute two distinct circles. Schoolmasters make up a circle of their own, as actors do theirs. Even the man of letters, who has up to now seemed to be an equivocal and dubious personage, has an entirely distinct standing. In short, it is as if an enormous stagecoach had rolled up to an inn, a stagecoach in which each passenger had sat muffled up the whole journey and now entered the common room only because there was nowhere else to go. Any attempt at establishing public societies has heretofore met with failure. The Petersburgher goes to a club only to dine, not to spend time. That Petersburg has not yet become an inn is due to some elemental inner quality of Russians, which remains idiosyncratic despite the constant polish derived from contact with foreigners. To describe each of these circles and observe the life pulsating through them with its amusements, recreations, hopes, sorrows, one needs must be one of those men who write absolutely nothing, because such gentlemen, as a result of their activity, have absolutely no time. Therefore, away with balls and parties! I shall address myself to those entertainments which linger longer in the memory and are accessible to all classes. Theater and concerts—those are the points at which the classes of Petersburg society coincide and have opportunity to stare at one another to their heart's content. Ballet and opera are the king and queen of Petersburg theater. Their appearance has been more brilliant, clamorous and magical than in previous years, and the enraptured spectators have forgotten the very existence of majestic tragedy that can inspire the consenting hearts of this speechless hearkening throng with involuntary feelings of sublimity, or of comedy, rigorously designed, which evokes laughter through the intensity of its irony—not the laughter engendered by superficial impressions, a glancing witticism or play on words, not that laughter which stirs society's ribald throng—with its need for convulsions and grotesque caricatures of nature—but that galvanic, vitalizing laughter which is wrested unbidden, freely and unawares from a soul smitten by a blinding flash of wit, born of the tranquil delight produced only by a superior intelligence. The spectators are right to have been enraptured by ballet and opera . . . The dramatic stage has been taken over by melodrama and vaudeville, transient guests who were masters of the house in the French theater, but played a singularly odd role on the Russian stage. It has long been acknowledged that Russian actors are somewhat incongruous when they impersonate marquises, vicomtes and barons, quite as ridiculous as the French would probably be if they ventured to imitate Russian peasants; but those scenes of balls, soirees and fashionable routs that show up in Russian plays—what are they doing there? And vaudevilles? . . . It's been a while now since vaudevilles crept on to the Russian stage, amusing folks of average quality, since it is easy to make them laugh. Who would have thought that vaudeville would survive on the Russian stage not only in translation but as an original play? A Russian vaudeville! It's really quite peculiar, peculiar because this feather-brained, insipid plaything could have originated only among the French, a nation temperamentally devoid of a profound, settled aspect; but when the still somewhat austere and ponderous Russian temperament forces itself to twirl around like a petit-maître . . . it calls to mind one of our corpulent, crafty, broad-bearded merchants, who has never been shod except with a heavy boot and who now dons a tight slipper and openwork stocking while he simply leaves his other foot in its boot, and in this fashion leads the first measure in a French quadrille.

It's been some five years now that melodrama and vaudeville have dominated the theaters all over the world. What apishness! Even the Germans—well, who would have thought that the Germans, that stolid race disposed to profound aesthetic pleasures—are now performing and writing vaudevilles, are adapting and slapping together bombastic and sterile melodramas! If only this pestilence had spread at the mighty bidding of a genius! When all the world was in tune with Byron's lyre, there was nothing funny about it; there was even something affecting in that aspiration. But Dumas, Ducange and their lot have become universal legislators! . . .[1] I swear the nineteenth century will be ashamed of itself for these five years . . . Oh Molière, great Molière! Thou, whose characters were developed with such breadth and abundance, who traced their nuances so profoundly; thou, austere and circumspect Lessing, and thou, noble, ardent Schiller, who illustrated the dignity of man so poetically! Turn your gaze to what is occurring on our stage in your wake. Behold what a strange monster, in the form of melodrama, has stolen in among us! Where is our life? Where are we with all our modern passions and quirks? Could we but see some of it reflected in our melodramas! But our melodrama tells lies in the most shameless manner . . .

The phenomenon is incomprehensible: only a profound, prodigious, extraordinary talent is capable of perceiving that which encompasses our everyday life, which is inseparable from us, which is ordinary. But the infrequent, the exceptional, the breath-takingly horrid, discordant amid concord, is latched onto by the mediocrity with both hands. And lo, the life of a profound talent flows in all its profusion, with all its harmony, clear as a mirror, reflecting with equal clarity both dark and light clouds, whereas the mediocrity's life courses toward turbid and muddied waters, which reflect neither light nor dark.

The bizarre has become the theme of current drama. Its whole concern is to relate some adventure, unquestionably novel and unquestionably bizarre, never seen or heard of up to now: murders, arson, the most savage passions, not an iota of which exists in modern society! It's as if the sons of torrid Africa had donned our European dress-coats! Hangmen, poisons—stage effects, everlasting stage effects, and not a single character to evoke any sympathy! Never yet has a spectator left the theater affected and in tears; on the contrary, in a rather overwrought state he hurriedly climbs into his carriage and for a long while cannot collect and coordinate his thoughts. Such is the style of show preferred by our refined and cultivated society! I cannot help but think of those bloodthirsty arenas where all Rome gathered to look on, during the period of its greatest sway and jaded glut. But, thank God, we are not yet Romans nor in the sunset of our existence, but only at its dawning! If a collection were made of all of the melodramas staged in our time, one might think it a cabinet of curios, where monstrosities and freaks of nature were deliberately assembled, or, better yet, an almanac in which, with almanacular dryness, all strange events were recorded, with a note after each date: today in thus-and-such a place thus-and-such a swindle was perpetrated; today the heads of thus-and-such highwaymen and incendiaries were lopped off; thus-and-such a shopkeeper slit his wife's throat on this particular date . . . and so forth. I can envisage the strange bewilderment of our posterity, thinking to discover our society in our melodramas.

No wonder ballet and opera are more cheering and promote relaxation: their pleasures are serene ones. We took to opera with avidity. Even now the enthusiasm with which all Petersburg rushed to the vivid, colorful music of *Fenella* and the wild, diabolically delightful music of *Robert le Diable* has not passed away. *Semira-mide*,[2] which the audience viewed indifferently five years earlier, *Semiramide*, now that Rossini's music is almost an anachronism, moves the same audience to utter rapture. There is nothing that can be said of the enthusiasm aroused by the opera *A Life for the Tsar*,[3] for all Russia already knows and understands it. Either a great deal must be said about this opera or nothing at all.

But I do not choose to discuss either music or singing. It seems to me that all musical treatises and reviews must be tedious to the musicians themselves: the greater part of music is ineffable and in-scrutable. Musical passions are not the passions of everyday life; sometimes music only expresses or, to be more precise, counterfeits the voice of our passions, so that, supported by them, it courses with the gushing, singing stream of other passions, to another sphere. I note only that melomania is becoming more and more widespread. Persons whom no one would suspect of having a musical sensibility never fail to attend *A Life for the Tsar*, *Robert*, *Norma*,[4] *Fenella* and *Semiramide*. The operas are performed almost twice a week, they sustain a countless number of performances, and even then it is often difficult to procure tickets. Is it our tuneful Slavic nature that is reacting in this way? Is this not a return to our good old days after peregrinations in the alien territory of European enlightenment where incomprehensible languages are always spoken and unfamil-iar people kept flashing by, a return to the Russian troika, with its jingling harness-bells, with which, rearing up as we run and waving our hats, we say, "It's fine to roam, but there's no place like home!"

What an opera might be composed out of our national melodies! Show me a people that has more songs. Our Ukraine rings with songs. Along the Volga, from its sources down to the sea, in every team of men towing the boats, bargehaulers' songs trill forth. To the accompaniment of song, cabins all over Russia are built out of pine logs. To the accompaniment of song, bricks are passed from hand to hand, and, like mushrooms, towns spring up. To the accompa-niment of peasant women's songs, the Russian is swaddled, mar-ried and buried. Everyone on the road, nobility and mobility alike, speeds to the song of the coachmen. By the Black Sea, the beardless, swarthy Cossack with his pitch-stiffened moustache sings an old-fashioned song as he loads his culverin; and way out there, at the other end of the world, mounted on an ice-floe, the Russian trapper harpoons a whale while striking up a song. Do we not have the wherewithal to compose our own operas? Glinka's opera is only a beautiful beginning. Fortunately he knew how to pour the music of two types of Slav into his compositions; you can hear at what point the Russian speaks and at what point the Pole: the free-and-easy theme of Russian song breathes in one, in the other the precipitant theme of the Polish mazurka.

Petersburg ballets are dazzling. Now about ballets in general: the staging of ballets in Paris, Petersburg and Berlin has made considerable progress; but it must be remarked that only the lavishness of costume and scenery has been perfected; the very essence of ballet, its theme, is not in the same class as its mounting; balletmasters have very little new to say in the dances. So far there is scant characterization. Look round you, there are folk dances all over the world: a Spaniard does not dance like a Swiss, nor a Scot like a German out of Teniers, nor a Russian like a Frenchman or an Oriental. Even in the provinces of one nation the dances differ. The northern Russian does not dance like the Little Russian, the southern Slav, the Pole or the Finn: one's dance is chatty, another's taciturn; one's is frantic, lascivious, another's placid; one's is straitlaced and pursey, another's light and airy. Whence originated such a variety of dances? It originated in the temperament of the folk, its life and style of occupation. A folk that leads a proud and warlike existence expresses that pride in its dancing; with a carefree and independent folk that untrammeled independence and poetical lack of self-consciousness are reflected in the dancing; a folk from a torrid zone preserves the same effeminacy, passion and jealousy in its national dances. Guided by a nice discrimination, the balletmaster can take as much as he wants from each to define the personalities of his dancing heroes. It stands to reason that once he has captured the central feature, he can develop it and soar incomparably above his original, just as a musical genius can create a whole epic from a simple song heard in the street. Then, at least, dances will make more sense, and thus that light, airy and ardent language, presently still rather constrained and constricted, may be better represented in vivid images.

Petersburg is a great fan of the theater. If you stroll down Nevsky Prospect on a fresh frosty morning, as the sky, sun-begilt and pink, is broken by transparent clouds of smoke rising from the chimney-pots, drop by the lobby of the Alexandra Theater about this time: you will be struck by the tenacious patience with which the folks gathered here forcefully besiege the ticket-seller, who pokes only one of his hands out of his wicket. So many footmen of all sorts congregate there, from the one who came wearing a gray greatcoat and a colored silk cravat but without a cap, to the one who has a three-story-high collar on his liveried greatcoat that resembles the particolored cloth butterfly used for wiping quill-pens. Also forcing their way through are those civil servants whose boots are blacked by their female cooks and who have no one to send for tickets. Here you will see how a forthright Russian hero, finally losing patience, bypasses the shoulders of the whole crowd, to its singular amazement, to reach the wicket and secure a ticket. Only then will you realize how manifest is our love of theater. And what do they put on at our theaters?—melodramas and vaudevilles! . . . I am fed up with melodramas and vaudevilles.

The plight of Russian actors is a sorry one. An untried population throbs and seethes all about them, yet they are cast as characters whom they have never ever seen. What are they to make of these outlandish heroes, who are neither French nor German, but merely hare-brained freaks with absolutely no well-defined passion or clear-cut demeanor? How are they to show themselves off to advantage? How is their talent to be developed? For heaven's sake, give us Russian characters, give us ourselves, our own scoundrels and cranks! On stage with them, subject them to general laughter! Laughter is a wonderful thing: it jeopardizes neither life nor property, but in its presence a guilty party is like a hare caught in a trap . . . We are grown so indifferent from watching insipid French plays that now we are afraid to look at ourselves. If we are confronted with some lifelike character, we start to wonder whether it is based on a specific person, because the character shown us is quite unlike the *paysan*, stage tyrant, rhymester and suchlike worn-out characters whom toothless authors haul into their plays just as they haul on stage the perennial supernumeraries who, with the same old smile, dance the spectators a *pas* evidently learned by heart over the course of forty years. If, for instance, someone says that in a certain town a certain aulic councillor is of inebriate habits, then all the aulic councillors are insulted, and some other, entirely different sort of councillor may even say, "How is this possible? I have a kinsman who's an aulic councillor, and a fine man! How can they say that an aulic councillor is of inebriate habits?" As if one could defame the whole corporation! And this sort of touchiness certainly extends to every rank of our society. Do you need an example? Recollect *The Inspector* . . .

It's aggravating. Truly, it is high time we realized that only characters depicted, not by cliché generalized traits, but by the forms they assumed in the course of national evolution, so striking in their lifelike quality that we exclaim, "Why, I believe I know that man"—only such a depiction will bring about real benefits. We have turned the theater into a plaything, much like those rattles used to attract children, and we have forgotten that it is a rostrum from which a living lesson is read directly to a mass of people, where amid the festive brilliance of bright lights, the thunder of music and unanimous laughter, a familiar but covert vice is exposed to view, and—to the clandestine acclaim of universal sympathy—a familiar, shyly hiding, but exquisite feeling is manifested . . .

But enough about the theater. I've been maundering on about it. A noisy week in Petersburg caps its winter carnival, when one half of its population soars on swings and hurtles like a whirlwind down the ice mountains, and the other half is turned into a long chain of barely moving carriages, kept in line by gendarmes, and when performances take place night and day and all of Admiralty Square is strewn with nutshells . . .

Lent is serene and austere. A voice seems to be audible, saying, "Halt, Christian! turn thy gaze upon thy life." The streets are empty. No carriages. The face of the passerby reads meditation. I love thee, time of prayer and thought! My own thoughts flow more freely, more reflectively. All the vapid and trivial people, I suspect, will lie abed drowsy and weary and forget to drop by and trouble me with vulgar conversation about whist, literature, promotions, theater.

Lent in Petersburg is a holiday for musicians. At this time they assemble from all corners of Europe. The vast concert for the veterans' benefit is always magnificent: four hundred musicians! There's something overwhelming about it. When the harmonious murmur of four hundred strains resounds beneath the shuddering vaults, then, I think, the soul of even the shallowest listener must quake with rare palpitation.

As Lent wears on, the sun peeps into the Petersburg atmosphere. The western seashore becomes brighter. The North glares with modulated severity from its Vyborg shore. Equipages halt more frequently in the streets to deposit promenaders on the trottoir. From 1836 on, Nevsky Prospect, that noisy, ever stirring, bustling and jostling Nevsky Prospect, fell entirely out of favor: promenades transferred to the English Embankment. The late emperor[5] loved the English Embankment. It is beautiful, to be sure. But only after the promenades began did I notice that it is rather short. Still, the promenaders all benefit from that, because half of Nevsky Prospect is almost always cluttered with a tribe of artisans and functionaries, which is why you get jostled there three times as often as anywhere else . . .

Where does our time, so irrecoverable, fly to so fast? Who is calling it homewards? Lent—how serene, how solitary is its hiatus! What cannot be accomplished in those seven weeks? Now at last I shall plunge deep into my work. Now at last I shall complete what the noise and general stir kept me from completing. But there, the first week is already drawing to a close; I had not the time to begin when the second is already flying after it; now it's the middle of the third, now the fourth, now the fair in the Gostiny Dvor is on, and a whole gallery of willows and wax fruit and flowers has bloomed beneath its shadowy arches. Whenever I walked past this brightly colored lane, in whose shade were heaped crudely carved children's toys, I grew vexed. I became angry with the red-cheeked nannies, toddling along in droves, and the children, joyfully halting before the piles of pleasing (to them) junk and the swarthy, stubby, mustachioed Greek, who had dubbed himself a Moldavian confectioner, with his dubious and nondescript preserves. The boot-brushes, little tin monkeys, knives and forks, gingerbread, miniature looking glasses lying on the little tables nauseated me. All the people were garish in hue and squeezed together in the same old way; the same old feelings were expressed on their faces; with the same old curiosity they gazed as they had gazed a year ago or two or three or even more—and yet I and everyone of these people have changed; one's feelings are different now from what they were last year; now one's thoughts are more serious; one's soul smiles less often on one's lips, and every day a bit more of one's former vivacity diminishes.

The Neva broke up early. The ice floes, undisturbed by the winds, almost had time to melt before the breaking-up, loose chunks had already drifted away, and broke asunder on their own. Lake Ladoga evacuated its ice at almost the same time. The capital suddenly altered. The spire of the Peter and Paul Belfry, and the fortress and Vasiliev Island and the Vyborg shore and the English Embankment—all assumed a picturesque aspect. Puffing smoke, the first steamboat sped by. The first boatloads of bureaucrats, soldiers, old nannies, English counting-house clerks, were borne from Vasiliev and back again. I cannot recall the last time it was so sunny and mild. When I walked up Admiralty Boulevard—the evening before Easter Sunday—when by way of Admiralty Boulevard I reached the port, at whose entrance two jasperware urns glisten, when the Neva was unveiled before me, when the rosy color of the sky smouldered with a pale blue mist from the Vyborg shore, the buildings on the Petersburg shore were clad in an almost lilac hue that concealed their unsightly exteriors, when the churches whose protuberances were fully hidden by the monochromatic veil of mist seemed painted or pasted onto rose-colored cloth, and in that lilac-blue mist only one thing shone out, the spire of the Peter and Paul Belfry, reflected in the infinite mirror of the Neva—it seemed to me as if I were not in Petersburg. It seemed to me as if I had moved to some other city, where I had been before, where I knew everyone and where there is something not to be found in Petersburg . . . Look, there's a familiar oarsman, whom I haven't seen for over half a year, rocking in his yawl by the shore, and familiar phrases ring out, and there is water and a summer that never yet existed in Petersburg.

I love springtime intensely. Even here, in this savage northland, it belongs to me. I do not think anyone in the world loves it as I do. With its coming my youth returns to me; with its coming my past is more than remembrance: the past stands before my eyes, ready to gush from them in the form of tears. I was so intoxicated with the bright, clear days of Holy Easter that I failed to notice the gigantic fair on Admiralty Square. Only from a distance did I see how the swings bore into the air some youth, sitting arm in arm with some lady in a smart bonnet; a sign on a corner booth, painted with an extra-large red-headed devil carrying an axe, caught my eye. Nothing more did I see.

On Easter, it seems as if the capital has closed down. It looks as if everything we see on the street is being packed for a journey. The post-Easter performances and balls are nothing more than the left-over tag-ends of pre-Easter performances and balls, or, to put it more neatly, guests who remain long after the rest have departed, and sit by the fireside, making a few more statements, as they cover their yawning mouths with one hand. The whole town has been drained dry, the trottoirs are dry. Petersburg gents wear a certain style of light frockcoat and carry all sorts of walking sticks; instead of cumbersome coaches, demi-calashes and phaetons dash along the wood-paved carriage ways. Books are read more desultorily. Instead of woolen stockings, summer foraging caps and riding crops are already making an appearance here and there in the shop windows. In short, throughout the month of April, Petersburg seems on the verge of flight. It is jubilant to dismiss the sedentary life and routine and think about a distant road under other skies, in green southern groves, in lands of fresh new air. He is jubilant who can make out, at the end of a Petersburg street, the cloud-capped mountains of the Caucasus or a lake in Switzerland or Italy crowned with anemones and laurels or Greece beautiful even in its desolation . . . But hold, my thought: Petersburg's dwelling places still loom on either side of me . . .

[1835/6]

A Theater Lets Out after the Performance of a New Comedy

by Nikolay Gogol

A theater lobby. Visible on one side are a staircase leading to the boxes and upper circle; an entrance, center, to the stalls and lower circle; on the other side the exit to the street. A distant crackle of applause can be heard.

THE PLAY'S AUTHOR* (*coming out of the auditorium*). It was like dragging myself out of a millpond! Acclaim and applause at last! The whole theater's in an uproar! . . . Such is fame! Lord, how my heart would have pounded, say, seven or eight years ago, how my whole being would have quickened! But that was long ago. I was young then and, like a stripling, harebrained. Blest be the vocation that prevented me from tasting ecstasy and praise in my immaturity! And now . . . But the judicious coldness of age would make anyone wise. At last you realize applause means little and is bestowed as a reward on anything: the actor who can fathom the whole mystery of human hearts and souls, or the ballet dancer who is skillful enough to doodle with his legs or the conjurer— applause acclaims them all! No matter if it be a thinking head or a feeling heart or the echoes in the innermost soul or feet working or arms juggling water tumblers—everything is drowned out by

---

*Of course I grant that the play's author is an idealized character. He represents the plight of the comic writer in society, a comic writer whose chosen assignment is to deride abuses within divers ranks and occupations.

This playlet was first published in volume 4 of the 1842 edition of Gogol's works, and first performed in 1902. The present translation is based on the text in N. V. Gogol, *Sobranie sochineniy v semi tomakh*, ed. S. I. Mashinsky, N. L. Stepanov and M. B. Khrapchenko (Moscow, 1967), IV. I have retained throughout Gogol's own technical nomenclature: a vaudeville remains a vaudeville and not a farce, for instance. However, a difficulty arises with the word *pobasyonki* on which the peroration turns; there is no equivalent term in English to convey contempt for a work of narrative fiction, and after toying with "mere fiction," "yarns" and "amusements," I have decided on "fairy tales."

an equal amount of acclamation. No, it's not applause I'd be wanting now. What I'd like now is to be transported suddenly into the boxes, the circle, the stalls, the gallery, to infiltrate all over the place, to hear all the opinions and impressions while they're still fresh and unspoiled, while they are still unchastened by the comments and appraisals of experts and journalists, while everyone is still under the influence of his own judgment alone. I need that sort of thing, for I am a comic writer. All other kinds of writing and literary genres are subject to the judgment of the elite; only the comic writer must submit to the judgment of all. Every spectator has a claim on him, any man of whatever calling becomes his judge. Oh, how I should like every man to point out my flaws and failings! Let him laugh at me, let malevolence, partiality, indignation, hatred govern his lips—what you will, so long as the words are uttered. A word cannot be uttered without good reason, and the spark of truth can be kindled anywhere. A man who means to point out another man's ludicrous aspects must logically consent to having his own ludicrous aspects pointed out. I'll give it a try, I'll stop here in the lobby while the house lets out. There's bound to be talk about the new play. Under the influence of his first impressions, a man is always vibrant and anxious to share them with others. (*He steps to one side.*)

(A FEW RESPECTABLY DRESSED PERSONS *appear; one addresses another.*) We'd better go now. There's a silly vaudeville coming on next.

(*They both leave.*)

(*Two* COMME IL FAUT *of portly mien come down the stairs.*)

FIRST COMME IL FAUT. I'll be lucky if the police haven't shooed my carriage too far away. What's the name of that pretty young actress, d'y'know?

SECOND COMME IL FAUT. No, but she's not bad.

FIRST COMME IL FAUT. Not bad at all; though she lacks a certain something. Say, let me recommend a new restaurant; we were served fresh green peas yesterday (*kisses his fingertips*)—exquisite!

(*They both leave.*)

(AN OFFICER *runs in,* ANOTHER OFFICER *restrains him by the arm.*)

FIRST OFFICER. Come on, let's stay!

SECOND OFFICER. Oh no, my boy. I wouldn't stay for a vaudeville for all the tea in China. You know the sort of plays they offer as a treat: lackeys instead of actors, and the women! One frump after another.

(*They leave.*)

A SOCIALITE, FOPPISHLY DRESSED (*coming down the stairs*). That rascally tailor has cut my trousers too tight, I live in fear of an accident whenever I sit down. Just for that, I think I'll hold off paying his bills for at least two years.

SIMILAR, STOUTER SOCIALITE (*speaks to another energetically*). Never, never, believe me, he'll never play cards with you. He won't play for under a hundred and fifty rubles the rubber. I know it for a fact, because my brother-in-law Pafnutiev plays with him every day.

THE PLAY'S AUTHOR (*to himself*). And still not a word about the comedy!

A MIDDLE-AGED BUREAUCRAT (*coming out, his arms outstretched*). What the hell was that supposed to mean! What a . . . what a . . . It's outrageous.

(*Leaves.*)

A GENTLEMAN SOMEWHAT NEGLECTFUL OF LITERATURE (*turning to another*). Of course it is—isn't it?—or so it seems, a translation!

ANOTHER. Bless my soul, what do you mean, a translation! The action takes place in Russia, with our very own customs and ranks.

THE GENTLEMAN SOMEWHAT NEGLECTFUL OF LITERATURE. I do remember, though, there was something in French, not quite the same sort of thing.

(*Both leave.*)

ONE OF TWO SPECTATORS (*also on their way out*). There's no way of telling right now. Wait and see what the newspapers say, and then you'll know.

TWO WINTER TOPCOATS (*one to the other*). Well, what d'ye think? What's your opinion of the comedy?

ANOTHER WINTER TOPCOAT (*moving his lips in the most extraordinary way*). Well, of course, you can't deny that it was the sort of thing . . . of its type . . . Why, surely, no one's opposed to this sort of thing, but, on the other hand, it shouldn't . . . wherever, so to speak, . . . and yet . . . (*Purses his lips affirmatively.*) Yes, yes.

(*They leave.*)

AUTHOR (*to himself*). Well, they haven't said much so far. Still, there'll be some discussion now: I can see some people in the front of the crowd frantically waving their arms.

(*Two* OFFICERS.)

FIRST. I never laughed so much in all my life.

SECOND. It's a first-rate comedy, I must say.

FIRST. Hold on, let's just see what the papers say. The critics have to pass on it first . . . Look, look! (*Nudges him.*)

SECOND. What?

FIRST (*pointing at one of two men coming down the stairs*). A literary man!

SECOND (*hastily*). Which one?

FIRST. That one! Ssh! Let's hear what they have to say.

SECOND. Who's the man with him?

FIRST. Dunno. No idea what sort of fellow he is.

(*Both* OFFICERS *stand aside and make room for them.*)

THE NO-IDEA-WHAT-SORT-OF-FELLOW. I can't judge it on its literary merits, but there seem to be flashes of wit in it. It's very, very clever.

LITERARY MAN. For heaven's sake, what's so clever about it? Such low persons put on the stage, such a tone! The crudest jokes, why, it's practically smutty!

THE NO-IDEA-WHAT-SORT-OF-FELLOW. Well, that's another story. As I say, I can't judge as to the literary merits. I only remarked that the play is funny and gave satisfaction.

LITERARY MAN. It is *not* funny. For heaven's sake, what's so funny about it, what's so satisfying? The plot is improbable to the nth degree. The whole thing is a tissue of incongruities: no intrigue, no action, no structure whatsoever.[1]

THE NO-IDEA-WHAT-SORT-OF-FELLOW. Yes, well, I wouldn't deny that. From a literary standpoint, a literary standpoint that is, it isn't funny. But from, so to speak, an outsider's standpoint, it's got . . .

LITERARY MAN. Does it really? For heaven's sake, there's not even any of that! What kind of conversational tone do you call that? Who talks that way in high society? Go ahead, tell me, do you and I talk like that?

THE NO-IDEA-WHAT-SORT-OF-FELLOW. That's true. You're very sharp to have noticed that. That's exactly what I was thinking myself: there's no refinement in the dialogue. It's as if none of the characters could disguise his low nature—that's true.

LITERARY MAN. Well, and you still praise it?

THE NO-IDEA-WHAT-SORT-OF-FELLOW. Who's praising it? I wasn't praising it. Now I can see the play is rubbish. But you can't tell that at first sight; I can't judge as to literary merits.

(*They leave.*)

ANOTHER LITERARY MAN (*enters accompanied by his own audience, to whom he speaks, waving his arms*). Take it from me, I know all about this kind of thing: it's a disgusting play! A squalid, squalid play! Not one believable character, all caricatures! Nature isn't at all like that. Believe me, no, I know better: I'm a literary man myself. People call it "lively," "well-observed," but it's nothing but rubbish. It's all his friends, his friends puffing it, all his friends! I've already heard it all but compared with Fonvizin, yet the play is simply unworthy to be called a comedy. A farce, yes, a farce, and not a successful farce at that. The most trivial, the most vapid comedietta of Kotzebue[2] is, in comparison, Mont Blanc compared with Pulkovo Hill. I can prove it to anybody, I can prove it mathematically like two plus two equals four. It's merely his friends and acquaintances who've praised him so extravagantly that I daresay now he thinks he's a regular Shakespeare. Here in Russia, friends always overdo the praise. Look at Pushkin, for instance. Why does all Russia talk about him now? Because of his friends, they ranted and raved, and then all Russia started raving in imitation.

(*He exits along with his audience.*)

(*Both* OFFICERS *step forward and resume their places.*)

FIRST. That's right, absolutely right, a farce, to be sure. I was the first person to say so. A stupid farce, puffed by his friends. I must admit it was quite disgusting to watch some of the things in it.

SECOND. But didn't you say you never laughed so much in all your life?

FIRST. That's entirely different. Don't you understand? I'll have to spell it out for you. What is there in the play? First of all, no intrigue, no action either, definitely no structure, utter incongruity, and what's more, it's all caricatures.

(*Two other* OFFICERS *behind them.*)

ONE (*to* THE OTHER). Who's laying down the law around here? One of your men, I think? (THE OTHER, *having peered askance into the face of the* ONE *laying down the law, waves his hand in dismissal.*) What, some fool?

THE OTHER. No, not exactly . . . He does have a mind, but only after the papers come out. But if the edition's at all delayed, his head is empty. Never mind, let's go.

(*They leave.*)

(TWO DEVOTEES OF THE ARTS.)

FIRST. I am certainly not one of those who has constant recourse to phrases like "squalid," "disgusting," "in bad taste" and the like. Take it for granted, for the most part, such phrases fall from the lips of those who are in bad taste themselves. They talk about drawing rooms and are never permitted beyond the front hall. But they're not our concern. I'm referring to the fact that there is absolutely no plot in the play.

SECOND. Yes, if you take plot to mean the usual thing, a love intrigue, then there is none indeed. But I think it's high time we stopped relying on that previously perennial plot-line. It's worth taking a good sharp look round. The whole world changed long ago. Nowadays the effort to obtain a lucrative post, to shine and so eclipse others in every way possible, to get revenge for being slighted or ridiculed would make a strong plot for a drama. Nowadays aren't rank, money and a profitable marriage more electrifying than love?

FIRST. That's all well and good; but I still don't see any plot in the play, even in that regard.

SECOND. I don't intend to argue whether or not there's a plot in it. I only say that people usually look for a plot about private lives and refuse to see one of public interest. People are naively accustomed to these everlasting lovers, without whose marriage no play can end. Of course that's a plot, but what kind of a plot? A tidy little knot in the corner of a handkerchief. No, a comedy should be trussed up in and of itself, in its totality, in one big all-embracing knot. A plot situation ought to encompass all the characters, and not just one or two. It should concern whatever moves all the parties in the action to a greater or lesser degree. Everyone in it should be a hero; the thrust and progress of the play will make the whole machine hum: not a single cog should remain, as it were, rusty and inoperative.

FIRST. But not everyone can be a hero. Surely one or two ought to control the others?

SECOND. Not exactly control, but rather predominate. In a machine, too, some cogs are more functional and efficacious to its working—they may be called the main ones. But a play is governed by its idea, its concept. Without it there is no unity. And anything can be used as a plot: terror, suspense, the threat of far-reaching law . . .

FIRST. But don't you end up investing comedy with a more universal significance?

SECOND. Why, isn't that its direct and real significance? In its very origins, comedy was social, a popular creation. At least its sire, Aristophanes, claimed it was so. Only later did it enter the narrow cleft of private concerns, and introduce love interest, the one and only perennial plot. And yet how dully our best comic writers handle this plot! How trivial these theatrical lovebirds and their cardboard romance!

THIRD (*stepping up and clapping him gently on the shoulder*).

You're wrong there. Love, like any other emotion, can be part of comedy.

SECOND. I didn't say it couldn't. But love and all the other, more sublime feelings can make an uplifting impression only when they are fully developed. If you concentrate on them, everything else will inevitably be sacrificed. Whatever constitutes the expressly comic aspect will then fade, and the significance of a social comedy will inevitably be lacking.

THIRD. Then I suppose the subject of a comedy is bound to be low? Comedy is already considered a low genre.

SECOND. For those who focus on words and do not probe meanings, that's true. But can't the positive and the negative share the same purpose? Comedy and tragedy can both express the same high ideal, can't they? Even the slightest devious twist in the soul of a vile and dishonorable man outlines by contrast the profile of an honorable man, doesn't it? So this whole conglomeration of turpitude, miscarriage of justice and perverted law instills in us a clear conception of the requirements of law, duty and justice, doesn't it? In the hands of a skillful physician both hot and cold water can effect cures of the same ailments with equal success. In the hands of a talented writer everything can serve as a tool of the beautiful, so long as it is guided by high-minded ideas of serving the beautiful.

A FOURTH (*walking up*). What can serve the beautiful? What are you talking about?

FIRST. We were debating comedy. We keep talking about comedy in general, but no one's yet said a word about this new comedy. What do you think?

FOURTH. Just this: it's obviously packed with talent and close observation of life, a good deal that's funny, accurate, drawn from nature. But by and large there's nothing to the play. You can't extract a plot or a denouement. 'S funny that our comic writers can never omit the government. Not one of our comedies can resolve a plot without its interference.

THIRD. That's true. But then, on the other hand, it's natural enough. We're all connected with the government, most of us work in the civil service; all our interests are more or less bound up with the government. So it's no wonder our writers reflect this in their work.

FOURTH. Maybe so. Then this connection ought to be emphasized. Still, it *is* funny that no play can end without the government stepping in. It never fails to put in an appearance, just like ineluctable Nemesis in the ancient tragedies.

SECOND. Well, you see, our comic writers probably do this without thinking. It's probably come to constitute a sort of distinguishing feature of our comedies. We cherish a kind of occult faith in the government in our bosoms. What of it? There's nothing wrong in that. Pray God that the government ever and everywhere heed its calling as an agent of Providence on earth and that we trust in it as the ancients trusted in Nemesis to overtake transgressors.

FIFTH. Good evening, gentlemen! I just heard somebody invoke "the government." This comedy's caused a lot of shouting and arguing . . .

SECOND. We'd better discuss this shouting and arguing at my place, and not here in a theater lobby.

(*They leave.*)

(SEVERAL RESPECTABLE AND DECENTLY DRESSED PERSONS *appear, one after another.*)

NO. 1. Uh-huh, I see. True enough, such things do happen here, and even worse things go on in other places. But what's the point, why put it on stage?—that's the question. Why shows like this? What good do they do? That's what I want to know! Why do I have to find out that there are scoundrels in such-and-such a place? I simply . . . I fail to understand the necessity for shows like this. (*Exits.*)

NO. 2. No, it is not a satire on vice. It is a revolting lampoon on Russia—that's what it is. It amounts to casting the government itself in a bad light, because if you expose corrupt officials and the abuses that go on in the various ranks, you expose the government itself. It's indecent to permit such performances. (*Exits.*)

(*Enter* MISTER A *and* MISTER B, *persons of no mean rank.*)

MISTER A. That's not what I'm talking about. On the contrary, we ought to be shown abuses. We ought to look upon our own behavior. And I certainly do not share the opinion of many overheated patriots; but it does strike me that there may be just the slightest excess of unpleasantness in it . . .

MISTER B. I really wish you could have heard the remarks of a very modestly dressed man, who was sitting behind me in the stalls . . . Ah, there he is in person!

MISTER A. Who is he?

MISTER B. Just a very modestly dressed man. (*Turning to him.*) We hadn't finished our conversation, and it was beginning to interest me.

VERY MODESTLY DRESSED MAN. Well, I admit I'm delighted to pick up where we left off. I've been hearing talk to this effect: it's all untrue, it's a lampoon on the government and our customs and it's indecent to perform it. That made me run the whole play through my mind again, and, I admit, the term "comedy" seems even more meaningful to me now. I think the laughter in it made an even more powerful and profound attack on hypocrisy—the mask of decency which disguises vileness and meanness, the scoundrel who assumes the look of a virtuous man. I admit, I was overjoyed when I heard how comical virtuous statements sounded on the lips of a scoundrel and how hilariously funny the mask he wore became to everyone, from the stalls to the gallery. And yet there are still people who say there's no need to put this on stage! I heard someone, a rather respectable man, I believe, make this remark: "What will the common people say when they see the kinds of abuses that go on in Russia?"

MISTER A. Forgive me, but I confess I involuntarily asked myself the same question. What do our common people say when they see all this?

VERY MODESTLY DRESSED MAN. What do the common people say? (*He draws to one side.*)

(TWO IN PEASANT OVERCOATS *cross the stage.*)

BLUE OVERCOAT (*to* GRAY OVERCOAT). I reckon them grafters was bigshots, but they got skeered when the Law showed up!

(*They both go out.*)

VERY MODESTLY DRESSED MAN. That's what the common people say, did you hear it?

MISTER A. What?

VERY MODESTLY DRESSED MAN. They said, "I reckon them grafters was bigshots, but they all got skeered when the Law showed up." Do you hear how faithful man is to his natural intuition and feelings? How unerring the simplest eye, if it is not clouded by theories and book-learning but plucks its ideas from human nature! And isn't it as plain as day that, after a performance like this, the common people will have more faith in the government? Yes, they need this kind of show. They must distinguish between the government and poor practitioners of government. They must see that abuses derive not from the government but from those who do not understand what government entails, and who do not wish to be responsible to government. They must see that the government is noble, that it regards all equally with its Argus-like eye, that sooner or later it will catch up to those who betray law, honor and man's sacred duty, that those with unclean consciences will tremble before it. Yes, they ought to see these shows; believe me, even if they happen to undergo extortion and injustice them- selves, they will leave comforted after such a show, with a stead- fast faith in the Argus-like, supreme law. I also like that remark, "the common people will get a bad opinion of their betters." In other words, people think that they will see their betters here in the theater for the very first time; that if some dastardly village bailiff at home gripes them in his clutch they won't notice it, but as soon as they come to the theater, they will. Honestly, people like that must think our common folk stupid blockheads—too stupid to tell the difference between a meat pie and a bowl of por- ridge. No, I do think it was a good thing that no honorable man was brought on stage. Man is vain. Point out just one good trait in a multitude of bad ones and he'll leave the theater with his head held high. No, it's good that we saw only exceptions and vices which so stuck in their craws that they don't want to admit that such characters are their compatriots or that such things exist.

MISTER A. But still, do such persons exist, to the letter, in our country?

VERY MODESTLY DRESSED MAN. Let me answer you this way: I don't know why I get depressed whenever I hear such a question. Let me speak candidly—there's something in your face that disposes me to be candid. A man always begins by asking, "Can such per- sons exist?" But when did a man ever ask, "Can I myself be un- tainted by such vices?" Never, never! That's how it is—I'm speak- ing to you straight from the heart. I'm a tenderhearted sort, and there's a great deal of affection in my nature, but if you knew how much spiritual fortitude and resilience I need lest I give in to the many vicious propensities a man is prone to involuntarily, living in this world! Then how can I say that at this very minute there may not exist in me the same propensity everyone was laughing at just ten minutes ago and which I laughed at myself?

MISTER A *(after a short pause)*. I must confess, I have to mull over your remarks. And when I think back, I recognize how proud our European education has made us, how, for the most part, it has hidden us from ourselves, how haughtily and disdainfully we stare down at those who have not received the superficial veneer we have, how each of us sets up to be virtually a saint, and constantly speaks of wickedness in the third person—then, I confess, I can- not help but get depressed . . . But forgive my rudeness—though you yourself are to blame—may I know whom I have the pleasure of addressing?

VERY MODESTLY DRESSED MAN. I am no more nor less than one of those civil servants whose functions dressed out the characters in the comedy, and I came here from my village only the day before yesterday.

MISTER B. I never should have thought it. Yet after this won't you find it offensive to live and work with such people?

VERY MODESTLY DRESSED MAN. Offensive? Let me say this: I admit I have often lost patience. Not all the civil servants in our little town belong to the honest ten percent; often I've had to move heaven and earth to do something decent. Many a time in the past I was on the point of resigning; but now, particularly after that show, I feel refreshed and newly fortified as well to carry on my work. I am consoled by the thought that here in Russia vileness does not remain concealed or indulged, that here it is attacked by ridicule in the sight of all noble persons, that there is a pen which does not hesitate to expose our ignoble actions, though it may not flatter our national pride, and that there is a noble government which permits this to be shown to all who ought to see it—and this alone makes me zealous to carry on my useful labors.

MISTER A. Let me make you a proposition. I occupy a rather important post in the government. I need a truly noble and honest assistant. I offer you a position in which you will have wide scope for action, will receive incomparably greater benefits and will be conspicuous.

VERY MODESTLY DRESSED MAN. Let me thank you with all my heart and soul for that proposition and, in so doing, let me turn it down. If I feel now that my present position is a useful one, would it be noble on my part to resign it? And how can I resign it, without the complete assurance that, after me, it will not be held by some young puppy who will start putting the screws on? If you made this offer with a mind to reward me, let me tell you this: I applauded the playwright as much as anyone did, but I did not call him before the curtain. What should be his reward? The play pleased—it was praised, and he—merely did his duty. True, in our country it's gotten to the point that a man considers himself God knows what sort of paragon of virtue not because he accomplished something, but simply because he refrained from playing dirty tricks on anyone in the course of his life and career, and he gets mighty angry if he is not singled out and rewarded. "For heaven's sake," says he, "I've lived my whole life honorably, almost never did anything underhanded—how can they not give me a promotion or a medal?" No, I think that if a man is incapable of being honorable without inducements—I don't believe in his kind of honor. His ratty honor isn't worth a groat.

MISTER A. At least you will accept my friendship? Forgive my importunity; you see for yourself that it derives from my sincere respect. Let me have your address.

VERY MODESTLY DRESSED MAN. Here it is; but be assured I shall not let you take advantage of it. Tomorrow morning I shall look in on you. Forgive me, I am not bred up to high society and I do not know how to speak . . . But to meet with such magnanimous attention from a member of the government, such striving for virtue . . . God grant that every sovereign be surrounded by such persons! (*He leaves hurriedly.*)

MISTER A (*flipping the calling card in his hands*). I look at this card and this unfamiliar name and for some reason my heart swells with pride. My earlier dismal impression has dissipated all by itself. May God preserve you, our Russia so unbeknownst to us! In the hinterlands, in one of your forgotten crannies, such a gem is hidden, and he is probably not the only one. Like flakes of golden ore, they are scattered through its rough, dark granite. There is a profound sense of reassurance in these phenomena, and my soul brightened after meeting that civil servant, as his own did after the performance of the comedy. Good-bye! Thank you for enabling me to meet him. (*He leaves.*)

MISTER V (*going over to* MISTER B). Who was that with you? He's a minister of state, I believe—isn't he?

MISTER P (*coming over from the opposite direction*). Dear me, old chap, what *is* going on, what's it mean? . . .

MISTER B. What?

MISTER P. Why, how can they put this on?

MISTER B. Why not?

MISTER P. Why, figure it out for yourself. I mean, how can they, really? Nothing but vice upon vice. What sort of example is that for the spectators?

MISTER B. But are the vices praised? They're targets for mockery, aren't they?

MISTER P. Why, that's all very well, dear chap, but say what you will: it's a matter of respect . . . why, they'll start losing respect for officials and government appointees.

MISTER B. People will not lose respect for officials or government appointees, but only for those who perform their duties badly.

MISTER V. Do let me get a word in: somehow or other this is an insult that affects everyone more or less.

MISTER P. Precisely. That's just what I was going to remark. An insult is exactly what it is, and it will spread. This time, let's say they put some titular councillor on stage, next time . . . uh . . . dear me, they'll put on . . . even an actual state councillor.[3]

MISTER B. What of it? Only individual personalities should remain inviolate; but if I concoct a character all on my own and invest him with some of the vices that exist among us, and pin a rank on him, whichever comes to mind, maybe even actual state councillor, and if I say that this actual state councillor is not all that he should be—what of it? You mean to tell me there are no bad eggs among actual state councillors?

MISTER P. Come, come, my dear chap, that's going too far. How can an actual state councillor be a bad egg? Of course, if he were only a titular councillor . . . No, you're going too far!

MISTER V. Why don't they show the good instead of the bad, show something worth imitating?

MISTER B. Why? That's a strange question: "Why?" Much might be said to such "why"s. Why did a certain father, who wished to wrest his son away from a life of debauchery, not mince words and precepts, but took him to a pesthouse where the ghastly results of a life of debauchery stood before him in all their horror? Why did he do that?

MISTER V. But may I remark: these are, to some extent, social sores which should be hidden and not revealed.

MISTER P. That's right. I agree with that entirely. We should hide our evils and not reveal them.

MISTER B. If anyone else but you had said that, I should have said those words were prompted by hypocrisy and not by true love of country. In your opinion all one need do is conceal and somehow doctor up the outward signs of our social sores, as you call them, so that they are not noticeable the while, but let the disease rage within—no need to bother with *that*. Never mind that it might have erupted and surfaced with these symptoms after it was too late for any treatment. No need to go that far. You choose to ignore the fact that without profound, heartfelt confession, without Christian recognizance of one's own sins, without magnifying them in our own eyes, we shall not have the power to surmount them, to soar with our soul above the despicable in life. You choose to ignore that! Let man remain deaf, let his life flow on like a dream, let him not thrill or weep in his heart of hearts, let him deaden his soul till it is so torpid that nothing evermore will cause it to palpitate! No . . . forgive me! Lips that frame such remarks are moved by cold egoism and not by a sacred and pure love of mankind. (*He leaves.*)

MISTER P (*after a short pause*). Why don't you say something? What do you think of that? Quite the orator, eh? (MISTER V *is silent.*) (*Continuing.*) He can tell himself whatever he likes, but all the same they're our sores, so to speak.

MISTER V (*aside*). May those sores blister his tongue! He'll be blabbing about them to every soul he meets!

MISTER P. I can probably talk heaps of that sort of thing too, but after all, what's the point? . . . Ah, here's Prince N. Listen here, prince, don't run off!

PRINCE N. What is it?

MISTER P. Why, let's have a chat, stop a bit! Well now, how'd you find the play?

PRINCE N. Funny enough.

MISTER P. Do tell me, though: how could they let it be performed? Whoever heard of such a thing?

PRINCE N. Why shouldn't it be performed?

MISTER P. Now really, just think, now really, how can they? What if there's a scoundrel on stage—after all, these are all our sores.

PRINCE N. What sores?

MISTER P. Why, our sores, so to speak, our social sores.

PRINCE N (*annoyed*). Keep them to yourself! They may be your sores, but not mine! Why lumber me with them? It's time I went home. (*He leaves.*)

MISTER P (*continuing*). Come to think of it, what *was* that tommyrot he was talking? He said an actual state councillor might be a bad egg. Well, let's grant a titular councillor, I'll go along with that . . .

MISTER V. Oh, let's go, that's enough talk. I suppose all the passersby have figured out by now that you're an actual state councillor. (*Aside.*) Some people have a genius for putting their foot in it. By repeating your idea, they can make it sound so crass that you blush for yourself. If you say something silly, it may slip by unnoticed—but no, some friend and admirer stumbles across it, invariably sends it on its way and makes it sound even more stupid than it is. It's really most aggravating: like being plunked in a mud puddle.

(*They leave.*)

(A MILITARY MAN *and* A CIVILIAN *come in together.*)

CIVILIAN. You military men are all alike! You say, "That's got to be put on stage." You're ready to have a hearty laugh at some civilian official; but single out some military man, just say that in such-and-such a regiment there are officers—don't even suggest vicious propensities, simply say there are ill-bred officers with rude manners—and just for that you lot are ready to lodge a complaint with the Privy Council itself.

MILITARY MAN. Now, now, do you really think I'm like that? Of course, we have a few such Don Quixotes in our ranks; but you can be sure there are plenty of levelheaded fellows, who will always rejoice to see a man who disgraces his calling made a laughingstock. Where's the offense in that? Show him to us, show him to us! We'll be delighted to look at any time.

CIVILIAN (*aside*). That's what they always shout: "Show him to us! show him to us!"—and when he *is* shown—they have a fit!

(*They leave.*)

(*Two* WINTER TOPCOATS.)

FIRST TOPCOAT. The French, for instance, put on the same thing, but with them it's all so charming. Why look, remember yesterday's vaudeville? He undresses, gets in bed, grabs a salad bowl from the table and puts it under the bed. Of course it's risqué, but charming. You can watch it all, it isn't offensive . . . My wife and children go to the theater every day. But this thing—well, really, what is it?—some good-for-nothing lout, a peasant I wouldn't let in my front hall, lolls about with his boots on, yawns or picks his teeth—what's that supposed to mean? It's disgraceful!

SECOND TOPCOAT. The French are another story. That's what's called *société, mon cher*! Out of the question in this country. None of our writers have the slightest sophistication; most of them were educated in seminaries. They're fond of their glass, and they're loose-livers as well. There was a writer of sorts used to call on my footman. Where would someone like that pick up a knowledge of good society?

(*They go out.*)

A LADY OF SOCIETY (*accompanied by two men: one in a dress-coat, the other in a uniform*). But the types, the characters they put on stage! If there were at least one attractive one . . . Why don't our authors write as the French do, for example, Dumas and the others? I don't insist on paragons of virtue. Show me a woman who may be seduced, who may even cheat on her husband, may give in to, oh, let's say, the most depraved and indefensible passion. But present it attractively, so that I'm induced to take her side, so that I fall in love with her . . . But in this all the characters—why, each one is more disgusting than the last.

UNIFORMED MAN. Yes, quite commonplace, quite commonplace.

LADY OF SOCIETY. Tell me, why is everything here in Russia still so commonplace?

MAN IN DRESS-COAT. Darling, you'll tell us later why it's commonplace; they're calling our carriage.

(*They leave.*)

(THREE MEN *come in together.*)

FIRST. Why not laugh? A person may laugh. But are abuses and vices fit subjects for ridicule? What kind of mockery do you call that?

SECOND. What else is there to laugh at? Virtuous people or a man's good points?

FIRST. No. True, that's no subject for comedy, dear boy! But somehow this casts aspersions on the government. Aren't there any other subjects to write about?

SECOND. Such as?

FIRST. Well, aren't there plenty of absurd goings on in society? Why, for instance, let's say I'm off on a jaunt to Apothecary Island, and the coachman goes and drives me to Vyborg or the Smolny monastery. Aren't there plenty of absurd happenings of all sorts?

SECOND. In other words, you want to extract all serious intent from comedy. But why make it an inviolable law? There are a great many comedies in just the style you prefer. Why not allow the existence of two or three of the variety performed today? If you're fond of the sort you were describing, simply go to the theater. Every day you see a play in which one man hides under a table while another yanks him out by the leg.

THIRD. No, listen, that's not the point. Everything has its limits. There are certain things which are, so to speak, unsuitable for laughter, which are, to some degree, sacrosanct.

SECOND (*to himself, with a sardonic grin*). 'Twas ever thus in the world: laugh at the truly noble, at what constitutes the soul's holy of holies, and no one will rise to its defense. Laugh at vice, vileness and baseness, and everyone starts shouting, "He's laughing at something sacrosanct!"

FIRST. Well, there, I can see you're convinced now: don't say another

word. Believe me, you can't help but be convinced: it's the truth. I'm utterly unbiased myself and I don't say this to . . . but it's simply not the author's business, it's no fit subject for comedy.
(*He leaves.*)

SECOND (*to himself*). I admit I wouldn't like to be in the author's shoes for anything on earth. Try and please people! Pick out trifling incidents in society and everyone will say, "He writes trivia, it's got no profound moral purpose." Pick a subject that has a modicum of serious moral purpose, and they'll say, "It's none of his business, let him write trivia!" (*He leaves.*)

(A YOUNG LADY OF HIGH SOCIETY *escorted by her* HUSBAND.)

HUSBAND. Our carriage shouldn't be far, we'll be able to go directly.

MISTER N (*coming up to the lady*). Do my eyes deceive me! You came to see a Russian play!

YOUNG LADY. What of it? Aren't I even the teensiest bit patriotic?

MISTER N. Well, if so, you can't have had your fill of patriotism this time. You *are* abusing the play, aren't you?

YOUNG LADY. Not at all. I found much of it to be very accurate. I laughed wholeheartedly.

MISTER N. Why did you laugh? Because you enjoy laughing at everything Russian?

YOUNG LADY. Simply because it was funny. Because they brought out into the open the vileness and meanness that would still be the same vileness and meanness no matter what costume it was clothed in, if it were in a provincial town or here around us: that's why I laughed.

MISTER N. A very clever lady just told me that she laughed too, but by and large the play had a depressing effect on her.

YOUNG LADY. I have no way of knowing what your clever lady felt. But my own nerves are not so sensitive, and I'm always delighted to laugh at whatever is intrinsically funny. I know there are others who would disagree with us and, although they are willing enough to laugh out loud at a man's twisted nose, have no mind to laugh at his twisted soul.

(*In the distance another* YOUNG LADY *and her* HUSBAND *appear.*)

MISTER N. Ah, here comes a friend of yours. I should like to know her opinion of the comedy.

(*The ladies take one another's hands.*)

FIRST LADY. I could see how much you laughed even at a distance.

SECOND LADY. Who wasn't laughing? Everyone laughed.

MISTER N. And didn't it depress you?

SECOND LADY. I admit I did feel quite depressed. I know that it is all quite true. I myself have seen much that resembled it and often, but for all that it oppressed me.

MISTER N. Then I don't suppose you cared for the comedy?

SECOND LADY. No, wait, who says so? I just told you that I laughed wholeheartedly, and even more loudly than all the rest. I suppose they must have thought me mad . . . I was depressed because I should have liked to linger over one good-hearted character. That excess, that plethora of vileness . . .

MISTER N. Go on, go on!

SECOND LADY. Listen, advise the author to put in at least one honorable man. Tell him that people implore him, that it will be a really good idea.

FIRST LADY'S HUSBAND. But that's exactly the advice you shouldn't give him. Ladies invariably want a knight in shining armor to make them all sorts of speeches about nobility, no matter how banal the style.

SECOND LADY. Certainly not! How little you know us! *You're* the ones for that! You're the ones who like nothing better than phrases and speeches about nobility. I overheard one of you give his opinion: a certain fat man was shouting so loudly that I think everyone had to pay attention to him. He was shouting that it was defamation of character, that such nastiness and vileness had never existed in Russia. And who was saying this?—the nastiest, vilest man, a man ready to sell his soul, his conscience and anything you please. I don't even want to mention his name.

MISTER N. Won't you tell us who it was?

SECOND LADY. Why should you know? And he wasn't the only one: I kept hearing the people around us shouting, "It's a disgusting travesty of Russia, a travesty of the government! How can they permit it? What will the common people say?" And why were they shouting? Because they actually thought and felt that way? By no means! Because they wanted to make a fuss, get the play banned, because they may have found something in it too close for comfort. That's what your true-life offstage knights are like!

FIRST LADY'S HUSBAND. Oh! A little malice is beginning to creep in.

SECOND LADY. Malice, of course, it's malice. Yes, I am malicious, quite malicious. How can one help but be malicious, when faced with the vileness that shows up in all shapes and sizes.

FIRST LADY'S HUSBAND. That's right. You're longing for some knight to burst in right now, leap over a precipice, break his neck . . .

SECOND LADY. By no means.

FIRST LADY'S HUSBAND. It's only natural. What does a woman need? She needs above all romance in her life.

SECOND LADY. No, no, no! A thousand times no! That's a banal, stale, antiquated concept that you're always foisting on us. Women have more real magnanimity than men. A woman cannot, a woman is incapable of perpetrating the vileness and nastiness that you commit. A woman cannot be hypocritical in the way you are, she cannot shut her eyes to those meannesses the way you do. She has enough nobility in her to say all this, without looking back over her shoulder to see whether anyone is displeased or not—because it has to be said. If something is vile, then it's vile, no matter how you disguise it and pretend. It's vile, vile, vile!

FIRST LADY'S HUSBAND. Ah well, I can see you've gone and lost your temper.

SECOND LADY. Because I am frank and cannot stand people speaking untruths.

FIRST LADY'S HUSBAND. Well, don't be angry, give me your hand! I was only joking.

SECOND LADY. Here is my hand, I'm not angry. (*Turning to* N.) Listen, do advise the author to put a noble and honorable man in his comedy.

MISTER N. But how can he? Why, if he does put in an honorable man, won't the honorable man stand out like a stagy knight in shining armor?

SECOND LADY. If he feels strongly and deeply, his hero won't be a stagy knight.

MISTER N. Yes, well, I don't think it's all that easy.

SECOND LADY. Why don't you simply say that your author has no intense, deeply felt impulses in his heart?

MISTER N. Why so?

SECOND LADY. Well, anyone who is forever laughing without a stop can have few sublime feelings. He cannot be acquainted with the things only a tender heart feels.

MISTER N. Is that so? Then, according to you, the author is not very likely to be a noble person?

SECOND LADY. There, you see, you instantly misinterpret my words to mean something quite different. I didn't say a word about the comic writer not being noble and not having a strict understanding of honor in its fullest sense. I only said that he could not . . . shed a heartfelt tear, love something intensely, with all the profundity of his soul.

SECOND LADY'S HUSBAND. But how can you say this with such certainty?

SECOND LADY. Because I know. Everyone who was laughing or mocking was conceited, but they were virtually egoists; noble egoists, to be sure, but egoists all the same.

MISTER N. Then no doubt you prefer the brand of writing that deals only with humanity's sublime actions?

SECOND LADY. Oh, of course! I have always ranked it higher, and I admit I have more spiritual trust in such an author.

FIRST LADY'S HUSBAND (*turning to* MISTER N). There, can't you see— it always comes down to the same thing. Feminine taste. For women the most vulgar tragedy is superior to the finest comedy merely because it *is* a tragedy . . .

SECOND LADY. Keep still or I'll be malicious again. (*Turning to* N.) Now tell me, didn't I speak the truth: mustn't a comic writer's soul always be cold?

SECOND LADY'S HUSBAND. Or hot, because an atrabilious temperament promotes mockery and satire too.

SECOND LADY. Well, or an atrabilious one. But what does that mean? It means that such writing is prompted by bile, bitterness, discontent, which may be entirely justified. But none of that proves it was engendered by a sublime love of humanity . . . by love, in short. Am I right?

MISTER N. Right you are.

SECOND LADY. Now tell me: does the author of this comedy resemble that portrait?

MISTER N. What am I to say? I don't know him well enough to be able to judge his soul. But, taking into consideration everything I've heard about him, he must be either an egoist or a very atrabilious man.

SECOND LADY. There, you see, I knew it perfectly well.

FIRST LADY. I don't know why, but I didn't want him to be an egoist.

FIRST LADY'S HUSBAND. And here comes our footman, the carriage must be waiting. Good-bye. (*Pressing the hand of the* SECOND LADY.) You're coming with us, aren't you? To take tea at our place?

FIRST LADY (*leaving*). Please do!

SECOND LADY. By all means.

SECOND LADY'S HUSBAND. I believe our carriage is here too.

(*They follow them out.*)

(*Enter* TWO SPECTATORS.)

FIRST. Try and explain this to me: why is it that when you anatomize each action, character and personality separately it all looks true and lifelike, grounded in nature, but taken all together it seems out of proportion, exaggerated, caricatured, so that when you leave the theater, you can't help but ask, Can such people exist? Yet they're certainly not what you'd call villains.

SECOND. Certainly not, they're not at all villains. They're as the proverb says, "His wrong's not grave, He's just a knave."

FIRST. And then, too, there's something else: that vast conglomeration, that excessiveness—isn't that a defect in a comedy? Tell me, where is there a society consisting entirely of such people, without at least some, if not half, decent folks? If a comedy is supposed to be a portrait and reflection of our social life, it ought to mirror it with total accuracy.

SECOND. First, as I see it, this comedy is by no means a portrait, but rather an emblematic frontispiece. You see, both the stage and the locale of the action are idealized. Otherwise, the author wouldn't have made such obvious blunders and anachronisms or have attributed to some characters speeches which wouldn't suit them if their personalities and status were taken into consideration. Only the audience's first outburst of annoyance took personally something which pertains not to the individual but more or less to all human personality. The play is a focal point: from all over, from every corner of Russia, perversions of truth, self-delusions and abuses have swarmed here to serve a single idea—to produce in the spectator a clear-cut and noble-minded revulsion from much that is vile. The impression made is all the stronger because none of the characters has lost his human aspect: one can sense the humanity throughout. As a result the heart shudders even more violently. And as he laughs, the spectator involuntarily turns around, as if he feels that the object of his laughter is close beside him, and every second he must be on guard to keep it from intruding into his own soul. I think the funniest thing of all the author hears must be the reproaches—"Why aren't his characters and heroes attractive?"—since he used every device he knew to alienate them from us. If even one honorable character were added to the comedy, fully empowered to attract us, all these people would link up with the one honorable character and would entirely forget the others who so frighten them at present. Then perhaps, at the end of the performance, those figures would not haunt them incessantly like lifelike beings, and the spectator would not carry away that melancholy sensation and exclaim, "Can such people exist?"

FIRST. Yes. Well, nevertheless, it takes time to understand this sort of thing.

SECOND. That's perfectly natural. Inner meaning is always appre-
hended afterwards. And the more vivid, the clearer-cut the images
in which it is enshrouded and fragmented, the longer general attention will linger on those images. Only by piecing them together will you derive the sum total and meaning of a work of art.
But not everyone can analyze and decode such ciphers rapidly,
reading them all at once and on the run; for a long time people will
see nothing but the ciphers. You see, I predict that before that happens, every provincial hamlet in Russia will wax furious in the
conviction that this is a malicious satire, a vulgar, nasty fabrication aimed directly at it.

(*They leave.*)

ONE CIVIL SERVANT. It's a vulgar, nasty fabrication, it's a satire, a
lampoon!

ANOTHER CIVIL SERVANT. It means that nothing's sacred any more.
No need for laws, no need to go to the office. This uniform I'm
wearing—it means I've got to throw it away: it's just a rag now.

(TWO YOUNG MEN *run in.*)

ONE. Well, everybody got angry. I've heard so many different comments by now I can tell what anyone thinks of the play just by
looking at him.

SECOND. What does that one over there think?

FIRST. The one putting his arm in the sleeve of his greatcoat?

SECOND. Yes.

FIRST. He's thinking, "A comedy like this should get you exiled to
Nerchinsk! . . ." But it looks like the upper regions are on the
move. I guess the vaudeville's over. Now the riffraff will be spilling
out. Let's go.

(*They both leave.*)

(*The noise increases. Down every staircase the tumult resounds.
Peasant overcoats, short fur wraps, mobcaps, merchants' long-
frocked German caftans, three-cornered hats and plumes, great-
coats of all varieties: coarse woolen, military, secondhand and
dandified, trimmed in beaver, scurry in. The crowd jostles the gentleman getting into the sleeve of his greatcoat; the gentleman
moves aside and continues to put it on in an out-of-the-way corner.
Gentlemen and civil servants of all genera and species appear in the
crowd. Footmen in livery clear a path for their mistresses. An old
woman's cry is heard: "Holy saints, they're squeegin' in on all
sides!"*)

A VERY YOUNG CIVIL SERVANT OF SHIFTY NATURE (*rushing up to the gentleman putting on his greatcoat*). Allow me, your excellency, I'll hold it for you.

GENTLEMAN IN THE GREATCOAT. Ah, good evening! You here? Come for a look?

VERY YOUNG CIVIL SERVANT. Yes sir, your excellency, comically observed, wasn't it?

GENTLEMAN IN THE GREATCOAT. Nonsense! Nothing comical about it!

VERY YOUNG CIVIL SERVANT. That's true, your excellency, absolutely nothing.

GENTLEMAN IN THE GREATCOAT. People should be flogged for such things, not praised.

VERY YOUNG CIVIL SERVANT. That's true, your excellency.

GENTLEMAN IN THE GREATCOAT. Look at the way they let young people into the theater. Much good'll come of that! You, for instance. Now, I suppose, you'll come to your office and start acting rude directly?

VERY YOUNG CIVIL SERVANT. How could I, your excellency! . . . Allow me, I'll go ahead and clear the way for you! (*To the common people, shoving this way and that.*) Hey you, one side, here comes a general! (*Stepping up with unusual civility to two foppishly dressed individuals.*) Gentlemen, be so good as to let the general get by.

(THE WELL-DRESSED PARTIES, *stepping aside and clearing the way.*)

FIRST. D'y'know which general? Somebody famous, d'ye s'pose?

SECOND. Dunno, never set eyes on him before.

CIVIL SERVANT OF A GARRULOUS NATURE (*catching up from behind*). Merely a state councillor, in a job only reckoned as fourth class. How's this for luck? After fifteen years' service, the Vladimir, the Anna, the Stanislas,[4] three thousand rubles a year plus two thousand in living expenses, and a bonus from the Council, a bonus from the Commission, and yet another bonus from the Department.

WELL-DRESSED GENTLEMEN (*to one another*). Let's be off!

(*They leave.*)

CIVIL SERVANT OF A GARRULOUS NATURE. Must be mamma's boys. Guess they work in the Foreign Office. I don't care for comedy; tragedy's more to my taste. (*He leaves.*)

VOICE FROM THE CROWD. What a crush!

OFFICER (*forcing his way with a lady on his arm*). Hey you, beards, what are you pushing for? Can't you see the lady?

MERCHANT (*with a lady on his arm*). We got ladies too, dear sir.

VOICE FROM THE CROWD. There she is, turning round, see, see? She's lost her looks by now, but three years ago . . .

ALL SORTS OF VOICES. Yes, three groats, get me, that's what he gave me in change.—A filthy, nasty play!—Amusing little piece!—You tryin' to crawl down my throat?

VOICE AT THE BACK OF THE CROWD. It's all drivel! Where can such things happen? An adventure like that could only take place on Chukotsky Island.[5]

VOICE AT THE OTHER END. Down to the very last detail the exact same thing happened in our little town. My guess is if the author wasn't there in person, he probably heard about it.

MERCHANT'S VOICE. What you got here, if you catch my drift, is more of a, so to speak, thing from the standpoint of moral rectumtude. O'course, it takes all kinds, so to speak, yessiree. But then again, if you think about it, even an honest man, when the time comes . . . But when it's a matter of moral rectumtude, why, you'll even find the gentry's doing it.

VOICE OF A GENTLEMAN OF A PROVOCATIVE NATURE. He must be a sharpy, a clever dog that author—unearthed it all, knows it all!

VOICE OF AN ANGRY BUT OBVIOUSLY EXPERIENCED CIVIL SERVANT. What does he know?—a hell of a lot he knows. He's lying, just plain lying. Everything he wrote, all of it—a pack of lies. That's not how to take a bribe, if you must know . . .

VOICE OF ANOTHER CIVIL SERVANT FROM THE CROWD. Why do you keep saying, "It's funny! it's funny!" Do you know why it's funny? When you come down to it, it's all portraits of real people. When you come down to it, he's put in his own grannies and aunties.[6] That's why it's funny.

UNIDENTIFIED VOICE. Stop, my handkerchief's been stolen!

(TWO OFFICERS, *recognizing one another, converse across the crowd.*)

FIRST. Michel, on your way there?

SECOND. Right.

FIRST. Me too.

CIVIL SERVANT OF IMPOSING ASPECT. I would prohibit everything. Nothing should be published. Use your education, read, but do not write. Enough books have already been written; we don't need any more.

VOICE FROM THE COMMON PEOPLE. So what, if he's a bastard, he's a bastard. Don't be a bastard, and people won't laugh at you.

A HANDSOME, STOUT GENTLEMAN (*speaks heatedly to an inconspic-*

uous puny one). Morality, morality suffers, that's the important thing!

PUNY AND INCONSPICUOUS GENTLEMAN, BUT OF VENOMOUS NATURE. But morality is relative, isn't it?

HANDSOME, STOUT GENTLEMAN. What do you imply by the term "relative"?

INCONSPICUOUS BUT VENOMOUS GENTLEMAN. The fact that every man's morality is measured in terms of himself. One man calls morality taking hats off to him in the street. Another calls morality shutting one's eyes to his thefts; a third calls morality favors done for his mistress. After all, what does one of our colleagues habitually say to his subordinates? He says patronizingly, "My dear sir, try to do your duty to God, your sovereign and your country"—and then you have to figure out for yourself, relative to what. Anyhow this sort of thing only goes on in the provinces, never in the capitals, right? Here if somebody winds up with two houses in three years, what's the cause? Sheer honesty, right?

HANDSOME, STOUT GENTLEMAN (*aside*). Ugly as sin and an adder's tongue.

INCONSPICUOUS BUT VENOMOUS GENTLEMAN (*nudging someone who is a total stranger to him, as he nods at the handsome gentleman*). Four houses in one street; sprang up right next to one another over six years! How's that for honesty promoting germination, eh?

STRANGER (*hurrying away*). Excuse me, I can't hear you.

INCONSPICUOUS BUT VENOMOUS GENTLEMAN (*nudging the stranger's neighbor*). Deafness is spreading all over town these days, eh? That's what it means to live in an unwholesome, damp climate.

STRANGER'S NEIGHBOR. Yes, and there's influenza too. All my children have been down with it.

INCONSPICUOUS BUT VENOMOUS GENTLEMAN. Yes, influenza and deafness; mumps, too, in the throat. (*Submerges into the crowd.*) (*Conversation in a group to one side.*)

FIRST. But they say a similar adventure happened to the author himself. He was imprisoned for debt in a small town.

GENTLEMAN ON THE OTHER SIDE OF THE GROUP (*breaking into the conversation*). No, it wasn't a prison, it was a tower. Anyone riding by could see it. They say it was something incredible. Imagine: a poet in the tallest of towers, with mountains on every side, a delightful location, and he reads poetry there. Don't you think a writer's idiosyncratic characteristics come to the fore at times like that?

GENTLEMAN OF POSITIVE NATURE. The author must be a clever fellow.

GENTLEMAN OF NEGATIVE NATURE. Not clever at all. I happen to know he worked in the civil service and was almost sacked: didn't know how to draft a petition.

A LIAR, PLAIN AND SIMPLE. A shrewd mind, shrewd! He couldn't get a post for the longest time, so what do you think he did? He wrote a letter straight to the minister. And the way he wrote it! The style of a Quintilian. Here's how he began: "Dear sir!" And then he went on and on and on . . . knocked off about eight pages at one go. When the minister read it, "Well," says he, "thank you, thank you! I can see you must have many enemies. Be head of the department!" And from clerk he zoomed right up to department head.

GENTLEMAN OF GOOD-HUMORED NATURE (*turning to a man of impassive nature*). What the devil is one to believe! He was in prison and climbed up a tower! Was sacked from the service and given a post!

GENTLEMAN OF IMPASSIVE NATURE. Why, it's all improvised.

GENTLEMAN OF GOOD-HUMORED NATURE. How do you mean, improvised?

GENTLEMAN OF IMPASSIVE NATURE. Just so. They don't know themselves two minutes beforehand what will come out of their mouths. Their tongues, unbeknownst to their owners, suddenly blab out the news, and the owner's delighted—he goes home as if he's just eaten a five-course meal. And the next day he's already forgotten what he himself invented. He thinks he heard it from others—and goes to broadcast it all over town.

GOOD-HUMORED GENTLEMAN. Why, that's unconscionable: to lie and not be aware of it.

IMPASSIVE GENTLEMAN. Well, some of them are aware of it. Some of them are aware they're lying but consider it a conversational requisite. "Lovely's the field fragrant with rye, lovely the speech adorned with a lie."

A LADY OF MIDDLING SOCIETY. What a malicious scoffer that author must be! I confess I wouldn't like to catch his eye: suppose he made fun of me.

A GENTLEMAN OF SOME AUTHORITY. I don't know what sort of man he is. He's a, he's a, he's a . . . The man holds nothing sacred; today he says such-and-such an official is no good, and tomorrow he'll be saying there's no God. It's but a step from one to the other.

SECOND GENTLEMAN. Ridicule! Laughter is no laughing matter. It means undermining all sorts of respect, that's what it means. Why, after this, anyone can beat me up in the street and say, "Hey, they're laughing at all of you, you hold the same rank, so now you'll get it hot and heavy!" That's what it means.

THIRD GENTLEMAN. Indeed it does! This is a serious matter! They call it a bagatelle, an airy nothing, a stage play. No, this is not a mere bagatelle; close attention must be paid to it. People get sent to Siberia for such things.[7] And if I had the power, I wouldn't let another peep be heard from the author. I'd stick him in a place where he wouldn't clap eyes on God's daylight.

(A GROUP OF PEOPLE *of God alone knows what nature, though of well-bred appearance and decently dressed, appears.*)

FIRST. We'd better stand here for a while, until the crowd thins out. What was all that about, really! Kicking up a rumpus, applauding as if it were God knows what! A trifle, some silly stage play, and they raise a racket, shout, call for the author—what's going on!

SECOND. Yet the play did amuse and divert.

FIRST. Of course it amused, as any trifle usually does amuse. But why such shouts and debates on that account? They discuss it as if it were something important, they applaud . . . Well, what's the point! I could understand if it were a soprano or a ballerina—I could understand that, because you admire the art, the suppleness, the dexterity, the native talent. But what was there in this? They shout, "Author! A man of letters! A writer!" And what is a writer? He happens to come across a witty remark or copies something from nature . . . What's so hard about that? What's there to it? It's all fairy tales and nothing more.

SECOND. Yes, of course, quite unimportant.

FIRST. Think about it. Now a dancer, for example—there's art in that, at any rate, you couldn't do what he does to save your life. For instance, suppose I wanted to: I simply couldn't lift my leg that high. Suppose I want to do an entrechat—I couldn't do it under any circumstances. But anyone can write without training. I don't know who this author is, but I've been told he's the most consummate ignoramus, knows nothing at all. I believe he's been sacked from somewhere.

SECOND. Even so, he must know something. Otherwise he couldn't write.

FIRST. For heaven's sake, what can he know? You know yourself a man of letters is the silliest ass going! The whole world knows that—he's unfit for any job. They've tried to put them to use but had to get rid of them. Judge for yourself, what do they write? It's all poppycock, fairy tales! If I wanted to, I could write the same stuff this very hour and so could you and so could he and so could anyone.

SECOND. Yes, of course, what's hard about writing? If you only have an ounce of brains in your head, you can do it.

FIRST. You don't even need brains. Why brains? It's nothing but fairy tales. Now if it were at least some academic science, say, some subject you never studied, all right, but what is this? It's something every peasant knows. You see it in the street every day. Just sit at your window and jot down everything that goes on—and that's the whole trick to it!

THIRD. That's right. Honestly, when you think of the rubbish people waste time on!

FIRST. Exactly, a waste of time—that's all it is. Fairy tales, poppycock! They simply should not be allowed to lay hands on pen and ink. Anyway, the mob's thinned out, let's go! Kicking up a ruckus, shouting, encouraging! And it's nothing more than poppycock! Fairy tales! Poppycock! Fairy tales!

(*They leave. The crowd thins out, a few loiterers run on stage.*)

GOOD-HUMORED CIVIL SERVANT. Regardless, he should have at least put in one honorable man! Nothing but scoundrels and more scoundrels.

ONE OF THE COMMON PEOPLE. Hey, wait for me at the crossroads! I'll run an' git my mittens.

ONE OF THE GENTLEMEN (*looking at his watch*). Why, it's almost one. I've never left a theater so late. (*He goes.*)

(*The lobby empties out.*)

THE PLAY'S AUTHOR (*emerging*). I heard more than I meant to. What a motley array of comments! Happy the comic writer born into a nation where society has not yet congealed into one inert mass or become encrusted by the uniform bark of old prejudice, enclosing all thought in one and the same shape and dimension, but where every man has his own opinion and everyone is free to mold his own character. What diversity in these opinions and how the stalwart and lucid Russian mind shone out in everything: In the noble aspiration of the husband in government! In the lofty self-sacrifice of the civil servant hidden away in the hinterlands! And in the delicate beauty of a magnanimous female soul! And in the aesthetic feeling of the devotees of art! And in the downright commonsensical instinct of the common people! Even in the grudging criticisms there is a good deal a comic writer needs to hear! What a living lesson! Yes, I am content. But why has my heart grown so heavy? Strange: I'm sorry that no one noticed the honorable character in my play. Yes, there was one honorable, noble character, who performed throughout from start to finish. This honorable, noble character was *Laughter*. Noble, because he decided to put in an appearance, despite the low esteem in which the world holds him. Noble, because he decided to put in an appearance, even though he earned the comic author an odious reputation—the reputation of a cold egoist, and even led people to doubt the existence of tender feelings in his soul. No one stood up for laughter. I am a comic writer, I served him honorably, and therefore must rise to his defense. Indeed, laughter is more meaningful and profound than people think. Not the laughter engendered by temporary irritation, by a splenetic and morbid frame of mind; nor the frivolous laughter which serves as holiday diversion and recreation—but the laughter which issues from man's brighter nature, because at its source lies an ever-gushing fountainhead which sounds a subject deeply and brings out clearly what would otherwise have gone unnoticed, without whose penetrating force the pettiness and vacuity of life would not so terrify man. The despicable and paltry which he passes by indifferently every day would not rise up before him with such terrifying, almost distorted force, nor would he exclaim with a shudder, "Can such people exist?"—when, by his own admission, even worse exist. No, it is unjust to say that laughter is disturbing. Only depressants are disturbing, but laughter cheers. Many things might disturb a man if they were set forth in their nakedness; but, illumined by the power of laughter, they conciliate his soul. Anyone who would wreak vengeance on a wicked man is almost reconciled with him as soon as he sees the base actions of that villain's soul ridiculed. It is unjust to say that a scoundrel will be the first to laugh at a scoundrel on stage. A scoundrel of some later age may laugh, but the contemporary scoundrel has not the power to laugh! He senses that everyone has already retained an indelible image, and that one vile action on his part is enough to turn that image into his eternal sobriquet; for a man who fears naught else in the world fears ridicule. No, only a profoundly virtuous soul can laugh a virtuous, bright laugh. But people do not hear the mighty force of such a laugh. "What is funny is low," says the world; only that which is uttered in a stern, tense voice is called sublime. But, Lord! the numbers of people who pass by, every day, for whom nothing in the world is sublime! They regard the creations of inspiration as poppycock and fairy tales; Shakespeare's works are mere fairy tales to them; the holy impulses of the soul are mere fairy tales to them. No, it is not a writer's petty and offended vanity that brings me to say this, nor is it because my immature and feeble works have just been called fairy tales—no, I see my shortcomings and realize that I deserve rebuke. But my soul could not endure it passively when the most perfect creations were honored by the titles of poppycock and fairy tales, when all the splendors and luminaries of the world are deemed creators of poppycock and fairy tales! My soul ached when I saw the number of unresponsive, lifeless creatures dwelling here in life itself, hideous in the inert frigidity of their souls and the barren wasteland of their hearts. My soul ached, when something that plunges a loving soul into heavenly tears could not make the ghost of an expression flicker across their impassive faces, and when their tongues did not freeze when uttering their constant byword, "fairy tales"! Fairy tales! . . . And lo, centuries have rolled by, cities and peoples have drifted past and vanished from the face of the earth, everything that once existed has evaporated like smoke—but the fairy tales live on and are repeated even now, and wise emperors, sagacious rulers, the handsome old man and the youth full of noble aspirations pay heed to them. Fairy tales! . . . And lo, the balconies and railings of the theater groan: from floor to ceiling everything is shaken, transformed into one emotion, one moment, one man, and all persons meet as brothers in a single spiritual impulse, and sympathetic applause thunders out a noble hymn to a man who departed this earth five hundred years ago. Do his moldering bones hear it in the grave? Does his soul, which endured the bleak misery of life, respond? Fairy tales! . . . And lo, amidst that overwhelmed throng seated in rows came one bowed down by grief and the unendurable weight of life, ready to lay hands on himself in desperation—and suddenly refreshing tears welled up in his eyes, and he went out reconciled to life and prays anew to heaven for grief and suffering that he may but live to shed more tears at such fairy tales. Fairy tales! . . . Why, the world would nod asleep without such fairy tales, life would grow shallow and men's souls would be overgrown with mildew and slime. Fairy tales! . . . Oh, may the names of those who sympathetically heed such fairy tales remain forever sacred; the wondrous hand of Providence was constantly hovering over the heads of their creators. Even in times of distress and persecution all that was noblest in their nations stood to be the first of their defenders; the crowned monarch shielded them with his royal buckler from the summit of his unapproachable throne.

Forge bravely onward! And may the soul be untroubled by censure, but gratefully accept any reminder of shortcomings, refusing to
be downcast even when people deny that it possesses sublime impulses and a sacred love for mankind! The world is like a millrace:
opinions and arguments whirl about in it eternally; but time is ever
threshing it out. Like husks, the false will fly away, and, like hard
kernels, the immutable truths shall remain. What once was regarded
as vacuous may then appear armed with stern significance. In the
depths of cold laughter, hot sparks of eternal and prepotent love can
be found. And who can tell? Perhaps, later on, everyone will recognize why, by virtue of those same laws, a proud and mighty man
seems paltry and weak in misfortune, while a weak man grows like
a giant amid sorrows—and why, by virtue of those same laws, he
who often sheds intense, heartfelt tears may seem to laugh more
than anyone else in the world! . . .

Dramatic Poesy
by Vissarion Belinsky

Drama represents an event in the process of being completed as if it were being completed in real time, before the eyes of the reader or spectator. A conciliation of the epos and the lyre, drama is not distinctly one or the other, but forms a special organic whole of its own. On one hand, the Self in drama is not enclosed in the circle of action, but, to the contrary, can break out of it and return to it. On the other hand, the presence of the Self in drama has quite another meaning than it has in lyric poetry: it is no longer an inner world concentrated in itself, feeling and contemplating, it is no longer the poet himself, but emerges and itself becomes an object of contemplation within the objective and actual world, which is structured by its peculiar activity; it has been fragmented and appears to be a living aggregate of many persons, out of whose action and reaction the drama takes shape. In consequence of this, drama does not admit of epic descriptions of locality, adventures, situations and characters which all by themselves must engage our contemplation. Even the demand for national qualities is much fainter in the drama than in the epic: in *Hamlet* we behold Europe and, through the spirit and nature of the characters, Western Europe, but not Denmark and—what's more—no particular period. Drama does not admit of any lyrical effusions; the characters must express themselves in action: we are no longer dealing with sensations and perceptions, but with characteristics. What are usually referred to as the lyrical passages in drama are only the energy of an exacerbated temperament, its *pathos*, which involuntarily inspires speech with special

"Dramatic Poesy" is a self-contained section of a longer essay, "The Classification of Literature into Genera and Species," which appeared in *Notes of the Fatherland* (*Otechestvennye zapiski*, no. 3, 1841). Belinsky had hoped to develop it into a full-length work on aesthetics which he never completed. The present translation is based on the text in *Belinskiy o drame i teatre*, ed. B. A. Ostrovskaya and A. M. Lavretsky (Moscow-Leningrad, 1948).

exaltation; or a character's secret, hidden thought which we need to know and which the poet compels him to *think aloud*. The action of a drama must be focused on a single point of interest and must eschew collateral interests. In a novel a character may have a place not so much out of actual involvement in the event as from his eccentric nature; in a drama there must be no one who is not indispensable to the machinery of its progress and development. Simplicity, orderliness and unity of action (in the sense of unity of the basic idea) must be among the most important conditions of drama; everything in it must be directed to a single goal, a single intention. The interest of drama must be concentrated in a single person, through whose fate its basic concept is expressed.

However, these things are most relevant to the sublime genus of drama, *tragedy*. The essence of tragedy consists in a clash or collision, a conflict between the heart's natural propensities and moral duty or simply an insurmountable obstacle. Associated with the idea of tragedy is the idea of an awesome, somber event, a fatal denouement. The Germans call tragedy *Trauerspiel*, a *sorrowful spectacle*—and tragedy is indeed a sorrowful spectacle! Even if bloodshed and corpses, dagger and poison may not be its ever-present attributes, nevertheless its conclusion always involves the shattering of a heart's most cherished hopes, as the happiness of a whole life is destroyed. That is the source of its somber grandeur, its grandiose monumentality: destiny reigns over it, destiny constitutes its foundation and essence . . . What is the clash?—fate's unconditional demand for victims. Should the hero prevail over the natural inclinations of his heart to the advantage of the moral order—then farewell, happiness, farewell, life's joy and charm! He is a dead man amongst the living; his element is the grief of a profound mind, his portion is suffering, his one and only outcome is either painful self-abnegation or imminent death! Should the hero of tragedy follow the natural bent of his heart—he is a transgressor in his own eyes, a victim of his own conscience, for his heart is the soil wherein the roots of moral law are deeply intrenched and not to be torn out, until he has first rent his own heart and made it bleed profusely. In this clash, the law of existence is reminiscent of Nero's edict, which punished as felons alike those who failed to weep over the tyrant's newly deceased sister—for they did not compassionate his loss—and those who did weep for her death—for she was numbered among the bevy of goddesses, and tears for a goddess can be only a sign of envy of her blissful state . . . And yet, no other genus of poetry holds such potent sway over our mind or attracts us with such irresistible fascination or procures us such sublime pleasures as does tragedy. And great truth, sublime intelligence, lies at the root of this. We deeply pity a hero who falls in battle or perishes in victory; but we are well aware that were it not for this fall or destruction he would not be a hero, he would not realize in his personality the eternal substantiality of forces, the universal and intransigent laws of existence. If Antigone had managed to bury the body of Polyneices, not knowing that an inevitable punishment awaited her for this, or without any danger of punishment befalling her, her deed would merely have been kindhearted and praiseworthy, but ordinary and unheroic. In such a case Antigone would not arouse all of our concern for her, and if by some chance she were instantly to die, we would not pity her death: after all, a thousand people die every hour on the terrestrial globe, and if a man is to pity them all, he'd have no time to drink a cup of tea! No, the untimely and violent death of the young and beautiful Antigone rocks our whole being only when we can see in her death an atonement of human dignity, the triumph of the universal and eternal over the personal and transitory, an exploit, the contemplation of which wafts our soul to heaven and makes our heart beat with sublime excitement! Fate chooses for the accomplishment of high moral tasks the noblest vessels of the spirit, the most exalted personalities who stand at the forefront of humanity, heroes who embody the substantial forces which hold together the moral world. Ismene was a sister of Polyneices too; her kind and kindred heart also suffered at the thought of her slain brother's disgrace; but in her this suffering did not overcome a fear of death. Antigone thought it easier to bear the torment of a cruel death than the disgrace of her own flesh and blood; she was sorry to part with her young life, so full of hope and charm; she proudly bade farewell to the allure of Hymen, whose sweetness fate did not allow her to taste; but she does not crave pardon or mercy, she does not flinch with loathing from the death that terrifies her, but rushes to clasp it in her embrace. Consequently, the difference between the two sisters lies not in feelings, but in strength, energy and depth of feeling, which results in one of them being a kindhearted but ordinary creature, and the other a heroine. Divest any tragedy of the fatal catastrophe—and you deprive it of all its magnitude, all its meaning; you turn a great achievement into something ordinary, which from the very first loses all its power of fascination over you.

Sometimes the clash may inhere in a man's false position, which results from the incompatibility of his nature with the situation in which fate has set him. We ask the reader to recall one of the heroes of Walter Scott's novel *The Fair Maid of Perth*,[1] a luckless clan chieftain, who—with his proud mind and intense passions, obligated on the eve of a battle to decide whether his clan is to take part—admits to his mentor that he is a coward . . . Hamlet is not a coward, but his inwardly contemplative nature was not created for the turmoil of life, nor for a struggle with crime and punishment of a malefaction, and yet fate summons him to such a deed . . . What is he to do? If he runs away, no one will know the difference and he will not be condemned; but is there anywhere in the universe, other than the grave, where he could hide from himself?—and poor Hamlet actually does find his refuge in the grave . . . Fate keeps watch over man in every byway of life: a youth may sometimes pay for the momentary glamour of a mad passion with the happiness of his whole life, poisoning it with the memory of an innocent victim who was destroyed by his love . . . And why is this so? Because deeply rooted in his soul are shoots from the seeds of moral law, whereas a fatuous, vile creature calmly enjoys the fruits of his debauchery and impudently prides himself on the number of ruined victims! . . . Only a man of the highest nature can be the hero or victim of tragedy: so it is even in reality!

Chance—for instance, the unexpected death of a character or some other unforeseen circumstance which has no direct relation to the basic concept of the work—can have no place in tragedy. One must not forget that tragedy is a more artistic creation than any other genus of poetry. Were Othello to delay one moment in smothering Desdemona or hasten to open the door to Emilia's knocking—everything would be explained and Desdemona would be saved; but, in recompense, the tragedy would be ruined. Desdemona's death is a result of Othello's jealousy and not a chance affair, and therefore the poet has the right to make a conscious choice and set aside all, even the most natural, events which might serve to save Desdemona. Desdemona could as easily have noticed the kerchief torn from her head by her husband, that kerchief which served for her downfall, as not notice it;[2] but the poet had every right to use this eventuality as it suited his purposes. The purpose of his tragedy was not to caution others against the dreadful consequences of blind jealousy, but to rock the soul of the spectator with the spectacle of blind jealousy seen not as a crime but as a phenomenon of life. Othello's jealousy had its cause and necessity imbedded in his fiery nature, his upbringing and all the circumstances of his life: he was as guilty of it as he was innocent. That is why this great spirit, this mighty temperament prompts us not to loathing and hatred of him, but to love, wonderment and compassion. The harmony of a peaceful life was wrecked by the dissonance of his crime—and he ennobles it by a voluntary death, redeems his own weighty guilt by it—and we end the drama with a sense of reconciliation, with a profound thought of the inscrutable mystery of life, and two shadows reconciled beyond the grave pass hand in hand before our enchanted gaze . . . Corpses and bloodshed upset our feelings only when we cannot see the necessity for them, when the author lavishly paves and inundates the stage with them for the sake of effect. But, thank God, frequent usage has weakened the power of these effects and now they evoke only laughter, not terror.

There is something imperfect and fatal in the conditions of life. Life is formed out of mobs and heroes, and these two facets are in eternal enmity, for the former hates the latter, and the latter despises the former. Every beautiful phenomenon in life must become the victim of its own quality. Barely have you finished reading the night scene in the garden between Romeo and Juliet, when a dismal foreboding steals into your heart . . . "No," you say, "such a love and such richness of life are not for this world, such creatures are not meant to live among people! How can they be so happy, when none of the others even suspect the possibility of such happiness? No, they must pay a high price for their bliss! . . ." And in fact, what is it that destroys Romeo and Juliet?—not villainy, not human perfidy, but human stupidity and triviality. The old Capulets are simply well-meaning if commonplace people; they are incapable of imagining anything superior to themselves, they judge their daughter's feelings by their own, they measure her nature by their nature—and destroy her, and then, when it is too late, they figure it out, grant forgiveness and even praise . . . O, woe! woe! woe! . . .

Macbeth's crime and the demonic nature of his wife stir us; but if he were to be asked how he carried out his villainous deed, he would certainly reply, "I don't know myself," and if she were to be asked why she is of so inhuman a disposition, she would certainly reply that she knows as much about it as her interrogators do, and that if it is owing to her nature, then it's because she had no other . . . These are questions to be resolved only beyond the grave, they are the realm of fate, the sphere of tragedy! . . .

Richard II arouses a hostile feeling in us by his behavior, which is degrading for a king. But as soon as his cousin Bolingbroke usurps the crown—then the king, unworthy whilst he reigned, looks to be a great king once he is despoiled of his kingdom. He departs fully conscious of the greatness of his office, the sanctity of his anointing, the legitimacy of his rights—and wise speeches and lofty ideas issue in a turbulent gush from his lips, and his deeds reveal a great mind, a kingly dignity. You no longer merely respect him, you venerate him; you no longer merely pity him, you compassionate him. Trivial in good fortune, great in misfortune, he is a hero in your eyes. But to bring out all the forces of his spirit, to become a hero, he had to drain to the dregs the cup of calamity and perish . . . What a contradictory, what a rich subject for tragedy, and, therefore, what an inexhaustible source of sublime pleasure for you! . . .

Dramatic poesy is the highest stage of development in poetry and the crowning glory of art, and tragedy is the highest stage and crowning glory of dramatic poesy. Hence tragedy contains the quintessence of dramatic poesy, encompasses all its elements, and, therefore, comic elements enter into it as well, by right. Poetry and prose walk arm in arm in human life, and the subject of tragedy is life in all the complexity of its elements. Truly, only the highest, most poetic moments of life are concentrated in tragedy, but only in regard to the hero or heroes of the tragedy, and not the rest of the characters, who may include villains and saints and fools and buffoons, because all human life consists of the collision of and mutual influence on one another of heroes, villains, average men, nonentities and fools. The division of tragedies into historical and nonhistorical has no fundamental importance: the heroes of both equally represent an embodiment of eternal, substantial forces of the human spirit. In modern Christian art man appears not as a member of society, but of humanity; tragedy is the crowning glory of modern art, and therefore King Richard II, Othello the Moor, the wellborn youth Romeo, Timon the citizen of Athens share the same equal right to occupy first place in it, because they are all equally heroes. That is why the distortion of historical figures which is less admissible in a novel is a sort of inalienable right of tragedy, derivative of its very essence. The tragic poet wants to present his hero in a particular historical situation; history gives him the situation, and if the historical hero of this situation does not correspond to the tragic poet's ideal, he has every right to change him as he will. In Schiller's tragedy *Don Carlos*, Philip is portrayed not quite as history portrays him, but this in no way diminishes the value of the play, but rather enhances it. Alfieri[3] in his tragedy portrayed the authentically historical Philip II, but his play is immeasurably inferior to Schiller's. As to Prince Carlos, it is absurd to take the distortion of his historical character in Schiller's tragedy as a serious fault, for Don Carlos is too inconsiderable a figure in history. Many are tempted by the free dealing of Goethe, who turned the seventy-year-old Egmont—father of a numerous family—into a hot-blooded youth, passionately in love with a simple maiden: the most legitimate license—for Goethe wanted to depict in his tragedy not Egmont but a young man impassioned by life to the point of intoxication and yet sacrificing life to redeem his country's prosperity. Every character in tragedy belongs not to history, but to the poet, even though the character may bear an historical name. Profoundly judicious are these words of Goethe: "So far as the poet is concerned, there are no historical personages; he wants to portray his own moral world and to that end he does a few historical personages the honor of sticking their names on his creations."

As to the division of tragedy into acts and their number, this relates to the external form of the drama as a rule. Tragedy can be written in prose or verse; but in most cases the blend of both will correspond to the essence of the content of the individual parts, i.e., the poetry or prose of life expressed in them.

Dramatic poesy evolves in a people with a matured civilization, during a period when its historical development is flourishing luxuriantly. So it was with the Greeks. Their most outstanding tragic poets are Aeschylus, Sophocles and Euripides. We have already denoted the essence and nature of Greek drama, and in describing the subject of *Antigone* have given the reader a datum for the verification of our remarks. Of the modern peoples, no drama has achieved so perfect and high a development as that of the English. Shakespeare is the Homer of drama; his drama is the highest prototype of Christian drama. In Shakespeare's dramas all the elements of life and poetry are melded into a living unity, boundless in content and superb in artistic form. All humanity, all its past and future reside in them; they are the luxuriant flowering and luscious fruit of art as it has developed among all peoples and in all ages. In them the plasticity and the relievo of artistic form, the chaste ingenuousness of inspiration and reflective thought, the objective world and the subjective world have interpenetrated one another and flowed into an indissoluble unity. To speak of the profound study of the human heart, the truth to nature and reality, the endless abundance and sublimity of creative ideas in this universal king of poets would mean repeating what has been said many times by thousands of persons. To define the value of his every drama would mean writing an enormous tome and yet not expressing a hundredth part of what should be expressed or a millionth particle of what they contain.

After the English, first place is held by German tragedy. Schiller and Goethe brought it to that stage of renown. However, German drama has quite another temper and even another meaning than the Shakespearean: it is for the most part either lyrical or philosophical drama. The breakthrough of spontaneous creativity may be observed only in Goethe's *Goetz von Berlichingen* and *Egmont,* and Schiller's *Wilhelm Tell* and *Wallenstein.* The meaning of German drama is closely connected with the meaning of German art overall.

Spanish drama is little known, although it can take pride in more than one glorious dramatic name, such as its Lope de Vegas and Calderóns. The reason for this seems to be the national tenor of its drama, which has not yet risen to general, universal subject matter.

The history of French literature glitters with many dramatic splendors. Corneille and Racine were for almost two centuries taken to be the leading tragic poets in the world, as were Crébillon and Voltaire after them. But now it is clear that the history of dramatic poesy in France relates to the history of dress, fashion and social customs of the good old days, and has nothing to do with the history of art. As for its contemporary dramatists, Hugo occasionally emits flashes of remarkable talent, but that is all.

Our Russian tragedy began with Pushkin and died with him. His *Boris Godunov* is a creation that deserves to take first place after Shakespeare's drama. Moreover, Pushkin created a special genus of drama which is to reality what a novella is to a novel; such are his "Scene between Faust and Mephistopheles," *Salieri and Mozart, The Covetous Knight, The Nixie* and *The Stone Guest.* In form and scope these are no more than dramatic sketches, but in content and development, they are tragedies in the full meaning of the word. In originality and spontaneity they are incomparable, but in profundity of concept and artistic form, testifying to the spark of inspiration in the creative act which gave them birth, their worth can be measured only by the dramas of Shakespeare. In our times a great poet cannot be exclusively epic, lyric or dramatic; in our times, creative activity is shown in an aggregate of all aspects of poetry; but for the most part, great artists commence with epic works, go on to lyric and conclude with the drama. And so it was with Pushkin: even in his first long poems the dramatic element is vividly evident, and many passages in them form excellent tragic scenes, especially in *Gypsies* and *Poltava.* His last works show that he had definitively turned to drama and that his "dramatic sketches" were only tryouts of a pen being sharpened for greater creations; and what those creations would have been! But death caught him at a time when his genius

was fully ripened and mature for drama—and his shade, full of suffering, bore away with it

A holy secret, and for us
The life-creating voice is stilled!

All other attempts at drama in Russian literature, from Sumarokov to Mr. Kukolnik[4] inclusively, have the right only to be remembered in the history of literature, where they will be mentioned in
their place, but not in aesthetics, where only works of art have a
right to be mentioned.

Comedy is an absolute species of dramatic poesy, diametrically
opposed to *tragedy*. The subject of tragedy is the world of great
moral phenomena, its heroes are individuals replete with substantial forces of spiritual human nature; the subject of comedy is fortuity, devoid of rational necessity, a world of phantoms or sem-
blances but not the reality that exists in actual fact; the heroes of
comedy are persons who have renounced the substantial bases of
their spiritual nature. Hence, the reaction produced by comedy is
hallowed terror that shocks the mind; the reaction produced by
comedy is laughter, at times mirthful, at times sardonic. The essence of comedy is the contradiction between the phenomena of life
and the essence and purpose of life. In this respect, life appears in
comedy as its own repudiation. Just as tragedy concentrates only the
sublime, poetic moments in the hero's doings in the narrow circle of
its action, so comedy predominately depicts the prose of everyday
life, its details and incidents. Tragedy is the cycle of revolution
of poetry's sun, which—when it reaches its zenith—stops, and—
crossing over to comedy—begins its descent. Among the Greeks
comedy was the death of poetry: Aristophanes was the last of their
poets, and his comedies are a dirge for the forever-lost universality of
life and the beautiful art of Greece that sprang from it. But in the
modern world, where all the interpenetrating elements of life do not
prevent one another from developing, comedy has no such mournful
meaning for art: its element has entered or can enter all types of poetry, and it can develop in step with tragedy and even precede it in
the historical evolution of art.

At the base of truly artistic comedy lies the most profound humor. The poet's personality is not only visible in its externals, but
his subjective contemplation of life is also present in it, spontane-
ously, as an *arrière-pensée*; and other faces, beautiful and human,
loom dimly from behind the distorted and bestial face of the comedy, and your laughter responds not to mirth, but to bitterness and

morbidity . . . Life is shown to us in comedy as it is, in order to bring us to a clear contemplation of life as it ought to be. The most excellent model for an artistic comedy is given us by Gogol's *Inspector*.

An artistic comedy must not sacrifice the goals a poet purposes to the objective truth of his depictions, or else it will cease being artistic and become *didactic*, as we shall explain the meaning of this term later. But if didactic comedy proceeds not from an innocent desire to crack a few jokes but from the life of a spirit deeply offended by vulgarity; if its mockery is dissolved in sarcastic bile, profound humor lies at its base and a turbulent animation is exuded in its expression—in short, if it is a creation achieved through suffering, it is as good as any artistic comedy. Naturally, such a comedy can be the work of none but a great talent; its character drawing may be distinguished by inordinate clarity and richness of colors but cannot be exaggerated to the point of affectation and caricature; it stands to reason that the temperaments of the characters must be created and not fabricated, and there must be more or less artistry apparent in the way they are depicted. The finest model of such a comedy we have in *Woe from Wit*, that noblest creation of a brilliant man, that ebullient dithyrambic effusion of bilious and fulminous dissatisfaction at the sight of a rotten society full of trivial people, whose souls have never been penetrated by any ray of divine light, who live according to obsolescent traditions of the past, according to a system of shabby and immoral rules, whose petty goals and vile aspirations are directed only at the phantasms of life—rank, money, scandal, the belittling of human dignity, and whose apathetic, torpid life is death to any living emotion, any rational thought, any noble impulse . . . *Woe from Wit* has a great significance both for our literature and for our society.

There is another, more inferior comedy, which can be elevated to the level of artistry by the creation of original types and by an accurate depiction of the manners of society, but which is based not on humor but only on comical mirth. Depending upon its quality, such a comedy may be related both to art and to polite letters, fluctuating between these two facets of literature. There are no models for such a comedy in our literature. Fonvizin's *The Minor* and *The Brigadier* are associated with the comedy of manners and satire, in the usual meaning of that term. A truly artistic comedy can never become obsolete simply because the social mores it depicts have changed. *The Inspector* and *Woe from Wit* are immortal.

There is another particular species of dramatic poesy which occupies the middle ground between tragedy and comedy: it is what is properly called *drama*. Drama derives its origin from *melodrama*, which in the last century set up in opposition to the bombastic and unnatural tragedy of the time and in which life found its only haven from moribund pseudoclassicism, much as it took shelter in the novels of Mrs. Radcliffe, Ducray-Duminil and August Lafontaine[5] from rhetorical poems like *Gonzalvo of Cordova, Cadmus and Harmonia*[6] and so forth. However, this provenance relates only to the name "drama," a specific but not a generic label, and even more to modern drama (such as, for instance, Goethe's *Clavigo*). Shakespeare, who always traveled his own road, following the eternal ordinances of creativity and not the rules of silly poetasters, wrote a great many works which should occupy the middle ground between tragedy and comedy and which may be called *epic dramas*. There are tragic characters and situations in them (as, for instance, in *The Merchant of Venice*); but their denouement is almost always happy, because the fatal catastrophe is not required by their nature. The hero of a drama must be life itself. No, despite the epic character of the drama, its form must be superlatively dramatic. Dramatic quality consists not only in dialogue, but in the vital action of the speakers. For instance, if two persons are arguing over something, this lacks not only drama but the dramatic element as well; but when a contentious party, in hopes of gaining the upper hand over his opponent, tries to affect a feature of the other's character or assail the tender chords in his mind, and when, as a result, their own natures come to light in the argument, and the end of the argument puts them in a new relationship to one another—that is the very essence of drama. But the main point in drama is to avoid long narratives and to see that every word be expressed in action. Drama must not be a mere copy from nature, nor a collection of individual scenes, however beautiful, but must itself form a distinct and exclusive world, where each person in striving after his own ends and in acting only for himself unwittingly contributes to the general action of the play. And this can occur only when drama has originated and developed out of the idea, and not been slapped together by the rational consciousness.[7]

A Type of the Current Drama

by Vasily Sleptsov

To my way of thinking, a time is now coming that will be particularly auspicious for the flourishing of art. The time has not yet come, but that doesn't signify—it soon must. I base my statement on the basic computations of a certain eminent European astrologer, who, at any time, can divine by the stars' trajectory the fates-to-be of renowned individuals and even whole nations. According to the sightings of this great soothsayer, there are two kinds of times particularly auspicious for the flourishing of all genres of art: either when humanity is oppressed by every conceivable calamity and is suffering sorely, or else when it is benefiting from peace and serenity and indulging in inoffensive pleasures. Likewise, other conditions, though wholly contrary to one another, equally promote the development of poetic creativity. On such grounds as these I too can assert that a propitious time is now heading our way and soon we shall see an end to that desolate scarcity of good men which has caused us willy-nilly to dub every Giles a gentleman.

As a matter of fact, it's about time it ended! For ever so long now, we've been hearing complaints, on one hand, about the paucity of new talent and, on the other, about the presence of old sneaks who force their way into Parnassus and turn it into a pothouse. Both complaints are equally fundamental: there are no new talents, but this cannot be helped; the only thing left is to wait and hope; as to the old sneaks, that grievance cannot be helped either, and in my opinion it's not worth bothering about, because sneaks on Parnassus are an anomaly and hence transitory. The garden of Russian literature has gradually gone to seed—well, naturally, weeds sprang up, as they tend to do. The history of this garden shows that the like has

The article was first published anonymously in *Notes of the Fatherland* (*Otechestvennye zapiski*) for February 1868. It was identified as Sleptsov's work and reprinted in *Literary Heritage* (*Literaturnoe nasledstvo*, LXXI, 1963), from which text this translation was made.

often occurred before; but as soon as circumstances took a turn for the better, the besom of Time swept this filth into oblivion on each occasion. And history demonstrates how futile was individual effort in such cases. Thus, the late Lomonosov, a famous savant but a poor politician, took a powerful stand against this evil in his time and even submitted a petition to the president of the Academy of Sciences recommending that appropriate measures be taken against anyone who, in Lomonosov's opinion, seriously discredited Russian science by his presence. Moreover, Lomonosov called attention to the danger science ran in such cases, and advised them to consider "how much the cattle allowed in were bedunging the place."[1] But if Lomonosov—who rejoiced in the purity of academic manners—was distressed and took a stand against the admission of mere cattle, it would be curious to know what he would do in our time, when quadrupeds of every imaginable species graze unimpeded in the garden of Russian literature, and not only are no petitions submitted about them, but—on the contrary—every day the quadrupeds themselves gain more and more self-assurance and have gone so far as to fancy themselves the masters of this garden. What Lomonosov would have undertaken had he seen such a disgraceful sight is hard to say. God knows, perhaps he and his petitions would start to be importunate and become such a nuisance that people would stop accepting them; or perhaps he would simply take a good look, and another good look, spit on it all and get back to his chemistry.

How are we, however, to act? Just what are we to do? To my way of thinking, the time has not yet come for us to do anything but wait. The stars make it clear that, with the advent of propitious circumstances, all this ugliness will be beautified on its own, and our garden will flourish and be restored. At least I, for my part, believe this steadfastly; all the portents suggest that we won't have much longer to wait. But in the meantime, while waiting for something better, we can divert ourselves at leisure with current events and for this once let us turn to the Russian theater.

Some enthusiasts of national drama believe that it behooves us to pay special heed to this institution, I mean the theater; they assert that every so often both audience and performers must be reminded about Parnassus, and the aims of art, and the theater being a great school for the people and other esteemed truisms; for otherwise Parnassus gets badly overgrown with nettles and the Pantheon of Russian muses might easily turn into a stableyard. I cannot concur with this opinion. I think that if art is really menaced by such a danger and can be saved from ultimate ruin only by constant chip-

ping away at it, then it isn't art and it isn't worth bothering about—
let it die a natural death. But the fact is, the Pantheon of Russian
muses is not quite as hopeless as all that; if truth be told, it is indeed
befouled and pretty badly befouled; but the calamity is not so grievous as to drive us to despair. The main thing, which ought not to be
forgotten, is that—under more propitious circumstances—the nettles will be uprooted, the livestock allowed in the Pantheon building
will be expelled, and even their having had time to "bedung" the
place will serve to manure future crops. It is all unimportant and
like the sands of the sea: today it piles up in drifts, but tomorrow is
no more; all is dust and decay, and not worth much concern. And
therefore we would do far better to turn directly to the Russian stage
and to observe what is being created there; especially since some
very funny things are going on there at the moment. First of all,
there seem to be two heroes of the current season: Tsar Ivan Vasilievich and Mr. Nilsky. Seriously. The stage of the Alexandra Theater is
still obviously much enamored of Ivan Vasilievich since last winter,
and he hasn't vacated it even now. He abides there still in the grand
style: he runs around, yells, bangs his staff and orders everyone
about, very much at home; sometimes he dies, sometimes he rises
from the dead and starts interfering in love affairs. Last year there
was an influx of pretenders on the stage; however, Ivan Vasilievich
would not tolerate them, and he has remained the sole master. No,
really, think of it: *Prince Serebryany, The Death of Ioann the Terrible, The Oprichnik, Vasilisa Melentieva*[2]—in all, four historical dramas with Ivan Vasilievich; and it now appears that if the late Mr.
Mey were still alive, there would probably be a fifth in readiness for
the current season, also with Ivan Vasilievich.[3]

But however prevalent the awe-inspiring conqueror of Kazan
was in historical drama, Mr. Nilsky[4] was equally prosperous in contemporary drama. Not that this means that Mr. Nilsky was exceptionally good this winter in his various roles and reaped the laurels.
Quite the contrary. I mean just what I say: just as Ivan Vasilievich
was portrayed in several plays all winter long, so Nilsky was portrayed in other plays all winter long, with this as the only difference:
Ivan Vasilievich was impersonated by two actors in turn, Vasiliev
and Samoilov,[5] whereas Nilsky impersonated Mr. Nilsky with no
substitutes, and only in one play—to wit, *Two Generations*—did
Mr. Zhulev play Nilsky.[6]

But because this may sound very odd and even bewildering to
those readers who do not frequent the Russian theater, I shall try
to explain more precisely and circumstantially. So far as I'm con-

cerned, there's nothing odd or bewildering about it and, if I may say
so, it's far from a novelty on the Russian stage for an actor to play
himself. In Moscow some twenty years ago this was practiced in a
most peculiar manner. The famous actor and dramatist Lensky[7] actually created a special sort of comedy, in which he really played
himself, Lensky, actor of the imperial theaters. There was such a
role. In this kind of play he would even sing verses and explain
to the audience that he did not write for fame but mainly for his
friends. And such plays were successful and long enjoyed the favor
of the audiences. After that, why shouldn't Mr. Nilsky play Nilsky?
Especially since he himself did not create it, but someone else devised what he has to say on stage. And I'll even tell you who created
this role: Ostrovsky. In *A Lucrative Post* Nilsky appeared for the
first time under the name of Zhadov. The drama *A Lucrative Post*
was performed in 1863, and ever since, the role caught on, and at
present there is not one serious drama of any sort that can dispense
with a Nilsky. Over the last two years several so-called "contemporary" plays have been written and revived, and without fail each of
these plays has a certain character or type of role, which, in all its
characteristics, was best incarnated by Mr. Nilsky. And all these
roles are as alike as two peas in a pod, despite the fact that in one
play this character appears as an arbitrator, in another as a bailiff, in
a third as himself, merely a young man; for in essence all these characters behave exactly the same; they are all, for the most part, of
humble origin, yet have graduated from the university with a bach-
elor's degree; they all say the same thing, in the same language, and
make use of the selfsame turns of phrase. Finally, their kinship goes
so deep that they all dress exactly alike: just as if the theatrical man-
agement had invented a special pattern and cut of clothing for them.
Such gentlemen are usually clad in a baggy black surtout and wide
black trousers: invariably black and invariably wide. And this pattern has become so standardized that in *Two Generations*,[8] when
Mr. Zhulev played this role, he dressed exactly the way Mr. Nilsky
dresses under similar circumstances. The similarity among all these
gentlemen has become so striking that they all blend together into a
single character, so that when you try to recall them, a single all-
round impersonation takes shape, one man, and his name is Nilsky.
Not the private individual Nilsky, who is a perfect stranger to us, not
Mister Nilsky or even the actor Nilsky; but the Nilsky type, the
Nilsky *emploi*. It probably is now an emploi, like, for instance, the
emploi dubbed "noble father" or "romantic lead," etc. And the costume serves as proof positive that such an emploi actually exists in

the Russian theater. I am thoroughly and seriously convinced that a certain standardized outfit is assigned to this emploi, just as *villains*, for instance, are assigned cloaks and hats with red plumes.

Now, what exactly is this new emploi? What use is it? Who and what needs it?

In my capacity as spectator, I think I have some right to express my personal opinion in this regard and therefore, placing hand on heart, and calling to mind all the plays in which I've seen it, I declare that I have observed no personal advantage at all for myself from it and have absolutely no use for it. Having watched this character in every one of his appearances, I see only that he demeans himself on stage with a certain self-confidence and does indeed behave rather decorously; but he has no organic influence on the unfolding of the drama; his very presence on stage betokens solely the outburst of more or less noisy verbal effusions which, by all appearances, are directed not at the other characters, but straight at the audience. And because I have never perceived any strong connection between these effusions and the drama (and besides, the ideas exploding in them are of the cheapest quality), I paid them scant attention and took more interest in the play itself. This is how it usually worked: let's say they are performing some contemporary drama (which one makes absolutely no difference); the play's getting on properly, just as it should; usually there's a superb maiden, swinish parents, domestic oppression, etc., just as there should be; add a hideous suitor; they're marrying her off against her will. At that moment, enter Nilsky, who casts a haughty glance at them all and stands to one side. I know already what will happen and think: all right, they've brought in the bottle. I wait. And meanwhile the parents yell, the maiden weeps, the suitor curses . . . suddenly Nilsky steps to the fore, one leg forward, one arm back, and rants:

"Weakness of will on the one hand, and despotism and lack of conscience on the other . . . Take this as an example . . . This is what such baleful afflictions will lead to, if they are indulged . . ."

The parents fly into a rage, the suitor runs off, Nilsky warms to his role and cries:

"Is it enough to *swerve* (?) people from this ill which evolved in our society over the course of its history? . . . Without a struggle against the affliction, the pains will first intensify, then grow numb . . ."

"Look at life," Nilsky continues, hearing nothing. "Here the despot is the husband, there the wife," etc., etc. However, as a result of this outburst, the maiden begins to reconsider and exclaims:

"Why, this is truly ghastly, it's horrible. Who, who is responsible for it?"

Nilsky: "Who? . . . Why, everyone, everyone without exception; myself and you among them . . . ," etc. Whereupon the bottle is drained dry, it is removed from the stage, and the curtain falls.

But it is curious that all these uncorked bottles and the torrents that pour from them evidently lead nowhere at all; and the dramatic action is in no way violated; the maiden is married off in due course all the same; while the bottle is refilled and taken to another drama, where once again it is carried on at the appropriate point, uncorked and so forth.

All these dramas produce a certain mental hodgepodge: domestic oppression, screens of some sort, thresholds, swinish parents, tears, hideous suitors . . . Everything gets mixed up, linked together, piled higgledy-piggledy, and on top of all this gibberish Nilsky stands in haughty grandeur and talks and talks and talks and talks . . .

And why has this bottle become so necessary to them?—I wonder but cannot understand. Can't these wretches think up anything better? . . . As a matter of fact, they probably can't. All these dramas are obviously the outcome of cunning contrivance. Respected authors, it must be stated, take up various contemporary problems and wrack their brains over them; but I partly surmise why they so fondly devote themselves to the domestic and ignore the rest. They have chosen the domestic problem because it is the one serious problem which, at first sight, seems the most accessible, and the one which all of them invariably set about deliberating. But that's where they get into hot water. The ensuing results are those various thresholds, screens, abysses, profligates and so forth, i.e., dramas in which the domestic problem is arraigned before the court of public opinion and is solved by each author to the best of his ability and understanding.[9]

Obviously, our dramatists' aim was respectable, at any rate; it's just a pity that not one of them could cope with his task; but that was because none of these gentlemen knew—let alone understood—how to approach it. Each of them has seen something in his era and recalls certain facts; but then they try to cook up a drama out of those facts. Nor is this the rub. A drama must be contemporary, and a few bare facts do not seem to suffice: one scene by itself isn't much: the scene must contain the *problem* per se. How is this to be done? Very simply: you must arrange the characters and organize the action so that problem itself permeates and works itself out in the drama. Now there's the rub. To write such a drama you need, first, a very great talent; second, the author himself must be steeped in the specific idea—the problem must long ago have ceased to be a problem for him and have become a settled matter. One way or another, the problem must be solved in advance. Do you see anything of the sort in the new dramas? No, there's nothing like that to be seen in them. On the contrary, every such play is performed as if made up of two heterogeneous sections, one consisting of the scene, the other of Nilsky. The scene stands on its own and Nilsky stands on his own. Why so? Because the idea which is taken to be the basis of the drama does not in fact lie at its base; the idea for such a drama is something extraneous, chosen for appearance's sake, something the author cannot conceal within his play. For, after all, this is no easy matter. A scene, after all—whatever else it may be—is fact, i.e., something palpable, but what is an idea? Some sort of vapor. How can they be linked together? He tried and he tried, but no, nothing doing; yet you can't do without an idea, that's quite out of the question. What's to be done? So he went and took that idea of his and corked it up in a bottle. Now, whenever the idea is required in the course of the play, the bottle is immediately brought on—pop! Out flies the cork and on goes the pumping. He released the whole idea and so he's relieved—well now, thinks he, it'll have its effect. What difference does it make if the audience swallows it along with the scene or separately: it'll all get mixed together in the stomach. That's why they need a bottle, that's why they can't manage without Nilsky.

As an example let's take one such drama, *The Guilty Woman,*[10] which is reckoned one of the best contemporary dramas. This play has a standard plot: a superb maiden is married off to a vile, repulsive but wealthy old man, under compulsion from her stupid and mercenary parents. She has been living with her husband for three years now and nothing's happened; suddenly, enter Nilsky. He looks around, plants one leg forward and uncorks the bottle. Mrs. Kutuzkina (that's the superb maiden's married name) immediately has second thoughts and yields to his influence, despite his having spilled only half in this act. In the next act he reappears and instantly spills the whole idea to the very last drop. This so reacts on her that she runs away from her husband and returns to her parents. But the parents immediately plunk her into a carriage and send her packing back to her husband. Now Nilsky appears for a third time, and this time only a raisin pops out of the bottle, in the guise of *contempt* for the maiden, probably because she was too weak-willed to be able to apprehend the idea. With this idiocy the play actually ends.

Nilsky's presence in this play cannot be explained, except by the author's clumsiness in instilling the idea into his work. Shabrov (i.e., Nilsky) is, essentially, not even a character, but a kind of overseer, set up by the author to supervise the other characters. No sooner do they start to get out of hand than Shabrov shows up and reads them a memorandum which he has learned by heart and which, in the author's opinion, contains all the latest wisdom. Precisely the same thing is repeated with staggering monotony in all the rest of the dramas of this year's and last year's seasons. But among these dramas is one which deserves a few extra remarks. This play is entitled *The Profligate.* This play merits attention for two reasons: first, for its own sake, and second, in regard to its author, Mr. Stebnitsky.[11] I have no intention of analyzing this play in detail, nor do I wish to investigate its author's personality, but now that I've started talking about this work, I cannot go on without involving its author; I absolutely cannot, because this is the kind of work about which you must either say nothing at all or else, once you have started to say something, you cannot fail to bring in the author. Necessity compels you to do so.

I do not have the pleasure of knowing Mr. Stebnitsky personally, and have certainly had nothing to do with his past activities; his present works interest me much more, and about them I do intend to speak. The author's personality is much more clearly present in these works, and I can find it out more surely here than through vague literary rumors, which can, moreover, always be suspected of partiality. No, I do not look at Mr. Stebnitsky's work that way; I cannot regard this personality with hostility; on the contrary, this personality arouses pity in me. To my way of thinking, Mr. Stebnitsky must be a profound sufferer. No, seriously, he must be unhappy; and other people's unhappiness always arouses my pity. I can see that his writing makes him unhappy. By now I've adapted myself to him a bit, and each of his new efforts convinces me all the more that I am right, that my view of Mr. Stebnitsky's writing is the most accurate one. All you need to convince you is attention, nothing but attention. Cast aside all preconceived notions and read in cold blood. If you follow these instructions, you will not fail to notice the following: first, you will notice that each of Mr. Stebnitsky's works, whichever you please, at first glance presents something integral, something fully finished, represents, in short, something. At first glance. But, scrutinized more attentively, this something appears to be somehow moth-eaten or corroded by vitriol. If you don't touch it and look at it from a distance, it appears, as I say, entirely whole; but

come a bit closer, pick it up and give it a tug, and nothing will be left
but tatters, it will all turn to dust. For a long time I wracked my
brains and wondered why that should be. Now look here, it seems to
have all it needs: the man's got the power of observation, and you
can make out the experience in it; why, there are individual pages
that are simply and even well written. What is this peculiarity? Why
doesn't it work, after all? I thought and thought and finally figured it
out. I realized that the cause of this failure must be hidden in the
author himself, in his personal characteristics; there is bound to be
some kind of organic flaw in him which spoils everything. That's
why I made the proviso above that, when discussing Mr. Stebnitsky's writing, you can't ignore the author's personality, you just
can't, otherwise you won't understand a thing. But what kind of
flaw is it? I don't know exactly what kind of flaw it is or what it consists in: I'm only sure that it exists, it must exist, because I can see
the traces of this flaw in Mr. Stebnitsky's work and can tell by the
traces the outward manifestations it assumes, specifically: each of
Mr. Stebnitsky's works presents a series of pictures, more or less
successfully copied from nature. How accurate they are is another
matter; in any case a penchant for life-drawing is visible in them,
and this life-drawing seems to compose the basis of the work; but
because of this his work never ends; he evidently cannot be satisfied
solely with life-drawing. What do I mean by life-drawing? It is, so to
speak, the mechanical transference of a picture from life to paper; it
does not involve any creativity, yet Mr. Stebnitsky insists on
creativity. So he sets about creating. How he does it, God alone
knows; all I know is that the picture that Mr. Stebnitsky copied
from nature and immediately after exposed to his own creativity
comes to light as if entirely corroded and disfigured by vitriol. What
he did with it, how he passed it through the crucible of his inspiration, is his secret; for our part we can only suggest that, in any case,
that crucible must contain stuff that virulently corrodes matter; and
this process probably occurs somehow unconsciously, without the
author's intending it. One cannot otherwise understand how a man
could spoil and disfigure with one hand what he creates with the
other. Now isn't this a misfortune? And shouldn't we pity such a
man? With this in mind, I made myself a rule, to approach each new
work of Mr. Stebnitsky only from this viewpoint: to observe in each
thing he makes, first, the material from which he made it, and, second, the damage wrought by the author on this material. Then and
only then can I gain a thoroughly clear understanding of what the
something is.

As an example I propose to apply this viewpoint to Mr. Stebnitsky's new work, the drama *The Profligate.*

The plot of this play is, I think, not so bad, it might even be said to be a good plot, and had it fallen into the right hands, something outstanding might have been made of it; it is obviously taken from real life. If not precisely this, something very like it probably happened somewhere, some time or other, and the author most likely heard or read about it. Here's the plot: young, intelligent, rich but spineless merchant and manufacturer Molchanov lives in a certain town and apparently wishes to devote himself to improving his workmen's living conditions; he even makes a stab at fraternizing with them and suggests that they organize on collective principles; but not only are these attempts failures, they even raise a hue and cry against him, and, finally, destroy him. And this comes about because Molchanov, a married man, has fallen in love with a working-class girl, who is also beloved by his former guardian, the eminent schemer and magnate Knyazev, who is also the "town's foremost man," as the playbill puts it. The dramatic action consists of the conflict between these two personages—a conflict in which almost the entire town takes part. The conflict ends with Molchanov's being accused of profligacy and his committal to a madhouse. There he falls into despair and determines to take his own life; finally, by some inscrutable means he escapes and sets fire to his factory, but dies.

The plot, as you can see, is meaty—there's something to sink your teeth into; and with a plot of that sort, you can twist it and stage it and light it any way you please. In short, a bona fide plot, if left to a master. Now let's look and see what Mr. Stebnitsky has made of it, and how it emerged from his crucible.

Let us begin with trivia, details, the playbill. Turn your attention to the names of the characters: *Molchanov*, which suggests *molchalivy* ["taciturn"]; *Myakishev* sounds like *myakish* ["soft crumbs"], a good man but pliable; *Knyazev* is the town's foremost citizen (a *knyaz* ["prince"]); *Guslyarova* is a poetic sort (*gusli* ["psaltery"]); Pavlushka *Chelnochok* is an unreliable fellow, an opportunist (a *chelnok* ["shuttle" in a weaver's loom]); Alyosha *Bosy* ["Barefoot"] walks around unshod; the Pole *Minutka* is a crook, but with no conviction (for a single little minute or *minutka*). How do you like that? Do you realize how powerful the demand for creativity is in the man, how it corrodes both himself and everything he touches? He cannot stand it, he cannot leave even a name in peace, he creates *his own* names so as to stamp his imprint on everything, absolutely everything. He even managed to get carried away by this insignificant trivia and create the impossible name "Minutka." Not only is there no such name, but there isn't even such a word as *minutka* in Polish. Even the playbill gets dragged through the crucible. He couldn't help it. What's to be done?

Now, please be so curious as to glance at the stage. Act 1, Knyazev's house. Knyazev is sitting and talking to himself, and then starts explaining his affairs to the audience, relating that he is in love with Guslyarova; Minutka arrives and they start talking about how to make some progress there. The longer you listen to this scene, the more you keep losing faith in Mr. Stebnitsky's creative capabilities, and finally you are definitely convinced that the whole first act is nothing less than a borrowing from *Krechinsky's Wedding*;[12] that Knyazev is Krechinsky in merchant's clothing, while Minutka is Raspluev, transformed into a Pole. The unique character attributable to the author in act 1 is a drowned man, a kind of scarecrow, who appears at a window in some strange way, and is supposed to serve Knyazev as a living reproof, while Molchanov at this time is buying the house. In act 2 the plot against Molchanov is laid; in act 3 he is denounced in his father-in-law's house, company gathers with the intention of accusing him of profligacy and of making Knyazev his guardian. All this is rather long-winded; the characters continually embark on intimate explanations with the audience, speak in "asides," crack inappropriate jokes, while Knyazev, in front of the whole audience, at Mrs. Myakisheva's, keeps trying to feel her pulse and she won't let him. Nilsky—i.e., Molchanov—in act 3 talks and talks and suddenly gets into a fight. This works out for the best, because it imparts an abrupt turning point to the whole affair, and the spectator is already guessing that they'll tie up this Nilsky right away. Yet they don't touch him and give him time to meet his beloved. Then somehow, God knows why, the factory workers debate collective organization and then begin to sing "In the Pockets"; the drowned man comes in again and it appears that it was Knyazev who drowned him. Then the merchants and kinfolk come in, seize Nilsky and pack him off to a madhouse. The fourth act ends; then comes the fifth—the denouement. But the things that go on in that fifth act—mercy on us! Obviously the author used up his whole stock of vitriol in it, because act 5 comprises the crowning glory of Mr. Stebnitsky's poetic creativity, i.e., everything gnawed into tatters. The curtain rises, a new setting by Mr. Bocharov[13]—an underground crypt. Terrifying, smoke-blackened arches, peeling walls, on the floor sit chests full of arsenic; the wind whistles and whines in the chimney. By the glow of a night-light we can see a woman sitting on a chest . . . Alone, all, all alone! . . . Behold her lift her head and, turning to the esteemed audience, report that she, the working-girl Guslyarova, has been languishing in this dreadful crypt for four months alone, all all alone! Dreadful. Suddenly a fresh gust of wind, bricks fall down the chimney. Alone! But then it appears that this whole gimmick, to be blunt, this solitude and all these horrors are only meant to scare the spectators, because after a while an old blind woman enters this crypt (probably the door wasn't locked); then a merchant comes in, then a factory-worker crawls down the chimney. No sooner has the merchant begun to recount that Nilsky has actually gone out of his mind and that it cost him lots of money to get in to see him than the door suddenly flies open and Knyazev enters. Guslyarova, not wasting a second, seizes a handful of arsenic from a chest and pops it into her mouth. So there stood a whole chestful of arsenic, ready for just such occasions. No sooner has she managed to poison herself than the police, too, drop in on the crypt; next the common people crowd in . . . suddenly there's a cry of "fire, fire," in the window crimson Bengal lights flare up and we can hear the alarm sounded; a sudden cry of "They caught the firebug, they're bringing him, they got him . . ." and people flock to the crypt in droves. They bring in the firebug; it turns out that Nilsky set the fire and dies as well. They lay him on the floor, while Guslyarova starts going into convulsions; the police hold her by the arm and cannot restrain her; she rants and raves, "Holy saints, I'm dying." She's dead. The town mayor arrives in a fur coat and beholds all this gruesomeness: the two deceased parties laid out and the drowned man sitting on them. For somehow he too has wound up here. The people stand in mute horror. The town mayor says: "Well, may they rest in peace, but you and I, Mister Knyazev, are now quite ruined. I've just received a telegram, that Minutka has ratted on us and opened himself a pawnbroker's shop on Big Copy-Clerk Street." The end. And now let the reader sort out for himself where truth lies and where vitriol.

More about Sarah Bernhardt

by *Anton Chekhov*

What the hell is going on!

We wake up in the morning, trick ourselves out, draw on our swallowtail coat and gloves and round about twelve we head for the Bolshoy Theater . . . We return home from the theater, bolt down dinner without chewing it and do some scribbling. At eight at night, it's back to the theater; from the theater back home, and more and more scribbling till about four. And it's like this every day! We think, speak, read, write about nothing but Sarah Bernhardt. O Sarah Bernhardt! All this folderol will end with our straining our reportorial nerves to the maximum, our catching, thanks to irregular mealtimes, a most virulent stomach catarrh and sleeping soundly for two weeks as soon as the eminent diva departs.

We go to the theater twice a day, look, listen and listen again, and won't be listened-out and looked-out until something special happens. For some reason it's all banal beyond expectation, hideously banal. We watch Sarah Bernhardt without winking or blinking, gluing our eyes to her face, and we strive, come what may, to see something in her beyond a good actress. We're crackpots! We've been tantalized by the expectation-raising publicity from abroad. We haven't even seen the slightest resemblance to the angel of death in her. This resemblance was discovered in Sarah (somebody said someplace) by a certain dying woman whom Sarah was watching and studying so that she might, at the end of a play, betake herself *ad patres.*

Then, what *did* we see?

Come along to the theater, reader, and you shall see what we saw. Come . . . well, at least to *Adrienne Lecouvreur.*[1] We go at eight. We approach the theater and perceive a countless multitude of

---

This squib first appeared in the *Spectator* (*Zritel'*, nos. 23–24, 6 December 1881). The present translation is based on the text in *Polnoe sobranie sochineniy i pisem v tridtsati tomakh* (Moscow, 1979), XVI.

two-eyed, rattle-trap carriages, cabmen, gendarmes, policemen . . .
The Indian file of cabbies returning from the theater is literally endless. The confluence reaches terrific proportions. A crush in the theater's corridors: Muscovite flunkeys on hand, every last one. They
don't hang up your wraps but, behind nameless hooks in the cloak-
rooms, they huddle them together, four to a heap, compressing and
stacking one garment on top of another like bricks. Let us enter the
very eye of the storm. Starting in the orchestra and ending in the
"gods," such a mass of every conceivable kind of head, shoulder and
arm swarms, crawls and flashes by that you can't help asking yourself: "Can there be this many people in Russia? Goodness gracious!"
You look at the audience, and the idea of flies around a honey-
smeared table pops right into your head. The boxes are jammed: on
one chair sits *Papa*, on *Papa*'s lap sits *Mama* and on her lap the kids;
and it's not the only chair in the box either. The audience, I ought to
mention, is not quite the usual one. Among the theatrical regulars,
the devotees and connoisseurs, you see no small quantity of those
gentlefolk who have definitely never been in a theater before. Here
you find desiccated cholera victims, made up of mere tendon and
sinew, physicians who never go to bed any sooner or any later than
eleven on the dot. Over there sits a nauseatingly grave professor of
differential calculus, who has no idea of the playbill's meaning or of
the difference between the Salamonsky Circus[2] and the Bolshoy
Theater . . . Here too are all those ultra-serious, ultra-clever wheeler-
dealers, who privately deem the theater poppycock and actors loafers. In one of the boxes are ensconced an old lady, stricken with paralysis, and her husband, a deaf prince with a speech defect, who
have not been in a theater since 1848. Everyone's mustered . . .

Three knocks. That was a whiff of Paris . . . In Paris they don't
ring, they knock. The curtain rises. On stage are Mme. Lina Munte
and Mme. Sidney.[3] The tableau that greets you is not unfamiliar. You
think you've seen something like it a year and a half, two years ago
in the pages of *Cornfield* or *Universal Illustrated*.[4] All that's missing is Napoleon I, standing behind the portière half in shadow, and
those rich, sumptuous forms French painters lay on so lavishly . . .
They begin clacking and jabbering in the French idiom. You listen
hard and your ears barely have time to keep up with the accelerating
tongues of the guttural-r'd Frenchwomen. You have the vaguest
knowledge of the plot of *Adrienne Lecouvreur*, you are getting just
the tiniest bit tired of watching the acting and start to inspect things
more closely . . . On stage are two Frenchwomen and a few French
gentlemen. Impeccably luxurious costumes, a foreign language, that

purely French knack of smiling endlessly convey your thoughts to "Oh Paris, my home town." Smart, neat and gay, it reminds you of a young widow who has put off her mourning, with its palaces, houses, countless bridges spanning the Seine. You can recognize in the faces and costumes of these frivolous French the Comédie Française with its first and second rows of stalls which enthrone a thorough-paced Paul-de-Kockian vicomte. You dream, and before your eyes flash, one after the other, the Bois de Boulogne, the Champs Elysées, the Trocadéro, Daudet with his long hair, Zola with his round beard, our Turgenev and our "warm-hearted" Mme. Lavretskaya,[5] carousing, tossing Russian goldpieces hither and yon.

The first act ends. The curtain falls. The audience is at a loss. A deathly silence, even in the "gods."

In the second act Sarah Bernhardt herself appears. She is handed up a bouquet (it can't be called a bad one, but it's not quite, no offense meant, a good one either). Sarah Bernhardt looks nothing like the Sarah Bernhardt you saw in the postcards you bought at Avantso's and Datsiaro's.[6] In the postcards she looks sort of fresh and personable.

The second act ends. The curtain falls—and the audience applauds, but so listlessly! Fyodotova and even Kochetova[7] get more energetic applause. But the way Sarah Bernhardt takes her bow! With her head cocked somewhat to one side, she comes out the door center, walks slowly and grandly down to the apron, looking in no particular direction, much like the *pontifex maximus* at a sacrificial offering, and with her head describes an arc in the air not visible to the naked eye. "Here you are, take a look!" seems to be written all over her face. "Take a look, wonder, marvel and say thank you for the honor of seeing 'the most original of women,' 'notre grande Sarah'!"

Wouldn't it be interesting to know the opinion our respected guests have of our audiences? The Americans drank up Lake Ontario, the English had themselves harnessed to her carriage like horses, the Indians used the entire army to guard the train she was traveling on, in order to steal her jewels, but our audience doesn't laugh or cry and applaud, it seems to freeze up and keeps its hands in its padded mittens.

"Bears!" that's what Sarah's companions might be thinking— "They don't laugh and they don't cry because they don't know French. They don't break their necks and seats with delight because these louts don't know beans about Sarah's genius!" It's quite possible that's what they're thinking. It's common knowledge that foreigners don't understand our audiences. We have observed this audience carefully, and therefore we may venture to state an opinion. The theater was teeming with bears who speak French every bit as well as Sarah Bernhardt herself. In the "gods" we noticed the kind of connoisseurs, experts and devotees who know how many hairs there are on Mr. Muzil's[8] head, who bespatter your face with spittle, knock over the lamp with their gesticulating hands and don't bother to say "pardon me" if you start arguing with them about which is better: Lensky or Ivanov-Kozyolsky.[9] In place of double basses, drums and flutes, the proverbial salt of the earth itself is installed in the orchestra pit, and price is no object. The audience that used to applaud Mr. Muzil because he "talks funny" does not attend Sarah Bernhardt's performances; why should it? It would far rather watch Tanti the clown[10] than Sarah Bernhardt. We saw an audience spoiled by the acting of the now-deceased Sadovsky, Zhivokini and Shumsky, a frequent viewer of Samarin's[11] and Fyodotova's acting, well-studied in Turgenev and Goncharov and, most important, having been through much instructive grief in recent years. In short, we saw an audience which is very hard to please, the most demanding of audiences. No wonder it doesn't fall into a swoon the minute that Sarah Bernhardt lets the audience know a moment before her death by the most energetic convulsions that she is now about to die.

We are far from worshipping Sarah Bernhardt as a talent. She has none of the stuff that makes our most respected audience love Fyodotova; she has none of the spark that alone is capable of moving us to bitter tears or ecstasy. Every sigh Sarah Bernhardt sighs, every tear she sheds, every antemortem convulsion she makes, every bit of her acting is nothing more than an impeccably and intelligently learned lesson. A lesson, reader, and nothing more! As a very clever lady who knows what works and what doesn't, a lady of the most grandiose taste, a lady deeply read in the human heart and whatever you please, she very deftly performs all those stunts that, every so often, at fate's behest, occur in the human soul. Every step she takes is profoundly thought out, a stunt underscored a hundred times over . . . She remakes her heroines into exactly the same sort of unusual woman she is herself . . . In her acting, she goes in pursuit not of the natural, but of the extraordinary. Her goal is to startle, to amaze, to dazzle . . . You watch *Adrienne Lecouvreur* and you see not Adrienne Lecouvreur in her, but the ultra-clever, ultra-sensational Sarah Bernhardt . . . What shines through all her acting is not talent, but tremendous, strenuous hard work . . . That hard work comprises the whole key to the enigmatic artiste. Not the slightest trifle exists in any of her roles great or small that has not been put through the purgatory of that hard work a hundred times. Extraordinary work. Were we as hard-working as she is, what wouldn't we write! We would scribble over all the walls and ceilings just in revising the most paltry scrawl. We envy and most respectfully kowtow to her hard work. We have no objection to advising our first- and second-rate artistes to learn how to work from our guest. Our artistes, no offense meant, are dreadfully lazy! For them, study is harsher than horseradish. We deduce that they, the majority of our artistes, work at practically nothing from the simple fact that they are at a standstill: they go neither forward nor . . . anywhere! Were they to work as Sarah Bernhardt works, were they to know as much as she knows, they would go far! To our great regret, our servants of the Muses, great and small, are sorely handicapped when it comes to know-how, and, if the old saw is to be believed, know-how comes only with hard work.

We watched Sarah Bernhardt and derived indescribable pleasure from her hard work. There were brief passages in her acting which moved us almost to tears. But the tears failed to well up only because all the enchantment is smothered in artifice. Were it not for that scurvy artifice, that premeditated tricksiness, that overemphasis, honest to goodness, we would have burst into tears, and the theater would have rocked with applause . . . O talent! Cuvier[12] said that you are at odds with facility! And Sarah Bernhardt is monstrously facile!

The company touring with Sarah is neither here nor, begging your pardon, there. Healthy, strapping, sturdy folk. Bearing in mind that anything might happen (an attack by tigers, Indians and so forth), Sarah has good reason to surround herself with this muscular bunch.

The French comport themselves exquisitely on stage. One Moscow reviewer, chanting praises of Sarah Bernhardt till he sweated blood, cited among other things her *skill at listening*. We acknowledge this skill as not only hers, but the entire company's. The French listen extremely well, with the result that they never feel at a loss on stage, they know when to move their arms and not stand in one another's way . . . It's not the same with our lot . . . It doesn't work that way in Russia. Here, Mr. Maksheev soliloquizes while Mr. Vilday,[13] listening to him, gazes at some point in space and coughs impatiently; it would even seem his face is inscribed with "This is none of my business, my boy!" The company is very attractive, well trained, but . . . untalented. Neither here nor there . . .

However, to get back to *Adrienne Lecouvreur*. Or else, look here, reader! You're fed up reading my gibberish, and I want awfully to go to bed. The clock is striking four, and the cock is bawling at my pretty neighbor-lady's place . . . My eyelids are sticking together as if smeared with glue, my nose is grazing my writing-d . . .

Tomorrow, back to Sarah Bernhardt . . . ugh!

However, I won't write any more about her, even if the editor pays me fifty kopeks a line. I'm written out! I quit!

Antosha Chekhonte

The Cherry Orchard
by Andrey Bely

In reproducing reality, the realist artist starts by working on its most general details, and then turns into a photographer of reality. His vision dilates. He is no longer satisfied with the superficial delineation of phenomena. After the definite and the perdurable, he will linger at the indefinite and the fleeting, of which each type of definition and durability is compounded. He then reproduces the texture of an instant. The isolated moment becomes the aim of the reproduction. Depicted in such a way, life is subtle, almost transparent lacery. An instant of life taken by itself as it is deeply probed becomes a doorway to infinity. Like a loop of life's lace, it is nothing by itself; it outlines an opening into that which is behind it. Infinite is the intensification of inner experience. The lace of life, composed of discrete loops, becomes a series of doors in parallel corridors, leading to something else. The realist artist, still true to himself, involuntarily sketches, along with the surface of life's texture, also that which is revealed in the depths of the instants' labyrinths, parallel to one another. Everything remains the same in his depiction, but is permeated by *something different*. He himself does not suspect whereof he speaks. Tell such an artist that he has penetrated *the world beyond*, and he will not believe you. After all, he worked from without. He studied reality. He does not believe that the reality he depicts is no longer, in a certain sense, reality.

The mechanism of life diverts the channel of inner experiences into a direction other than the one toward which we strain, and surrenders us to the power of the machine. Our dependence begins with common causes unbeknownst to us and ends with trolley cars, telephones, elevators, railway timetables. In our midst the staccato

This article first appeared in the symbolist journal *Balances* (*Vesy*, no. 5, 1904) and was reprinted in Bely's collection *Arabesques* (*Arabeski* [Moscow, 1911]), since reprinted by Wilhelm Fink Verlag (Munich, 1963). It is from this last text that the translation has been made.

mechanical cycle, from which it becomes increasingly difficult to break loose, evolves ever more and more. *A* kills himself for *B*, *B* for *C*, but even *C*, to whom *A* and *B* devote themselves, remaining zeros instead of life organically cohesive through inner experiences, devotes himself to *A* and also turns into a zero. The machine is formed out of the aimless slaughter of souls.

The power of the instant is a natural protest against the mechanical organization of life. To free himself, man delves deep into the fortuitous moment of freedom, directing all the might of his soul toward it. Under such conditions man will learn more and more how to see into minutiae. The minutiae of life will appear ever more clearly to be the guides to Eternity. Thus, realism imperceptibly crosses over into symbolism.

Instants are pieces of stained glass. Through them we gaze at Eternity. We must stop at one pane of glass, or else we will never descry distinctly what lies beyond the fortuitous. Everything will get overly familiar, and we shall tire of looking at anything. But once we have experienced a particular instant intensively enough, we want a repeat performance. Repeating the experience, we will delve more deeply into it. Delving more deeply, we will pass various levels. A particular instant will become for us an unexpected outlet into mysticism: our inner path will be marked out and the wholeness of our psychic life restored. The mechanism of life will be controlled from within, discrete instants will no longer have any power. The lace of life, woven from discrete instants, will disappear when we discover the outlet to that which had earlier shown through behind it. By recounting what we see, we shall arbitrarily deal with the materials of reality.

Such is mystical symbolism, the reverse of realistic symbolism which presents the world beyond in terms of circumambient reality.

Chekhov is a realist artist. It must not be inferred from this that he uses no symbols. He cannot help but be a symbolist, if the conditions of reality in which we live have changed for modern man. Reality has become more transparent, owing to a refinement in the nervous system of the best of us. Without abandoning the world, we move toward what is beyond the world. This is the true path of realism.

Not so long ago we stood on a firm foundation. Now the earth itself has become transparent. We walk as if on slippery transparent glass; below the glass everlasting perdition dogs our footsteps. And lo, it seems to us that we walk on air. It is terrifying on this pathway of air. How can there be talk now of the limits of realism? Under such conditions can realism and symbolism be contrasted? Nowadays fugitives from life have reappeared in life, for life itself has changed. Nowadays the realists who depict reality are symbolists; at the very point where everything once ended, everything has now become transparent, pellucid.

Such is Chekhov. His heroes are outlined by external strokes, but we apprehend them from within. They walk, drink, talk rubbish, while we behold the spiritual poverty transpicuous within them. They talk like men confined in prison, but we have learnt something about them that they themselves have not noticed in themselves. In the minutiae by which they live, a certain secret cipher is revealed to us—and the minutiae cease to be minutiae. The banality of their life is in some way neutralized. Something grandiose is revealed throughout in its minutiae. Isn't this called seeing through banality? But seeing *through anything* means being a symbolist. *Seeing through,* I associate the object with what stands behind it. In such a relationship symbolism is inevitable.

The spirit of music is extremely diverse in its manifestations. It can penetrate all the characters of a given play equally. Each character is then a string in the general chord. Chekhov's *plays of mood* are musical. Their symbolism is a guarantee of this, for a symbol is always musical in an abstract sense. Chekhov's symbolism is distinguished from Maeterlinck's by its very essence. Maeterlinck makes the heroes of a drama vessels of his own mystical subject matter. His experience is revealed through them. To indicate the approach of death, he makes an old man say, "Is there not someone else amongst us?"[1] Too glaring a symbol. Isn't this allegory? Too abstract in its expression. Chekhov, attenuating reality, unexpectedly comes across symbols. He barely suspects them. He has put nothing in them with premeditation, for he has hardly undergone a mystical experience. His symbols therefore have unintentionally sprouted up in reality. Nowhere is the spider's web of the phenomenal torn. Thanks to this he manages more profoundly to reveal symbols reverberating on a background of minutiae.

Here sit these enervated people, trying to forget the terror of life, but a *tramp walks by . . . Somewhere a bucket drops in a mine shaft.*[2] Everyone realizes that here is the terror. But mightn't it all be a dream? If we scrutinize *The Cherry Orchard* with a view to totality of artistic effect, we will not find the polish of *Three Sisters.* In this respect, *The Cherry Orchard* is not so successful. But it provides a more perfect presentation of the psychological depth of discrete instants. If our first glimpse was of the transparent lace texture viewed from afar, the author now seems to have drawn nearer to a few loops of that web, and to have seen more clearly what these loops outline. He skims over other loops. Hence perspective is violated and the play is rather uneven in tone. Relatively speaking, this is a step backward for Chekhov. Absolutely speaking—he has not stayed in one place, attenuating his technique. In some passages his realism is even more subtle, even more transparent with symbols.

How terrifying are the moments when fate soundlessly sneaks up on the weaklings. Everywhere there is the alarming leitmotiv of thunder, everywhere the impending storm-cloud of terror. And yet, it would seem there's good reason to be terrified; after all, there's talk of selling the estate. But terrible are the masks behind which the terror is concealed, eyes goggling in the apertures. How terrible is the governess cavorting around the ruined family, or the valet Yasha, carping about the champagne, or the oafish bookkeeper and the tramp from the forest!

In the third act there seems to be a crystallization of Chekhov's devices: in the foreground room a domestic drama is taking place, while at the back, candle-lit, the masks of terror are dancing rapturously: there's the postal clerk waltzing with some girl—or is he a scarecrow? Perhaps he is a mask fastened to a walking stick or a uniform hung on a clothes tree. What about the station master? Where are they from, what are they for? It is all an incarnation of fatal chaos. There they dance and simper as the domestic calamity comes to pass.

A detail is touched in with a certain brushstroke never seen before. Reality splits in twain: it is and it is not, it is the mask of another, and people are mannequins, phonographs are profundities—terrible, terrible . . .

Chekhov, remaining a realist, here draws back the folds of life, and what at a distance seemed to be shadowy folds turns out to be an aperture into Eternity.

1904

Drama at the Lower Depths

by Innokenty Annensky

I have not seen Gorky's play performed. The performance was probably excellent.[1] I am willing to believe that the realism, subtlety and sensitivity of the performance will turn over a new page in the history of the Russian theater, but for my present purpose it is perhaps preferable that I can use Gorky's text without theatrical glosses, without a stage illusion which is obtrusive and vivid, but despotically narrows a poet's conception.

I think that in our time, for the most part, the clash between poetry and the stage is becoming ever more frequent and inevitable. On stage the increase in realism and objectivity of interpretation advance concurrently.

The theater grants ever more scope to the creative individuality of *each performer,* and thereby the school and tradition which had formerly united and restricted these individualities by means of convention are retreating ever farther from our stage. Meanwhile poetry is becoming ever more *individualized* and *concentrated.* In our day the poet expresses himself freely and fully, but the manifestation of his personality is becoming far too whimsical, especially when we consider that both his own nature and the life around him have grown more complicated. The boundaries between the real and the fantastic have not only dwindled for the poet, but in places have become quite illusory. Truth and wish-fulfillment not infrequently blend their colors in his mind. Life begins to seem mystical and stage scenery to seem lifelike.

Besides, the stage, instead of presenting the poet's one complex personality, presents at best a whole gamut of them, and these indi-

---

This essay, along with two others on Pisemsky's *A Hard Lot* and Tolstoy's *The Power of Darkness,* appeared under the rubric "Three Social Dramas" in Annensky's *Kniga otrazheniy I* (St. Petersburg, 1906). This translation follows the photostatic reproduction made by Wilhelm Fink Verlag (Munich, 1969).

vidualities, as they constrict one another, reduce the free play of creative thought to an illusory reality.

Even though the word as a suggestive symbol has always been sharply differentiated from the word as intonation and gesture, and poetry as the highest indivisible manifestation of individuality from poetry as something mirror-like, combinatory and histrionic, in our day this differentiation has occasionally begun to take on an almost morbid tinge.

I know that I personally would be prevented from closely examining the interesting texture of Gorky's poetic conception by that chaotic hum of life, the inconsequential talk, the slamming of doors, the fleeting glimpses of damp hemlines, the rasp of the file, the crying of a baby, in short, everything that is unavoidable in life and may perhaps constitute a triumph of stagecraft, but which impedes thought in the theater just as it does in real life.

And yet to appreciate Gorky's play and enjoy it, one must think about it intently, because the individuality that created it is complex and manifested in the most idiosyncratic ways.

The impression the play makes is a direct one; while the reader is puzzling out its internal conceptual harmony, which lights up for a moment and then goes out, he seems constantly either to be lured into a labyrinth or else incapable of ever extricating himself from the nagging contradictions.

In my opinion, Gorky, after Dostoevsky, is the most graphic of the Russian symbolists. His realism has nothing in common with that of Goncharov, Pisemsky[2] or Ostrovsky. As you contemplate his pictures, you recall the remark of the author of *A Raw Youth*, who once said that there are times when the most commonplace milieu seems to him a dream or illusion. Such an impression was made on him, for instance, by a muddy, yellow autumn morning in the Petersburg streets.

A certain theater critic made what I consider a very apt statement about Gorky's characters, that they are like devils. Of course, I do not take this simile to imply the notorious demoniality of our modern-day heroes of fiction: it may mean nothing more than the enigmatic quality and idiosyncrasy of those masks behind which the poet's mind is fleetingly glimpsed, that tantalizing vagueness of outline, which somehow gets strangely disguised as the typical stereotypes of the theater.

A cardsharp, beaten up for his cheating and stupefied by drink, and although in the throes of an emotional upheaval, passionately discusses the truths that stir the finest human minds. An old man, who has been pushed around all his life and nothing more, manages to salvage compassion and spontaneity from his plight. A twenty-year-old girl, who has never seen anything in life except filth and atrocity, somehow keeps her heart as pure as a lily and as open as a child. And what about Pepel, the professional thief, spawn of the prison colony, but at the same time so womanishly sensitive, bashful and even dreamy? This internal discrepancy between people and their situation, life conceived by the poet as a layer of dirt smeared over the free human soul, imparts to Gorky's realism a peculiarly fantastic and yet wonderfully Russian coloration. For good reason in the old folktales the mother-lode of strength and daring turns out to be, all unawares and to everyone's surprise, a kind of bumbling simpleton, and the tsarevna's diamond is found wrapped in dirty rags on the person of a derided booby, hidden somewhere in a dark oven. But Gorky has ceased to be Dostoevsky, for whom the diamond was God, and a man might be a fortuitous and fragile vessel of divinity; for Gorky, at least for appearance's sake, everything exists for and within man, including the tsarevna's diamond. And if Dostoevsky's motto was "Submit and let God speak," Gorky's chimes forth proudly, "Fight and thou shalt prevail over the element of death, if thou knowest how to wish."

On rereading Gorky's play, I am convinced that the last thing he has in mind is to tease the reader's brain with a realistic depiction of beggary, degradation and mental breakdown.

Generally speaking, he does not fit in with those genre writers who try to familiarize the reader with their characters' environment. He never seems to have cared much for life-drawing, and even his imagination barely provides him with the kind of clear reflections of reality which made Goncharov, for instance, suffer in his creative moments. Gorky's novels are ideological sketches, related to an *urgent problem*, rather than artfully composed narratives of the human heart. There is something strange in the way Gorky relinquishes his heroes—sometimes he kills them off, sometimes he abandons them at an early age when there would still be plenty of time to start on a novel. He does not seem to be particularly interested in "a man's typical foibles or intriguing episodes." He is induced to make his drawings not by persistent observation or interest in problems of individual psychology, but by ideological questions posed by his intuitive artistic nature.

When, for the twentieth time, I read about Goncharov's Zakhar, or Flaubert tells me about Pécuchet or Charles Bovary, or Thackeray methodically and unhurriedly unfolds the chronicle of Becky Sharp's life for me,[3] I do not ask *why*. First, I am concerned with a concrete person: I like to picture him even down to details of dress, the sound of his voice, I look around to find those like him, sometimes it even seems as if I had met and lost him in a crowd or had once been acquainted with him. When I put down the book, I am bored for a while, missing my fictional friend, even though the novelist may have been telling me about the most uninteresting man in the world. Our bond with the world of Zakhars and Charles Bovarys and Pickwicks sinks somewhere deep into the very recesses of the unconscious mind and, remarkable for its great staying power, at times even draws tears.

But, on the other hand, take one Stepan Petrovich Verkhovensky out of Dostoevsky's *The Devils*, at a moment when this old man stoutly plays hearts as trumps or makes a declaration of love or complains or confesses. His French accent and his attack of cholera, his ingenuousness and his frivolity are all so beautifully written and so artistically composed, and yet do you not feel that there is something that prevents you from relating to Dostoevsky's hero as you do to Oblomov or Kalinovich?

Beyond Verkhovensky, as beyond Lyovin, Pozdnyshev, Ivan Karamazov,[4] in the aftermath of their appearances, something new burgeons which is more sublime and more significant than they are. Beyond Verkhovensky, for instance, you sense Dostoevsky's spiritual anxiety, which we see gradually change into a severe and grievous verdict on that charming past which engendered such a present horror as Shatov's murder.

Gorky is precisely this type of writer: when a new character makes an appearance you do not expect details, you want to know not *what* but *why*? When you read him, you think not about reality and the past, but ethics and the future.

The Lower Depths is a genuine drama, although far from an ordinary one, and with more modesty than accuracy Gorky has called his play *scenes*. What unfolds before us is something integral and strictly unified by the poet's thought and mood.

Into a flophouse, where a strange and dependently cohesive family has huddled together, enters a man from another world. His wholly special charm is infused into the slow death of these "ex-persons"[5] almost like a life-supporting injection, but it is dangerous for an inhabitant of this cellar to look at himself too closely.

As a result Luka's arrival merely quickens momentarily the pulse of a dying life, but it can neither save nor uplift anyone. The

realm of the humdrum triumphs impudently: to replace two mur-
dered persons it latches onto two new ones, the Tatar and Kleshch,
who had previously held out and preserved their bonds with the
past. Gorky's drama is clearly social in character; the love story of
Pepel and Natasha is merely an episode, skillfully linked by the author to the general chain.

If you prefer, the love of Vasily and Natasha has almost nothing
to do with the murder of Kostylyov. The cause of this event lies in
Luka, who stirred up the stagnant water of the swamp. Jittery Pepel
is only a vagrant stone flung up by the new waterspout, and Kostylyov only the toad who thought he would quietly wallow till the end
of his days in the slimy waters now suddenly turbulent and fatal, if
only for a moment and only for one old toad.

Gorky's very *Depths*, as an element of tragedy, represents nothing new. It is the ancient *destiny*, that εἱμαρμένη, which once
gouged out Oedipus' eyes and suffocated Desdemona—only now it
turns out to be a rather well read lady artist *du nouveau genre*, and
her palette flashes fleeting glimpses of hitherto unseen colors of degeneracy, depraved heredity and the iron laws of the market.

Once she had plumbed the lower depths, of course protected by
a diving bell, this lady turned out to be far more garrulous than she
had been when she lived above our heads and only occasionally
showed the world her dire red claws.

In earlier times Destiny would select royal victims as her prey;
she might require the hoary age of a Lear or the lily-white virtue of a
Cordelia. Nowadays she has perceived that the game need not want
for piquancy even with more common specimens, and so she is satisfied with the Kleshchs and Satins. Nowadays she does not disdain
even the most humdrum milieu for her little affair, but, to make up
for it, having dispensed entirely with romantic effects and the world
of superhuman passions, nowadays she is capable of putting to exquisite use the data of psychopathology and police-court statistics
for her purposes.

Along with this transformation of Destiny's aspect, the drama
itself in Russia has lost its grounding in individual psychologies.
Like the novel, it seeks a social footing. The drama was already ripe
for alteration from the very fact that the mind of the modern spectator and reader encompasses more scientific ideas and public concerns and, of primary importance, has grown more sensitive to
aesthetic questions and generally more timorous. So dramatic techniques had to be reformed as well.

Thus, the precious relic of the mythic period, the *hero*, a person of godlike nature, a chosen one, a favored victim of Destiny, has now turned into a typical group, a specimen of a class.

We simply stopped being interested in a plot because it had become banal. Life, which we are condemned to substitute for dramatized myth, also causes serious emendations in the structure of drama.

Life is now kaleidoscopic and complex, but, most important, it has begun to be impatient of constraints, the encrustations of rules and the bathos of isolated action and a grossly palpable harmony.

The wholeness of a modern drama is exclusively embodied as the *author's concept*, a poetically attuned individuality—that is the only unifying factor for the kaleidoscopic impressions of life, the only power over itself which life, as dramatized by a poet, cannot help but acknowledge.

There are a few characteristic features in the playwriting of *The Lower Depths*. The play contains three main elements: (1) the power of Destiny; (2) the soul of the ex-man; and (3) a man of different status, whose advent effects a clash of the first two elements, a clash detrimental to the ex-men, and a violent reaction on the part of fate. The center of the action does not always remain the same, as in older dramas, but is continually shifting: our attention is therefore caught more particularly by temporary heroes. At first these are Anna and Kleshch, then Luka, Pepel, Vasilisa, the Baron, Natasha, Satin, Bubnov and finally the Actor. Personal dramas now smolder, now flare up from beneath the ashes, and from time to time their flames intermingle very intricately.

To be precise, there is no ordinary opening or traditional denouement in Gorky's drama. The play is like a river in the steppes, which imperceptibly originates somewhere in a marsh to die away in the sands. But pay closer attention to the opening and closing scenes, and you shall see that *The Lower Depths* is far from being a spangled gray patch snipped out of reality for some unknown reason and gaudily tarted up, but is an authentic work of art.

The opening is the awakening of the flophouse. Right at the start the old man with the long shaggy salt-and-pepper beard existed, like anyone else, like you and I, because he was asleep. But he awakes and instantly turns into an *ex-man*.

The whole flophouse comes to life at the very moment the curtain rises. Night delivered its inhabitants over to an indisputable illusion, that of life; as they sleep the very existence of this hell-hole has seemed somehow chimerical.

And then there's the Actor. Half-asleep, he is obsessed by his alcoholism, as a kind of license for general attention, he sees it as an actor's last laurels. After all, he is like everyone else, he is even more important than the others, even though he may have lost his name, he is more important because his *organism is polluted with alcohol*, and the rest of these bums don't even understand what that means. Perhaps Nastya's kerosene-lamp burned all night long, and she is drunk on *Fatal Love*. On the other hand, with the dawning the hope of living a little longer awakes in Anna: she is not alone now, they won't let her die. In short, what could be a more natural and dramatic opening for the new tragedy of Destiny? The play's conclusion is also wonderful. It is, if you like, the reconciliation of an ex-man's soul with Destiny. Destiny has her own way, of course. Taking revenge on an ex-man for his mutiny, she acquires three new little victims: first, Kleshch, who from this day forth will stop talking about honest labor and will abstain from arrogance, as he grows inured to little drams of vodka and to swindlers; second, the Tatar who today is to receive from the claw of Destiny a fiery baptism in alcohol so that, little by little, he may forget the Koran and the faraway Tatar maid "who kens the law." The third victim is comic, the dethroned monarch, Medvedev, who has today exchanged his constable's whistle for a woman's bedjacket, and thus becomes an ex-man too.

The reconciliation of the rebellious soul with Destiny is consummated by a characteristic funeral game: the weakest, most gullible, most feebleminded of the ex-men—the Actor—perishes with a noose around his neck. All that remains above the smooth ripple of the quiescent creek is poetry, that creature tenacious of life that makes no distinctions between stall and swill, young and old, christening and funeral. Its forms are endlessly variegated. Just now it hung over the stagnant ripple like the yellow fog of a convict song. Is this then not the proper curtain for the finale of a contemporary play?

I spoke above of the somewhat mystical nature of Destiny which turns men into ex-men; Gorky has demonstrated clearly in one of his latest narratives* that this is on his mind.

The story concerns a certain Goncharov, a tax assessor who, one holiday eve, found the bosom of his family and his surroundings exceptionally boring and routine, and how this gentleman, in his fur coat and with some cash in his pocket, was for no apparent reason

---

*"Christmas Eve," in the books of narratives and verse, published by Kurnin (Moscow), pp. 29 *et seq.*

attracted to bums. After seeking out a couple of men who have struck him as adequately ragged and vagrant, Goncharov begins, so he truly thinks, to join the begging and tells the bums about his spiritual lassitude. Here is part of his conversation:

> "Anyway, you're all low-lifes and can't understand this."
> "I do understand what you mean!" said I to the assessor.
> "You? Who're you?" he asked me.
> "I too was once a respectable man," said I. "I too enjoyed the charms of a serene and placid way of life. But its triviality wrung the life out of me. It squeezed and crushed out of me my soul and everything in it . . . I got depressed the way you are now, and took to drink, and turned into a lush . . . May I introduce myself?"
> The assessor turned his goggling eyes at me, and long feasted them on my person in lugubrious silence. I could see his fat red lips twitch squeamishly beneath his fluffy moustache, and his nose wrinkled up in a manner that did not imply affection for me.
> "Help me on with my fur coat."

That is all that the ill-starred romanticist of vagrancy still had the spirit to exclaim. But Gorky proceeds, not without tragic *Schadenfreude*: "I looked at his lengthening face and said nothing more. *Destiny has prepared each beast his stall according to his nature,* and no matter how much fuss the beast kicks up, he will be in the place prepared for him . . . heh-heh-heh!"

However, the fate of bums is not quite inscribed on their faces, as it is with the heroes of Marlinsky.[6] It all boils down to the fact that Gorky, having peered into even our philistine soul, can now and then discover traits of a bum's psychology there.

Then why did Maksim Gorky write his *Lower Depths*? Was it to scare the Goncharovs? Or perhaps so that bankers in tuxedos might gaze at the Barons from their boxes and think, "Thank you, God, for not making me like that publican and sinner"? After all, do we, who have been nurtured on the pen of Dostoevsky, have still to learn pity? Or did Gorky want to fortify our feeling of vicarious and general responsibility, as V. G. Korolenko did splendidly in his sketch "Not So Scary?"[7] No and no again. Gorky is Gorky. He is not a moralist like Korolenko, and, unlike some of his colleagues, he will not pluck at our heartstrings with callous fingers and rosin the bow to play Chopin nocturnes on these strings at his leisure.

Gorky's individuality represents an interesting combination of a feeling for beauty allied to profound skepticism.

Hence his feeling for beauty is not limited to skill at describing the sea, the steppe and a song—it comprises part of his nature and wells up from beneath his pen; perhaps Gorky himself is not aware how much he loves beauty; and yet the most sublime form of this feeling, when a man understands and loves the *beauty of an idea*, is accessible to him. It is this capability of Gorky's which can make a sublimely aesthetic impression out of such horrors as the story of the cruel lackey from the brothel, and which seems to add depth to such clumsy, childish things as "Varenka Olesova."

Gorky's brand of skepticism is also special. It is not dark despair, nor an ailment of the spleen or the spine. It is a lusty skepticism, eternally questing and thirsting, and hence it has two characteristic features. (1) Gorky seems to love no one; (2) he is afraid of nothing. If moralizing artists, like doting mothers, are at times inclined to overindulge an unattractive child, the spokesman and heir of their ideas, their dream—I do not believe that Gorky holds anything hallowed and sacrosanct, especially in the sense of not allowing people to scrutinize the subject. Gorky examines everything with his eyes wide open. Of course, how is one to know what will happen next? But meanwhile no Andreevs with their "abysses" and "walls" can attain his simple boldness. They want to persuade us that Gorky considers Nil in *The Lower Middle Class* an average man. But this is an entirely arbitrary assertion. If that were the case perhaps Gorky would not have made Nil such a nitwit. To my mind, one must take these Artyoms, Nils and Gordeevs[8] as they are offered, *cum grano salis*. As we watch them, we think these are forceful and, in their own way, fine human beings; but can they really be blamed for not accepting our bureaucratic prescriptions, compounded of scraps of philosophy and religion and even written in Latin? They become drunkards and money-grubbing brutes not because vodka and brutality were thought by Gorky to be the normal outlets for the energy of his forceful people, but because vodka and power at least provide a surrogate life, and all we can provide is its rejection by proposing that people choose between red tape or a slavish morality. Can one blame a brawny miller for regarding an overtaxed and consumptive schoolteacher as nothing more, ultimately, than a piece of machinery?

Among the characters in *The Lower Depths*, the finest and most interesting specimen is, of course, Vasily Pepel. He partly resembles the Gordeevs and millers, but is the most extreme development of this key type. Pepel has a complex temperament. A thief by trade and heredity, he bears no stamp of the oppressed worker with his spiteful and obtuse arrogance. His expertise has taught him to reason and, moreover, rewards his ratiocination. It has developed in Pepel a peculiar keenness of instinct and even an odd edginess. He is afraid of the dead, afraid of words, memories and loneliness; there is something feminine in Pepel's nature, a certain chaste sensitivity that connects him with Gordeev and the vendor from the novel *The Trio*. Vasilisa disgusts him when he recalls that she seduced him.

Perhaps, in this instinctive protest of a youthful temperament against the narcotic of a lewd woman's passion, Gorky is slightly drawing aside the curtain on an entirely new world order—the future lovelessness of human beings, i.e., their true freedom and pure high-mindedness.

Set beside Pepel is the image of Natasha; with what rueful humor Gorky draws us a silhouette of the "modern soul" in this victim, early marked-out by Destiny's dirty finger.

Natasha is that proud and bashful virginity which fears curses and blows less than the hot breath of passions which humiliates her even as she fails to understand it. Natasha's young soul is all—expectation . . . all—questioning . . . all is in the future; it does not need Nastya's drug, because it lives by its own tacit intuition.

> NATASHA. I'm imagining . . . I'm imagining and—waiting . . .
> BARON. For what?
> NATASHA. Well, y'see, I'm thinking, tomorrow . . . someone will show up . . . somebody special . . . Or something will happen . . . and it'll be different . . . I've been waiting ever so long . . . I'm always waiting . . . Oh well . . . after all . . . what *can* a person wait for?

If Gorky had singled out *only this* pastel-drawn Natasha against the background of his *Lower Depths*, he would still have remained one of the "prophets in Israel." It is difficult to conceive of a more tremulous and more terrifying symbol of the modern Russian soul than Natasha, the sister of Vasilisa Kostylyova. Exactly like her, we all go on waiting with a kind of tragic naiveté.

"Then something will happen . . . and it'll be different . . . someone will show up . . . somebody special . . ."

And like her we know all the time perfectly well that our future holds nothing in store.

In the lower depths all the fundamentals of bourgeois order and happiness are reduced to such rudiments that there can be no doubt about the dramatist's attitude toward them.

Here is family—its emblem, of course—Vasilisa Kostylyova . . . Here is religion—her husband's icon-lamp and the means of filling it

. . . and lastly, here is government . . . Medvedev the cop in his bucolic relations with the tenants . . . But among these fundamentals of bourgeois well-being which they connote there is one which cannot be so easily verbalized, because for so long it has been beautifully idealized by our consciousness, and that is—labor. I once read in a book by a German philologist that the tragedy of Phaedra could ripen to such a pitch of ghastliness only thanks to an environment where blessed labor was unknown. Gorky's milieu does not know blessed labor either, because it does know hated and accursed labor, and one need hardly blame its poet if, having made an abstraction out of the utopia of his great teacher, he wrests from the hands of the philistines their weapon, *allegedly blessed* by Tolstoy.

The workingman Kleshch is the most evil person in the whole flophouse. Even Kostylyov can be forgiven two-score sins on account of his Vasilisa. After all, what is Kostylyov? A weak, putrid and hypocritical little old man, he is ever so much easier to take than Kleshch. Kostylyov is a chatterbox, he trims the icon-lamp and unburdens his soul with the fatuous banalities of Yudushka Golovyov,[9] and at heart is scared of everyone . . . Not so Kleshch . . . After tormenting his wife to death, he is sorry only that her funeral cost him the tools of his trade. Kleshch boasts about his honesty. He despises loafers, and when something goes wrong, he shouts out hysterically that it isn't fair because he, an honest man with horny hands, is dying of starvation, but the crooks are drunk!

Bubnov is an *ex*-workingman and businessman. Once he was a furrier, and he cannot scrub from his hands the yellow dye in which the dogs' pelts were put to soak. What with all this blessed labor, scrimping and saving and dyed martens, Bubnov almost committed a murder. But suddenly he came to his senses in time and discarded the happiness labor had scraped together, along with his wife and the yellow dogs. Now he's a cynic, a petty cardsharp, at moments a kind of inspired, almost ecstatic drunkard—but he no longer kills anyone or scrimps and saves anything, because he has forever renounced householding, scrimping and saving and conjugal rights, having left them to his competitor along with his wife and the "imitation marten" dye.

Nor did work have a happy ending for the honest Tatar: blessed labor broke his arm, and before our very eyes he descends to the lower depths.

I am neglecting Anna. The ancient Hellenes aptly called such persons as she κεκμηκότες—which means both *dead* and *done with suffering*. There are two of Gorky's characters to whom labor is alien *organically.* One is Nastya. Lord, how far our poetry has come since Sonechka Marmeladova, her sloping yellow room at the tailor Kapernaumov's, the raising of Lazarus and the romantic emblem of human suffering![10] Here she is, our modern-day Sonechka Marmeladova—an almost grotesque creature. She lives on prostitution and novels. There is nothing in her past . . . nothing in her future . . . her life is a chimera . . . an impossibility.

Her pimp is the Baron, an ex-man with an aristocratic drawl, and, I suppose, limpid blue eyes, who has sunk to the lower depths after a series of episodes in a hectic life, a meaningless marriage, carouses, prodigality, forgeries. He still imposes on the flophouse with vestiges of breeding, bearing and broad shoulders. Superficially the man is habitually, elegantly indifferent and at moments curtly haughty, but a kind of hazy trepidation has already burrowed into his soul.

"You're thinking things out," he says to Satin, "good for you, I suppose it warms your heart . . . None of that for me . . . I don't know how! I'm scared, old boy . . . sometimes . . . D'y'understand? . . . In a funk . . . Because . . . what comes next?" The Baron's hazy *What comes next?* is, again, not remote from our psychology.

But in the lower depths labor has opponents other than the semi-conscious, instinctive, hereditary and, so to speak, elemental ones. Satin is its foe on principle.

SATIN. Hey, widower! why're you down in the dumps? What's on your mind?

KLESHCH. I'm thinking . . . about what I'll do. Got no tools . . . The funeral swallowed 'em up!

SATIN. Take my advice: don't do a thing! Just fill up space.

KLESHCH. Swell . . . You can talk . . . I'd be ashamed to look people in the face.

SATIN. Cut it out! People aren't ashamed that you live worse than a dog . . . Think it over—you stop working, I stop . . . a hundred more . . . thousands . . . everyone! . . . get me? everyone quits working! Nobody'll want to do anything—then what'll happen?

or

Work? What for? For a full belly? (*Roars with laughter.*) I've always despised people who worried too much about a full belly. That's not what it's all about, Baron! That's not what it's about! Man's higher than that! Man is higher than full bellies!

To Satin, the most subjective of Gorky's characters, the idea of work is distasteful, not because he's a drunkard, an ex-man rattled by the shock, afraid to discuss his past, but because his moral nature is opposed to labor, seen first as a reflex of bourgeois happiness, and second as the brand of slavery. Labor, like conscience, as he puts it, is something every man asks only of his neighbor. Labor does not equalize people but estranges them, turning them into Kleshchs and Kostylyovs. He is right about a good deal. I confess I am not quite sure what blessed labor means. Be it Lyovin's gymnastics or my writing, we regard it as life and enjoyment and not labor at all . . .

There is more than a little that is petty and vile and obtuse and most often even pointless in labor. Still, what can be done about it? Satin's philosophy contains that stirring question, but does not move us a step further in resolving the agonizing problem of conscience.

Luka is a fugitive. He has a full life: he has been manhandled till he's soft, prowled every corner where Russian is spoken, probably worked at things like sweeping out the flophouse, just by chance, got drunk when other people stood treat, dallied with peasant women, lay low, gave comfort, teased, pitied and, most of all, *lied pleasantly* and told fairy tales.

Ultimately he came to regard all people as good, but this is Gorky, nevertheless; he loves no one and cares for no one. He is loveless. Even persons as persons fail to interest him. Long ago he ceased to care about their individual affairs, because he lives on the sidelines, like Socrates among the Athenians. Besides, why spend a long time caring for the same people if the world is wide and there are lots of *every sort of man* in it.

Luka loves not people, but what is concealed behind people, he loves the riddle of life, the tricks of adaptation, the fantastic sects, the capricious combinations of existences. He likes Satin.

"You're a merry sort, Kostyantin . . . a pleasant fellow . . ." Luka, like a Tolstoyan workingman, likes to tell people agreeable things, but he does not do so out of any particular spiritual delicacy or misty-eyed idealism. A skeptic and a passive observer, Luka has noticed that on the dungheap, praise causes every soul to blossom forth and reveal itself the more. This is why he praises, this is why he inquires, investigates, and this is why he indefatigably strides the earth with his old man's legs. For the most part, he's a sly little old gaffer, but he loves the man who's frank, expansive and daring: that's the kind he calls *merry*. Narrow-minded persons, of Kleshch's sort, are not to his taste. "There ain't no work, he shouts . . . No nothing." Luka is used to lying, and without it his dealings would be impossible. For in the world he roams, people could no more get on without lies, in all probability, than they could without vodka. Luka consoles and lies, but there is nothing of the philanthropist or moralist in him. Except for woe and a victim, Luka has left nothing behind him in Gorky's Lower Depths . . . But what are we to conclude from this? First, it is worthwhile, whatever the outcome may be, to stir up the Lower Depths every so often, and second . . . second, what would our life be, this life of most placid philistinism, tell me, if every so often various Lukas had not lied to us about a land of righteousness, and troubled us with questions, albeit the most hopeless ones.

Yet I do realize that in a few minutes I can boldly ring a bell and be pulled out of the depths and into a fog that is more decorous for the race of mammals to which I have the honor to belong for the time being. Listen once again: here is Satin as he sings a paean to freedom and, out of Bubnov's winnings as a cardsharp, drinks to mankind.

"When I'm drunk . . . I like everything. Ey-yup . . . He's praying? Fine! A man can believe or not . . . It's up to him! Man is a free agent . . . he pays for it all himself: for believing, for not believing, for love, for brains. A man pays for it all himself, and that's why he's free! Man—why, he's truth! Just what is man? He's not you or me or them . . . No! he's you, me, them, the old man, Napoleon, Mohammed, all in one! Understand? He's tremendous. He contains all beginnings and endings. Everything's in man, everything's for man! Nothing exists but man—all the rest is the work of his hands and brain! Man! A man should be respected! Don't pity him . . . don't belittle him with pity . . . he must be respected! . . ." etc.

I hear Gorky's Satin and I say to myself: yes, as a matter of fact, it all has a *splendid resonance* to it. The idea of *one* man containing all men within him, a God-man (isn't that a fetish?) is very beautiful. But then tell me why these same gusts of alcoholic breath, these thoraxes of short-winded chests immediately send a wild convict song soaring and spiraling somewhere aloft in superhuman space. Ugh, look, Satin-Gorky, won't man be terrified and, more important, won't he be immeasurably bored when he realizes that he is everything and that everything is for his sake and for his sake alone? . . .

On Drama

by Aleksandr Blok

I

Only a supple, shrewd and wily lyric poetry is capable of recording contemporary uncertainties and contradictions, the vagaries of
drunken wits and the vaporings of idle forces. We are living through
an era of just such lyric poetry. The spacious lyricism of a placid epic
or stormy ballad enlivened by heroes, or even the long and mournful
lay in which a nation's soul sheds its tears: this type of poem has
been shivered into tiny glittering streams. The monotonous roar of
the waterfall has given way to the enchanting song of many tiny
rivulets, and the spray of those lyric rivulets sped in all directions:
toward the novel, the short story, the theoretical discourse and, finally, the drama. And the influence of contemporary lyric poetry
(that art of transmitting the subtlest sensations) was perhaps particularly detrimental to the drama. It seems the very air is impregnated
with lyricism, because both free actions and strong passions have
disappeared, and the loud voice has given way to the whisper. The
subtlest lyrical poisons have corroded the simple columns and
sturdy chains that uphold and bind the drama.

The last great European dramatist was Ibsen; in the wake of the
King of Scandinavian Drama, the works of Hauptmann, D'Annunzio, Maeterlinck, even Hofmannsthal or Przybyszewski and
Schnitzler have declined to a sunset.[1] Some of these writers have already been doomed to extract the hero from the drama, deprive it of
action and eschew dramatic pathos, reducing the brazen voice of
tragedy to the hoarse whisper of life. But in the West this followed

This article first appeared in *Zolotoe runo* (*Golden Fleece*, nos. 7–9, 1907).
The present translation is based on the text in A. Blok, *Sobranie sochineniy v
shesti tomakh* (Moscow, 1971), V. I have not attempted to reproduce the
meter or rhyme scheme of the verse quotations, but, since they are quoted as
bad examples, I have tried to capture the flaccidity of image and vocabulary.

some unalterable law; Western drama moved toward its own crises with a sort of mathematical precision, by way of cultural evolution.

Now, take Maeterlinck. The writer is far from brilliant, though, like all Western writers, possessed of his own quite special brand of pathos [*pafos* in the Belinskyan sense of "attitude toward the material" or "point of view"—*tr.*]. When we utter the name "Maeterlinck," we conjure up a distinct image; we no longer feel the thrill of novelty; many of us are fed up with Maeterlinck, others find him flat; but we know what Maeterlinck is and by now his very name is dogma, one of those dogmas that some maintain and others challenge. Even Russian proponents of staging Maeterlinck's plays are already daring to cavil, if only in whispers. (Sometimes the show is absurd. The actors strive with all their might to be supersubtle, so nothing can be heard and occasionally, all for subtlety's sake, nothing can be seen, while the audience listens attentively and applauds; but neither actors nor audience understand any of it at times.)

Then what is the reason for this rapid dogmatization of the author of what is probably the most "decadent" poetry in the world? I think the reason lies in the nature of Maeterlinck's own work and culture. Maeterlinck arrived at just the right moment, neither too soon nor too late. He suffered some minimal persecution, became famous and rested on his laurels, having put to good use his own brand of pathos, the very special but minor pathos of a subtle, clever but far from brilliant lyric poet. His native culture spawned him and schooled him, showed him the ships in the sleepy canals; like a strict mother it trained him up and rocked him to sleep in his own automobiles. As to life and death, a prophet being persecuted, talent gone unrecognized—things hardly went so far as that. And one sophisticated critic, Rémy de Gourmont, was still capable of making these simple, savory remarks about Maeterlinck no more than ten years ago (*Livre des masques*):

> Literature had become melancholy and wearisome; revolt was considered pointless, cursing puerile; mankind, disillusioned by fruitless struggles, slowly resigned itself to knowing nothing, understanding nothing, fearing nothing, hoping nothing except very remotely.
>
> Somewhere in the mists there is an island, and on this island a castle; in the castle there is a large room lit by a small lamp; and in the large room people are waiting. Waiting for what? They themselves don't know. They are waiting for

someone to knock on the door, waiting for the lamp to go out.
They are waiting for Fear, waiting for Death. They talk. Yes,
they utter words, disturbing the stillness for a moment, then
fall to listening once more, leaving their phrases unfinished,
their gestures incomplete. They listen and wait. Maybe it
won't come. Oh no, it will come. It keeps drawing nearer. It's
late, maybe it won't come until tomorrow. And the people,
gathered in the large room beneath the small lamp, begin to
smile and are on the verge of hoping. There is a knock at the
door. That's all: that is an entire lifetime.

In this respect, Maeterlinck's brief dramas, so deliciously
unreal, are profoundly lifelike and true . . . they are real by virtue of their irreality.[2]

This is one brief and modest excerpt, yet how simple and eloquent.

Now let us hear from Maeterlinck's opponents in the West;
their statements are equally simple and distinct. For instance, here
is "a vote of censure by the Social-Democratic party"—a pamphlet
on Maeterlinck by Henrietta Roland-Holst:[3] "Maeterlinck appears
to be a representative of senescent Western European capitalism . . .
The content and essence of Maeterlinck's poetry is this: ignorance,
lack of any desire to know, fear, uncertainty, unawareness and weari-
ness with life—everything the capitalist class is rife with. And the
forms of his poetry had to be accommodated to the form reaction
takes in his country—Catholic and priest-ridden. Hence the caress-
ing, lulling and flaccid character of Maeterlinck's poetry, hence his
idealizing of humility and meekness, a confirmation of the eternal
and unsettled discord between body and soul . . ." Nothing in this
quotation contradicts Rémy de Gourmont; the difference is that the
critics act as exponents for different parties, and so one praises and
the other finds fault. But even Rémy de Gourmont says that Maeterlinck is "monotonous," that his "language is impoverished and
timid," "the outlines of his dramas are infantile," "it is hard to put
up with his habit of repeating phrases"; while Henrietta Roland-
Holst calls Maeterlinck a "sophisticated and profound talent" and
hopes that a study of nature will yet rouse him "to seek true beauty
and the grandeur of the human world, that is, our social organism."
So *that*, plain and simple, is how things stand with Maeterlinck.
Friends and enemies alike praise and blame him. And finally, he
himself with enviable serenity passes sentence on his own dramas in
one of those articles of his, in which he always wittily, subtly and
charmingly discusses God, death, his lapdog, his automobile and

human sin. This verdict declares that the drama is afflicted with a
"paralysis of external action"; that there is a tendency to penetrate
deeper and deeper into human consciousness and to attach great significance to problems of morality. The less violent and extraordinary
the event, the less "material" are bloodshed and passion. Death is
no longer the *ultima ratio*. There are no more external embellish-
ments, they dare not compete with the godhead; no predestina-
tion by fate, for action is consummated in the very depths of consciousness where duty and desire (*devoir et désir*) wrestle together, a
principle initiated by Dumas *fils*[4] with his elementary moral problems of infidelity, arranged marriages, adultery, divorce when there
are children, etc. Indeed, the deeper one plumbs human consciousness, the fewer "conflicts" exist, because *in the deepest recesses and
in the darkness everything is at one* (how calm and simple it all is,
like "twice two makes four," like the guttering bonfire of dramatic
pathos, like the praise and blame of Maeterlinck himself by his critics!). And Maeterlinck praises Ibsen—without diminishing his "admiration pour le grand poète scandinave," he finds that Ibsen possesses an "orgueil injuste, une sorte de folie chagrine et maladive"
["an unjustified arrogance, a sort of peevish and sickly madness"—
tr.]. And it all ends with the desire "to think about the new theater
of peace and beauty without tears" (Maeterlinck, "Le Double jar-
din," *Le Drame moderne*). Yes, this is very simple, very calm and
very civilized. But where is life with its contradictions and its acute
and profound struggles, and where is the sublime drama that reflects
these contradictions? They have ceased to exist. A wholesome
meaning exists, all by itself, and a lyrical refinement (and occasionally perversity) exists, all by itself. This is referred to as "peace and
beauty."

   Yes, everything is different in civilized nations. Maeterlinck
knew how to employ his talent, he did all he could. His work is an
original minor art, his plays are the original *petits drames*. No one
in the West would have tried to construct philosophical theories on
such lyrical foundations, and no writer-journalist would ever have
started writing lyrical dramas. But in Russia such is not the case.
Georgy Chulkov devised the theory of "mystical anarchism," while
Evgeny Chirikov writes "dramatic fantasies" in verse.[5] But the further and deeper you go, the more different things are. For example, I
think that *Woe from Wit* is a Russian play of genius; but how star-
tlingly *fortuitous* it is! And it was born in a kind of fairy-tale surrounding: amid Griboedov's other plays, which are quite undis-

tinguished, in the brain of a Petersburg bureaucrat with a heart full of Lermontovian spleen and malice and an immobile countenance that gave no signs of "life"; worse yet, a straitlaced fellow with a frigid, pinched visage, a venomous scoffer and skeptic dreamed up *Woe from Wit*. He had a vision—and wrote a brilliant Russian play. He had neither precursors nor successors equal to him.

Where did "dramatic technique" come from—that great and mysterious mainspring which has been wound tight in Europe for ages? In Russia it is fortuitous, it simply does not exist here.

Thus, dramatic technique is fortuitous in Chekhov, who said that "new forms are needed"; intuition alone, it would seem, eliminated from Russian drama what Maeterlinck eliminated from European drama. Chekhov went a good deal farther and a good deal deeper in some directions than did Maeterlinck, but his drama did not become dogma; he had no precursors, and his successors do not know how to do anything *à la* Chekhov. The symbolist drama in Russia is also fortuitous and not native, but nurtured by foreign fads, such as Bryusov's *Earth* and Vyacheslav Ivanov's *Tantalus*.[6] Russia has room only for odd fortuitous occurrences such as, for instance, the fact that Ostrovsky's immense talent, focused exclusively on drama, produced works less striking than the plays of Sukhovo-Kobylin, a writer admittedly less important than Ostrovsky. While Ostrovsky often stretches out a canvas of the naturalist school for pages on end, Sukhovo-Kobylin rivets our attention suddenly with a single, unanticipated trait, and in the satiric farce *Tarelkin's Death* the ancient lineaments of symbolic drama are perceptible.[7]

If Russian drama itself is fortuitous and unexpected, treatises on drama in Russia are even more unexpected, as was, for example, L. N. Tolstoy's article "On Shakespeare and the Drama" which appeared not so long ago.[8]

At a time when dramatists of every country, even the most minor, were studying Shakespeare (if only to confute him, like Ibsen and Maeterlinck), Tolstoy "over the course of fifty years ventured many times to test myself, by reading Shakespeare in every conceivable format, in Russian, English, German and Schlegel's translation . . . and I never failed to experience the same old thing: disgust, boredom and perplexity." The Shakespeare "epidemic" is ascribed by Tolstoy to chance; Shakespeare's world view he considers "the most vile and vulgar." "The works of Shakespeare, their outward imagery borrowed, skillfully pieced together like a mosaic from bits and snatches, fabricated at the moment of writing, have nothing in common with art and poetry." Finding nothing of value in Shake-speare, Tolstoy demands of art and especially drama as its highest form a religious content:

> By religious content in art I do not mean a direct inculcation of a religious truth in artistic guise, nor an allegorical depiction of such truths, but a well-defined attitude toward the world, which corresponds to the most sublime religious comprehension at that particular time and which, serving as the incentive for the writing of drama, permeates an author's every work even though he may be unconscious of it. So it has always been with true art, and so it is still with every true artist in general and dramatist in particular. So, as matters stood when drama was a serious business, and as they ought to stand by their very nature, the only man who can write drama is the one who has something to tell people, and that something of the greatest importance to people: the relationship of man to God, to the world, to all that is eternal and infinite.

Reading these words, you feel about the same as when you stand on a high hill in a wintry snowstorm. While down in the valley below echo quiet and passive words we can understand about "theater of peace and beauty without tears," here on the heights we catch our breath in bewilderment. The piercing snowstorm is about as serene as the words of this seventy-five-year-old sage, the only genius now extant in Europe, a *genius who lacks pathos:* "the only man who can write drama is the one who has something to tell people."

Thus Tolstoy overthrows Shakespeare and talks about condign art. Arguing with him is like arguing with a blizzard. In fact we stare, our vision blurred, at both Tolstoy and Shakespeare from a kind of infinite distance; do we have any idea at all how to penetrate the hidden meaning of their simple statements? Or how to get round them? Perhaps we shall be supplanted by people who will not be enthralled by them, but by something else we know not of, something even more remote and sublime than Shakespeare and Tolstoy.

In the meantime we can forget neither Macbeth nor Anna Karenina. We live by their breath, without it we would not have strength enough to keep from dying. Therefore we have not the strength to solve the riddle of Tolstoy or Shakespeare—and can only store them in our hearts. Let tragedy ripen in the heart that can contain the opposition of these two elements. Other hearts will perish, unable to withstand the doubts and contradictions of unfathomable profundities: Wisdom or madness? Pity or contempt? Religion or mysticism? Life or the word (the *Word*)? Or can it be that

> The living well of unveiled mysteries will
> Intoxicate them with a sleepless thirst for knowledge,
> And beauty's transformed visage will
> Satiate their *uttermost* desires?

In other words, can it be that those desperate cries that people now emit will abate somewhat, and the close-packed roofs of the universal city, which conceal "the terrestrial globe as under a serpent's scales or a glittering glass" will start to crack—"to live forever in springtime's warm caress"? Or can it be that *magic* will subdue *tragedy* and life will become a dream, just as in our time *lyric poetry* is subduing *drama,* and action is ceasing in the very depths of human consciousness—*"in the darkness"* where *"everything is at one"*?

II

So it follows that Russian dramatists do not have a true technique for playwriting. Wholeness is almost always wanting in their works: not only are the individual acts unconnected but even sections within the acts are stitched together any old way, by chance. There are very few writers in whose works the whole play and its every act are entire of themselves—like a brimming chalice. Such was the drama of Ibsen, in whose hands dramatic material was like malleable wax. Ibsen's dramas are arranged in the order of the questions that came to his mind; and in this sense each of his plays serves as a sequel to the preceding one, and these plays are linked like chapters of an autobiography, so that anyone who wishes to know Ibsen's mind in its entirety was recommended by the playwright himself to read through *all* his works *consecutively.* Even in Russian drama it happens that one play may serve as sequel to another, though not in the best, the Ibsenite sense. For instance, Gorky's *The Lower Middle Class* and Naidyonov's *Vanyushin's Children*[9] are continuations one of the other and might almost be read as one play in eight acts; but, in the first place, this is because both writers analyze exactly the same question ("parents and children") from exactly the same viewpoint borrowed elsewhere, or, to put it more precisely, without any *personal* viewpoint; in the second place, because both have a singularly feeble technique; and in the third place, because they are virtually indistinguishable one from the other in the matter of language (in these particular plays).

Besides Russian drama's lack of technique, language and pathos, it has no action. It is paralyzed by lyricism and, more often than not, merely because this lyricism of Russia's wide open spaces is so dear to us, we are prone to prize plays and other works quite unworthy of artistic consideration. Lyricism is especially prevalent in Chekhov's plays, but his mysterious gift was not passed on to anyone else, and his innumerable imitators have given us nothing of value. Those Chekhovian realists who, as I have mentioned elsewhere, concentrated on the details of everyday life and foraged in trivial experiences have not yet started writing plays, luckily. Therefore stuffy air, claustrophobia, cloying flesh, libidinousness and perversion are for the moment absent from drama. It is principally the contributors to Znanie[10] who devote themselves to playwriting, and their countless dramas proliferate, from most of which one cannot extract anything of value with any consistency. These dramas are written at considerable length and tedium; they give the impression of having been churned out with great effort. The acts are of "normal" length, that is, short enough, as experience teaches, to keep the audience from falling asleep. And whole volumes of these plays give the impression that they are not so much plays as compilations of roles already assigned to actors. There are usually so many of these roles that one cannot possibly remember the cast of characters and, while reading the play to its conclusion, must keep flipping back to the pages where they are listed. The cast list is usually provided with psychological or physical data—why this is so is quite beyond me: apparently more for the actor's sake than the reader's. I cannot understand why they should be plays at all and not short stories or editorials or law reporting; only one explanation comes to mind: the author wants the public to hear from the stage, not read in a book, how he has treated the given problem. That's understandable—nobody objects to going to the theater. But who would ever read a pamphlet? Understandable yes, it's understandable, but what has this got to do with art?

Half a score of the latest plays and playlets lie before me. A few characters or situations can be gleaned from some of them. But only two works, which have nothing in common, can be taken seriously in a discussion of drama. They are Leonid Andreev's *The Life of Man* and Mikhail Kuzmin's *Comedy of Eudoxia of Heliopolis*. I will first speak of the remainder.

III

Gorky has already written six plays, of which only the second is noteworthy, *The Lower Depths*. As a *drama*, *The Lower Depths* has its shortcomings, but Gorky's favorite characters have not let him down. The writer keeps to the standard of *Foma Gordeev* and *The Trio*. His first play, *The Lower Middle Class*, is the most painstakingly written of the lot; on the other hand, starting with *Summer People*, Gorky appreciably goes to pieces.[11]

Gorky is certainly no dramatist; he has splendid individual scenes, lifelike dialogue and remarkable characters, but he has none of drama's special requisite. When he writes plays he almost always loses his own point of view. Gorky does not know how to dispense with a "hero" as Chekhov did, but then none of our current realists do. However, Gorky stands apart from the majority because he *doesn't want* to dispense with a hero. His hero is always someone noble, strong and despairing, apparently without kith or kin. In the last few years, this man has begun to degenerate into the abstract "Human Being" (in Gorky's lyrico-journalistic pieces) or else into a moralizing workingman (in his fiction: *Mother*). This happened, most regrettably, just at the time when Gorky had taken up playwriting; and in only one drama, *The Lower Depths*, did Gorky's real heroes occur, the people who perish from *dramatic necessity*, alive, powerful, well characterized by a few clearcut traits, which is how a play's characters should be characterized. The remarkable words "Honor the lunatic who tosses mankind a golden dream" are worthy of the play *The Lower Depths*, because their voices and their struggle can be heard from the theatrical boards and because they perish tragically.

Whenever Gorky's dramas show us merchants, scholars, intellectuals, workers, engineers, capitalists, no dramatic conflicts occur, and they all speak in faint voices, barely audible from the stage, somewhat more audible from the pages of a story, and, most likely, *highly audible* from the pages of an embattled magazine article. For instance, in *The Lower Middle Class*, he presents the obsolescent generation and the younger generation in such a way that it is immediately apparent whose side truth is on, and the man who perishes is smashed between these two forces, one of which is unreal. There is no eternal contradiction with its roots deep in reality, which is why there is no genuine impetus to the drama, which goes on only so long as the younger generation, meant to prevail, limply tarries. In *Children of the Sun*, there is not even that much conflict, and all the events and discussions are allocated among weaklings of one degree or another. To conform with this, the play is heavily adorned with "tenderness," lyricism (the same is true of "The Edelweiss" in *Summer People*), but tender lyricism is, notoriously, not Gorky's strong point.

Even less admissible as drama are the "scenes," *Enemies*; this is simply the labor question treated banally in a dramatic format. We no longer get even one of the real contradictions associated with art in general and drama in particular. On one hand, we have angelic workers who strike for the sake of justice, do not betray their comrades, take the boss's children for walks, and, on the other hand, the capitalists, intellectually enfeebled or mindlessly cruel, as well as the police, portrayed with the same incomparable banality, straight out of a newspaper exposé. Meanwhile, everything is moving and sentimental, but it has no relevance to art.

Prior to *Enemies*, Gorky wrote the play *Barbarians*; it is a play of types and characters, written with consummate shoddiness and an incredible number of characters, many of whom are repetitions of the old ones. Moreover, they all come in, go out, drink tea, hold conversations; there is absolutely no action. Certain individual lines are as effective as ever, and, in addition, there is the feeling of a county seat: a river, a roadway, a fence, gardens, a few dusty leaves. To this provincial town comes a "barbarian" engineer who destroys its way of life—and that's that. But in the entire play there is only one character remarkable enough to stick in the memory. This character is the excise officer's wife, Nadezhda Polikarpovna Monakhova, "a very beautiful, stately woman with huge, unmoving eyes." She exudes an original Russian strength and freedom. She is a demi-bourgeoise who has read her fill of novels; she knows plenty of love stories and they are all "like a young girl's dreams." She speaks quietly, simply, confidently, ponderously, somewhat "metaphorically," like a bourgeoise. She is sure that she is highly intelligent, and yet can think or talk of nothing but love. The locals shoot themselves and lose their heads for love of her; the ladies of the district treat her severely to admonitions and exhortations. She falls in love with the newly arrived engineer Cherkun, a coarse man who has, in her words, "fascinating eyes and flamelike hair, and he is all in all a distinguished man . . . once you set eyes on him, you can't forget him." Smitten, she follows him around persistently, gazes weirdly and horribly at him and, as soon as she sees he does not love her, quite simply shoots herself "outside." Everything about her is strangely and beautifully integral, she has a kind of great power, simultaneously attractive and repellent. She is powerful with a kind of bleak, bestial fascination. I fancy that the whole play *Barbarians* was written for the sake of this character. It may be thought that she too is a "Human Being"—the true *heroine* of the play—for want of a hero. "Gentlemen, you have killed a human being," says Monakhova's husband at the play's end. If such women, reminiscent of Varenka Olesova, Sasha and Malva, are to play the *human being* roles in Gorky's plays, at any rate they are more interesting than Pavel Vlasov and the rest of that virtuous crew.[12]

The rest of the Znanie dramatists (except Andreev) are inferior even to Gorky. Their themes are far less remarkable, and it is difficult to distinguish their "viewpoints" one from another; they cope with dramatic technique every bit as badly as Gorky does. What chiefly distinguishes them from Gorky is that they eschew a *hero* entirely and in that respect follow Chekhov's lead. But they are not even worthy to "loose the latchets" of Chekhov's sandals. They dabble but do not create; they are toilers of life, not creators of literature.

Of the lot, Naidyonov is the most cultured. But this culture is purely relative and is expressed in the most skillful construction of Naidyonov's plays and in his writing plays exclusively. The idiom he uses is in no way distinguishable from the idiom of the rest of the Znanie playwrights: tedious, long-winded, all about people whose life has been a failure, who seek life but cannot find it, who perish from their own or someone else's lack of understanding, distrust or inertia. None of these people has the least trace of heroism, and almost all are weak-willed mediocrities. Similarly, there are no "villains," but their place is taken by sluggish, frigid persons, intent on their own welfare. Not only is there no attitude to art, but no attitude to life. Life rolls along to the theme of misery; here a merchant's family squabbles, there a man with a past full of failure loses home and family and the woman he once loved; here an anonymous streetwalker enters a bookkeeper's hotel room to get warm, there a rich eccentric with honorable intentions fails at art, love and good deeds. Nobody succeeds at anything and sorrow reigns supreme, but it is vain to look for Chekhovian depths, and novelty is restricted to details. For instance, it is modish to end an act with a phrase of general significance or one that is in some way striking, pronounced loudly "as the curtain falls." Now in Naidyonov on these occasions the words uttered are deliberately commonplace; for example,

"KLAVDIYA (*points to her hair*). It's turned gray" (*Vanyushin's Children*, end of act 1).

"ANNA NIKIFOROVNA. Go on, have some pie" (*The Prodigal Son*, end of act 1).

Another "novelty" of Naidyonov's is psychological stage directions, for instance: "Vanyushin is sorely hurt by his daughter's remarks; he would like to tell her how unfair she is, but doesn't know how to put it into words" (*Vanyushin's Children*); or "Artamon's naive 'Pardon me' has echoed strangely in this house. Somehow everything has become awkward and pleasant [*sic*]. From this moment on Olga Ivanovna grows especially fond of Artamon" (*Walls*). These psychological stage directions are numerous and ultimately shatter the psychology of the characters, turning them into pale shadows of the shadows of life, instead of clear images of art. If the author needs such an abundance of explanations, which are absolutely alien to the stage, why does he write plays and not stories? This question crops up again and again. In fact Naidyonov's plays are woefully spent evenings in the theater at best.

Naidyonov's latest drama, *Walls*, is no better and no worse than the rest. The leading character Artamon Suslov, a spineless son of a merchant family, discovers America in act 4: "Have to search . . . search for another life . . . And perhaps real life lies there, in the searching." There is the madam of a brothel (for decency's sake referred to as a "guesthouse"), a debauched overseer, a moribund clerk, a noble schoolteacher with a revolutionary daughter; "authentically Russian people" they are dubbed, in reproof. In short, everything is in place: people are snatched out of the impenetrable gloom of life, described fumblingly and thrown back into the gloom without faith or hope; it is a pity that these people are the way they are, but it is also a pity that the writer and all his ilk write as helplessly as their heroes live. Yet a great deal might be made even of this Artamon Suslov! In a few passages Naidyonov reminds us that his grandfather was a schismatic and founded the "Suslovian creed"—what he recalls it for is unclear, since not a single schismatic trait is to be found in Artamon; the writer unconsciously comes up with something good, something profound, but he holds onto it for a while, turns it about a bit, and then throws it away; he doesn't know how to deal with it, even though he perhaps senses something; but he doesn't have enough power of conceptualization, imagination, generalization.

Even more unprepossessing than Naidyonov is S. Yushkevich.[13] The same old impoverished, hopeless life—such is his entire dramatic trilogy, *In Town, Hunger, The King*. Take only the last play, *The King*; it's the Jewish labor question; there is the preachment that Russian and Jewish workers are brothers, that together they ought to crush capitalism and arrange things so that the surplus profits don't go into the factory-owner's pockets. Why in the world is this written as a play, what is its theme? The theme takes shape as the following *worker's speech*:

> Let each man recall how we live. Behold here a worker's flat. One room and a kitchen. Here live myself, my sister, a working-girl, my father, a workingman, my brother Nakhman and the shoemaker Shmuil. We are asphyxiated by the stench that issues from the walls and we asphyxiate each other with our own breath. We sleep on the floor like dogs, and lice devour our bodies. We eat stale bread and only on holidays do we see meat. Our recreations are either drink or billiards or the sleep of the dead. Such is our plight . . . And how does Grossman live? Grossman's family consists of four persons. These four persons live in twelve rooms, which cost sixty thousand rubles. For these persons everything is available. Theater, music, education, good books, the best food, whilst for our children there is no milk in their mother's breasts, whilst we perish of exhaustion, filth and disease.

Why were these notions—perfectly fair notions (who hasn't thought them?)—crammed into a drama? Why, they are even poorly phrased. What worker would ever say "whilst" or "the stench that issues from the walls"? Drama is not forthcoming, despite it all, despite the fact that the son of the implacable factory-owner is on the side of the lower classes and the workers, or the fact that the workman's wife is related to the factory-owner's wife and entreats her aid in the name of their common Jewish blood and kinship or the fact that toward the end, the factory-owner's plant catches fire, all are shouting or keeping still, stamping their feet and cowering in horror.

When Yushkevich yearns for Europe (in both *In Town* and *The King*), it is Chekhov's three sisters yearning for Moscow. Except that they yearn in a highfalutin and wishy-washy way with what seems to be a dash of Dostoevsky. The general tone of Yushkevich's plays is an appeal to human abasement; in *The King*, for example, everyone speaks the language of the oppressed tailor Ersh: "So there I am, I come into the hall already, there I sit already, and nobody even knows already that I've come." They talk the same way in *In Town*. Because the characters are Jews, there is no way of knowing what this "already" means: is it a word to evoke pity or is it Jewish dialect? I suppose it's both.

The third dramatist is E. Chirikov.[14] His distinction lies in the fact that his characters are "naturalistically colloquial." A family, gathered in summer around the tea-table, speak just the way a family is supposed to speak:

> SERAFINA SERGEEVNA. Only, please, none of that chocolate Papa brought back today!
> NATASHA. Monpensier, Mamma dear. Nobody likes it.
> COOK. What'll you have for third course? Ice cream or frozen pudding?
> GORODETSKY (*angrily*). Definitely not frozen pudding! I'm sick and tired of your frozen pudding.
> SERAFINA SERGEEVNA. And no ice cream either! Seryozha will overeat himself and then get sick . . .
> COOK. All right, ma'am . . . Young miss is fond of waffles . . .

In addition to this dialogue (in the drama *Peasants*), there is the dialogue of an inadequately liberal landowner and his inadequately radical children, and the corresponding peasant dialogue. The landowners argue and bicker, are unable to decide whether to make over a forest to the peasants or not and how much to make it over for, while the peasants also talk, bicker and then set fire to the landowners' sheds and smash up the barns. Reading it attentively may indeed be very instructive, but what makes this a drama? These are merely rural dialogues, original though they be. And the "drama" *Ivan Mironych*—domestic dialogues and squabbling—is the same thing all over again. And yet, of late, Chirikov has begun to write "dramatic fantasies" in prose as well as verse; for instance:

> Aye, the sun draws nigh . . .
> It ascends and tenderly beguiles
> The slaves of earth with a longed-for new day . . .
> And gives them strength anew
> To forge themselves their iron fetters,
> To heap unneeded rubbish on the toiling backs
> While all keep hoping sometime to get somewhere! . . .
>
> (*Red Flames*)

Well, all right, there's no law against fantasizing. Except that you never get anywhere with it—not even "somewhere sometime."

Besides the "Znanian" dramas, there are others somewhat shorter, somewhat more modish, somewhat more modernistic. And they are all published in different ways—either in decadent wrappers, or with some sort of blazon. At Znanie four acts are taken for granted, but here it's up to the author's free choice. At Znanie they write: "The action takes place at Such-and-Such, on So-and-So's estate, and the chairs are arranged thus and so," but here: "Time: yes-

terday, today, tomorrow . . ." (Sholom Asch, *The Time of the Messiah*). I suppose it's the influence of the decadents.

The best of these dramas is *Hear O Israel!* (*Schma Isroel!*) by
Osip Dymov.[15] Even though the history of the oppressed Jews is tiresome and humdrum, there is something solemn in the scheme of
the play, while the dialogue possesses the author's customary vivacity and fruitiness. Army Doctor Silkin is taken outright from Chekhov, but Dymov knows how to imitate Chekhov well. However,
even he is no dramatist and if *Hear O Israel!* is better than *The
Debt*, both of them and the rest are vastly inferior to Dymov's fresh
and enjoyable, if very neurotic, book of stories, *Sun Gate*.

Beneath contempt is another poor play of Jewish life, *The Time
of the Messiah* (*On the Road to Zion*) by Sholom Asch.[16] In the
course of three acts old Jews assemble to go to Zion, while their
multi-tribed posterity unloads every conceivable vulgarity and sen-
timentality—either in Yiddish or in abominable Russian; as, for instance: "The clouds, like unto a flock of wingéd sheep, bathed their
fleece in the pellucid grey *coloring* of the waves." The author makes
use of the expression "to keep an eye out" and so forth. There is not
a whiff of Zion, despite the plethora of Yiddish words, talk about
Uganda and Palestine, Jewish costumes and the like.

Sergey Rafalovich[17] in his play *Don Juan Spurned* portrays Don
Juan not as victor, but as victim. Any effort to understand the deadly
dull debates is hindered by exemplarily flat and facile verse, as in the
following:

Since thou hast spurned life on earth, dreamy one,
Since thou hast devoted thy passion to God,
Folks think thee in heaven, folks think thee a saint.
But the ruse of heavenly reveries has died with thee.

In each of the three acts, such verses are interrupted by others,
proving graphically that it is impossible to imitate Valery Bryusov,
no matter how slavishly, if you lack talent:

All was humbly purpos'd for etern.
Life is created at every moment.
In the straitness of the earth's ravines
He loves passion, who has attained passion . . .
Longs for bread and seeks for power,
Thirsts for glory: thus does man,
Happy he who by passion alone
Has sanctified himself for aye.

If Mr. Rafalovich's language is merely infinitely insipid, the language of his verbose commentator Miss Vengerova[18] is inaccurate as well; in her commentaries, which fill more than twenty pages, such phrases crop up as, "But just how can a relationship to *Don Juan Spurned* be presumed? . . ." or "He is victorious with a strength sprung up against him," or "Don Juan . . . encounters the limit of himself."

The play *Taiga* was not a success for Georgy Chulkov. Apparently, it was to have been a "lyrical" drama, the sort in which a mist hovers over the action, and out of the mist emerge characters—doubles who resemble one another; at least, the Doctor looks like Yury, while Sister Lyubov looks like the Yakut girl Sulus, and, moreover, all the characters exchange nothing but "meaningful" remarks and are constantly cross-questioning one another and wondering at each other. But the lyrical prophecies are cold, abstract and incomprehensible—for instance: "Taiga is becoming the sun. Taiga is merging with it. They will blaze together eternally, in one kiss, like lovers"— and they create the most perfect muddle right up to the play's conclusion; this is not lyrical ambiguity, but mere obscurity. *Taiga* is inferior to some of Chulkov's stories, but there is less rhetoric in it than in some of his verse.

It would be a thorough waste of time to recall Mr. Gidoni's[19] "dramatic etude" *In the Garret*, were it not for the extraordinary lack of formality with which, not knowing how to write Russian, he undertakes to solve problems. Mr. Gidoni's "concept" consists of artists' having to abandon art and rush to the barricades on the premise that on the barricades all hearts—"be they full of empty trumpery or precious fire, cowardice or self-sacrifice"—undergo a "resplendent rebirth." To this profound and novel idea the objection may be raised, first, that ruffians and cowards are out of place even on barricades, and, second, that Mr. Gidoni's "artists"—who exclaim "What contrastful lighting effects! No exaggeration—it's picturesque!"—are the average no-talents and the above-average philistines; their fitness for the barricades remains unproven, but their unfitness for the "garret" is proven brilliantly, as if very badly translated from the French, by the torrent of commonplaces they utter, so that the author's first postulate is correct: his "artists" and himself among them ought to abandon art.

IV

Mikhail Kuzmin is the author of *The Comedy of Eudoxia of Heliopolis, or The Converted Courtesan* (published in "The Or Flowerbed," 1907, "Pannier the first").[20]

Kuzmin—at the present time—is a writer unique of his kind. There were none such in Russia before him, and I doubt whether there ever will be again; at least I cannot see him as the founder of a school, as journalists, their mouths agape with bewilderment, try to do. By this I do not mean to say that Kuzmin is a writer without any roots in the Russian past or that he is a blossom doomed to wilt. On the contrary, Kuzmin's creativity does have roots, maybe the deepest, most forked, crooked ones that burrow into the dense darkness of the Russian past. For me the name "Kuzmin" is always associated with the awakening of Russian Dissent, with the murky religious presentiments of fifteenth-century Russia, with memories of "trans-Volgan elders" who came from the dense swampy marshlands to squat, smoky huts.[21]

I believe deeply in the genealogy I have devised for Kuzmin. If it be so, then how can his writing fail to be associated with everything in eighteenth- and nineteenth-century Russian literature that gropingly drags itself along the dark trunk of sectarian despair? One of the branches of this living trunk is Kuzmin's writing; much about him leads us to forget his lineage and to think of Kuzmin as an exclusively adventitious phenomenon, imported from the West. But this is a ruse: it is merely the superficial aspect of his writing, the means he uses to lay on lavishly his favorite cosmopolitan hues and his themes, which are perfervid in a non-Slavic way.

The name "Kuzmin," presently surrounded by a certain reputation for gross, tame barbarity, is an enchanting name for us. It is associated with the "Alexandrian Songs," *recherché* little narratives which revived the adventure novel (*The Adventures of Aimé Leboeuf*) and, finally, the mystery play that lies before us. True, for us Kuzmin's name is also associated with a few passages in his novellas, *Wings* and *House of Cards*, passages in which the author paid tribute to gross barbarity and which were leaped upon with delight by the guardians of journalistic morality. But if our unhappy times are such that "middle-class morality" actually has to be protected in some cases, it would be entirely misleading to raise a hue and cry after Kuzmin, an *artist* to the marrow of his bones, most subtle in lyricism and most witty in dialectics in his art. The barbarity which even I cannot deny is present in Kuzmin, is utterly sublimated by the limpid and crystalline solvent of art.

The Comedy of Eudoxia resembles the genres "lyrical drama," "mystery play," "holy farce." It is made up of an indefinite number of individual scenes, written in playful prose and airy verse. The melodiousness of the mystery play rings like a silver chime in the cool evening air. It is the most perfect achievement in the realm of *lyri-*

cal drama in Russia, permeated with a kind of enchanted melancholy and suffused with the most subtle poisons of that irony which is so peculiar to Kuzmin's works.

The harlot Eudoxia—the "rose of Heliopolis"—in a moment of inner melancholy, which cannot be fended off by the magic salves, scents and simples and the adoration of all Heliopolis, hears the voice of a monk uttering words from the Gospel, "and took the heavenly light unto herself"; after giving away her valuables, she dedicates herself to God and enters a holy cloister, whither the youth Philostrate, enamoured of her, finds his way. His entreaties that she return to the city that adores her are unavailing, and Eudoxia compels Philostrate to take the tonsure, promising him that he will be able to see her across the stream that runs through the valley, from the walls of his monastery.

Throughout this uncomplicated fable from an ordinary "vita," Kuzmin has embroidered colorful patterns; he made a worthy townsman argue with his wife, illumined Eudoxia's garden with a bright evening, enumerated her gold-embroidered garments, draperies, caskets of precious myrrh, planted with flowers the monastery garden, where Eudoxia and the nuns gather posies. Aristocratic taste and artistic restraint reign throughout, and are especially palpable when one compares *The Comedy of Eudoxia* to the previous play *The History of the Cavalier D'Alessio, A Dramatic Poem in Eleven Tableaux* ("Green Miscellany," 1905). This latter play shows a complete absence of harmony among the individual episodes, despite a wealth of precious details. The worldly melancholy predominant in *Eudoxia* corresponds to the somewhat dark, at times profane weight of earth in *The History*, where Scheherazade's spirit fails to redeem the operettacality of the Elders of the Thebaid and the far too easy victories of the frivolous cavalier over the lady nun, lady courtesan and lady sultana, whose "heavy black eye peers from beneath the coverlet." But the courtesan's lovely song does give promise of those songs sung to us by the most recent Kuzmin, as the lively, laughter-provoking dialogue of the townsmen does of the light, pointed, brief scenes in *Eudoxia*.

Current criticism tends to regard Kuzmin as a *proselytizer* and to consider him the propagator of certain dangerous ideas. I once heard the opinion expressed that, in our times, *Wings* corresponds to Chernyshevsky's novel *What Is to Be Done?*[22] I do not believe that such an opinion, not devoid of wit, though very tendentious, will withstand the slightest criticism. Anyway, the far too frequent charge against the writer nowadays for something he never dreamt of smashes in this case against Kuzmin's crystalline humor. This humor puts an impassable gulf between Kuzmin's work and the tendencies he is accused of; it sets him in the realm of pure lyricism unassailable by the poorly aimed shafts of ostensibly humane criticism.

When Eudoxia asks a priest whether she may seal a letter about the donation of her property with a bejeweled ring on which "a flaming heart and two billing turtledoves" are depicted, the priest replies, "They may be interpreted as Christian symbols too. I think Master Theodotus would not be offended by the charming emblems." While Eudoxia tells Philostrate, "I forgave you before you came here. You will see me: you will be tonsured by Abbot Germanius, who undertakes your instruction. Only the valley stream will separate us; the walls of our convent are visible from your walls; we will behold the same clouds, feel the same rain, and when the same evening star rises, I will pray for you, and you will think of me"—we would like to see Philostrate, genuflecting in an affected posture in the tight-fitting garb of Beardsley's Fanfreluche,[23] teetering on red heels. And when the Angel, the invariable accompaniment of the climactic event in a "holy farce," speaks his beautiful words—Lord knows whether they are comic or mournful—that "all things are led salvationwards by Heaven in different ways," and talks about the "easy yoke" of faith, Eudoxia's taking the veil and Philostrate's amorousness, and the unknown, unknowable end and submission—behind those speeches we hear tinkling, crystalline, inoffensive laughter. Are we to take offense at this inoffensive laughter, this mercurial lyricism and the elegant gallicisms of an author who permits us, in calm repose and admiration, to swim along "the bright surface of the watery deeps" amid flowery banks, reminiscent of the artificial estates where Edgar Poe's monstrous fancy went to take its rest? Kuzmin is utterly integral. We are free to accept or reject him, but to demand bread of him is the same as to demand gracefulness from Gorky. Other writers will hurl us, dissatisfied and cursing, into the very depths of ideas, contradictions, life, confusion, and chief among them in our time is Leonid Andreev.[24]

V

Even though a fair amount of time has gone by since the first appearance of *The Life of Man*, up to now it has not been easy to write about it. Aside from the fact that it is unusually innovative in itself, it is, in addition, even more innovative for Andreev himself, and sharply differentiated from the rest of his pieces. The work, merely called "A Presentation in Five Tableaux and a Prologue," contains traces of a powerful dramatic technique which Andreev's coevals never dreamt of and which, in that respect, immeasurably excels not only *To the Stars*, where the shade of Ibsen is too faint, but also *Savva*, a work of Gorkian pathos. On the other hand, *The Life of Man* seems to have been written by an inexperienced, even a tyro, author, so imperfect is its technique, and so primitive the sense of a writer who appears to be opening his eyes to the world for the first time.

But wisdom is concealed behind the primitiveness. This is obviously not the first time these eyes have opened to gaze upon the world, for there is nothing horrible, strident, perplexed or childishly drooling about this gaze. The author's persona, hidden behind the drama, recalls the persona of Man, the drama's hero; neither Man nor the author utters the lacerating cry that, up to now, invariably composed the pathos of almost every work of Andreev, or the perplexed "Good grief, what is this all about?" Both in Man and in the author there is a wholesome and steadfast resolve to fight on to the close, "to let the swords clash," "to let the shields clang," "to cast a white-hot volley of blazing thoughts at a brow of stone, devoid of reason." Only in the fifth and last scene do both Man and the writer undergo a change. Written stridently, hysterically, messily, this scene is unlike the others. It is powerful, like everything Andreev writes, but it contains a certain *covert lie*, the same lie that always compelled us to anticipate each new work by this writer in agony and secretly to fear for him. I don't know how to define the essence of this lie, nor do I think it can be defined as "pessimism" or "anticivilization"—the two weightiest accusations leveled at Andreev these days. These two accusations, which suggest to me the cloying and repugnant odors of a particular brand of partisan feeling, lead me to love everything that Andreev has written all the more deeply, and to fear all the more deeply for his covert lie as it remotely and sporadically beckons to me. Wherefore and wherefrom does it proceed? Is it not because there is *a limit set to cries of suffering, despair, rage and grief*, though there is no limit set to suffering itself? And does not Andreev surpass this limit in some of his works (*Red Laughter*, for instance) as well as in the fifth scene of *The Life of Man*? It is one unbroken cry. Cannot a cry be broken and fade away when the voice itself grows weak? The heart falls silent not in submission, not in weakness, but often because suffering has already filled its cup to the brim, and a rending cry only *insults* this suffering, deadens and profanes it.

Can it be that Andreev emits these cries in fear of submission and weakness and only by some miracle has hitherto failed to insult majestic suffering? Or perhaps he has already insulted it? The future will reveal how accurate my suspicions are; may Andreev pardon me for them—they come from the heart.

The first four scenes of *The Life of Man* present a great harmony between the internal and the external. Observe how technically perfect they are: Man does not appear at all in the first scene and crosses the stage in silence in the third; he actually does something only in the second and fourth scenes. And yet the spectators' full attention is focused on him, and all the other countless characters, as countless as the characters in life itself, and vivid in themselves, are infinitely inferior in vividness to him. Great skill is required to achieve this indispensable condition of wholeness and proportion between the parts in drama, if only because the hero is not apportioned any supernatural attributes. His outer and inner forms are limned in the same description: "a proud handsome head, with flashing eyes, a lofty brow and black eyebrows, which arch away from the bridge of his nose like two audacious wings. Wavy black hair, loosely flung back; a low, white, soft collar reveals a well-proportioned neck and part of his chest. In his movements Man is supple and brisk, like a young animal; but he adopts poses peculiar only to men: energetically proud and free." And not a single specific detail: not mind or heart or willpower predominates, all are allotted to Man in equal degree, and with all his attributes he wrestles alone with his "faithful companion"—"Someone in Gray."

Man's wife is much the same—"very beautiful, graceful, delicate." This is the wife of middle-class Man in the best and fatal meaning of that concept: probably, as I picture her, a housewife with large simple gray eyes and an enormous, tightly plaited braid. The braid comes undone—and it falls to her skirt; when plaited it conceals part of her neck with a large knot of tiny golden tresses. The wife is Man's faithful mate, his inspiration, his mistress, his dear and quiet companion—a greater defense of Man against the gray companion than are his mind, heart and will.

The rest of the characters are written in an entirely different style. The old women are meaninglessly horrible, foul Celestinas and Lepestinas.[25] The relatives are caricatures. The guests of both sexes at "Man's Ball" are wooden, the musicians look like their instruments. The Nanny is literally an extension of that cobweb-covered chair in which she sits. And lumped all together they compose a sort of quiet nightmare, a sullen oblivion of life, flowing like

heavy metal, hemmed in by steep banks. All these people are like
the occasional utensils of life, contemptible junk, floating down the
metal river; they are not so much people as fading shadows or dolls
come to life by chance. This is why none of them is allowed to commune with the suffering permitted the hero Man. Yes, the only *non*-
cardboard hero of recent drama is a man whose average humanity is
emphasized with the same obstinacy with which Chernyshevsky
emphasized the ordinariness of Lopukhov, Kirsanov and Vera Pavlovna.[26] He is the most realistic of real people, without any admix-
ture of the bizarre or fantastic, and entirely capable, like Lopukhov-
Beaumont, of writing in favor of the abolition of slavery in the
American *Tribune* and becoming "a citizen of Massachusetts." Instead of writing for the *Tribune*, Andreev's Man builds a house, for
he is an architect by profession; the only thing that distinguishes
him from Lopukhov is that he, who knows how and "what is to
be done" in life, also knows that standing ever beside him, on the
borderline of life, is that ghastly stone-gray being, and that a can-
dle-flame is burning before his tightly compressed lips and square
chin. And *a second time* the question arises—and this time without
Lopukhov's love of life and rose-colored unselfconsciousness—the
question "what is to be done."

The question, posed as children might pose it: *cruelly*; with age
questions mellow, and the grown-up audience in the theater, whose
faces I gazed into more than once during a performance of *The Life
of Man*, is perplexed: just what is there to get upset about? And
what's this play about? And why is everything so mysterious? And
why do we need to be consoled? "Poppycock, an imitation of Maeterlinck." But the questions are beside the point: *there is no Maeterlinck in The Life of Man*, there is only a semblance of Maeterlinck,
or, in other words, Andreev has probably read Maeterlinck—and
that's all. But Maeterlinck never achieved such cruelty, such coarse-
ness, crudeness and naiveté in posing questions. I love *The Life of
Man* for that very crudeness and naiveté and I think that it will be a
long while before another play as important and vital comes along.

While on the subject of *The Life of Man*, we must not neglect its
Petersburg production. It is, without any question, Meyerhold's[27]
best production. The concepts of author and director have merged.
The Life of Man is truly a work for the stage, written with a certain
"knack" for the stage. I think a great deal is lost in merely reading it.
On the other hand, a few lines were changed in the production and,
to my mind, for the better. At least Andreev's stage directions about
the ballroom (third scene) are dubious in a *theatrical* context: that

"irregularity in the correlation of parts" is too literary—doors disproportionately small in relation to windows, and the "unnerving impression" they produce: no audience will be unnerved by any such disproportion. Meyerhold did far better to set up a squat grayish-white colonnade in a semicircle and to seat staggeringly idiotic ladies and decrepit old men at the base of each column.

I had the opportunity to see *The Life of Man* from the stage. I never shall forget the stupendous effect made by the first scene. It was played "in cloth"—the entire enormous expanse of stage was covered with cloth to its full depth and width. At the back stood a small divan for the old women and a screen, downstage a round table and chairs set round it. And nothing else. The stage was lit only by a lamp and a narrow circular patch of light from above. By standing at the back of the stage, almost next to the characters, one could see the entire theater and be completely hidden from it. And *The Life of Man* unfolded there, beside me, for nearby I saw the dim shadows of old women creeping in and out, heard the piercing cry of the mother in her birth pangs, observed the silhouettes of relatives bustling about, barely made out the apron of the doctor, smoking a cigarette and nervously running on a diagonal, and almost felt the cold emanating from the motionless back of "Someone in Gray" who, standing in a narrow shaft of suffused light, cast into the circumambient gloom the never-to-be-forgotten words: "Look and listen, ye who have come hither for mirth and amusement. Man's whole life will pass before you now, with its dark beginning and dark ending. Hitherto nonexistent, mysteriously buried in the infinitude of time, undreamt of, unintuited, unknown to anyone . . ."

And later, ". . . an icy wind from infinite space impotently whirls and soughs; a flickering flame on a candle blazes brightly and clearly. But the wax melts, consumed by the fire.—The wax melts . . ."

". . . *And ye, who had come hither for mirth and amusement, ye, doomed to death*, look and listen: here with a *distant and phantasmal echo* the fleeting life of Man will pass before you with its sorrows and its joys."

Then the shaft of suffused light was extinguished, and "those doomed to death" adjusted their opera glasses and saw how the lamp in the corner flared up and the muttering old women crept in and out. These opera glasses, lit from the stage, were like ruby eyes. When Nina Zarechnaya in *The Seagull* recites her soliloquy,[28] which is somewhat similar to the soliloquy of "Someone in Gray," beside a lake that stretches out behind her delicate profile, the same eyes glare in just the same way—the vacant eyes of eternity. And Treplyov calls out, "Mama! Mama!" Just so does the audience want to cry out and stamp its feet in the intermission.

This theater, hushed throughout the act, as keyed-up as a ship in perilous straits, with the whispering prompter, the measured tread of the characters, the stage manager's bells, the motionless levers jutting out in the control room, the stagehands quietly chatting and seeming to float as they chat; those glowing red eyes of the opera glasses in the auditorium and the hoarsely perplexed intermissions; an Armenian, overgrown with blue stubble, cynically cackling at an unattractive girl graduate; that everlasting gloom on stage and the gossamer light, creeping down from the ceiling. Blocks of wood instead of people in the auditorium, and people portraying blocks of wood on stage; Man, seeking, like Siegmund, with sword and buckler, cursing in sobs and whispering in anger and reproach which rend the heart: "You have insulted a woman. You have killed a child." Afterwards—those gray days, all solitary, encounters with "discriminating" people, with those who didn't understand, *worse*—didn't want to understand all the horror, all the grinding rage, all the sincerity of the curse. Days of secret grief, astringent despair. So it was with me and, I hope, many "witnesses" of *The Life of Man*. And then—the light, flooding in, in streams; the firm assurance that *Man was victorious*, that he is *right* who challenges implacable, four square, accursed Fate to do battle.

For a long time no "work of literature" has caused such acute reactions as has *The Life of Man*. Yes, it is full of darkness and despair. But light emerges from the darkness.

> Light out of darkness. On the black clod
> The visages of Thy Roses
> Could not arise
> If in earth's murky bosom
> Their dark sunken root
> Did not imbibe.

Now let them tell me that I am not being critical, that I am uttering a lyrical "digression." I am well aware of that. I am in no condition to criticize, although—the old women's conversation may be too drawn-out, the second act may be "naive," the dialogue of the guests at the ball may be monotonous. But the *light* is overwhelmingly dazzling, and the source of this light lurks in *The Life of Man*. Let those who wish to satisfy themselves with documentary evidence that Andreev does not want to put down life and "plunge into the gloom of nonbeing" read the following statement from his articles (James

Lynch, "Under the Influence of the Art Theater"):[29] "If Man weeps, sickens or kills himself, this in no way means that he does not want to live or does not love life." Or again: "To refute all of life is to seem its unintentional apologist. I never believe so much in life as when I read the 'father' of pessimism, Schopenhauer: the man could think such things—and go on living! It must mean that life is potent and invincible . . . Neither truth nor falsehood wins out; the winner is what finds itself joined with life itself; that which invigorates its roots and justifies it. Only that which is useful to life survives, everything harmful to it perishes sooner or later . . . If today it stands as an indestructible wall and the heads of the most noble persons smash against it in fruitless struggle,—tomorrow it will fall! It will fall, for it thought it could keep back life itself."*

However, these words convince me far less than do Andreev's darkest and, it may appear, most futile works. And *The Life of Man* stands pre-eminent among them, clear proof that Man is a man, not a puppet, not a pitiful creature doomed to decay, but a miraculous phoenix, surmounting "the icy wind from infinite space." The wax melts, but life does not wane.

August–September 1907

*Not having the articles at hand, I quote from V. F. Botsyanovsky's[30] pamphlet on Andreev.

The Theater of a Single Will

by Fyodor Sologub

"On the vessel is a seal, and on the seal a name; what is hidden within the vessel is known to him who set the seal, and to the initiate."—E. C. Wiesener, *The Silence of the First Bride*, a novel[1]

"You philosophize like a poet."—Dostoevsky, *Letters*

Of all that human genius has ever created, perhaps the creation superficially most accessible and most terrible in the profundity it can achieve is the theater. A fateful sequence runs from play to spectacle to sacrament . . . Light comedy and raucous farce no less than high tragedy.

With equally irresistible force both tragic horror and farcical laughter flutter before our eyes the threadbare but still alluring veils of our world, which seems so familiar, and then suddenly, by means of volatile playacting, so unwonted, uncanny, startling or disgusting. The tragic mask or the comic fail equally to deceive the alert spectator, just as they have failed to deceive the participant in the playacting at the same time they fascinated him; nor will they deceive the participant in a mystery cult at the same time that they initiate him into the arcana.

This essay first appeared in the collection *Theater: A Book on the New Theater* (St. Petersburg, 1908), from which this translation is made.

A key wordplay in Sologub's essay is that on *igra* (play, game, acting on stage, gaming) and *igrat'* (to play, to gamble, to act on stage), for he begins by using the word to mean "child's play" and then develops it into "playing on the stage." To indicate this ambiguity when it occurs I have used "playacting," which may be too specific but conveys the double sense. Another linguistic problem lies in the pronouns used to characterize the Theater of a Single Will: *Moy, Moego, Menya* (my, mine, of me) are regularly capitalized when Sologub distinguishes this special aspect. But better to preserve the abstract, impersonal sense, I have had recourse to the ungrammatical "of I, to I" in most cases, since it is the Ego and not the bump of acquisitiveness to which he refers.

Behind the rotting false-faces and the rouged grimace of the fair-ground mountebank and behind the pallid mask of the tragic actor a single Visage may be descried. Ghastly, beckoning irresistibly . . .

The fateful sequence. We playacted when we were children, and now we have lost our enthusiasm for frivolous play and come, out of curiosity, to see a show—and the hour is drawing nigh when, soul and body transfigured, we shall arrive at true unity in the liturgical enactment, the mysterious ritual . . .

When we were children, when we were alive—

alive are the children and only the children,
we are dead and long have been—

we playacted. We cast ourselves in roles and played them out—until we were summoned to bed. Theater for us was partly based on every-day life—we were very imitative and observant—partly symbolic with an undeniable penchant for decadence—we so loved fairy tales and the words of strange old incantations and the whole absurd and unnecessary (pragmatically unnecessary) ritual of game-playing. So charming were the conventions, naiveté and absurdity in game-play-ing. We knew perfectly well that it was not for real, that it was in fun. We were not demanding, either of the set designer or the prop-man. We would harness up a chair and agree: "Let this be a horse." Or if we ourselves felt much like running around, we would say: "I'll be the horse."

We were not exclusive or singleminded about the nature of our playacting. There was playacting for a large audience with many people, noise and rowdiness, in hallways and reception rooms, in garden and field—"it's a fight but it isn't really, it's a game but it isn't really"—and there was intimate playacting, in cosy, secluded corners, where grownups and strangers did not intrude. In the one situation it was exhaustingly jolly, in the other scary but jolly too, and our cheeks flushed more crimson than with boisterous running, and dim fires kindled in our eyes.

We playacted—unaware that our playacting was only hand-me-down garments from the life of grownups. We were replaying as new what had been played even before we came on the scene. And in this replaying of other people's games we became infected with the deadly poison of the threadbare.

Nevertheless, the meaning of playacting was not restricted to its content. The drops of corrosive poison dissolved in the vernal nectar of young life. The exuberance of new life got tipsy on light, sweet potations, our feet were fledged with rapid flight—and the

oppressive burdens of oppressive earthly time were consumed in
the rapture of a glowing unselfconsciousness. The keen, quick moments were consumed, and from their ashes a new world was erected—our world. A world ablaze with youthful ecstasy . . .

Yet even then did we want nothing else from playacting, which
by that time had become little more than spectacle in our eyes,
nothing else from tragedy and comedy? We are such enthusiastic
theatergoers—especially to first nights of famous plays—but what
do we want from the theater? Do we want to learn the art of living or
be purged of sinister emotions? Do we want to resolve a moral, social, aesthetic or any other problem? Do we want to see "a stick,
blown about by the wind? Or a man clad in loose garments? Or a
prophet?"

Of course, all that and much more besides can be brought into
the theater, and not without reason, not without point—for it all
must be consumed in the true theater as old rags are consumed in
a bonfire. And no matter how various the extrinsic subjects of a
drama, what we always desire from it—if we have remained even
the slightest bit alive since the carefree days of our childhood—is
the same thing we once desired from our childish playacting—
ardent rapture that can ravish the soul from the heavy shackles of
boring, bare-bones life. Enchantment and ecstasy are what lure each
of us to the theater, the means by which the genius of tragedy en-
tices us to take part in its mysterious design. But just what is it that
constitutes that design?

Either I am totally ignorant of what drama means to man, or else
its meaning is only to bring man to I. To transport him from the domain of featherbrained Aisa, the world of strange and ludicrous for-
tuities, the realm of comedy, to the domain of austere and consoling
Ananke,[2] the world of necessity and free will, the realm of high tragedy. To do away with the allurements of life, and to crown her who
eternally comforts, does not lie and does not deceive.

A theatrical spectacle, which people attend in search of amusement or distraction, will shortly cease to be merely a spectacle in
our eyes. Ere long the spectator, wearied by the alternation of spectacles alien to him, wants to become the participant in a mysterium,
as he once was the participant in playacting. Expelled from Eden, he
will ere long knock boldly at the door behind which the bridegroom
feasts with the wise virgins. He participated in innocent playacting
when he was still alive, when he still dwelt in paradise, in the beautiful garden of I between two great rivers. But now the sole means of

his resurrection is to participate in a mysterium, a liturgical ritual in which he can join his hand to that of his brother and sister and press his lips, eternally parched with thirst, to the mysteriously filled chalice in which *I* "shall mingle water and blood." To consummate in a bright public temple what is now consummated only in the catacombs.

But the theatrical spectacle is a necessary transitional state, and in our time, regrettably, the theater is capable of being only a spectacle, and often an empty spectacle. Nothing but spectacle, except in the intimate theater which is yet to be created but to talk of which—well, how are we to talk about it? After all, it may prove tantalizing to the uninitiate . . . Perhaps only in hints and images.

The contemporary theater in fact wants to be spectacle above all else. Everything in it is intended only for spectacle. Spectacle is the reason for professional actors, footlights and curtains, cunningly painted scenery which tries to supply an illusion of reality, the clever contrivances of the realistic theater and the ingenious devices of the conventionalized theater.

However, if a trail has now been blazed in our consciousness, the trail the development of theater must travel if the theater is to fulfill its great mission, then the task of the worker in the theater— be he dramatist, director or actor—consists in elevating the theatrical spectacle to a level of achievement only spectacle can attain, so that it can approximate the ecclesiastical enactment, mysterium and liturgy.

I think the first obstacle to be overcome on this trail is the performing actor. The performing actor draws too much of the spectator's attention to himself, and obfuscates both drama and author. The more talented the actor, the more insufferable his tyranny over the author and the more baneful his tyranny over the play. To depose this attractive but nonetheless baneful tyranny, two possible remedies exist: either transfer the central focus of the theatrical presentation to the spectator in the pit or transfer it to the author backstage.

The first idea, conceivably the result of acknowledging the theater as an arena for ecclesiastic enactments, also seems to imply that the footlights must be eliminated, the curtain perhaps removed and the spectator made a participant or even a creator of the performance. To replace one-dimensional scenery, leave four decorated walls or the open space of a town square, a street, a field. Turn the spectacle into a masquerade, which is an amalgam of playacting and spectacle. But then, what is the reason for this concoction? To make sure that "the people get extreme unction," as one modern ditty puts it? Not a bad occupation, of course, but where will it lead?

True, mysterious elements do mingle with playacting and spectacle in a masquerade. It contains allusions and secrets. But it is still no sacrament. Just as the uncanny fears occur at midday, when the evil Dragon tells fortunes hidden in his lair behind violet screens, so the very deepest secret emerges only when the disguises are dropped.

All meridians converge at one pole (or two, if you insist—but according to the law of the sameness of polar opposites, it is always sufficient to refer to but one pole), all earthly roads invariably lead to the same eternal Rome—"only I is all and in all things, and there is no Other, and never was and never will be"—every union of persons has meaning only insofar as it brings man to I, from futilely alluring disunity to genuine unity. The pathos ["inspired enthusiasm"—*tr.*] of a mysterium is nourished by a random myriad of beings mysteriously transformed into a necessary unity. It reminds us that each individual existence on earth acts only as a medium for I—a medium for exhausting in the infinity of *ad hoc* experiences the innumerable multitude of I's—and only I's—possibilities, an aggregate which makes laws but is itself activated by freedom.

And therefore, in tragedy only one person acts and wills, because he amplifies the unity of action, place and time, as well as the unity of willed aspiration in the drama.

(Perhaps the transitions in thought here may seem rather abrupt—but I am not arguing rationally [not that I am incapable of doing so], but simply propounding my one idea. "I philosophize like a poet.")

He who acts and wills in tragedy must always be but one, not in the sense that he leads the choric action, but in the sense that he appears as the exponent of the inevitable, not as the tragic hero but as his fate.

The modern theater presents a sorry spectacle of fragmented will and therefore disunited action. "There are all sorts of people," thinks the simpleminded dramatist, "each man in nature / Has his own form and feature." He goes to different places, takes notes on the ambience, life style and manners, observes different persons and depicts it all very faithfully. Kosmodemyansky and Nalimov, and Vaksel too, recognize themselves and their cravats, and are delighted if the author—for friendship's sake—has flattered them, or get angry if the author has suggested that he does not like their looks and behavior. The director rejoices that he has plenty of raw material for the staging and lots of business. The actor rejoices, too, because he can devise a nice, interesting makeup and imitate the outward appearance of *H* the painter, *U* the poet, *A* the engineer, *V* the lawyer . . . The audience is ecstatic—it recognizes those it knows and those it doesn't, and feels itself at a distinct advantage; no matter how endemic the peccadillos put on stage, still every spectator, including the small number of those on display, sees clearly that not he, but someone else, is being portrayed.

Yet none of this is necessary. None of the everyday life and none of the mores; the only thing that has to be performed is the eternal mystery. None of the story-lines and intrigues, nor all the plots long since plotted, nor the denouements long since predicted; the only thing that has to be consummated is the eternal liturgy. What of all the words and dialogue?—one eternal dialogue is held, and the questioner himself both answers and hungers for a reply. And what are to be the themes?—only Love, only Death.

No assortment of people—there is only one man, only one I in the whole universe, willing, acting, suffering, burning in the inextinguishable fire and fleeing from the frenzy of a ghastly and hideous life to the cooling and consoling embraces of the eternal comforter—Death.

Many are the disguises I don depending on the will of I, but always and in everything remain myself—just as a certain Shalyapin[3] is ever the same in all his roles. Behind the ghastly mask of the tragic hero and the ridiculous clown-face of the buffoon derided in a comedy and in the motley, floppy coat of polychrome tatters that bedecks the body of the show-booth clown making a spectacle of himself to tickle the groundlings—behind all these concealments the spectator must discover I. The theatrical spectacle is presented to him as a problem with one unknown factor.

If the spectator has come to the theater as the simpleminded gaper steps outside to "see the sun," I, the poet, create a drama in order to recreate the world in accord with the new concept of I. Just as the unique will of I reigns supreme in the macrocosm, so in the little circle of the theater spectacle only one unique will should reign supreme—the will of the poet.

The drama is the product of a single concept just as the universe is the product of a single creative idea. Fate in tragedy or chance in comedy turns out to be none other than the author. But is his will supreme in all things? It shall be as he desires it. He can, by his own free will, unite lovers or part them woefully, exalt a hero or cast him down into the somber abyss of despair and perdition. He can extol beauty, youth, truth, audacity, reckless daring, self-denial—but nothing prevents him from glorifying hideousness and debauchery, and setting the perfidious Judas above all the apostles.

> . . . To rebuke the days of iniquity
> Over the world shall I extol blasphemy
> And seduce by means of witchery.

But the actor is vainglorious. He obscured the author with his haphazard interpretation, the contingency and inappropriateness of psychological observations from life, and transformed the drama itself into an assortment of roles for various emplois. Then came the director and made off with the stage directions. So the fate of the dramatic enactment, the hollow tones of imperious Moira, is, at the behest of a theatrical manager, stowed away in a cramped prompter's box. And when the rehearsals have been sparse, everyone on stage stares at a fixed point from which a voice audible to the first rows of spectators issues and grates on them. And the words of the poet are ruthlessly garbled.

Do I really want my voice to issue from a narrow cellarage? Or, by a director's whim, have the on-stage window I envisaged turn into a column that means nothing to me? Or have my comments in the stage directions embodied only in the painted scenery?

No, my comments must sound loud and clear. The visitor to the theatrical spectacle must hear the poet before he hears the actor.

Here is how I envisage the theatrical spectacle: the author or the reader who stands in for him—or best of all, a reader, impassive and calm and unruffled by an author's shyness in the presence of spectators who may shout praise or blame at him (both equally unpleasant) and have perhaps brought their latchkeys for high-spirited whistling—a reader sits near the stage, somewhat to one side. Before him a table, on the table the play which is imminently to be presented. The reader begins at the beginning:

He reads the title of the drama. The author's name.

The epigraph, if there is one. Interesting and useful ones abound. For instance, the epigraph to *The Inspector*: "Don't blame the mirror if your mug is crooked. Folk proverb." The epigraph is coarse—as the author himself was—but accurate and suitable for establishing a necessary bond between spectator and stage action.

Next the cast list.

The author's preface or commentary if there is any.

Act 1. Setting. Names of the characters discovered on stage.

Entrances and exits of the actors, as they are designated in the play script.

All stage directions, not omitting even the slightest, be it but a single word.

And even as the reader reads beside the stage, the curtain parts, on stage the setting indicated by the author is revealed and lighted, the actors come on stage and do what the author's stage directions prompt them to, as they are read aloud, and speak what the play script sets down. If an actor forgets his lines—and when does he not forget them!—the readers read them, as calmly and as loudly as all the rest.

And the action will unfold before the spectator as it unfolds before us in life itself: we walk and talk according to what we think is our will; we do what we have to or what it occurs to us to do, and we try to actualize our seeming desires, to the extent that we are not prevented by the laws of nature and the desires of others. We see, hear, smell, touch, taste, use all our senses and all the faculties of our intelligence to learn what exists in the real world, what has its own being and its own laws, partially comprehensible to us and partially bewildering to us. We experience love for one and hatred for another, and are stirred by still other passions, and in accord with them we order our relations to the world and other people. And ordinarily we do not know that our will has no independent existence, that each of our movements and each of our statements is prompted and even predicted well in advance, once and for all, in the daemonic creative blueprint of universal playacting, so that we have neither freedom nor choice, not even the charming ad-libbing of an actor, because that too is included in the script of the universal mysterium by some unknown censor. And this world, which we come to know, is nothing more than a stage set, wonderful to look at but concealing the slovenliness and filth backstage. We playact as best we know how the role we are prompted with, simultaneously actors and spectators, alternately applauding or hissing one another, borne as the sacrifice and at the same time bearing the sacrifice.

Can the theater provide us with any spectacle other than that provided by a world too vast for our capacities and too narrow for our will? Should it? Play the way you live, transfer life to the stage—isn't that the very thing the realistic theater is after?

But then what is left of the actor's playing? Indeed, the actor is turned into a talking marionette—and this cannot please the actor, who loves showy roles and the attention the pit lavishes on him, and the howls of the simpleminded gallery and the newspaper chatter that surrounds his name. Such a theater would be unacceptable to a modern actor. He would say contemptuously:

You can't call this a theatrical performance, it's simply a literary reading, abetted by speech and movement. You might as well be honest about it and open a marionette theater, a children's amusement. Move the crudely daubed puppets about, have one man behind the scenes speak in seven voices—speak and jerk the strings.

Yet why shouldn't the actor resemble a marionette? It doesn't humiliate a man. Such is the unalterable law of universal playacting that man is like a wonderfully constructed marionette. And there is no way he can avoid this or even forget it.

When the hour ordained for every man comes, each of us, in full, will turn into an inert and unbreathing puppet, no longer capable of playing any kind of role . . .

There it lies on sackcloth for the final ablution, a puppet outworn and of no further use to anyone—its arms folded by others—and its legs outstretched by others—and its eyes closed by others—a poor marionette for only one tragic bit of playacting? Yonder, behind the scenes, an indifferent being pulled you by an invisible string, a cruel being tortured you with the fiery ordeal of passion, an evil being terrified you with the livid horrors of odious life, to an unrelenting being you directed your grief-stricken gaze in the anguish of your dying hours. And here, in the pit, someone was entertained by your clumsy movements—controlled by the yanking of the dreadful string—your addled words—so quietly whispered by the concealed prompter—and your idle tears, and your equally pitiful tears and laughter. Enough—somehow all the dialogue in your part gets spoken, all the stage directions are followed reasonably closely—the string is wound up—and vainly your desiccated lips try to utter a new word—they have parted and closed mechanically—and fallen silent for ever and aye. You will be hidden away, interred, forgotten . . .

Even the most brilliant actor is no more than a man. Even the most effective role is inferior to life, and easier. So, of course, it is far better for him to be a talking marionette and move to the dictates of a reader's distinct and impassive voice than to botch his role desperately while following the hoarse whisper of a prompter concealed in a box.

The one even and impassive voice of the "man in black" conducts the whole theatrical action, and everything on stage must cooperate with it and strive for the indispensable unity, lest it be diverted in any way from the uniquely essential feature of the theatrical spectacle—the revelation throughout the action, in manifold and multiform disguises, of the one unchanging visage of I.

He who consummates the action is never on stage alone. Even when the other actors are not visible on stage, he who remains before the spectator's eyes carries on a running dialogue with someone. A striving toward the one, the I, can result only from the polar opposite to I—the many, the non-I. But all streams must flow together into a single sea and not trickle away in the quicksands of individuated multiplicity. The unique Visage, hidden behind disguises, must be made lucid for the spectator over the course of the theatrical action. Hence the dramatic requirement of only one hero, one character who essentially consummates the action—only one point at which the spectator's attention is concentrated. All rays of stage action must coincide in a single focus, so that the bright flame of ecstasy can flare up all at once . . .

Other characters in the drama ought merely to be necessary steps leading up to the unique Visage. Their meaning in the drama depends entirely on the degree of their proximity to the unity of willed aspiration in the drama, revealed through the hero. The only rationale for their individual distinctions, their differing temperaments, which would otherwise be totally unnecessary to the drama, inheres in this, their arrangement along the descending steps of the one staircase of dramatic action. Desdemona is so relevant to a tragic situation, not because hers is a great and moving role, not because it was she whom Othello loved and slew, but because she was the fatal creature whose hand stripped away his disguise and disclosed to him the fatal mendacity and duplicity of the world.

Since in essence there must be no more than one actor in tragedy, it follows that the theater must be freed of the actor's playacting. Playacting, with the whole spectrum of accurately observed and precisely reproduced gestures and intonations, along with the whole theatrical tradition and whatever a talented actor's ingenuity or intuition can acquire through assiduous training or can invent anew, this playacting we know so well, whether inspired or carefully preplanned, presents a facsimile of the clashes and conflicts of wholly different persons, each of whom is self-sufficient. But there are no such autonomous personalities on this earth, and therefore there can be no conflicts between them; there is only the semblance of a conflict, a fatal dialectic within the characters. A conflict with fate is unthinkable—there is only daemonic playacting, fate's sporting with its marionettes.

The better the actor plays the role of Man, the more pathetically he exclaims: "Let us clash shields, let us clank swords"—the funnier is his inappropriate acting, the more obvious his misreading of the role. "Someone in Gray" has never yet accepted a challenge to a duel from anyone whatsoever.[4] A little girl does not fight with her dolls—she tears them and breaks them, and does the laughing or crying herself, depending on her mood.

An actor's wholehearted playacting already strikes us as ludicrous, and magniloquent declamation, grandiose gesture and inordinate scrupulosity in reproducing the particulars of everyday life—all these blandishments are even starting to get on our nerves a bit. Just as someone in high society gets on our nerves when he suddenly starts talking loudly and feverishly and gesticulating. It is not worth the trouble to playact wholeheartedly. Only the gallery roars with laughter and weeps at what happens on stage—the pit blandly smiles, sometimes ruefully, sometimes almost gaily, always ironically. It is not worth playacting for its sake.

Tragedy strips the enchanting disguise from the world, and there where we had marveled at harmony, pre-established or in the making, it reveals to us the world's eternal contradiction, the eternal similarity of good and evil and of different polar opposites. It confirms all sorts of contradictions; to every one of life's pretensions, true or not, it utters in like manner an ironic *Yes!* Tragedy says a lyric *No!* to neither good nor evil. Tragedy is always ironical and never lyrical. That is how it must be staged.

And so there is to be no playacting on stage. Only an even transmission of one word after another. A calm reproduction of situation, one tableau following another. And the fewer of these tableaux there are and the more slowly they change, the more clearly the tragic concept will emerge for the enthralled spectator. Do not let the tragic actor emote and show off—overdone gesture and bombastic declamation must remain the portion of the buffoon and mountebank. The actor ought to be cool and collected, every one of his words ought to ring out evenly and resonantly, every one of his movements ought to be slow and graceful. The performance of a tragedy ought not to remind us of the flashing images in the cinema. Relieved of this irrelevant and annoying flashing, an attentive spectator should travel the very long road to an understanding of tragedy.

At the furthest point from the spectator stands the tragic hero, leading exponent of the will of I—longest of all is the path to understanding him. The spectator must ascend to him along a steep staircase, and overcome and conquer much that lies both within and without himself. But the further one is from the hero, the nearer one is to the spectator and the more comprehensible to him, and at last the characters of the drama become so close to the spectator that they more or less merge with him entirely. They come to resemble the chorus in ancient tragedy, stating what anyone seated on the tiers of the amphitheater might say.

Behold, the pacific and smug bourgeois has come to the theater. How will he figure out the drama's plot and denouement and what sense will he make of it, if all the speeches that echo from the stage are alien to his understanding? Just as Shakespeare's tragedies could not do without the fool, so modern drama cannot do without those hackneyed mannequins whose faces are blurred, the mechanism slightly defective and creaky and the words tarnished and trite. And if the bourgeois himself winces at their unbearable banality, that's good. We can read it as a reassuring sign that even he is coming to an understanding of the unique Visage concealed behind all the disguises, wounded but not slain by the banality of mundane commonplaces. This veritably justifies light comedy, farce and even show-booth highjinks. Even pornography. There is another meaning in this—because to date this is the sole medium for a public theater, accessible to all (I am not referring to chamber theater, which we hold most dear and most desire, but which is difficult to discuss)—the sole medium for uniting the spectator with the action. The sole and perhaps, in many cases, sufficient medium.

Even the mysterium itself, being an enactment that is ecumenical in a high degree, still requires one performer, both sacrificator and sacrifice, for the sacrament of self-immolation. Not only the mysterium, the highest sort of public activity, but all public celebrations are wholly individualized as well. Every common cause is executed according to the idea and plan of one man—every Parliament heeds its Speaker and does not kick up an ecumenical rumpus, ecumenicizing in a jolly ecumenic uproar. "On the vessel is a seal, and on the seal a name; what is hidden within the vessel is known to him who set the seal and to the initiate." The temple is open to every man, but the builder's name is engraved in stone. One who approaches the altar must leave his iniquity outside the threshold. And so the mob—the spectators—can be united to tragedy only by burning away their outworn platitudes within themselves. But passively. He who consummates the action is always one.

What interest can the stage take in being swamped by a multiplicity of characters, each one laying claim to his own personality and his own particular role in the drama? Their flashing-by annoys anyone who understands drama, for it is both difficult and pointless

to keep them in mind. That is why even reading plays is difficult—
one has constantly to turn back to the cast list. Consequently plays
are out of favor in the book market.

For what do I care who is hustling and bustling about on stage,
Shuisky or Vorotynsky, so long as I know that a tragedy of impos-
ture, so brilliantly conceived by the genius of Russian history (and
still so pallidly sketched by the geniuses of Russian literature) is
about to unfold before me![5] One man speaks and then another—
aren't those thy words, simpleminded spectator? Aren't those thy
tarnished silver coins, long since rubbed thin and yet dear to thee,
rolling about on the stage floor beside the goldpieces of poetry?

The money-changing is ingenuous—but canny and accurate.
Greedily snapping up his silver coins, the theatergoer will also
pocket the weighty gold of I, and in exchange sell to I his soul,
lightweight but charming to I all the same. Even so, I wish there
were less small change littering the stage floor—a wish directed at
dramatists.

One man wills in drama—the author. One performs the action—the actor. The spectator should also be one. In this respect the
mad king was right, who listened alone in his magnificent theater as
his actors performed, hidden behind the heavy brocades in the stillness and darkness of the royal box.[6] In the tragic theater every spectator ought to feel that he is that mad king, hiding away from everyone. And no one ought to see his face, and no wonder that

in mystery he veiled
the play of his passions,
at times gay at the graveside
and gloomy at the feast.

And if he dozes off and even falls sound asleep—art is a golden
dream—and why shouldn't drama be a rhythmic dreaming?—no
one will laugh at him, and no one will be upset or shocked by his
startling snores in the most pathetic passages.

And he himself must neither see nor hear anyone—not those
whose faces naively reflect their every emotion, mood, chagrin and
sympathy, nor those who pretend to be understanding and intelligent. Nor must he see the handkerchief dabbing at the bloodshot
eyes, nor the glove nervously wadded in restless hands. Nor hear
those who blow their noses and sob, nor those who laugh when it's
time for laughter and also when it's time to cry. In stillness, in darkness, in solitude, the spectator of a tragic spectacle must dwell. Like
the prompter in his cramped box. Like the theater mouse.

The spectator who is undistracted by things extraneous to the stage must not be then distracted by anything on stage that fails to constitute a strictly necessary feature of the drama. Whether the stage is set with gorgeously painted scenery or with draperies that only swag and droop over it, it must be one-dimensional. The spectacle must be like a picture, so that the spectator need not gaze beyond the actor into the depths of a multidimensional stage, that sphere where something casually concealed may turn up just at the moment when it is most pertinent to find what is revealed in the acting, willing and contemplating being.

Scenery is pleasant enough on stage—it instantly supplies a proper mood, gives the spectator all the extrinsic hints—and why not use it? Especially if the wide world outside is much the same:

And suddenly all looked to me
As if it were flat scenery;—
Like a strip of paper the dawn stretched far,
Like a tawdry sequin shone the star.

But someone lost in a world of outward scenery comes to the theater to find himself—to arrive at I. And his sight must not be overly distracted by a sumptuous profusion of stage settings. Therefore, it is also best that all dramas be played in a single setting. At any rate, at each specific moment the spectator must know what he should be looking at, what he must see and hear on stage. He will be assisted in this by the author's stage directions, loudly uttered by the reader, and of course by the whole technique of mechanical contrivances. Everything that the spectator sees on stage must be significant, each detail in the production should be rigorously deliberated, so that nothing superfluous confronts the spectator, nothing beyond the most indispensable.

In line with this, perhaps, the lighting design is both pertinent and wholly functional: the spectator should perhaps be shown only what he is meant to see at any given moment, with all the rest submerged in darkness—just as in our consciousness, everything impending that does not immediately catch our attention falls outside the threshold of consciousness. It simultaneously exists and seems not to. Because the only thing that exists for me is what is in I and for I, all the rest, despite its potential reality for someone else, resides only in the world of possibilities and waits its turn to be.

Such is the outline of the theatrical spectacle I project. And the content, given shape by this outline, will be the tragic playacting of Fate with its marionettes, the spectacle of the fateful melting away of all mundane disguises, the mystery of perfect self-assertion. When I playact, I play with dolls and disguises, and the disguises and veils drop off for all the world to see, and mysteriously the unique image of I is revealed, and the unique will of I triumphs, exulting. My fatal error ties all the knots, and I thrash about in the constricting shackles of mundane and ineluctable contradictions—and the fatal knots are cut through by a sharp stiletto that pierces the heart of I. By merry playacting *I* has sublimated the world—and I is the sacrifice and the sacrificator. Ardent love comforts and, in consuming, is consumed, and the ultimate comforter is Death.

Of course, the theater is gravitating toward tragedy. And is bound to become tragic.

In our era every farce turns into tragedy, our laughter rings in a sensitive ear more hideously than does our weeping, and hysterics precede our ecstasy. In days of yore the merry and sane laughed. The winners laughed. The losers wept. In our world the sorrowful and insane laugh. Gogol laughs . . . The insanity of I has twinkling eyes.

To put it plainly, our comedy is simply an absurd and amusing tragedy. But even tragedy strikes us as funny.

The sorrows of young Werther?[7] No—the sorrows of a hypersensitive high-school student. It is very funny, but most serious as well. He should have been thrashed with birch-rods—but he shot himself instead. Little girls cluster round the grave dug for him, and drop roses on his coffin—the parents weep and blow their noses. They meant to thrash him, but didn't get around to it. It isn't their fault.

Quavering laughter floats about us like music. It may be rhythmical. It wants to dance. Is it only Death who dances on fresh graves? We know how to dance too. We are a terribly merry people— we dance like a family of undertakers in plague-time . . .

Whatever the content of future tragedy may be, dance is bound to be part of it. Even now shrewd dramatists who know what they're about fill their plays with the cakewalk, the maxixe and other fiddle-faddle of the kind.

But I do hope the dances will be choric. And that is why the footlight-rows in theaters must be removed.

If the modern spectator can take part in the theatrical spectacle only when he recognizes himself in the more or less distorting mirrors set up for him on stage, the next step in his participation in the tragic action must be his taking part in tragic dance.

Luckily Isadora Duncan dances,[8] fledging bare feet with dancing . . .

How sweet to know there is another life besides our own!
(Valery Bryusov)

But soon we all will be infected by this "new life" and, like whirling dervishes, will spin onto the stage and start twirling in frenzied zeal.

The action of a tragedy will be accompanied by and interspersed with dance. The merry kind? Perhaps. In any case, more or less frenzied dance. Because dancing is no more than a rhythmical frenzy of body and soul, plunging into the tragic element of music.

If you watch someone dancing and think that he is spinning, drenched in sweat, and therefore loves to be drenched in the dulcet fragrance of perfumes, you will, of course, be mistaken. He is not doing the whirling before your eyes—the world is gyrating around him ever faster and faster, dim and blurred, decomposing, melting into the quick, free, easy movement. But you do not see this universal gyration, because you are timid and cautious and do not indulge in the frenzied rhythm of the dance, which breaks the shackles of the quotidian. All you see is the comic aspect—an extremely red face, an arm held awkwardly or curved grotesquely, soaking wet locks of hair and those repulsive little droplets on young skin. You do not know that this is the world's gyration, which fans sweet fire on the entranced body that abandons itself to the universal dance, and within the dewdrops of Eden are blent soothing coolness and soothing heat.

The black ringlet bounces off the white neck, the veriest tip of a white pump flashes from beneath a white gown, the smile on vermilion lips gleams merrily and darts away, the train trails behind and rustles by. Draw on your gloves, invite the lady of your choice, fear not—this is only a ballroom dance and you are not on the Brocken but in the salon of the Baroness Jourfixe. The floor has been waxed—"with that gift of the wise bee"⁹—but is by no means unsafe. "Young Miss Snandulia dances only with men of her own set" (Wedekind, *Spring's Awakening*)—she is a well-bred young miss, although "the gown she wore was cut low fore and aft—in back down to her waist and in front low enough to drive you crazy. She can't have been wearing a shift."¹⁰

This ballroom dance is only a hint of what tragic dancing ought to be. True, the corset, gloves and pumps of the dancing lady partially, if only in small degree, correspond to the mask of the ancient tragic histrion. But by now we are well aware that we do not need the mask made by the theater's prop-man, no matter how fine it is.

We always wear our own disguises, and they perform their function so well that often we deceive not only others but ourselves with the playacting of their expressions.

The whole world is merely the scenery that stands in front of the creative soul—the soul of I. Every mundane face and every mundane body is merely a disguise, merely a marionette brought on for a word, a gesture, a laugh or a tear. But tragedy enters, attenuates the scenery and the face-making, and through the scenery glows a world transfigured by I, the world of the soul of I, the fulfillment of the unique will of I—and through the disguises and face-making glow the unique Visage and unique transfigured flesh of I. Flesh made beautiful and liberated.

The rhythm of liberation is the rhythm of dance. The pathos of liberation is the joy of the beautiful, undraped body.

The dancing spectator of either sex will come to the theater and at the threshold he or she will doff the coarse, philistine clothing. And dash about in the light-footed dance.

So the throng, which came to look on, will be transfigured into the choric round dance, come to participate in the tragic action.

Theater and Modern Drama
by Andrey Bely

Drama is the ultimate and supreme employment of poetic creativity. Therefore, the furthest aims of poetry are revealed and crystallized in it. The outpouring of creativity is not limited here to the images of the imagination. It flows further, far beyond the bounds of the imagination: it irresistibly impinges on life and is realized in outward action. The imagination impinges on life. Life becomes imagination, imagination life. In drama the format of art seeks to expand until it achieves the possibility of being life, in both the literal and figurative senses of the word.

That is why performance on stage is a necessary precondition of dramatic art. The drama cannot be read. What sort of drama would that be? The action portrayed must be viewed ocularly, the words enunciated must be heard. For the stage is the embodiment of dreams. On it the fiction of dramatic poesy haunts you with overwhelming force. It steals into your soul and, when you leave the theater, you will convey this fiction into life. Moreover, you will test life against fiction. Life is becoming populated by the images of fiction. Like vampires, the images of fiction drink the blood of life—and there they are, right beside you—Lear, Ophelia, Hamlet! And there is the actor, a living man, hypnotized by fiction, imbuing it with his own private life, recreating himself as the hero of the action portrayed. Dramatic fiction infects people as with a fever, by inventing roles, by creating a life that is sublime and significant. And, with its light, the life of fiction illuminates the actor's private life with a reflection of the extraordinary. At this point human beings become mythical creatures. They are exalted as gods, in the light of myth. And myth, repeated an infinite number of times, exalts to an infinite number of degrees. How far does it exalt? Beyond life? But are we to abandon life? Does fiction draw us away from life? And now

This essay was first published in the collection *Teatr: Kniga o novom teatre* (St. Petersburg, 1908), which text is the basis for this translation.

there steals into the mind transfigured by myth a doubt as to whether what it is abandoning is indeed life and whither it goes is indeed death. Try to expunge Hamlet, Lear and Ophelia from your life, and your life becomes more insipid. And yet Lear and Ophelia are mere phantoms. The creative idea becomes a life you value more than the life bestowed on you. Why is this so? Is it not because you have been sleeping a deep sleep, and it was fiction that wakened you to life? And you will not give up fiction to gratify life, because when fiction departs it takes with it a kind of lore of life inculcated in humanity by dramatic action centuries old. Dramatic poesy, like a cynosure, focuses all the rays of poetic fiction. Perhaps the ultimate purpose of drama is to contribute to man's transfiguration in such wise that he will begin to create his life on his own, populating it with fateful events. In such a case a man's life is the role in which he is cast, and it is up to him to make sense of this role and elucidate it through creativity. But a life elucidated by creative activity is beautiful. Therefore, a life spent in creating overcomes fate. And thus drama's mission—to portray man's struggle with fate—is a master-plan for life's creativity: the actualization of this struggle. But what is the use of it? Does not life itself contain all the elements of drama? Why drama, when we are given life? Yes, but drama is life expanded by the musical sensitivity [literally, *pafos*, meaning an awareness of another world—*tr.*] of the soul. Yes, but life's self-awareness, like the musical sensitivity of the soul, is itself a first step toward the transfiguration and intensification of life. We could never sustain that awareness within ourselves so lucidly, so proudly, if the instincts of dramatic culture did not exist in our lives. The creative works of Sophocles, Shakespeare, Calderón, Corneille and Ibsen illumine our lives with momentary brilliance. But this brilliance fades, growing ever dimmer and dimmer. Only the soul, amid our everyday concerns, retains a memory of that brilliance. And the brilliance of dramatic sensitivity will illumine once more. And a vague presentiment creeps into the soul that life is not life, and that we, as dramatists, create it. And therefore, fate is not fate but merely a dream born of our inactivity; and we shall rise above the dreams, as befits us as human beings, while the storm-cloud of fate encircles our breast, and our brow, ablaze with brilliance, ascends to another life—a living life. And the black clouds of fate that enshroud our dreams shall appear as snow-white waves of soft sublunary silk, lapping at our breast. Fate is not fatal! Whenever this rallying cry is openly bruited over mankind, life will become dramatic creativity.

But will we not say then that life has become life, and that we have wakened from a deep slumber? A deep slumber surrounded us with the chimeras of fate, a dream-vision of death. And life flew away from us, while the dream became incarnate: hark how the dream, mechanized by millions of weak-willed lunatics, rages at us with the multisonorous roar of a machine. The machine devours life, the machine takes on a soul, and man, within the machine, turns into a machine—into a cog in the works. Like a machine, man submits to the iron law of necessity.

Such is the immutable course of a constellation, and such is the immutable course of history. A heavy fate was laid on us in the form of space and time. But in spirit we have overcome all space and in spirit we have overcome all time. Spirit tells us that the creative wellspring of life is within us. Time and space not only choke up our creativity, they even spew out our very selves onto the surface of life, as the insignificant refuse of meaningless meaning. All art begins when the human spirit, albeit unconsciously, proclaims the pre-eminence of creativity over cognition. The free will is the creative will. Only creativity, in whatever form it takes, possesses free will. Any other noncreative (not disinterested) will is only a ruse of vacant fate—vacant, because fate ceases to exist wherever creativity triumphs. Fate does exist wherever time-honored submission exists.

That is why the drama, when it depicts fate, uses the creative forms of fiction to depict the occult principle of our enslavement. Drama holds the first acknowledgement of the hidden springs which control artistic creativity.

Art occurs whenever a summons to creativity is also a summons to create life.

Life must be understood both in its superficial aspect as it crystallizes in the fixed forms of social, scientific and philosophical relationships, and in the source of those forms that lie beneath—creativity. Life too is creativity. Moreover, life is one of the categories of creativity. Life must be subordinated by creativity, re-created creatively wherever it breaks in upon our freedom with its jagged edges. Art is the origin of life's melt-down. It melts the ice of life into the water of life. An artist is an artist only because, as he penetrates life to life's alpha and omega, creativity, he does not truckle to life's visibility. In creating idols (forms), he shields himself and us, by means of these visible idols, from the idol of the invisible—fate, which has shackled our life with what seems to be iron but is in fact spectral laws. In opposition to the worship of the invisible spectre, he sets the visible forms he has created himself. In every art the idol (form) is a means. In every submission to the invisible idol (fate) which accepts hecatombs of bloody victims, there is implied a worship of the idol as an end in itself. The creation of life abolishes all idols. But in the struggle with the idol of fate, the creation of artistic idols is indispensable: with its help, to use a vulgar expression, the artist fights fire with fire.

The artist is indefatigable in his struggle with fate. Even artistic creations are doomed to perish as is the creation of dead forms (works of art). Drama provides us with the first portents that all temporal conditions of the struggle with fate will perish along with us. Art will perish. What of that? The first ranks of warriors always perish. Man, in becoming godlike, will topple both life and the images of the gods, and the facsimiles of those images are the marble statues of Apollo and Dionysos. Human beings will become their own personal forms of art.

The drama is the first to raise the curtain on the future. But the drama has its own particular aims: it is a form of art. It sublimates the living water of artistic creativity into a resplendent rack of sub-solar clouds. And the clouds, gilded by the sun, look to us like a new city—the Jerusalem of eternally creative life. Remaining an art form, the drama redirects the channel and transmutes the development of the arts. It strives to become life, but a life of creativity. Dead life and dead forms of creativity are liable to decompose, and this is particularly true in the drama.

Art is a temporary measure: it is a tactical strategy in mankind's struggle with fate. Just as the liquidation of class distinctions requires its own type of class dictatorship (by the proletariat), so in eradicating the nonexistent, dead life of fate, dead form must be emblazoned on the banner of life. By means of this worship, the artist's soul is inculcated with an unconscious repudiation of fate. At the very moment when fate transmutes and shrinks the universe into this narrow prison of ours, the artist escapes prison by occupying the term of his incarceration with certain idle amusements. These amusements are artistic creativity. No, they are not really amusements; they are the manufacture of explosives. A day will come when the artist will hurl his infuriate missile at the prison walls of fate. The walls will be demolished. The prison will turn into the world.

By creating dead forms which the artist packs with his soul as a kind of dynamite, art hurls explosive missiles at the prison wall. The evolution and development of art forms are only the trajectory of the explosive missiles as they leave the creator's hand and hit the prison wall. In drama the creative missile comes in contact with these walls. An explosion takes place underneath the drama. Art forms are trying irrepressibly to expand, irrepressibly and strenuously. In this case art must detonate, disintegrate, cease to be.

But how do we know that our whole life, subjugated to fate, must not also detonate, disintegrate, cease to be? Then that new creativity will fuse with new life. Life will become life indeed, for the creation of dead forms will become the creation of living forms.

In the drama, the occult summons to create is realized first as a summons to create life. But fate blocks the path to this act of creation. Therefore drama depicts the struggle with and triumph over fate. And if there is no premonition of this triumph in the drama, it is not a tragedy. The refulgence of tragedy lies in its prediction that the drama of humanity is not to end as drama. The refulgence of tragedy is the principle of the return to life. By depicting the struggle with fate, the radical antinomies of cognition impinge on the radical antinomies of life itself. These same antinomies unconsciously summon the artist to create a world of art as a new world, intended to loose from our feet decrepit necessity (ἀναγκη). But the antinomies of life are predetermined by the antinomies of pure reason, and the norms of that reason, predetermined by moral obligation, necessarily depend on value. And only the energy of creativity can be of value.

And that is why the artist-dramatist, proclaiming the pre-eminence of creativity over cognition, and, conjointly, developing his art until it impinges on life, comes to betoken the creation of new life, as if illumined by the rainbow of tragedy's refulgence (καθαρσιζ).[1] But a new life is impossible without the triumph over fate. And antecedent to this is the struggle for liberation: neither cognition nor life in its enslaved modes exists any longer as a means of struggle. The creation of life becomes an end in itself.

It is first realized as drama.

Drama is the communicative principle of creative energy in art. The principle of synthesis is contained in drama. In drama the basic stem, from which the magnificent corona of multifarious art forms has fanned out in all directions, seems to be feeling its way. But when drama is realized as the collective principle of art forms, its living meaning diminishes. Nowadays we are often told that the mysterium is the synthesis of art forms, and that modern drama resembles a mysterium. For me this illustrates the danger threatening modern drama. A pyramid of idols is crushing the drama. Its musical principles are replaced anew by eclecticism. All these sweet appeals to the mysterium in our time are suspect. They lull to sleep the valor of the spirit. And we need this valor, as we need troops of heroes, because a cruel struggle lies before us. In struggle, and not in dreamy supplication, are we to be transfigured. Drama contains the tactics for the coming battle with fate. Dramatic culture *is* culture. That is how Nietzsche, that great theorist of the new drama, conceived of culture. And he conceived it more accurately than did Wagner or, for example, Schuré.[2]

In Wagner's music-drama, Nietzsche beheld the actual struggle for mankind's liberation. But even Nietzsche did not grasp the fatal contradictions of modern drama. He sensed the call of life it holds, before he had first distinguished this call from the form in which it issued forth. A return to life by means of newness in drama cancels out drama itself a form of art. First worshipping the call to life that is in drama, Nietzsche then canonized the form the call took—the stage. A monstrosity was born: the call to life *from* the stage turned into the call of life *to* the stage. Drama as form was worshipped by Nietzsche in the first phase of his enthusiasm for Wagner. For him the dramatic form became a byword for dutiful creativity. The effect of the explosive missile was attributed to the bomb's casing. He forgot that life itself will be the moment of explosion, and not the moment of dramatic action. The music-drama, that token of the event, was worshipped by Nietzsche as the event itself. He set himself up an idol. And therefore he tore Wagner's brilliant music out of his soul, just as he tore his own brilliant work *The Birth of Tragedy* out of his soul, as his declaration testifies. Zarathustra—now there's a dramatic actor, drunk with mythopoeia, and not the wooden yahoo Siegfried, waving a cardboard sword about on stage and stupidly tooting on an inverted horn. Zarathustra was born on stage and began acting for the spectators. The stage represented the town of "Brindled Cow," the virtuous Zarathustra walked into "Brindled Cow" and taught. Then he dismissed it and walked off stage into life. The third and fourth parts of Zarathustra are the drama of life in earnest. The actual principle of explosion subsists here in the substantiation of the occult inner experiences of Zarathustra's life, and not in the splendid theorizing about operatic Siegfried.[3]

But the explosive missile will not detonate until all mankind is gathered beneath a single banner of tragedy. The true visage of fate will be revealed at the moment when man overcomes the class struggle, that impediment to all true affirmation or negation of life. The fetish of industrial productivity is, of course, not fate but a guise of fate. Nor does the struggle for liberation consist in repudiating or accepting forms of economic slavery. It begins in new forms of social slavery. When the mask falls from fate, all mankind will go to battle for life and its own happiness. Only then, out of the shattered forms of art, as from the shattered forms of private life, will the sacred flame of life's creativity flare up. Then the explosive missile of drama, launched by the dynamite of the spirit, will detonate. This is what Nietzsche failed to perceive. A comprehension of social drama was alien to him. At first he toyed with the missile's casing—as the regeneration of modern forms of dramatic action; then, extracting the dynamite of life's creativity from drama as an art form, he unwittingly defused the missile. The missile exploded not where it was supposed to—against the prison walls—but in the hands of the inventor. And for fifteen years Nietzsche—the inventor of explosives—sat on the balcony of a quiet villa with his brains blown out. And now they point out to tourists the place on the balcony where crazy Nietzsche whiled away the hours.

Such was the fate that befell the greatest theorist of new drama.

The most recent theorists of drama take special relish in analyzing Nietzsche's mistakes. They prescribe their own paths for drama, as they correct the blunders of the insane genius. Instead of freeing modern drama from the morbid excrescences of the mysterium mania, which Nietzsche had adduced in such fury, they are prompt to confirm Nietzsche's errors and reject his sane protests against mass Wagneritis. Remember—in the cave of Zarathustra even "the most foul of men" had hidden himself away, there to strike up the anthem of despondency. There, where the healthy song of the tragic actor Zarathustra had resounded, the foulest and most sickly-sweet songs can now echo forth.

The most recent theorists of drama,* perhaps correctly, establish a bond between the modern conditions of the dramatic enactment and the conditions for the rise of ancient drama (it is easy to carry on this work by following in Nietzsche's footsteps). They help us to establish the profound, sometimes forgotten meaning of dra-

---

*I hasten to make the reservation that in my analysis of the latest views of drama's trend, I do not have in mind the subtle and profound theory of V. I. Ivanov, with whose details I do not agree, but whose fundamental theses I accept. I have no intention of analyzing his theory. Such an analysis would be bound to take up too much space. I absolutely protest against the vulgarized interpretations of this theory and the too-easily-made deductions from V. I. Ivanov's basic propositions. But these facile deductions are only to be met with in the ranks of discreditable modernists. While giving a serious thinker his due, I cannot help but view with alarm the rapid popularization of his ideas.

ma's individual components; they point out that drama developed out of sacrificial offerings, as a form of religious cult, and they attempt to organize a worship service in modern drama. The theater, it appears, should become a temple. But why should the theater become a temple, when we have both temples and theaters? Divine worship takes place in a temple. So does the sacrament. "Let the sacrament be performed in the theater as well," so say the latest theorists of drama. But what are we to understand by "sacrament"? And what are we to understand by "divine worship"? The existence and persistence of religion provide us with a definite, not a figurative, answer to this. Whether or not we discount this answer, we understand its meaning. We also understand the connection between the ancient Greek drama and the religious cult of Dionysos. But in Greece the drama developed by moving away from religion. Drama was emancipated from religion. The legacy we received was an emancipated drama.

The European theater expanded and gave precise definition to the form this emancipation took. Now when we are told that the stage is divine service, the actor a priest and watching a drama will communicate the sacrament to us, we take the terms "divine service," "priest," "sacrament" in an imprecise, ambiguous, almost meaningless sense. What is divine service? Is it the public performance of a religious enactment? What god are we to pray to? Are we or are we not invited to return to those primitive forms of religion out of which drama evolved? It all remains hidden by the murk of uncertainty.

If that *is* the case, give us a goat to immolate! But what are we to do with a goat, once we have had Shakespeare? If this implies some kind of new divine service, tell us the name of the new god! Where is he, who is he? Where did you, the founders of the theater-to-come, discover a drama with the name of this new god on it? If the name of this god is not given us, if the religion of such a god is wanting, all intrinsic statements about the path of modern drama, the new theater as a temple, remain figurative statements which change nothing in the modern theater. The "temple" is still the Mariinsky Theater and rhetoric is still rhetoric.

But the matter is not so simple.

The ingenious conceit that the stage acts as an obstacle between actor and spectator, between the mythic enactment and the contemplation of it, that the spectator must enter the circle of the plays performed, like a chorus member—these conceits compel us to pay close attention to what the theorists of modern drama are telling us. Their answer to the objection that we have temples enough, even without the stage, is rather sound: a temple is a link to a religious cult; all historical forms of cults, which conceal a meaning profound and important in its dynamics, are deprived of life by religious scholasticism and dogmatism. Dogmatism paralyzes the free development and differentiation of a cult, whereas the theater is a hearth which, once it has embraced the mentality of the historical creativity of religions, will kindle with the fire of unhampered creativity.

All this we might grant, if such reasoning were grounded in reality. But the reasoning is diametrically opposed to the creative processes of the modern dramatist. Modern dramatists have not even dreamt of uniting the audience and the stage.

Where is the *orchestra* [the ancient Greek choric dancing-floor—*tr.*] in Ibsen? And where is the *orchestra* in Maeterlinck? How is the dramatic enactment in Ibsen to be converted into a divine service? Following the recipes given by the latest theories, should we not stage the famous scene in *Enemy of the People* (when the "enemy" makes a speech) so that the auditorium stands for the town meeting? But then the choric element of the spectators turns Ibsen's drama into farce. If anyone considered reviving the form of ancient drama, it was Schiller, not Ibsen or Maeterlinck. But even in *The Bride of Messina*, the choric element is introduced in a conventional and therefore an admissible sense.[4]

Granted, the modern drama developed out of the ancient. Does that mean it has to revert to it? The objection is made that the ancient drama is drama's thesis. Modern drama evolved as its antithesis, and is now approaching synthesis. But synthesis is not the same as thesis. Granted, the Greeks wore tragic masks and staged sacrifices in the theater; granted, there are vestiges of Greek culture in our culture. But does that make us Greeks? Are we then to eat olives and dance around a goat? I should notice if such a thing were taking place. So the most recent interpretations of drama remain unimplemented. Many talk about what drama is obliged to be. But where is this *obligatory* drama? It will come, is the answer they give us.

But it would be better if such drama did not develop. Here is why.

Suppose that we, the spectators, have reverted to the choric element. And, moreover, that the choric element indulges in dances of prayer. Then, however, the distance of our states of prayer from a life unrecreated through prayer will be emphasized with particular acu-

ity. For life will overwhelm prayer. We must not escape from life to
the theater, to dance and sing over the dead tragic goat and then, re-
lapsing into life, be astonished by what we have done. That would
consummate an avoidance of fate. Yet fate bursts into the theatrical
temple right on our heels and disembodies our songs and dances for
us. We must convert life itself into drama. Otherwise, we shall enter
the theater-temple, drape ourselves in white garments, crown ourselves with clusters of roses, to act out a mysterium (whose theme is
ever the same: a godlike man struggles with fate); at the proper moment we shall take one another by the hand and dance. Picture yourself, reader, in this role for just a moment. Is that us spinning around
the sacrificial altar—an *art nouveau* lady, a stockbroker, a workingman and a member of the Privy Council? I am sure that our prayers
will not tally. The *art nouveau* lady will pray to some poet in the
image and likeness of Dionysos, the workingman will pray for a
shorter workday, while the state councillor—to what star does his
gaze aspire? No, it is better far to whirl around in a waltz with a
pretty young miss, than to lead a choric dance with an actual privy
councillor.

They protest in reply that this is just what we shall do in the
democratic theater of the future, that the premises of social organization are rooted in independent communes where everything is
active creativity, that *orchestras* are the demiurgic focus of these
communes. Furthermore, we are told that all our skepticism erupts
because we are representatives of a cellular, isolated (alias bourgeois)
life and that in the people's theater unimpeded mythopoeia will take
place. But the people's theater is a fairground booth where, from
time immemorial, the bandit Churkin has held the stage,[5] and the
cinema aspires more and more to fill the role prescribed for the democratic theater of the future. True enough, the cinema is full of
mythopoeia: a man sneezes and explodes—an edifying victim of the
fatal struggle with . . . the common cold. And besides, if you want to
talk about collective creativity, it exists even now. Why don't they
consider the round dances in any peasant village an *orchestra*? Poor
Russia—they threaten to cover her with *orchestras*, when she has
been covered with them from time immemorial. Go out for an evening's stroll in the country and you will encounter both the choric
element and collective creation . . . of uncensored remarks. So much
for deductions from a theory that does not take into account the
concrete forms of life. They plan to cover Russia with *orchestras*,
when they have long been planning to deliver her from those very
orchestras.

So long as the class struggle goes on, these appeals to aesthetic democracy are grotesque. And absurd, absurd in the highest degree, is this democratic, congregational-mythopoetical temple-theater (God be praised, it won't come into existence for some time yet). Since no such theater exists, they turn back to the past. They revive Aeschylus, Sophocles and Euripides on the stage. Sometimes they successfully imitate the methods of Aeschylus (as V. Ivanov does, for instance).[6] But where is the democracy in that? Is it not aristocratic boredom that drives us to seek aesthetic pleasure in the religious significance of foreign dramas? And if the altar to Dionysos were to be solemnly set up in the new theater, would it not turn into a symbol of the most supreme profanation of theater, of ourselves, of art, of the sacred beliefs of a noble people?

Thank God, the emblematic appeals to Dionysos remain remote from the personal lyrical life (oh, how profound and beautiful!) of the theorists of new theater. But these appeals cause no destruction. The temple is still the Mariinsky Theater.

The fatal contradiction in which the most recent theorists of art became entangled is that, when they issued invitations to the theater as a temple, they forgot that a temple presupposes a cult, and a cult presupposes the name of God, i.e., a religion. And so long as they have no name, their attempts to create a religion are ungrounded. There can be no talk of a new cult, born on the boards of a stage, and least of all of a templelike theater and a drama resembling a divine service. Divine service, when it has no purpose or form, merely intrudes an actor's posturing into the sacred realm of spirit, where hope burns to the creativity of life. If the actor seems to be nothing more than an actor in the modern theater and only in the theater, that very disparagement of the actor's function may perhaps contain his great freedom as the creator of a given role. The priestly tiara might crush the actor, were he unable to turn it into a fool's cap. At present, when he enters a role, an actor comes in contact with those prototypes of living creativity which dimly agitated the dramatist as well. Even as he remains an actor to us, in himself he is the precursor of something different and vital. So we go and exalt him as the tragic sacrifice; the very sacrificial quality, in return for being itself a prototype of future life, will turn *him* into a counterfeit. And man will be defiled in the actor.

What is tragic about those who theorize about a path for new drama is that, as they note Nietzsche's error (confusing the occult fire of drama with its form), they promise us a detonation of the explosive missile within the confines of the theater (transfiguring form) that will shatter the dead forms of life and creativity. A stage-effects explosion of Bengal lights takes place on stage: life remains life, theater remains theater.

Modern art is defined as symbolist art. Symbolism in art affirms the living totality of experience, as the elective principle of image-clusters. The power of art lies in expressing experiences through images, and not in a system of images utilized by experience. Symbolism is precisely that method of expressing experience through images. In this respect, every art is overtly or covertly symbolist. But experience, understood as an end in itself which subordinates the image as a means, invests the artist with the right to be a creator of images. Modern art turns this individual right, so to speak, into a plank in its artistic platform. Symbolism, as a literary school of the latter half of the nineteenth century, is more or less based on hypothetical psychologies and a theory of cognitive awareness. And just as some theoretic-cognitive schools presume cognition itself to be creativity, so the revolutionary force of symbolism lies in its declaration that artistic creativity is the unique principle capable of creating life. The meaning of life is in the creation of it and not in the cognition of it. Life is a form of artistic creativity. The mission of art is to stimulate creative activity. This mission certainly does not lie in the contemplation of aesthetic phenomena, as Schopenhauer stated. Symbolism emphasizes the dynamics of creativity. That is why it opposes academic pedantry as a principle of stasis in art. Symbolism's point of view illuminates the existing schools of art. Justifying the existence of multifarious schools as the result of creative activity, it stands up against them whenever those schools pass themselves off as the norm that regulates creativity. Stasis in the arts is regarded in the light of symbolism as a special case within the dynamics of the arts.

Art itself is an anticipation of the victory over fate, at the moment of the spirit's fatal struggle with form. Grounding creativity in symbolism, as the eternally motive principle of life, is the most stable form of grounding. Art is there affirmed as a means of struggle for the liberation of mankind. Therein lies the religious sanction of art.

These notions come into particularly harsh and tragic collision with the ideology of the modern theater, as a form into which they try to pour the symbolist drama and—alas!—cannot. All the strength and all the frailty of modern art are traduced to us by the drama. And we begin to sense that modern art is a degenerate art, because we realize ever more clearly that modern drama cannot exist within the confines of the theater.

Why is this so?

A symbol is the union of two orders of sequentiality: the sequentiality of images and the sequentiality of the experiences which evoke images. All strength is on the side of the sequentiality of experiences. Images are the emblematic inventory of experiences, nothing more. Experience burgeons with images. In symbolism the real connection between them lies behind the frontiers of visibility. The moment we learn how to subordinate the world around us to inner experience so that the current of the visible does not cut discordantly across our soul; and, conversely, the moment the soul has transubstantiated the visible to its own image and likeness, the victory over fate will be accomplished. Gnosiology liberates the subject of cognition from time and its measurement theoretically. The problem of mankind is to realize this freedom pragmatically. And the problem is solved in principle by creating values. But the theory of values *is* the theory of creativity. It is also the theory of symbolism.

As it notes the soul's involuntary impulse toward freedom in the sphere of art, the theory of symbolism recognizes this impulse *as a duty*. It issues an order to implement this duty of freedom, by turning life into the object of creativity. And therefore, symbolism, which may be the most conscious school of art, regards art itself only as the beginning of a vital path to freedom. Poetry orders us, "Behold the dawn. Hymn the dawn." For the poet, symbolism turns the dawn breeze into an actual summons: "The dawn is calling—greet the dawn!" So John Gabriel Borkman picks up his stick, puts on his galoshes and goes to wrestle with life; Solness climbs up a tower; Brand leads the villagers up a glacier; Rubek, flying in the face of death with Irene, goes into the mountains, as if one had to ascend some thousands of feet to defeat Death, so that they die on Mont Blanc; Ellida hears the call of the Stranger. They all do this— these heroes, who take the measure of Eternity almost by the square yard, just as in the Apocalypse we take the measure of the future temple.

The symbolist drama of Ibsen,[7] that patriarch of the newest drama, consciously rips the veil from the visible everywhere: the visible, remaining visible, becomes as transparent as glass, displaying the incredible meaning of what takes place within the visible. The power of audacity in Ibsen's dramas lies in this incredibility of meaning. Here symbolism is so far realized that, while they remain inscrutable in essence, all these Rubeks, Borkmans and Solnesses are yet the algebraic signs of some apocalyptic equation of life.

Not so in Shakespeare's drama. There symbolism is either involuntary or overly allegorical, as in *The Tempest*, for example. Shakespeare's dramas depict the profoundly real action of passion, of jealousy. There the symbolism is an inadvert rainbow on the waterfall of the real. Symbolism changes the rainbow into a sunbeam, the sunbeam leads back to the sun—to that reality which created both the earth and the waterfall. Realistic drama guides the sunbeam of symbolism back to the waterfall of reality. Symbolist drama turns the sunbeam into the condition necessary for the creation of a waterfall. It turns the striving for freedom, presentient like the dawn, into duty: "Thou seest the light—then rise thou as the sun." And Oswald gibbers, "The sun, the sun . . ."[8] The entire force of Ibsen's drama is not in Rubek's climbing onto the glaciers, for this action is meant to create an external emblem for adumbrating his ideas, but in the fact that the striving for victory over death must have an entirely realistic sense. If allegory is potential in realistic drama (for instance, love scales the heights), in symbolist drama such allegory is asserted to be reality, while reality (love) becomes an emblematic condition of the fact that to rise a few thousand feet by certain inner experiences is indeed to fly in the face of death.

But any man can walk over precipices who has turned life into a pedestal for creativity. He might succeed in beaming with sunshine like a child of morning. The solar city of the new life—the *Civitas solis*—is a colossal living symbol. Both the Apocalypse and the fire of social-democracy, Nietzsche and all religions have proceeded in divers way toward this promised end. Art, proceeding to the focus of human aspirations, is acquiring unwonted mastery. It is beginning to create Rubeks like this, who may perhaps sit for a year stony-faced over a glass of beer, and then suddenly start trudging to the heights, and with billions of miles and days between each stride. It is clear that they are striding through time and space not in Greek chitons, but in overcoats and top hats. Rubek was sitting at a restaurant table and then trudged to a new heaven, a new earth. True, he did manage to cross the frontier and so was crushed. But the audacity itself shows that Ibsen's drama, through its symbols, speaks to us of the transfiguration of flesh into spirit. The Apocalypse of human flesh comprises the symbolism of Ibsen's dramas. Symbolist drama can depict one thing only: the transfiguration of organs of mundane perception and thereby the regeneration of the world of necessity as the world of freedom. Fate's role in it is as a danger threatening the human organism into spasms that change it psycho-physiologically into a superhuman organism. And therefore the Rubeks, Solnesses, Brands in Ibsen are surrounded by a pack of degenerates of both sexes, leading us to think that the Rubeks are also degenerates.

The artist doffs his laurel wreath at this point, but he is beginning to glow with the rays of his prophet's mitre. By affirming in drama the symbol's objective reality in forms of freedom, symbolism prescribes that its heroes must with stern resolve substantiate the objective reality of the symbol by going beyond the visible ("all or nothing"). Thus, by undermining noncreative morality, symbolist drama imputes amorality to its heroes in forms of the categorical imperative. It tells us: "If thou art Rubek and hast beheld the ultimate blinding light, then become blinding light thyself, as the countenance of Moses, having spoken with God, came to dazzle the children of Israel." And perhaps once Mr. Rubek awakened that morning in his hotel, like everyone else, and shaved and dressed, like everyone else, and finished his breakfast or luncheon and had taken affectionate leave of the ladies he knows at the *table d'hôte,* he then went to commit his folly: to rise above death by momentarily becoming a Titan. A Titan in a restaurant, the ancient Greeks never dreamt of such a thing! Here mythical symbolism turns into eschatological symbolism; here Ibsen in his aspirations is more essential to us than ten Sophocles, even though we knew no more before than we do now how we are to stage such a monstrous theatrical phenomenon, the symbolist drama of modern times, which only Ibsen could crystallize as something entirely new and hitherto unknown to us.

Rubek and Solness are only the first fighters for the actual liberation of mankind. They are victims of the struggle with fate, because victory will be won only when all mankind walks across the precipices through death to the azure-laved isle of children, promised both by apocalyptic prophecy of remote antiquity and by the theomachistic daring of Nietzsche. And meanwhile? Meanwhile Rubek falls off a tower [Bely means Solness the Master-Builder—*tr.*], Eyolf chokes on a salt-sea wave and his crutch floats over him, and the Stranger vanishes from Ellida's path. Does not the Stranger call us too, and are we incapable of following him? As incapable as Ellida is, when the Stranger calls to her. She is afraid that when she comes to him on the steamboat, the invocatory appeal that draws her will be dispelled. She does not understand that the Stranger calls her not for his sake or for hers, but for the sake of the appeal overshadowing all of us: she forgets that she is a lady from the sea and that a steamboat does not linger in port—it sails off to sea toward a new land, flesh transfigured. It sails away in the wake of death. And Brand falls because of doubt. Once he is left alone on the glaciers, he says to himself, "What happened? Why am I here?" The ability to soar has shriveled up within him and he no longer dared, against the will of all, to replicate his ecstasy. Because of a thought ("Why am I here?"), not because of a madman's gunshot, the avalanche comes crashing down. And "He is the *Deus caritatis*" echoes not in the rumble of the avalanche, but in the brain of dying, doubting Brand. And Solness, climbing up the tower, suddenly realizes that a confrontation with God must now inevitably take place, and he does not know what to say to God. Solness does not know the *word* any more than Ibsen does, any more than the modern drama of symbols does. For the modern drama of symbols is pledged to an Apocalypse without a Second Coming. The world will be forthcoming only when the flesh is subtilized down to the form of new creativity. Meanwhile the forms of modern art are frail earthen vessels.

We ourselves are the marble blocks which we must carve into sculpted statues. The statues of Apollo, Dionysos and Venus are not the symbols; we—we are the symbols of Apollo, Dionysos and Venus. We ourselves, our very selves are still unwilling to accept and realize that already something stirs within us. Worshipping a graven image (art), we overlooked the transubstantiation already taking place in the recesses of our soul, and the fact that we are the most beautiful of all art forms old and new. Art raises us to the known limits and teaches us to walk in beauty with unsteady gait. But we shall grow and our gait will become ever more confident. Art is the mother of our striving for life's transfiguration. She nourished us as sucklings. But when sucklings cease to be sucklings and yet go on feeding at mother's breast, we are right to wean ourselves away from her.

And so it is time for the best, the most sophisticated among us, to bid farewell to art, if they are faithful to the path they once chose. Do they not know that they have already passed through the gateway called Art into the open field of life's creativity? The blacksmith's bellows has been admired long enough. It is time to take up the bellows and fan the fire in which their life is to be forged.

Symbolist drama on stage is a phenomenon of rare hideousness. It puts on stage those things that take place within us far beyond the confines of a stage. It teaches the best of us to dissemble. It objectifies in us or, to put it more simply, picks out of us that which ought to be hidden away in us until it has consolidated. Like music, it is the lightning-rod of heroism.

Many of us have already come as far as the fatal frontier beyond which the creativity of forms is replaced by the creativity of life. Instead of learning how to incarnate creativity in life, we pursue it on stage. This can still be done in poetry and painting. One can say, "This is what I experienced." One can say and seek in life the forms for experience. But after all, the whole power of drama lies in realized action. The symbolist *bond of images* and not the symbolist images taken individually would seem to be the essence of drama. This symbolist bond is realized in drama as a bond of new relationships in life. In life these relationships are still no more than potential. They are not realized. The symbolist drama is a peep into the future. And so those images conveyed into the circle of the dramatic enactment are *not real or actual on stage.* They are a sermon about the future, nothing more. As a sermon, modern drama is proper for the stage; as a mysterium of new life, never. When Ibsen shows us his Rubeks, he speaks what he knows: the day will come and the dead will awaken. But *how* this is to be, Ibsen does not know. Had he converted his own life into an experiment and sought all life long for forms of ascension that really, concretely transfigured himself, he might perhaps have learned about something more than emblematic glaciers and John Gabriel Borkman rushing out in his galoshes to wrestle with life, where the icy hand that clutched at his heart is the icy hand of fate: it clutches at us too. But the problem of creativity lies not on stage, not in the portrayal of icy hands clutching at the heart. One must throw one's body and soul into the creative furnace that melts down life. Had Ibsen-Borkman not written dramas, but lived the drama of the struggle for transfiguration, perhaps the icy hand clutching at his heart would have melted away and lain at his feet, a vernal runnel. Had he been a mystagogue of the new life, he would not have written dramas. But he too, like all symbolist dramatists, hastens in the meantime to trade his sunny birthright for a mess of the pottage of fame.

Symbolist drama, symbolist enactment—that is indeed the bond, the covenant of people who rack their body and soul for a new love, a new creative life. The symbolist bond is the religion of a confederated path to happiness. There everyone is a participant, everyone a creator, everyone a symbol. There are no actors or dramatists or directors or spectators there. There drama is a creative relationship with life, and consequently no one seriously needs symbolist theater. Some do not need it because they regard symbolist stage images merely as an invitation to peek at life: they have learned more on their own. If they do go to the theater, it is not to see Ibsen but their own past: they go to recall how art once opened their eyes. The neophytes, those actually seeking, prefer to read Ibsen and not to see him on stage. Even those who have not yet reached the fatal frontier separating art from life's creativity go to the theater. They go and get confused by contradictory styles of staging. Finally, the majority have absolutely no use for Ibsen and his drama, but do need his ideology, which is infernally difficult to extract from any symbol. With a certain knack, this ceases to comprise a difficulty.

Symbolist drama is not drama but a sermon about the great, ever-burgeoning drama of humanity. It is a sermon about the approach of the fatal denouement. And the best images of symbolist drama must be read and not seen on stage. The theater is no place for symbolist drama. The European theater is rather too adept technically. They are quite wrong who attack it. Theater remains theater when we watch Shakespeare, Sophocles, Corneille. And theater ceases to be theater when we attend Ibsen and Maeterlinck. But it does not become a temple, though perchance a preacher's pulpit.

A book is a far better pulpit.

People may object: a concrete depiction of images, animated by a modern dramatist, may bring those images closer to us. Oh, if only it were so. *De facto* it always distances them: that is what gives rise to the fatal question of how to stage symbolist drama.

This question does not exist for the staging of realistic dramas. Portray a passion as best you can, portray the hero's psychology. The subject of the portrayal is life intensified to the level of drama. Unintentional symbolism, inherent in art, will come through on its own. But how is an actor to relate to Solness, climbing up a tower with a wreath in his hand to talk to God? How is one to portray a realistic man behaving unrealistically? As a psychopath? But Ibsen certainly does not regard Solness as a psychopath. Does Ibsen mean him to be a psychopath? But then why stage a psychopathic drama? And so they try to make the spectators swallow the symbolist pill all unawares, and obscure the central topic of the drama with a portrayal of everyday life, as we have seen in the production of *The Wild Duck* on the stage of the Moscow Art Theater.[9]

But this means distorting Ibsen. The actual task of the actor in the new theater is almost infeasible: to portray the hero's psychology with soul and flesh transfigured and with all the psychophysiological spasms that accompany rebirth. One must be a new man oneself, not in word, but in deed. And where among us are there such performers? There are none, there can be none. And so new wine is poured into old bottles.

In the best symbolist drama we hear a sermon about new relationships of life, calling these relationships to collective creativity. The participants in collective creativity must possess new individuality. The actor who incarnates the path preordained by the dramatist must have an entirely realistic knowledge of the new man in his ephemeral actions. And these actions are so hidden in new men beneath the prosaic and ordinary that you cannot even recognize who or where a new man is. The actor must himself *be* a new man. Second, the actions of new men must be coordinated into one cohesive whole—into the symbolist bond. Without violating the freedom of creativity, the symbolist bonding of the whole is, nevertheless, the norm. How can one reconcile freedom with necessity? That is another stumbling block. The modern actor trips over these blocks. When he does manage to avoid them, Ibsen is taken for Ostrovsky, Ostrovsky for Ibsen.

And therefore, quite inadvertently perhaps, the theater uses a new means of maintaining its dignity: it uses the director to repress the individual actor. This is a compromise between the need to stage symbolist drama and the impossibility of finding performers for it. It would be preferable to avoid compromise and to banish Ibsen and Maeterlinck from the stage. As poets, they can both but gain from the stage's neglect of them.

In repressing the actor's individuality, the director instinctively endeavors to conceal the glaring fact that, when an actor enunciates the text of a drama verbatim, he in no way speaks those things its author considers worthwhile. And so, to gloss over the embarrassment, the actor is turned into a stiff-jointed puppet. But the glaring fact remains a glaring fact. Every so often the actor pops out—and forgets that he is a puppet; well, say he gets carried away by the speeches in the play and, as he gets emotionally overwrought, he bursts into psychology, but almost always messes up the rhythm of his own relationship to the symbolic bond. And the director hastens to declare that not the actor's personality but the common bond is the crux of the matter.

Thus the director's creativity increases within the restrictions of staging symbolist drama. The director is now the autocrat of the theater. He towers above actors, spectators and dramatists. He segregates them from one another. Thus he usurps the author's prerogatives and meddles in the creative act. In that case, he ought to be even wiser than the dramatist and know not only the dramatist's secret inner experiences, but even how to mount these experiences in the proper setting. In such a setting he will enhance the author for the audience. Simultaneously he must contend with the actors, correct the author's mistakes by means of his staging and instruct the audience in a new life—such is the task of the modern director; and, naturally, it is impossible to fulfill this task. Hence the duty is imposed on the director to be a mystagogue of the crowd.

Finally, the author himself will aspire to be the director.

The influence of the director simply introduces *de facto* a new distortion of the meaning of symbolist drama, which has already been unavoidably distorted by the actors. It invests this distortion with integrity, i.e., it ultimately displaces the drama's center. When staged, symbolist drama, being for the most part a compromise, comes across in a doubly distorted guise. And, of course, we get not a glimpse of the real Rubeks, Solnesses and Mélisandes. One must be Rubek to impersonate him. Let Ibsen himself, and not some provincial Ivan Ivanovich, be Rubek. Anyone who knows Ibsen only from the stage has never known the real Ibsen.

The author must be his own director. His real creativity comes not at the moment of writing the play, but in staging it. And if this is impossible in practice, he had better provide a rigorously cut stencil for the performance. The author must describe to us how Rubek eats, sleeps, brushes his top hat, if he does not want Rubek to be played by a puppet; this would curtail the personal creativity of director, actors and audience. In practice this could be done in a marionette theater. The method of turning a man into a marionette is also the method of technical stylization. Stylization is also a method of conventionalized presentation to the spectators of the symbolist *bond* between the images of the drama, possibly involving the extensive elimination of the *images* themselves. The symbolism of imagery must be subordinated to the symbolism of enactment.

But such stylization thoroughly isolates the stage from the audience. The stage turns into an illustration of a play read out loud. And dreams about collective creativity within the confines of the theater and the transformation of the spectator into the choric element would become patently absurd and overstated. Far better if the spectator came on stage to voice approval or disapproval, something like the inscriptions found scrawled in old library books: "I enjoyed reading this book. Ivan Andronov," followed by the postscriptum, "I didn't. Marya Tvorozhkova."

Yes, even the modern drama of symbols is not a stage play but merely a sermon about the potential drama. Least of all is it a divine service, but at most a surrogate divine service—a hieratic pose. But one cancels out the other, and all together cancel out drama. No, it is better openly and honestly to admit in principle the ineffectiveness of the symbolist drama in the theater, and give up straying in the shadows once and for all.

The trouble starts when a director or an actor or even an author, while acknowledging that the symbolism in a play is a summons to the mysterium of life, begins to approximate the stage itself to a mysterium: the stage disintegrates and the dreams of life's mysterium—a dream deeply etched on the soul—is defiled. This dream may even conjure up for us the ancient forms of theater with an altar and a choric element: but that is false nostalgia. We recall Zarathustra. Even he might be tempted by sugarcoated despondency. Mankind moves toward a mysterium never dreamt of by the ancient Greeks. A return to the past would repudiate this, our own mysterium.

Heaven forbid!

There will be dramas, indeed there will, with spectators coming on stage and an actor as hierophant, prostrate before the altar, summoning all to prayer. But such dramas leave the soul nothing to do except blaspheme.

Once it was all richer and livelier. The Eleusinian mysteries played an enormous role in enlightenment. But the people prepared themselves, purified themselves for the mysteries; they prayed, there were degrees of consecration. Not everyone was allowed to enjoy the holy night of Epopteia.[10] Before the golden effigy of Demeter the hierophant was the sun, the hierophanta the moon, the Epopteia the constellations; the world was there within these souls transubstantiated by creative experience. No lessons might be imparted there. There was no need for it. Lobeck[11] is correct to maintain this. But there they knew, they understood, if only for a twinkling they could transubstantiate their own body and soul. The mystery of Eleusis has receded into the past. There is no way to bring it back to the stage; indeed, that would be an outrage.

For the great night of Epopteia will not come to us on stage. This night is now descending over human existence. During the final insights of our life we shall cross its frontier. And neither life nor art shall help us escape the ordeal. Even now, once in a while, we get beyond visible life, beyond art, beyond religion—we sail on the last ship to the fatal battle: our flesh is being reborn. We shall be altered or die. Before initiation into the Epopteia, the Mystai[12] stopped by the temple. Lightning flashed from the temple: the gates swung open, and ghosts with dogs' heads came out to greet the initiates. We initiate ourselves into a new life and lo! its gates swing open, but from the gates come ghosts with dogs' heads: they are phantoms of horror and degeneracy. But some of us, initiated in the silence of this great night, link arms, and the dog-headed ghosts bark and then commingle with the night.

That is why the symbolic theater of modern times is singularly anachronistic. The innovators of life look with contempt upon the forced clamor for stage reform. On the contrary: a regressive reform of the modern theater, back toward the heroic theater of Shakespeare, engages their full sympathy. Let the theater remain a theater, and the mysterium a mysterium. To mix the two together is to create without destroying, to destroy without creating. It is flirting with vacancy.

And the vacancy of nonbeing is already fast infiltrating the modern theater as the abomination of desolation. Talk about revolution will fall silent on the stage. The traditional theater will be resurrected in its modest dignity.

The modern theater will be wrecked against either the Scylla of the Shakespearean theater or the Charybdis of the cinema.

The sooner the better!

Realism and Convention on the Stage
by Valery Bryusov

[ROUGH DRAFTS AND EXCERPTS]

Note: The rough drafts presented here are borrowed from an extensive work on the theater which I am preparing for the press. Therefore many statements made here may not be supported well enough and many essentially important questions are referred to only in passing. These shortcomings will, I hope, be corrected when my work reaches the reader in its entirety. I note that the section entitled "The Theater of the Future" was delivered as a public lecture in the spring of 1907 in various halls in Moscow, and the first portion of this article, a critique of the realistic theater, reiterates the premises I set forth as early as 1902 in the article "Unnecessary Truth" (*World of Art*, no. 4, 1902).

I

The production style at modern theaters can be divided into two kinds: realistic and conventionalized.

Historically, stage convention preceded stage realism. The ancient theater knew only conventionalized staging, being reconciled to kothurnoi, masks and megaphones and scenery that almost never changed. Conventionalized were the stage productions of the medieval theater and the theater of the ages of Shakespeare and Corneille. Even in the mid-nineteenth century, when realism triumphed

---

This essay was first published in *Teatr: Kniga o novom teatre* (St. Petersburg, 1908) and reprinted in Bryusov's *Sobranie sochineniy* (Moscow, 1975). This translation is based on the former source.

The term *uslovnost'* is translated throughout as either "convention" or "conventionality," although others have Englished it as "stylization." J. B. Woodward has pointed out (in *Canadian Slavonic Papers*, VII [1965]: 177) that it "has the alternative meaning of 'conditionalism.' In reference to the theatre the term implied 'conditioned reality,' that is, the reality conditioned by the subjective viewpoint, by the viewpoint of the artist."

even in literature and the graphic arts, theater directors remained faithful to convention, which had degenerated into a pernicious tradition: in depicting a room or a forest, in turns of speech, in gestures, in makeup. Only in the last twenty-five years have attempts been made to turn the stage into a kind of mirror which would reflect reality. The Meiningen theater in Germany, Antoine's theater in France, the Moscow Art Theater here in Russia,[1] all attempted to free the stage from all these conventions. Their productions might be considered the last word in theatrical realism; their failures ought to be acknowledged as fatal for all theories.*

The ideal of the realistic theater is to make everything on stage as it is "in life." The realistic theater contrived to put an entire apartment on stage, in lieu of the traditional three-walled "box-set" with white draperies: the spectator faced a room with a ceiling, a hanging lamp, furniture arranged just as it ordinarily is in private homes: through the window a town or garden was visible, other rooms could be seen through the open door. In place of trees painted on the wing-and-border pieces, quaintly intertwining their branches up to the sky, the realistic theater plants a sort of real garden or forest on stage, with paths, grass, asymmetrically staggered tree-trunks. If rain is to fall during the play, the spectators in such theaters hear the sound of water; if the play takes place in winter, bits of white paper are sprinkled behind the windows or between the trees; if there is wind, the window curtains billow; if there is supposed to be a street on stage, the noise of a crowd and carriages or even the whirring and bells of an electric trolley reach our ears. The actors in such theaters wear costumes that correspond exactly to the epoch or social stratum depicted; their vocal intonations, accents and gestures copy exactly what they have seen and heard in life; in delivering dialogue, crossing the stage, positioning themselves in groups, they pay no attention to the audience, but pretend that they are living, not acting, etc., etc.

Nevertheless, it should be noted that, despite all these innova-

---

*This is no place to revive the old argument about "realism" in art, in general. The question may claim to have been resolved, until the defenders of realism find new arguments. Only those who refuse to hear and understand can still aver that art should "reproduce" or "reflect" reality. It has long been proven that art, in the first place, has never performed that function; in the second, cannot perform it; in the third, were it to perform such a function, it would create something wholly unsuitable. A popular synthesis of all the relevant arguments can be found in J. Volkelt's clever little book, *Modern Questions of Aesthetics*[2] (first German edition, 1895; Russian translation, published by the journal *Education*, 1900).

tions, even in the realistic theater a great deal fails to appear to be "life as it is." While it pays heed to details, it leaves untouched the basic scenic conventions. The stages of realistic theaters are lit, as before, by footlights and spotlights from below, above and the side, whereas, in reality, light either falls from the sky—from the sun or moon—or filters in through a window or issues from a lamp or candle. Not one theater has yet dared to portray night by plunging the stage into total, real darkness. In just the same way, all theaters continue to make sure that everything spoken on stage can be heard in the auditorium, even though it be spoken in a whisper. Even when a large number of people is on stage, invariably only one actor does the talking, and when a new group of performers starts to speak, the preceding group never fails to fall silent and only pretends, by frantic gesticulation, to be carrying on its conversation. Thus, at every step individual realistic details in the production are revealed to be out of keeping with others: when, for instance, rain is depicted, they forget to devise runnels of rainwater and leave the actors in dry clothing; in portraying a sunset, they let the shadows of things and persons fall to the side opposite the footlights, right in the path of the sun, etc.

Of course, an ingenious and highly intelligent director may perhaps succeed in avoiding all these pitfalls and eliminating all these imperfections (for instance, by taking advantage of the phonograph and the cinematograph, which are, as yet, barely used in the theater). But, even so, no director will be able to "deceive" the spectator or make him believe that what he sees is life and not a "show." By all sorts of trifling signs, by the brightness of colors or the movement of shadows, our eyes almost always and unmistakably distinguish the make-believe from the real. Unlike Zeuxis' stupid birds,[3] we never take painted fruit to be the real thing; we never walk up to a landscape painted on a wall with the idea that it is an open window where we can inhale fresh air; we never nod to a marble bust of an acquaintance. When an avalanche composed of cotton wool buries two lunatics at the end of a performance, we see perfectly well that they are not the actors who just now were playing their roles for us, but dummies stuffed with straw.[4] And none of the spectators sitting in the pit and the balconies, having paid from two to six rubles for his seat, believes that Hamlet, prince of Denmark, is actually standing before him and later lies dead as the curtain falls.

The most realistic productions remain in essence conventionalized. In Shakespeare's day they would put up a sign with the inscription "A Wood." Not so long ago we were content with a painted backdrop of a wood and wing-and-border pieces representing implausible trees. Nowadays they begin by constructing a forest out of artful plastic trees with three-dimensional trunks, hinged branches and fake foliage. Possibly the next step will be to confront the spectators with living trees, whose roots are concealed beneath the stage floor. However, even this will remain only a conventional symbol for a forest to the spectator; he will never believe that, behind the curtain during the intermission, pines, oak and birches actually sprang up—and he will merely assume a forest in the shape of what he sees, as the Elizabethan spectator assumed it when he read the inscription "A Wood." In the ancient theater, when the actor portrayed a man come from foreign parts, he entered from the left. On the modern stage the actor is left in a little vestibule, where, in sight of the spectator, he removes his overcoat and puts down his umbrella, to show that he has entered from the street. But who among the spectators forgets that the actor has entered from the wings? How is the convention of removing an overcoat, donned in the dressing room a minute before going on stage, subtler than the convention that an actor, entering at left, has come from foreign parts?

Moreover, all the technical improvements of the realistic theater not only fail to enhance stage illusion, but vitiate it. A beautiful stage-set rivets the attention as an independent work of art, and distracts it from the course of action. Period and true-to-life objects, flaunted by Messrs. the Directors, arouse interest as museum curios and fill the mind with notions irrelevant to the drama. By giving free play to machinery, such as the sound of rain, the chirp of crickets or curtains billowing in the wind, one arouses curiosity and compels the whole audience to wonder and ponder: where is the gramophone or the wind machine located, behind which curtain are they jerking wires? Little by little the spectators grow accustomed to these improvements in stage realism, which have now ceased to be novelties, but this is not the result of spectators starting to accept cotton wool as snow and a length of cord as wind, but of all these contrivances having passed into the roster of ordinary stage conventions. In the world, emotion and nature are the active elements; in the theater they are replaced by the artistic creativity of the performers and the craft of the machinist. The more we conceal this distinction between life and stage, the more palpable it will come to be.

II

The shortcomings of the realistic theater of late, when realism was put in effect on the stage in a logical fashion, were so striking and pronounced that they prompted a reaction. The blatantly antirealistic movement, which, at the end of the last century, regenerated all forms of art, finally invaded the theater. Attempts were made to transmute the very principles of stage production and, to replace realistic theaters, theaters arose that called themselves "conventionalized." The Théâtre de l'Oeuvre in Paris, Max Reinhardt's theater in Berlin, V. F. Kommissarzhevskaya's theater in Petersburg with productions by V. E. Meyerhold, the Moscow Art Theater in its latest productions,[5] one after another made *conscious* efforts to return to conventionality on stage. Their productions are only the first steps on the path of exploration, but they mark out the road on which stage art is stumbling.

Conventionalized theaters, starting from the accurate premise that total illusion on stage is unattainable, eschewed the hope of deceiving the spectator and mimicking life and nature. These theaters exchanged the realistic depiction of place of action for pictorial allusion. Instead of a box-set of a room, for instance, they put only a window; instead of a forest, a few trees; instead of a tower, a piece of cardboard with a crudely marked pattern of stones. The stage is furnished with only those objects absolutely necessary during the course of action: a bench, a bed, the bank of a stream, with the walls of the room or the outskirts of a park or the back of a street left entirely empty. In the new theater, the acting corresponds to the décor. Instead of reproducing those vocal intonations and gestures observed in life, they "portray" only various psychic upheavals and various behavioral actions: for instance, weeping is an inclination of the head, running is a slow floating movement, a kiss is a bringing together of lips that do not touch one another. The directors of these theaters take special care to see that everything consummated on stage be beautiful, regardless of the subject of the drama performed. All of the actors' rhythmical movements and their groupings are subordinated to the general concept, the general tempo chosen, to harmonize with the style of the décor, etc.

However, it must be noted that these would-be conventionalized productions in fact seem, for the most part, semirealistic. The directors of conventionalized theaters, thinking to free themselves from unnecessarily realistic detail, present, rather than all of the ambience, only a few of its components, but often those few are presented with complete realism. The former theater depicted a whole room, the new one depicts one wall; the former theater depicted a forest, with sunlight streaming between the tree-trunks and birdsong, the new one, in its stead, puts three saplings on the forestage. This semirealism rivets the spectator's attention with heavier shackles than the old stage realism did. Seeing only part of a room in front of him, one wall without a ceiling, one window beside a bed, the spectator sees *only* that wall, *only* that window beside a bed, and it is much harder for him to imagine the room than if it were either depicted in entirety or not depicted at all. The Elizabethan spectator, reading "A Wood," could conjure up a dense, impenetrable grove, wherein the action takes place; the spectator at a "conventionalized" theater, with three trees set before him on stage, sees only these three trees and nothing more.

In just the same way the actors' conventionalized acting in fact seems, for the most part, inconsistently performed. The actors at "conventionalized" theaters perform ordinary dialogue wholly naturalistically and switch to conventionalized acting only in the most dramatic passages. In dialogue during the scenes their voices correspond accurately to what we hear in life; conversely, in screams and exclamations, they do not imitate an actual scream but "depict" it. Walking across the stage, sitting on a bench, closing their eyes, raising an arm, the actors of the "conventionalized" theater move like living people; at a moment of emphasis or intense dramatic action, they suddenly lose this ability—of being living creatures—and turn into mannequins. In conventionalized productions these shifts from realism to stylization in the acting checker all the actions, shatter all the effects, transform the show into an excruciating alternation of clashing colors and dissonances.

Of course, one can combat semirealism and inconsistent acting style; conventionality might be more logically injected into *all* set-pieces and *all* details of the acting. Aware that the depiction of objects cannot, in any case, give an illusion of the originals, some "conventionalized" theaters have already begun deliberately to distance the scenery and set-pieces from the forms of reality. Not walls or trees or clouds are portrayed on stage, but a suggestion of walls, trees, clouds—stylized reality; the furniture put on stage, the props put into the actors' hands are intentionally unlike the originals, obviously only depictions, only symbols, and not the things themselves. The actors at such theaters, in all the scenes, significant and insignificant, strive to deport themselves like mannequins. Recollecting that, in the emotional passages, they nonetheless will fail to deceive the spectators or compel them to believe that they [the actors] are suffering, enjoying bliss or dying in actual fact, for the sake of a total effect, they pretend that they are not walking, not looking, and not talking, but depicting walking, looking, talking . . . In these theaters everything must be conventionalized from start to finish, and as in the old theaters they constantly strove to convince the spectators that they were watching reality, so here they constantly strive to remind them that this is only representational . . . Nevertheless, not one theater has yet succeeded in implementing such a plan in full measure. At every point, realism kept breaking through the conventionality all the same: the sky, for instance, was conventionalized, with its stripes, but the crags were realistic; the walls were conventionalized, but the staircase real; the portières conventionalized, but the actors' costumes real. Finally, at every moment the actors themselves mistook the tone and suddenly, after sweeping the floor with "conventionalized" gestures, they started moving like living persons, etc.

We grant, however, in theory, that a brilliant director and an ideal company may succeed in surmounting all the difficulties and create an entirely "conventionalized," "stylized" theater; they may succeed in avoiding the most minor realistic details in scenery and set-pieces, in dressing the performers in costumes that will also be nonrealistic and will not contradict those things they depict, in training the performers in movement that will harmonize with the stationary clouds on the painted sky and the leaves on the constructed trees and so forth: will the harmony necessary to all-round conventionality result? No. Even after this, one entirely insurmountable contradiction is left. The actors' living, actual bodies will never jibe with the conventionality of the scenery, set-pieces and acting. Against a background of daubed canvas which merely delineates a house, a bush or a sky, there always stands the alien and inapposite figure of the actor, which does not delineate a man but is, in actual fact, a man. One may do away with realistic gestures and intonations, but how can one do away with the living quality of the voice itself, with the living color of the face, with the living radiance of the eyes? The only way left for the "conventionalized" theater to triumph ultimately is to replace actors with puppets on strings, with gramophones inside them. This would be logical and a possible solution to the problem—and there is no doubt that the modern "conventionalized" theater is leading by the most direct route to a theater of marionettes.

But the more logical the conventionalized production and the more it tallies with a mechanical theater, the less necessary it will be. By gradually depriving the actor of the possibility of acting and of artistic creation, theatrical conventionality will finally eliminate the stage and art as well. In reading a dramatic work, of course, we conjure up the action taking place through the power of our imagination. "Conventionalized" theater will aid imagination only some-what: in its performance, as in the mere reading of a book, the action itself will only be implied. If the conventionalized theater gains a foothold, the only persons to visit it will be those with feeble imaginations, persons for whom books are not enough; for those persons imbued with fancy, the theater will seem superfluous.

III

Both methods of staging now practiced in theaters—the realistic and the conventionalized—lead to insoluble contradictions. To elucidate the question, one must translate it from the realm of pragmatism to the realm of theory, to define more precisely what the art of the stage is and how it differs from other arts.

It is erroneous to think that the arts are differentiated by the materials they use. A work of sculpture can be created from various materials, marble, bronze, oak, plaster—but it remains sculpture nonetheless. Conversely, sculpture and architecture are quite distinct arts, although they often use the same materials: stone, metal, wood. Arts are differentiated by those aspects of the visible world and reality to which each of them directs its primary attention. Sculpture is concerned exclusively with shapes; painting and drawing with colors and lines; music knows only sounds; epic poetry, human life and events; lyric poetry, fluctuations in emotion; and so on. True, the ancient carvers painted their statues (as some moderns do), but this decoration played an ancillary role. A statue painted does not turn into a painting any more than poetry spoken aloud turns into music.

The ultimate aim of art is to apprehend the universe by a special artistic intuition. To this end it strives, singling out one aspect of reality, isolating it, making it possible to fix all our attention on it. Out of the infinitely multitudinous world of colors, sounds, actions and emotions surrounding us, each art selects but a single element, as if inviting us to bestow contemplation on it alone, to seek in it a reflection of the whole.* A statue which represents Sophocles gives

---

*The theory of "art as cognition" is only glanced at here. It is developed in somewhat more detail in my article "Keys to the Mysteries" (*Balances*, no. 1, 1904), which has required, however, significant emendations. Similar ideas, deriving from different premises, have been developed by A. A. Potebnya (see an account of his view of art in the books and pamphlets of D. Ovsyaniko-Kulikovsky). The question of dividing the arts by the aspects of reality on which they concentrate is examined rather thoroughly in Karl Groos' book *Introduction to Aesthetics* (Russian ed., F. Ioganson, 1899).[6]

us, first of all, a depiction of the shapes of his body, without telling us what color his hair was or what timbre his voice. Admiring a landscape by Levitan,[7] we do not know exactly who lived in the manor house he has drawn or how the rooms in it were arranged. Shakespeare portrays the development of Othello's jealousy, but says nothing about the views Othello held as a military commander.

Art always "abbreviates reality," showing us only one of its aspects. This method must be admitted as fundamental to art, its constant "modus operandi." At first sight, it may be thought that stage art contradicts the general law. In the theater everything is as it is in life: shapes and colors and sounds and movements and events and emotions. It is sculpture, but brightly painted in natural colors, it is painting, but moving and speaking, it is music and lyric poetry, but personified in outward images. It may be asked, does not the theater transgress against the fundamental requirement of art, by becoming a kind of color photograph of reality, transplanting it to the stage, so to speak, with the roots and soil intact? Is not the theater like a panorama, presenting an illusion of truth, or waxwork figures in a museum, touched up with rouge and dressed in real costumes—like all those artifacts to which we deny the name of art? Is it not misconceived on our part to ascribe stage performances to the realm of art?

These charges would be valid if the theater did, in fact, lay claim to concentrating on several different aspects of outward appearance at the same time. Then it would only be a blend of the various genres of art and would lose the right to an individual place in their ranks. But, not being a synthesis of the arts as some theoreticians claim, the theater is nevertheless a true art, because the essential token of artistic creativity is characteristic of its very authenticity. The essence of theater, as of any art, was beautifully defined, once and for all, by Aristotle two thousand years ago, in his treatise on poetics. "Tragedy," said Aristotle, "is the imitation of a single, important, self-contained action"—and these words, with striking precision, distinguish the art of the theater from other types of art. As shapes are to sculpture and line and color to painting, so action, direct action appertains to drama and the stage. The dramatist wants the actor, by his playing, to incarnate the action as it develops before the spectator's eyes, much as the sculptor wants to show the spectator the inert shapes of a body in marble or bronze.

The dramatic works of all ages and countries confirm Aristotle's definition. Leaving aside the Greek tragic poets, whose works served him as points of departure for his theory, all later masters of drama incarnated in their works primarily action: Kālidāsa, Shakespeare, Calderón, Corneille, Ibsen, Wedekind.[8] What is Othello, for example? He is not a statuesque image, immediately taken in by the sight, like D. G. Rossetti's "Beata Beatrix,"[9] he is no outpouring of emotion like Shelley's poetry, he is the image of a man in action. We learn of Othello not from his outward guise, not even from his speeches, but precisely from his behavior on stage.* Even those dramas which could seem to contradict Aristotle's definition essentially affirm it. Such are the early plays of M. Maeterlinck, who wrote a great deal against the theater of action, and in defense of static theater. The immobility and inactivity of those dramas are notorious. Although all the characters, throughout the course of all the plays, remain in almost one and the same posture, the possibility of action keeps growing in their souls, to burst forth in the last scene as the catastrophe.

In order to show the spectators action protracted over time, an "actor" is indispensable. Therefore, the incarnation of drama on stage can appertain only to a performer, a living creature capable of action, or else to an ingenious mechanism which depicts action. In the latter case the theater, as an individual art form, disappears and becomes only a second-rate auxiliary for the dramatist, just as typography is for the poet. In the former case, the sole legitimate monarch of the stage remains the artist-performer. There is no third option. Once the performers have been retained, one cannot force them to act like machines; a living creature is incapable of it, to any great degree. Once machines have been utilized, one cannot elevate their workings to the level of creativity: we do not have the power to inspire the dead with life. If in the past the theater ever revealed its mighty influence as an artistic activity, this was always due to the creativity of the performers. Stage art and the actor's art are synonymous; the director and machinists have no more meaning in the theater than editor and copy-reader have on a newspaper. Scenery and set-pieces for the acting are the same as a frame for a painting, and woe betide if the frame dominates the foreground.

Each art has its own degree of realism and its own—conventionality. That aspect of the visible world on which the attention of a given art is primarily concentrated must be incarnated with all the realism available to it. So, sculpture tries to be realistic in reproducing form, letting the body be the color now of marble, now of bronze, now of cast iron. In just the same way, in a black-and-white

---

*The theory of drama as "action" ("in the process of being accomplished" [*sovershayushchagosya*] and not "having been accomplished" [*sovershevshagosya*]), propounded by Aristotle, is worked out in greater detail by the German critics, beginning with Lessing.

engraving, the drawing may be realistic but the coloring is conventionalized. A performer's acting may be realistic, too, when it embodies the stage action, but this realism must not turn into naturalism. The actors' vocal intonations, gestures and mime must correspond to the truth of life only insofar as the form of a statue corresponds to the form of the human body. We do not consider a sculptor's creations to be unlike life because they are more or less than life-size in proportion—be it the gigantic Zeus of Phidias or a tiny golden statuette by Cellini. We do not consider the caricatures of Leonardo da Vinci to be untruthful, although he portrayed deformity seldom met with in real life. But we withhold the name of art from creations which contradict our notions of the possible: statues which break the laws of anatomy, paintings which break the laws of perspective. Acting ought to be realistic in the sense that it must show us possible actions, even if exaggerated in one direction or another: in comedy, toward vulgarity, in tragedy, toward grandeur.

But the very act of choosing performers to act out the drama predetermines the nature of the stage décor. Side by side with living persons, both counterfeits of reality ("realistic" productions) and its stylization ("conventionalized" productions) are inappropriate and impossible. The natural human figure can harmonize only with actual objects and not their representations. Theatrical realism, dimly aware of this, was mistaken, however, in thinking to achieve its goal by perfecting its counterfeits of reality. A more decisive step had to be taken and representation replaced directly by reality itself. But the objects surrounding the actor must in no way be those very ones which, given the play's subject, might surround its characters in life. The conventionalized theater understood perfectly that the spectators' imagination can create the necessary picture better and more accurately than can all the contrivances of scene designers; it was mistaken only in thinking that the imagination had to be assisted by all sorts of inappropriate hints. Portières, particolored rugs covering the stage floor, benches covered by cloth or fur, rows of columns, massive pediments, steps ascending aloft and so on—these are the possible accessories of dramatic performance. None of these objects can have a direct relation to the drama performed; they can be associated with it only by a unified style, and their selection must depend on the discretion and taste of the director.

The ancient Hellenes, possessed of a subtle dramatic flair, had their actors play against the background of an actual building. In Shakespeare's time actors played against a background of tapestries and draperies which did not pretend to the spectators to be anything else. Neither the spectators of the ancient theater nor those of Shakespeare's theater found it difficult to use their faculty of imagination in picturing Scythia, the brink of earth, where Prometheus was fettered to his rock, and the clouds where the action of Aristophanes' *Birds* takes place, and all those courts, hovels, seacoasts, woods and mountains that alternate with such cinematic rapidity in Shakespeare's tragedies. The attempts made by some German and Russian theaters to play Shakespeare and the ancient drama on dual-level stages and similar experiments of the French open-air theaters with unit sets[10] have shown that even for the modern spectator such exertion of the imagination is not at all difficult. After the manifest failures of all the "realistic" and "quasi-conventionalized" productions, it is definitely time to turn to the techniques of the ancient and Shakespearean theaters. Only then shall we be returning the art of the stage to its rightful owner—the artistic creativity of the performers.

Introduction to Monodrama
by Nikolay Evreinov

When some event unfolds before me on the theatrical boards that stand for the world, I regard it as drama in the highest sense of that word only when I myself become, as it were, a participant in what is transpiring on stage, when I myself share the illusion of becoming an active participant, and not a secondary one at that, ever since I became acquainted with the pleasure that resides in the most powerful, most profound emotional reactions of my responsive spirit. In other words, I accept as drama only such "action" as I can, without violence to my imagination, call "my drama."

The rest which I am unable to accept as my own drama I consider the spectacle of someone else's drama, no matter how beautiful, amusing or absurd it may be, only "spectacle" and not drama.

What does the aesthetic force of true drama rest on, or rather, lean on? A sympathetic emotional experiencing of what happens on stage. Indeed, the basis of such an emotional experiencing, according to the just remark of Professor K. Borinski,[1] appears to be an inner recognition of the identical essence inhering in all things; "thanks to the power of sympathy, a man put himself in the charac-

---

Evreinov delivered this lecture in Moscow at the Circle of Art and Literature, 16 December 1908, and in St. Petersburg at the Theatrical Club, 21 February 1909, and the V. F. Kommissarzhevskaya Theater, 4 March 1909. It was published as a pamphlet in 1908 and in a cut version as the introduction to his play *The Performance of Love.* As he half-jokingly remarked, the ideas contained in it were in the air, and he definitely wanted credit for distilling them. The essay has never been reprinted, and the pamphlet has become extremely rare. This translation has been made from a copy kindly lent me by Alma Law.

Evreinov keeps referring to the Ego on stage with whom the spectator is to identify as the *deistvuyushchee litso,* literally the "acting personage" or "dramatis persona," the usual term for any character in a play. It may be rendered as the "protagonist," but I have translated it as "active participant" to indicate the dynamic role which Evreinov assigns it.

ters' place, seems to forget that they are only playacting, suffers with
them and undergoes all the emotions that move them." In short, the
spectator "co-experiences" along with the active participants. The
ideal of a dramatic performance is to be found in an experience
shared equally on either side of the footlights. Through this initia-
tive, an emotional experience which by its nature has no great
meaning can be relevant both to the actor and the spectator.

I have said that the spectator co-experiences along with the active participants. But is this so? Can we simultaneously share experience with even two active participants who are not attuned to one
another at a given moment? . . . Naturally, when the villain and his
victim, say, stand before us, out of an innate penchant toward the
relatively good, we put ourselves in the place of the victim who appeals to our sympathy and we will co-experience only with her. But
what if both "active participants" are equally sympathetic, near and
dear to us, and yet their dramatic conflict stirs up in each of them
emotions which are different not only in nuance but in their very
essence? Whose experience are we to share? . . . The question is
more serious than it may seem. After all, if it is impossible to co-
experience the emotions of two active participants with all possible
completeness, isn't the playwright, the culprit in this case, relegat-
ing us to mere spectacle, to the status of mere curious eyewitness,
and depriving us to a large extent of that sublime pleasure in art,
whose essence, according to Karl Groos,[2] lies in the exercise of inner imitation or, what I consider the same for dramatic art, in co-
experiencing.

What constitutes this "inner imitation" of another person's psychic state, which I call "co-experiencing"? Here is how K. Groos
illustrates this concept: when we listen to Faust's second soliloquy
and yield fully to the "magical power" of his speech, we feel as if the
words do not fall on our ears from outside us, but seem to issue from
our own breast. We do not perceive them in the ordinary way as
something irrelevant to ourselves, but let ourselves be carried away
by them as by a mighty flood: we inwardly perform every movement
along with him, every tremor of thought, feeling, passion . . . We accompany Faust in his feeling of dreadful self-contempt, we progress
with him to the decision to drink of the poisoned chalice and our
resolution falters when his does, when the joyous tidings reach us—
the greeting of the Easter bells.

Naturally, when a drama's expository scene is so successful, we
are so capable of living "soul for soul" with Faust that we actually

see the entrance of Mephistopheles through Faust's eyes and hear through his ears, as the sense of the tragedy requires.

But we can call to mind scores of other expository scenes with two, three, a great many characters. In such cases can we live "soul for soul" with several characters at a time? Can we co-experience with them in such completeness as to view all of them through the eyes of each of them?

Dissatisfied with the negative answer made by sane common sense, we turn to science.

Psychology teaches us that our mind's capacity for perception is limited insofar as it concentrates its activity invariably on some one thing to the exclusion of another. A shift from unclear perception to clear apperception occurs only when the mind wholly yields to the power of one specific impression. If I regard a man through the eyes of a painter, I cannot at the same time regard him through the eyes of a sculptor; becoming interested in the musical quality of his speech, I cannot easily appreciate its political meaning. When, as the saying goes, we stop, look and listen, essentially we are not really doing all this simultaneously but consecutively: we fluctuate back and forth, nonstop, between a visual apperception and an aural, again and again. The result may be a certain danger of fatigue and defective pleasure. "If a work of art," says Goethe, "compels me to too rapid and abrupt an adjustment, then, for all my willingness, I cannot go with it." And this is because man has a limited perceptual ability.

We all would agree that as a true work of art is the product of aesthetic contemplation, so the pleasure we take in it has the self-same source. And what is aesthetic contemplation but the concentration of the consciousness on a specific and individual object!

It may be protested that in that case, the stage performer has to choose between success as a declamator or as a mime; because if the precondition for aesthetic reactions is concentration on a specific and individual object, then the stage embodiment of an image visually and aurally at the same time entails a reduction in the effective power of one method by the other.

This is quite correct: only one specific aspect of reality can occupy the center of our consciousness, but, naturally, this does not exclude the possibility that the remaining facets of an emotional sensation may contribute to the aesthetic reaction in a subordinate role.

As Groos wittily observes, "a stately and deferential retinue enhances the splendor of a monarch, but of course it ought not to be so numerous and magnificent that the monarch cannot be instantly recognized." And if the artistically intoned word is meant to seem a "monarch" at a given moment, it does not behoove mime to overstep its role as servant and auxiliary.

In the last analysis, the true "monarch" of our aesthetic pleasure in a dramatic performance must, in my opinion, be an *emotional experience*, and everything else is simply the auxiliary "entourage" that enhances it. And my preceding remarks should make it obvious why I say *experience* and not *experiences*, singular, not plural.

I repeat—our mind is limited in its capacity for perception; the basis of aesthetic contemplation is the concentration of attention on a specific, individual object; moreover, a readjustment in the objects of our concentration provokes mental fatigue and consequently a weakening of the ability to perceive. So the true object of a dramatic performance must be seen to be an emotional experience, and, in the hope of facilitating perception, it should be the emotional experience of a single mind, not of several.

This brief résumé should suffice in swaying adherents of the old architectonics of drama to prefer one "proper active participant" over several "equally active participants"; in other words, to prefer an "active participant" who, like a focal point, would concentrate the entire drama and perhaps even the emotional experiences of the rest of the active participants. But I will not stint further proof of the excellence of this new—I may say, "self-evident"—architectonics of drama, since such proof is part of my plan. To be brief, it is this: diversity, when not reduced to unity, splits a whole into several individual, less powerful impressions and thus prevents an aesthetically significant moment from occurring. Therefore, with Fechner,[3] we must invariably aim at unifying diversity, in order to bring about an easily perceived simplicity, and thereby make the total impression a pledge of aesthetic significance.

Now I shall try, as clearly as I can, to substantiate my doctrine as to the form of stageworthy dramatic creation that modern drama ought to take, the drama which is to become "my drama," i.e., the drama of each of the spectators, a drama which, I am finally persuaded, belongs to the immediate future. I refer to *monodrama*.

This word (having become the property of the scholastics, the word is at present utterly forgotten and its meaning lost to any but the sedulous philologist) used to mean a certain kind of predominantly melodramatic work, which from start to finish was performed by one actor alone. Even now we are able to make acquaintance with this type of performance through the appearances of a new kind of quick-change artist, in the style of Fregoli, Francardi and their ilk.[4] This art is of very ancient derivation; its originator appears to be the immortal Thespis, who more than twenty-five hundred years ago, after writing plays with several characters following a certain plan, took to performing them as one-man shows, with the help of linen masks and distinctive costumes of his devising.

However, as one might easily surmise from my preceding statement, I should like to see the term "monodrama" embrace an entirely different concept of dramatic presentation.

And of course I should not have had to rouse this term from its age-old slumber, if another one had managed to arise, to better define this species of dramatic presentation which sooner or later will take its rightful place in the history of the theater.

But when one is talking about creating new values, it is ridiculous to invest much importance in creating new words as vocables. Moreover, a new pearl glows all the more brightly in an old, tarnished setting.

Now by "monodrama" I mean to denote the kind of dramatic presentation which, while attempting to communicate to the spectator as fully as it can the active participant's state of mind, displays the world around him on stage just as the active participant perceives the world at any given moment of his existence on stage. Thus, we are talking about an architectonics of drama based on the principle of the drama's stage coalescence with the way the active participant is presented.

As I have already explained, the conversion of theatrical spectacle into drama is conditional on emotional experience, whose contagious nature which evokes co-experience in me, turns a drama alien to me into "my drama" at the moment of its enactment on stage.

The theatrical means of expressing dramatic emotional experience are reduced, as we know, first of all to words; but the unsatisfactory nature of this means is rather obvious. Anyone who has paid close attention to his behavior in the theater stalls will admit that we hear more with our eyes than with our ears; and this, in my opinion, is natural to the theater. Przybyszewski,[5] for instance, makes the direct assertion that "one cannot possibly express oneself in words; subtleties and elusive nuances can be shown only in gestures." I will not expatiate on literature's subjection to theater; A. R. Kugel[6] has proven this subject status soundly enough in a whole series of articles in *Theater and Art*. Although I am far from agreeing with him in his individual instances, I nevertheless tend toward his explanation that the theater declined when literature, by usurping a dominant role for itself, overloaded the stage. Therefore Gordon Craig comes close to my way of thinking, for he is driven frantic by the lack of stage training in modern authors; I applaud him whole-heartedly when he declares: "We shall do without them, since they fail to provide us with the most important thing—something that is beautiful in a stage sense."

And so, as Przybyszewski says, "One cannot possibly express oneself in words." There remain gestures, artistically expressive gesticulation, a language of movements, common to all human races, mimicry in the broad meaning of the word, that is, the art of reproducing movements expressive of our passions and emotions by means of one's own body. Charles Aubert[7] justly remarks that pantomime would seem pre-eminently to be the basic element of theater because it represents action in its own form, i.e., the element of action that is clearest, most effective and most infectious; because when a spectator sees a more or less profound emotion portrayed in mime, he is, by virtue of the law of imitation, stirred to share and feel the emotion whose outward signs he beholds. And this latter circumstance is the most essential in the theater, because, by promoting co-experience with the active participant, it thus implements the conversion of "drama alien to me" into "my drama."

However even this potent means of contact between the stage and the audience is limited in its potency. I freely grant that the mimic art of Quintus Roscius Gallus was so great that the enthralled Cassiodorus[8] believed the eloquent hands of this performer to have a tongue in every fingertip, but when it is reported that this same Roscius managed to translate into the language of gestures all the orations of Cicero, I am inclined to think, with Ch. Aubert, that the Roman public's power of imagination at least equaled the talent of its favorite performer.

And so we see productions in which the dramatist, unable to rely on the performer's mimic art, in some cases adds to highly expressive words and highly detailed directions for the leading participant's miming the very object that motivates both those words and mime, and personifies this object on stage in all its garishness. So, in a whole series of dramas, both classical and modern, a feeling of horror is sometimes instilled in the spectator not only by verbal and mimic means of communication, but also by the presentation of the very object of that horror, for instance, a ghost, an apparition, this or that hallucinatory image. The dramatist's reasoning is very clear: if the spectator is to experience approximately the same thing that the active participant does at a given moment, he has to see the same thing.

In such cases there comes a moment which I would call *mono-dramatic*, despite all its lack of preparation and scenic groundwork. Why, in fact, is the spectator suddenly obliged to see what only one of the protagonists sees and what goes unnoticed by the other characters, who are only stricken by the fear that distorts the features of the one who beheld the ghost? That's the first thing; and second, if the spectator is to see only what the man frightened by the ghost sees, to wit, the very image of the ghost, why is he shown the other characters, those personages whom a terror-stricken man is in no psychological state to see in all their distinctness? . . . and what is more, why does the room, clearing or forest—the place where the ghost appears—not alter at the moment when terror is suggested, in its features, coloring, lighting, as though nothing had happened and the man stricken by unspeakable terror continues to behold its undisturbed contours?

Puzzling questions of this same kind can be applied as well to the use of the "ineffable light" visible to the active participant and invisible to those around him, to the mysterious voice or celestial music, intelligible only to one of the participants in the drama. Finally, one more relevant case is that in which the characteristics of one of the characters are shown to the spectators as they look to another character; when, for example, the villain is represented on stage in the way his victim sees him; for the other characters, even those most astute throughout the play, he is "charming Ivan Ivanovich," despite the patently criminal cast of his whole figure, his ominously hoarse voice and, perhaps, if the drama is played at the Tsarevokokhaisk Theater,[9] his fiery red hair, because a "ruddy red-haired man is dangerous." Only the hapless victim, oppressed by an evil foreboding, mistrusts the sweet smile of this villain, who is obvious even to a spectator born yesterday. There is no doubt as to the reasoning of the author of the play and the author of the production: the audience must feel wholehearted compassion for the virtuous victim, the heroine of the whole drama, and therefore the villain must be perceived from her viewpoint; and so vice is represented the way the virtuous regard it! There are variations: for example, in a fashionable "style moderne" drama with a Nietzschean tinge, the victim would be represented as a silly little shopgirl, whose whole function is to perish beneath the heel of a red-headed Übermensch; however, let me stipulate that this is not an absolute—for he would not in that case be red-headed, but have jet-black hair, the wind-swept ringlets of a prophet, the blazing eyes of a demon and the lofty brow of a genius—as everyone knows, theatrical wigmakers, no less than gods, set their seal on nature's noblemen.

Despite the crudeness of all these examples and their somewhat comic grotesquery, I am pleased to adduce them as testimony that great masters of the stage, as well as their apprentices, are stead-fastly striving to make it possible for the audience at some crucial moment in the drama to begin to see and hear with the eyes and ears of one of the active participants. And this alone says a great deal for the intrinsic nature of my theory, which might seem ephemeral, were it not for historical support by specific experiments.

The greatest similarity to monodrama as I interpret it can be seen in those plays which represent a dream or a lingering halluci-nation, such as Hauptmann's *Hannele*, Maeterlinck's *Blue Bird*, L. Andreev's *Black Masks* and others.[10]

However, despite the artistic worth of these plays, it is easy to see that they confuse objective representation through (sometimes) the most absurd images with a representation dependent on the ac-tive participant's subjectivity. And if you object that conventionality is indispensable to the theater, my reply is that even stage conven-tions should be subject to strict artistic logic and expediency.

According to a report in the Belgian *Literary Monthly*, Maeter-linck has just completed a poetic drama which, to my mind, comes even closer to being a play with monodramatic architectonics; how-ever, once more we have on stage a kingdom of reverie, a kingdom of magical dreams, where some sort of "everyman" acts outside of time and space, in short, a life of illusion and not an overt life, through the portrayal of which the power of monodrama's attrac-tions must be proclaimed.

I fear I may be too hasty in my resolve, but I have to make sure that the refreshing notion of monodrama hangs, as it were, in the musty air of the senescent theater at this moment, and I act as spokesman for what, perhaps tomorrow, another person or persons may propound. History teaches us that this happens on occasion. For instance, the "idea of the eternal recurrence" must have been *in pendente* in its time, if three savants, unbeknownst to one an-other—Nietzsche, Blanqui and Le Bon—almost simultaneously hit upon it in their labors.[11]

As I have already explained, my concept of monodrama must designate that very dramatic work in which the world outside the active participant looks just as the active participant perceives it at any given moment of his stage existence.

Thus, the basic principle of monodrama is the principle of the stage representation's coalescence with the active participant's representation. In other words, the external spectacle must be an expression of the internal spectacle.

Monodrama requires each of the spectators to stand in the participant's shoes, to live his life, i.e., to feel as he feels and have an illusion of thinking as he thinks, and therefore to be the first to see and hear the same thing the participant does. The cornerstone of monodrama is the participant's on-stage emotional experience producing an identical co-experience in the spectator, who, through this act of co-experience, becomes one with the participant. To induce the illusion in the spectator that he is turning into the participant is the chief task of monodrama. To accomplish this on stage, there first must be but one object of action, not only for the reasons given earlier, but also because monodrama's aim is the representation of an external performance that corresponds to the internal performance of the object of the action, and it is not within our feeble powers to be present at two performances at once.

To enable the spectator on any given occasion to say yes or no inwardly along with the participant on stage, it is sometimes not enough for the spectator to see the participant's eloquent figure, hear his expressive voice and know that he is speaking within a room. He must be shown, in addition, if only allusively, the participant's relationship to his environment. We often say yes instead of no when the sun shines, but it sometimes shines more brightly in our mind than in the sky; and that sunshine, no less than actual sunshine, can brighten up my shabby environment with regal comfort. I can say my yes or no in profound meditation, remote in my thoughts from this environment, which then almost ceases to be and becomes veiled by my apathy toward it. Can it be that Hamlet, as he pronounces "To be or not to be," sees at that moment the rank luxuriousness of the court furnishings? And were not you, hard-bitten theatergoers, angered at such a moment by the intrusive splendor of this scene-shop luxury, all this superfluous precision of outline, so meaningless to Hamlet? . . .

And is not Fyodor Sologub right when he demands that the spectator know at each given moment where he is to look, what he is to see and hear on stage. And how candid those lines in his "Theater of a Single Will" sound when he speaks of the expediency of designing the lighting so that the spectator sees only what he ought to see at any given moment, and all the rest is submerged in darkness "just as in our consciousness, everything impending that does not immediately catch our attention falls outside the threshold of consciousness."

Lately there has been much clamor in favor of abolishing scenery. And indeed it ought to be abolished in drama as soon as it hinders more than it helps. But can it not develop into something else? For monodrama this is almost a question of life and death. Can it not become changeable? I affirm that it can. Nowadays, with the invention of transparent scenery, veritable "magic lanterns," improvements in techniques of lighting in all possible hues and intensities, pure transformations which earlier dramatists did not even dream of, excellent screening effects and so forth, we can boldly discuss monodrama as a concept that is wholly feasible.

But I have hurried ahead, before I had exhausted those potentialities for whose sake it is worth "fomenting a revolution" in the backstage world of the modern theater. I have not yet presented the rather weighty circumstance in favor of monodrama as a presumptive form of modern drama, that a man's environment, perceived by his consciousness, does not appear as something inert and dead, lying outside him.

"Is not all nature," exclaims Hofmannsthal through the voice of one of his heroes, "only a symbol for the mood of our souls? Do we not seek traces of ourselves in her? Do we not regard everything as reflections and images of our torments and our aspirations?" This question is the insight of a poet into that domain which the savant has long and rightfully assumed to be his field of competence.

Any psychologist takes it to be elementary that the world around us inevitably undergoes transmutations, due to sense impressions; and the notion that the object of an impression inherently is what it in fact borrows from the subject of an impression is not an exclusively psychological phenomenon. All our sensory activity undergoes the process of projecting purely subjective transmutations onto an extrinsic object. I do not know what color cherries are; I only know that in my eyes they are red; whether your eyes color them exactly the same shade of red as mine do, I do not know; I know only that the Daltonists color them green.[12] It seems to us that the world itself is full of sounds, although sounds, like colors, are nothing but our subjective transmutations of extrinsic qualities. That which in an inanimate object suddenly emerges as an animating force is by no means so alien (as K. Groos explains it) and mysterious, because

this animating force is our own familiar "ego" with all its peculiarities; here, according to Vischer's[13] apposite remark, "soul lend-
ing" takes place—we, as it were, lend the needed particle of our soul
to the constitutionally inanimate object at the time we perceive it.

The world around us borrows, as it were, its character from the
subjective, individual "ego"; and we understand what Goethe meant
about Hebel, when he remarked that the latter endowed nature with
"a peasant quality";[14] nature can be peasantlike when Hebel perceives it, but it can also be "chivalrously beautiful" when Wolfram
von Eschenbach perceives it.[15] And it is modified as we modify, as
our mental mood alters: the cheerful glen, the cornfield and the forest that I admire as I sit carefree with my beloved will become nothing more than a bright green patch, yellow stripes and a dark border,
if at that moment I am brought news of a misfortune befalling someone close to me. And the author of a modern drama, in my interpretation, will fix both these moments in the character's environment in a stage direction; he will pedantically demand of the
set-designer an instantaneous transformation of the cheerful landscape into a meaningless medley of a clamorous green, unnerving
yellow and sullen olive, and he will be right in his pedantry.

In particular, monodrama reveals to us a special refinement in
the depiction of objects which the protagonists perceive purely aesthetically. As Hermann Siebeck wittily demonstrated in his *Das
Wesen der aesthetischen Anschauung*,[16] every aesthetically scrutinized object appears to us to have a personality—not only human
beings, which is only natural, but inorganic objects, as well. Aesthetic contemplation occurs whenever a sensation materializes in a
form which usually expresses a manifestation of personality; extracting from the object its natural essence, aesthetic contemplation
turns the object into a mood expressed in extrinsic form. The inanimate object is made into a personality . . .

Naturally, monodrama makes wide use on stage of this person-
ification of objects, conditioned by the active participant's perception of them in his aesthetic moods. It does not remain apathetic to
the participant's vision of mystically beautiful images in a river
mist, to those pictures cast on nacreous rose-pink clouds which
haunt him in the twilight hours, and, if the participant is filled with
the yearning of Wilde's Narraboth, it will perhaps reveal in the
moon the seductive lineaments of the princess; or a dead woman, if
he is overcome by a presentiment of death; or a drunken profligate,
if the participant has begun to live as Herod; or a virgin, if this is the
hour of his chastity; or, finally, it will be the actual moon, mere

moon, if the hour has struck within the character's soul for that indifference to nature which pervaded Herodias when she came into
the garden to summon her husband to his guests.[17]

Returning from the particular to the general, i.e., from a purely
aesthetic perception of objects to a perception unqualified in this
way, I maintain that even in the latter, more frequent case the monodramatic method of denotation will remain the prevailing method.

The artist of the stage must on no occasion show objects on the
"drama"'s boards as they are in themselves—only when represented
as experienced by or reflecting someone's "ego," his torment, his
joy, his wrath or indifference, will they become organic parts of that
desired whole which in truth we are right to call total drama. Expressing itself in images, the participant's blood must somehow cir-
culate in the objects represented on stage and the stoniest of stones
must not keep silent beside the participant—the revolver which I
admire as a glittering plaything is not the same when I am cleaning
it efficiently for my master and of course no longer the same when I
pick it up to shoot myself; on just what grounds am I shown from
the stage, in all three cases, the same inexpressive, farcically scary
revolver! I was promised drama and not a "mere spectacle," wasn't
I? I want to live the same life the protagonist lives—the moment has
come for the most intense co-experiencing with him! So do not distract me, do not cool me off with your "criminal" stage-props!

"But it's a convention!" our theatrical brakes will screech—"a
necessary convention which cannot hinder the attunement of our
soul in unison with the participant; when the spectator comes to
confront the author's concept, he will see the object in its real light,
because he can easily imagine the form the object has to take from
the tendency of the play." But in that case, I reply, you need show
nothing! It is much easier to imagine it all, if there are no impedi-
ments to the fancy!

"But," the modern dramatist waxes indignant, "can furniture
and a room and trees and the rest be treated as objects of theatrical
creativity?"

Yes.

Look at this bench (you hear?—a "mere bench"), where you
have long sat with your beloved. Now the two of you have broken
up, fallen out of love . . . It is autumn . . . windy . . . and the leaves
drift down in a yellow tedium. You wander aimlessly . . . you're
drawn back to the bench (you hear?—a "mere bench"). Look! something has happened! It is no longer the same! It seems to have grown,
to have become vast and meaningful; it has become so serious and

sorrowful in its stoniness. When you go away, maybe it will begin to whisper to the faded grass about "those" moonlit, dew-drenched nights, about "that" first kiss. It is shamming dumbness! It is alive! But it is reserved, and understands everything. And if it is worth weeping anywhere, then it is here on this bench; and if it is worth kissing anyone right away, let it be this bench . . . And let the dramatist exhaust all the words potent enough to express this "sentient" bench and its physiognomy. And let the director ply all his craft to show it with the same meaningful and authentic truth with which the dramatist dreams he sees it. I have no doubt that under these conditions, a "sentient" bench like this will first render superfluous a score of words in a soliloquy (which is in the interests of economizing stage time) and yet, it will explain the necessary words, their tempo, their rhythm, their inflection better than any commentary could do. And let the scene designer help the director with his inspired rendering, and let the property man and the scene painter, confronting the common concept of dramatist, director and designer, piously carry out their assignments. We ought to see that bench, feel it, understand it and be shaken up, and not simply hear about it. I repeat—we come to the theater first as spectators, and afterwards as auditors; and we invariably want to see all the essentials, to contemplate them with both the corporeal and the mind's eye. Grant us this satisfaction, if this is indeed a stage, and not a pulpit or a concert platform!

In the last analysis, it should become clear to the dramatist that if he wants to represent the life of the mind, he must operate not on extrinsic realities, but on intrinsic reflections of actual objects. For what is important to the psychology of a given character is his subjective vision of the actual object and not the object itself in a relation irrelevant to him.

Heretofore we have been talking about scene-changes as the natural *effect* of a given emotion, a given mental condition, which, when represented on stage, produces in the spectator the desired fullness of co-experience with the active participant. Thus the *cause* of scenic transformations is taken for granted. But some of our emotions, our feelings, are so tenaciously associated with this or that characteristic of our environment that occasionally we learn the cause from the effects.

In his study of personality types, the psychologist Ribot[18] cites this remarkable fact: "After holding a sorrowful pose for some time, one may feel overwhelmed by sorrow; by joining a gay throng and imitating its outward demeanour, one can stimulate a temporary gaiety in oneself. If you position the arm of a hypnotized man in a threatening gesture with a clenched fist, a corresponding play of the features and movement of the other parts of his body will occur of themselves to complement this. Here motion seems to be the cause, and emotion the effect." Therefore, Ribot concludes, there exists an indissoluble partnership between certain movements and their corresponding emotions; moreover, not only are specific emotions capable of stimulating specific movements, but, conversely, some of the subject's movements evoke the emotion that corresponds to them. And I suppose that we will not overstep the bounds of experimental psychology, if we apply the concept of "motion" even to scene-changes in a monodramatic sense. Under this condition the gain in time-saving—a most essential element in modern drama— will be indubitable: instantly shifting from effect to cause, i.e., from the given nature of the environment to the psychic state of the protagonist that causes it, the spectator will sometimes have absolutely no need of an introduction to the protagonist's "psychology" by way of words or mime. Speed and precision aside, the idiosyncratic charm of such an abbreviated stage transmission of emotional experiences turns out to be an additional merit of the monodramatic method.

As already explained above, all our sense activity is subject to a process of projecting purely subjective changes onto an extrinsic object. By extrinsic object, monodrama means not only the inanimate surroundings of the active participants, but also that of living persons.

As we already know, in total drama, which becomes "my drama," only one active participant is possible in the proper sense of this term, only one subject of action is conceivable. Only with him will I co-experience, only from his viewpoint will I perceive the world around him, the people around him. Thus these people must appear before us in exactly the same way, refracted through the prism of the proper participant's mind; in other words, the spectator of monodrama perceives the rest of the participants in the drama only as they are reflected by the subject of the action, and consequently, their emotional experiences, having no independent significance, are presented as theatrically important insofar as the perceiving "ego" of the subject of the action is projected onto them. On these grounds we cannot grant a meaning in monodrama to the drama's other characters as participants in a strict sense, and by rights we must reduce them to objects of action, taking the word "action" to mean their being perceived, their being related to by the true participant. What is important here is not what they say and how they say it, but what the participant hears. How they seem to themselves must remain concealed; we see them only in the form in which they are imagined by the participant. It is highly possible that the latter ascribes to them attributes which they might not possess in our eyes. They will necessarily stand before us transfigured. They will go unnoticed, merged with the background or even absorbed into it, if at any moment they cease to be relevant to the participant. They will efface the entire setting by their appearance, if the participant is wholly engrossed in gazing at them. They are good-looking, intelligent and kind, if the participant imagines them to be so at the moment, and they will stand forth as hideously ugly if the participant is disappointed in them and perceives them from a different angle of vision.

Finally, as the architectonics of monodrama would lead us to expect, the subject of the action himself must appear to us as he imagines himself to be at any given moment of the stage action. After all, we always regard our corporeal outward appearance as something that is at once "ours" and "outside" ourselves; thus we can relate to ourselves in various ways. And this constant or variable relationship to one's own person must, of course, be clearly indicated in the monodrama equally with the other subjective notions of the leading participant. Makeup, mime, lighting are the most available means to achieve that.

As I have already explained, the task of monodrama is almost to transport the spectator himself onto the stage, to see to it that he feels himself at one with the true participant. And therefore I would very much insist that the active participant be designated by the simple but expressive first-person pronoun "I," in contrast to the rest of the participants in the drama, who are my friend, my wife, my acquaintances and so forth. I should prefer this not only for the reason that Przybyszewski's novella *Requiem Mass*[19] is narrated in the first person, i.e., because in that form, as he asserts, "the most intimate pulse can best be felt," but simply out of practical considerations. The spectator should know from the playbill itself with whom the author invites him to share experience and in whose image he, the spectator, must appear. The designation of the subject of the action as "I" is his own bridge from the auditorium to the stage. The leading participant enters and the bridge is crossed; a dual performance begins. Let us suppose that the leading participant, the one designated in the playbill as "I," has begun to squint; the result is darkness; the spectator experiences this result, because the lighting man at that instant in the monodrama turns out the footlights and the border lights and the strip lights, everything; however, by proceeding from effect to cause, that is, from one's own sensation of darkness to whatever caused it, the spectator by the gradual power of imagination will realize that the darkness was caused not by switching off the electric current to the stage but by his, the spectator's, closing his eyes. The leading participant's head is swimming and green spots flash before his eyes . . . The spectator sees these green spots on stage too, and because he knows from his playbill that the leading participant is "I"—that is, he, the spectator—not only green spots but any sight seen by the leading protagonist must be accepted as his own. These are crude examples—illustrations.

In summation, we must reach the conclusion that monodrama, among other things, solves one of the burning issues of modern theatrical art, namely the issue of the paralyzing, ardor-dampening, estranging influence of the footlights. Suppressing them in actuality, as some propose doing, does not mean suppressing them in our imagination: a nasty experience from time to time forces us mentally to re-create the obliterated line of demarcation. This must be done in such a way that, although it is visible, it seems to be invisible, exists yet seems not to exist. And once the director, through an illusion-filled manipulation of the images of the leading participant, achieves a fusion of his "I" and the spectator's "I," the spectator, as if coming on stage, that is, the place of action, will lose sight of the footlights—they will remain behind or, in other words, be obliterated.

In this short introduction to monodrama I have pointed out only a few advantages of the monodramatic method, but it is not difficult to foresee that when monodrama receives a practical application, i.e., when this kind of play is written and staged, yet other advantages, other scenic advantages of this method, when compared to the method of modern drama, will come to light, advantages whose aesthetic significance may be difficult to grasp at the present time.

I do not dispute that, like everything imperfect in this world, even the applied architectonics of drama will require many improvements. So be it! Nonetheless, bear in mind that it is absolutely necessary to extricate essential drama from spectacle and that the only conceivable way to do this is the way I have demonstrated.

And I have one more request to make, a request of a demanding sort!—do not attempt to read signs of naturalism, so ruinous to art, between the lines of my theory of monodrama, even a naturalism of purely subjective hue! When I speak of an architectonics of drama based on the principle of its stage coalescence with the way the active participant is presented, I stress the expression "stage coalescence," as antithetical to realistic coalescence, because I know full well that if a technique for art in general presents an inevitable and yet desirable simplification, it will apply even for theatrical art. Finally, all the positive things that I have said about theatricality* should serve, I believe, as sufficient proof against any suspicion of that antiartistic tendency that is utterly insupportable for modern aesthetics.

And let my last word be the ardent wish that monodrama, actualized in practice, when on its fascinating voyage to a new horizon, will steer clear of that submarine reef ringed round by the songs of treacherous sirens.

*See my article "Apology for Theatricality" in *Morning*, no. 15, 1908.

Russian Dramatists

by Vsevolod Meyerhold

(An Essay at Classification, with a Supplementary Table
of the Development of Russian Drama)

The repertory is the heart of all Theater.

The truth of this assertion is affirmed by the Golden Age of the theaters in Spain, Italy and France: the theater of the sixteenth and seventeenth centuries flourished all the more brilliantly because its heart (its repertory) beat with an infusion of vigorous blood.

The Repertory is already Theater.

We know the Spanish theater of the seventeenth century because it bequeathed us the plays of Tirso de Molina, Lope de Vega, Calderón and Cervantes.

We know the French theater of the seventeenth century because it bequeathed us a splendid collection of texts by Molière.

This is not simply a matter of the talented abilities of the masters of drama I have cited.

The repertory came into being as an individual entity, an aggregation of plays united by a common intellectual schema and common technical devices.

The plays of the Spanish theater are thoroughly steeped in an elemental sense of national power, constantly trumpeting honor, both national and personal. The Spanish dramatists of the seventeenth century marched in step with the religious predilections of

The translation is based on the text published for the first time in V. E. Meyerhold, *Stat'i, rechi, pis'ma, besedy* (Moscow, 1968), I. The manuscript is the draft of a letter which Meyerhold sent to the English translator George Calderon, who was planning an article on the contemporary Russian drama and who had asked him to recommend the most important or interesting playwrights working at the time. One finds, by consulting Calderon's finished article in the *Quarterly Review* (July 1912), that he read many of the authors Meyerhold had indicated but reserved his own strong opinions about them.

the people. The striving to liberate the individual from the shackles of medieval scholasticism is manifested in an original manner in the Spanish theater.

This relates to the ideological plane.

On the technical plane, the repertory of the Spanish theater is united by one task: to concentrate the rapidly unfolding action into *intrigue*. Thus, a radius firmly fastened at one end to a central point can move along its circumference at the other end. And while this theater strives to raise tragic pathos to the highest pitch, it has no fear of destroying the harmony by injecting comic grotesquerie into it, even going so far as the reverberant personal idiosyncrasy of caricature.

The plays of the French theater are bound together by the same attitude toward the individual struggling for liberation from the shackles of religious inertia. They are also allied to a common progressive mode of philosophic thought. This relates to the ideological plane; on the technical plane, the French theater follows the traditions of the Italian and Spanish theaters.

In Russia during the reign of Empress Anna Ioannovna, the public was lucky enough to see the original plays of the *commedia dell'arte* performed by outstanding Italian actors.*[1]

And throughout the playwriting of the eighteenth and early nineteenth centuries one can trace how tightly knit was the influence of those visiting Italians. Knyazhnin[2] made use of Italian plots, but the most resonant echoes of the Italian comedies presented at the court of Anna Ioannovna are heard even now in the showbooths of central Russia. The *commedia dell'arte* tradition, wholly rejected by the Russian actor, is firmly rooted in the showbooths of the Russian folk. And even though Knyazhnin had no heir, the Italian theater nevertheless left the imprint of its influence on the remotest fate of the Russian theater.

Traits of the *commedia dell'arte* rebound to us from the French and English, who were firmly attached to elements of the Theater of Masks.

Although the Russian theater never experienced an efflorescence like that of the Western theaters of the seventeenth century, nonetheless it did have a period of remarkable upsurge. And these upsurges always occurred whenever dramatists sought to recover el-

---

*As members of the companies that visited the court of Anna Ioannovna we find Constantini, Pedrillo, Casanova, Vulcani.

ements of the historical past and took revivals, enlightened by age-old experience, to be an inevitable condition of progress.

The Russian theater of the nineteenth century inscribes three glorious names in its annals: one of them has already been generally acknowledged—that of Gogol; another is too meagrely recognized (on the theatrical plane)—that is Pushkin; a third is not recognized at all (also on the theatrical plane)—that is Lermontov.

Gogol forges a link with the French theater of the seventeenth century by instinctively injecting into Russian comedy an element of the humor and peculiar mysticism of Molière.

Pushkin, in dealing with drama, learned from Shakespeare, but when he comes to praise his master, he soon begins to carp that he did not read Calderón and Lope de Vega. When he himself begins to write plays, he outstrips his master on the path of traditional theater, instinctively following the precepts of the Spaniards.

The Spaniards always tended to subordinate dramatic works by cleaving to the rules of ancient drama.

> The history of literature tells us that in the period of Renascence, in the early sixteenth century, at least from the time of Bartolomeo de Torres Naharro,[3] in Spain an attempt was made to subordinate works of art to the codes of ancient drama, but such attempts were dashed on the medieval spirit and the prerogatives of popular taste, which were too powerful to allow the scholars of the Reformation to achieve their ends. It was under these conditions that Spain enjoyed Lope de Vega and Calderón. In France the attempts succeeded, and resulted in Racine and Corneille, immense talents who, in the opinion of many (e.g., [Marius] Sepet, author of *Le Drame chrétien au moyen âge* [1878]), might have been more beneficial to national art had they been less subservient to the despotic pressure of theory, and might then have better preserved links with *the national heritage of dramatic art.**

What might Pushkin have produced for the theater if he had known the Spaniards, since, after studying with Shakespeare, he nevertheless traduces the Theater of Character in favor of the Theater of Action? "Is tragedy possible without action?" asks Averkiev,[4] and answers, "No." And is it possible without characters? "Yes, it is still possible in their absence."

Chrestomathy of the Russian Language and Literature Department of the Imperial Academy of Science, vol. 59 (St. Petersburg, 1895), p. 25 (my italics).

Averkiev,* when comparing Pushkin and Shakespeare, says, "Shakespeare is a dramatist, Pushkin a poet in the widest sense of the word, with all kinds of poetry equally available to him. Shakespeare drew man in the grip of the passions that overwhelm human beings; Shakespeare's heroes stir terror in us at seeing the unequal struggle with passion.

"We would seek in vain anything similar in the ancient tragic poets; they have a different conception of the tragic"; while arousing tragic terror, they also awake compassion, which, according to Averkiev, is the sole function of tragedy. In Pushkin the motif of *overcoming passion* found its poetical expression in the character of Tatyana.[5] Pushkin's special quality is the serene *contemplation of reality*, and a poet who masters serene contemplation can more clearly and fully express to others those ideas whose essential characteristic is serenity. In *Boris Godunov*, Pushkin delineates a character not by means of passions, as Shakespeare does, but by means of the fateful and inevitable destiny evoked by Boris' heinous crime. This motif likens Pushkin's tragedy to the tragedies of the ancient Greeks and the Spaniards, insofar as the latter tried to follow the laws of ancient tragedy in this regard.

Lermontov, whose *Masquerade* was banned by the censors for its excess of passion, tries first of all to create a Theater of Action. By the demoniacally charged atmosphere of his plays, in scenes that rapidly flit by one after another, Lermontov unfolds a tragedy of persons struggling to avenge offended honor, flailing about in love manias and the fatal ring of gamesters, tearstained murders and posthomicidal laughter. The whirlwind of Lermontov's tragic talent bears us a reminder of Lope de Vega's *Punishment No Revenge* down to the best pages of Tirso de Molina's *Proscribed for Want of Faith*.†[6] *Two Brothers*, a play which many of Lermontov's respectable publishers expelled from the poet's complete collected works, no doubt adjudging this drama to be a piece of juvenilia—this, Lermontov's best drama after *Masquerade*, introduces us to the quintessence of Spanish theater, sharply drawn characters and keen intrigue. And Lermontov begins his attempts at playwriting by endeavoring to compose a Spanish tragedy.

These three dramatists—Gogol, Pushkin and Lermontov—

---

*"On Drama, a Critical Dissertation by D. V. Averkiev, with an Introductory Article 'Three Letters on Pushkin'" (St. Petersburg, 1893).

†An excellent translation of this play (in the original meter), wrought by the poet Vl. Pyasty, will soon appear (M. and S. Sabashnikov, pubs., Moscow).

forged out of durable metal the first links of that chain which must securely form a bridge between the unified Western theaters of the Golden Age and the Theater of the Future.

In the 'sixties a new link for that chain was wrought by Ostrovsky, and his plays, along with the comedies and dramas of Gogol, Pushkin and Lermontov, make up the basis of the Russian repertory. (Ostrovsky makes his debut as the creator of the Theater of Real Life, an achievement which his followers will later and inaccurately claim as the natural evolution of the Russian theater.)

And Ostrovsky, like Gogol, Pushkin and Lermontov, bolstered his peculiar strengths by his acquaintance with models from the great theatrical ages of the West. Ostrovsky translated from Spanish the interludes of Cervantes,[7] and when you compare Ostrovsky's Theater of Real Life with Lope de Vega's Theater of Real Life, you realize the lesson Ostrovsky learned from Cervantes.

The heart of the Russian theater is contained in the repertory, which, as in the period of the Western theater's superb efflorescence in the seventeenth century, has rendered these traits indispensable: on the ideological plane, a pulsation to the beat of folk experience, on the technical plane, the creation of both a Theater of Action with the music of tragical pathos (Lermontov) and a Theater of the Grotesque, which transmogrifies every "type" into a tragicomic grimace, now in the spirit of Leonardo da Vinci, now in that of Goya (Gogol).

Despite the firm foundations laid for the Russian theater by Gogol, Pushkin, Lermontov and Ostrovsky, some of the heirs of these dramatists would not, others could not build on these foundations the magnificent edifice of Russian drama.

It is as if a superstructure had to be constructed on top of Ostrovsky's Theater of Real Life, in the shape of Chekhov's Theater of Mood; but this superstructure instantly revealed its absolute insubstantiality.

Chekhov's theater was born of the seed of Turgenev's theater. Turgenev, almost simultaneously with Ostrovsky, initiated the second (as it were, parallel) stream of the Theater of Real Life, adding to Russian realistic drama a new element—musicality; for a long time this component was relegated to the shadows and only subsequently was it genially developed in the works of Chekhov. But what was only a minor embellishment in Turgenev was developed by Chekhov to its furthest extent.

Turgenev's theater was too intimate, seemingly created only for the amateur stages of old-fashioned drawing rooms or the platforms of outdoor theaters, surrounded by bosky thickets on the estates of the 'fifties and 'sixties.

Beneath the birch trees that border weed-grown footpaths and in portrait galleries, a lacework of unending dialogues is entwined, with no movement and no pathos. This is the way the lyric epos of a great novelist devolves. But is it Theater?

Such is the so-called Theater of Mood.

That the original elements of the Russian theater were replaced for a long while by alien elements is partly Chekhov's fault and partly the fault of an epoch of intense stagnation of Russia's spiritual powers. The 'nineties did indeed impress a fatal stamp on the destiny of Chekhov's theater.

The link between Chekhov's theater and Turgenev's tradition also compels the former to remain associated only with the epoch which created it. No wonder, for Chekhov's theater dies along with the general apathy which the year 1905 takes to its grave.[8] And just as the link of Turgenev's theater seems at one end unattached to the principles of traditional theatricality and at the other unprepared to be fastened to the Theater of the Future, so Chekhov's theater cannot fasten its link to the chain of the great triad (Gogol, Pushkin, Lermontov), for the metal of the Chekhovian link was durable only for one decade. Turgenev and Chekhov did not know how to couple their plays to the repertory, which was born out of the nadir of primeval theatricality.

The theater of mood, thanks to energetic propaganda for plays of this tendency by the Moscow Art Theater, so dominates the Russian stage that a whole series of Chekhov's imitators, headed by Maksim Gorky, are following in his footsteps in the theater. These dramatists appear to be epigones of the Theater of Mood, yet have destroyed its integrity by a propensity to make superficial connections between the attributes of the Turgenevian-Chekhovian theater and the theater of Ostrovsky (Naidyonov is typical).

If these dramatists not only lacked the know-how to forge new links to the inchoate chain of Russian theater but, what is worse, allowed the first spot of dreaded rust (the predominance of literary elements in the theater) to blotch it, dramatists of the newer movements made a conscious effort to multiply these spots and corrode the sacred chain.

Wholesale ruin of the great cause of Russian literature which had been constructed by the efforts of the best dramatists of the 1830s and 1840s was personified by the notorious Viktor Krylov.[9]

Apparently eager in his own time to rot the underpinnings of the Russian theater as deeply as possible, this prolific dramatist boggles the Russian stage by inundating it with his handiwork. He writes dramas, comedies, vaudevilles, farces, translates and adapts French comedy of the decadent period and has for a long while arrested the progress of the Russian stage. In this he is abetted by a whole phalanx of his followers, who are not to be outdone by their leader either in productivity or potent "talent."

The epigones of the Theater of Real Life arrived. Muscovite dramatists reprise over and over the themes of Ostrovsky; Petersburg is ruled by dramatists who either follow the precepts of Krylov or take Ostrovsky's genre-descriptive manner to be a technique for photographing life.

And so the foundations of the Russian theater are shaken loose, the audience's taste is corrupted to the nth degree, the Russian actor has lost all ties to his predecessor, the great actor of the mid-nineties.

Whatever bold experiments on the path of discovery are carried on by the talented youth of the new literary movements and by those who tag along for the ride, the theater stands muffled in a fog of the greatest insipidity and utter lack of principle.

THEATER OF THE "DECADENTS"

As our century begins, a host of dramatists, devoted to daring experimentation, is trying to break with theatrical traditions. These dramatists (who have written more for the reader than for the stage) produce works that are *antitheatrical*, however interesting they may be in themselves. The outstanding among them appear to be Balmont, Bryusov, Minsky, Zinovieva-Annibal (*Rings*), Z. Gippius (*Sacred Blood*), Chulkov and Leonid Andreev.[10] The last (one need only compare his *Black Masks* with *Days of Our Life*) may be grouped with the "decadents" in a purely superficial way, for, by the nature of his taste, outlook and, by and large, his whole literary makeup, he belongs rather to the circle of writers following Maksim Gorky.

NEW THEATER

The founders of the New Theater try first of all to revive this or that aspect of one of the theaters of the original theatrical periods. *Vyacheslav Ivanov* is trying to resuscitate the attributes of the ancient theater, with dreams of doing away with the footlights and recreating the classical Greek orchestra in their place.[11] *Aleksandr Blok* follows the traditions of the Italian popular comedy, associating his explorations with the Weltanschauungen of the German romantics (Novalis, Tieck).[12] *Aleksey Remizov* makes a stab at a modern mystery play patterned after the mysteries of the early Middle Ages.[13] *Mikhail Kuzmin* writes plays in the spirit of medieval drama, and also reconstitutes the French comic theater.[14] *Andrey Bely* tries to create an original style of modern mystery play.[15] *Fyodor Sologub* either apes the forms of ancient theater (*The Gift of the Wise Bees*) or the principles of the Spanish dramatists (*The Triumph of Death*).[16] *L. Zinovieva-Annibal* tries to adapt the manner of Shakespearean comedy (compare her *The Singing Ass* with Shakespeare's *Midsummer Night's Dream*).[17] *Evgeny Znosko-Borovsky* in his play *The Transformed Prince* begins to convey to Russian drama characteristic attributes of the Spanish theater, by condensing the mannerisms of the grotesque.[18] *Vl. N. Solovyov* in his plays *The Devil in Green* and *Harlequin Marriage Broker* returns the theater to the Comedy of Masks.[19]

Contrary to the decadents, who created a theater without foundation, the dramatists of the New Theater are striving to subordinate their creativity to the laws of traditional theaters of the original theatrical epochs.

Note: This sketch [on the following pages] was a result of my friendly correspondence with the English researcher of Russian theater George Calderon, concerning the latest trends in English and Russian theater at the present time. Calderon brilliantly translated two plays by Chekhov, *The Seagull* and *The Cherry Orchard* (London: Grant Richards, 1912). See his article "The Russian Stage," in the *Quarterly Review*, no. 432 (July 1912).

Theater of Real Life

I. A. N. Ostrovsky (1850s–1870s)   II. I. S. Turgenev
                                             (1850s–1870s)

III. Ostrovsky's Pleiad (1850s–1870s)
   1. Pisemsky (1850s and 1860s)
   2. Sukhovo-Kobylin (1850s)
   3. N. Potekhin (1860s–1870s)
   4. A. Potekhin (1850s–1870s)
   5. Dyachenko (1860s–1870s)

IV. Count L. N. Tolstoy   V. Viktor Krylov
    (1880s–1890s)   (1870s–1890s)

EPIGONES

VI. Moscow (1880s and later)	VII. Petersburg (1880s and later)	VIII. A. P. Chekhov (1890s)
Shpazhinsky	Gnedich	IX. Maksim Gorky
Boborykin	M. Chaikovsky	X. Epigones
Nevezhin	E. Karpov	Chirikov
Vl. I. Nemiro-vich-Dan-chenko	Suvorin	Naidyonov
A. F. Fedotov	Potapenko	Yushkevich
Vl. Aleksandrov	Trakhtenberg	O. Dymov
Timkovsky	Timoshevsky, etc.	B. Zaitsev
Goslavsky, etc.		Aizman
		A. Fyodorov
		L. Andreev (*Days of Our Life*), etc.

Theater of "Decadents"

I. K. Balmont (*Three Blooms*, 1905)
II. V. Bryusov (*Earth*, 1905)
III. Minsky (*Alma*, 1900)
IV. L. Zinovieva-Annibal (*Rings*, 1904)
V. Leonid Andreev (*King Hunger, Black Masks*, 1908)
VI. Z. Gippius (*Sacred Blood*, 1903)
VII. G. Chulkov (*Taiga*)

New Theater

I. Vyacheslav Ivanov
Tantalus, 1905
II. Aleksey Remizov
The Play of the Devil, 1908
Of Judas, Prince of Iscariot, 1909
George the Dragon Killer, 1912
III. Mikhail Kuzmin
Comedies
(a) *of Eudoxia*
(b) *of Alexis*
(c) *of Martinian*
The Chimes of Love
Liza the Dutch Girl
The Prince from the Cottage, etc.

IV. Aleksandr Blok
The Little Showbooth
The King in the Square
The Incognita
The Song of Destiny
V. Fyodor Sologub
The Triumph of Death
The Gift of the Wise Bees
Night Dances
The Petty Demon
Vanka the Steward and the Page Jehan
Hostages of Life
VI. L. Zinovieva-Annibal
The Singing Ass, 1907

VII. Andrey Bely
He That Is Come, fragment, 1903
VIII. Evgeny Znosko-Borovsky
The Transformed Prince, 1910
IX. Vl. Solovyov
The Devil in Green, 1910
Harlequin Marriage Broker, 1911

The Essence of Tragedy
by Vyacheslav Ivanov

I

Nietzsche was right to begin his book on Tragedy with the assurance that our aesthetics will make great strides if we accustom ourselves to distinguishing in every work of art two omnipresent, mutually opposed, but also mutually interacting principles, which he chose to designate by the names of the two Hellenic deities who define just this aesthetic polarity—the names "Dionysos" and "Apollo."[1]

This statement of an idea not new in essence (on the contrary and fortunately, profoundly ancient, but for the first time propounded with such precision, its precision intensified by its being kept within the bounds of aesthetics and psychology, all else that the spheres of speculative thought and religious mysticism have invested it with from time immemorial having been eliminated), this statement might justly be called a discovery: so fruitful did it seem for the comprehension of both the nature of the arts and the enigma of Hellenism. Furthermore, it would appear that it possessed as the distinctive mark of an original discovery—an independence from the conception as it first arose in the consciousness of the thinker, freedom to exist outside him.

In fact, we can and to some degree must describe both principles differently than he does, evaluate them differently, conjecture a different content for them, examine them in different cultural-historical and philosophical correlations. But no longer can we fail to see and distinguish them, no longer can we deny the dual, double-natured composition of every work of art. A kind of chemical formula has been posited, which remains constant, no matter what

---

This article first appeared in the journal *Works and Days* (*Trudy i dni*, no. 6, 1912) and was reprinted in Ivanov's second collection of essays, *Borozdy i mezhi* (*Furrows and Landmarks* [St. Petersburg, 1916]). The present translation is based on the reprint of that book by Bradda (Letchworth, Herts, 1971). I have tried to be faithful to Ivanov's gnomic prose style.

conclusion we may reach as the result of investigations into the nature of the two elements that enter into it. And what is more, these elements were correctly named: their equation with certain definite values of ancient thought has been verified by the latest researches and served as a key to open many doors to the proscribed sanctuaries of antiquity.

Therefore one can proceed from recent observations, independent of the formulated theory, of the nature of the worship of Apollo and Dionysos among the Hellenes—and if these observations are correct, one may be sure in advance that they will provide inferences in aesthetics that concur with Nietzsche's basic premise about the duplex nature of every art form.

II

In the following reflections on the essence of tragedy, we shall begin with the idea—popularized in the form of a philosopheme only after Plato's day, but in its gist much older than Plato—the idea that Apollo is the principle of unity, that his essence is a monad, while Dionysos signifies the principle of multiplicity (which is even depicted in myth as the sufferings of an agonized, lacerated god).

The god of structure, co-ordination and harmony, Apollo is the connective and re-uniting power; the god of ascension, he rises from discrete forms to the higher form that embraces them, from a fluctuating coming-to-be to a static and abiding state of being. The god of disruption, Dionysos, by descending, sacrifices his divine integrality and wholeness, imbuing all forms with himself in order to permeate them with an ecstasy of repletion and rapture—and again, to divert living forces from the amorphous unity achieved by escaping oneself and, consequently, abolishing oneself, and toward the imaginary inner experience of discrete existence.

But if the natural symbol for unity seems to be a monad, the symbol for discreteness within unity, as the source of any multiplicity, has been suggested by the teachings of the Pythagoreans from time immemorial: it is the doublet or dyad. Thus, the monad of Apollo is opposed to the Dionysian dyad; just as the feminine principle opposes the masculine, and from earliest times also signified its opposition to the "unit of man" by the number 2.

Dionysos, as everyone knows, is pre-eminently the god of women—a babe pampered by them, their bridegroom, their daemon, filling them with his presence, inspiration, might, now blissful, now tormented by the mindless excess, the object of their lust, transports, adoration—and, finally, their victim. Tragedy, by its very nature, origin and name, is the art of Dionysos—a simple modification of the ritual of Dionysian worship.

Hence the feminine soul of tragedy is implicit, as is its religious and aesthetic essence, as the fullest revelation of the dyad in art.

III

If we ask ourselves, "what should the art be like, by virtue of its concept, whose content and concern consists in the revelation of the dyad?"—naturally, our answer is, an art which should be internally dialectic. It will portray passions and events whose linkage will form a dialectical chain.

The more consciously the life reconstituted by this art issues forth, the greater part the element of logic will play in its reproduction. The more persistently the age demands consciousness from art, the more certainly this art will gravitate toward theory. (Let us recall the French drama of the seventeenth century.)

The less consciousness the creator of this art injects into his creation, the more decisively the logic of the elements and the mechanism of blind passions will predominate, the more emphatically the struggle of chaotic forces will be shown and, with them, the more urgently the need for purely mechanical means of depiction will be sounded. (Let us recall the tragedies of Aeschylus, who, for good reason, required theatrical machinery much more than did Sophocles.)

Furthermore, an art devoted to the revelation of the dyad will, of necessity, be an art of action, an "act"—if not of pure music. The monologue principle inherent in the epic and lyric precludes the complete revelation of the dyad (which these types of poetry represent, more or less approximately, only by its reflection in some monad); it constitutes an impediment to the spontaneous influence on the mind of the receptor. The purpose of the art of the dyad will be to show us an embodiment of thesis and antithesis; what Hegel called "becoming" (*Werden*) will take place before our eyes; art will be an impression of life.

Resolution of the process depicted must consist in the "removal" or annihilation of the dyad. Insofar as the dyad is to be represented in art by living forces, incarnated in human characters, they themselves are consequently liable to be annihilated: it is up to them to divest themselves of their selves, to become in essence something other than they were before—or perish. This logically inexorable end must make the art devoted to revealing the dyad catastrophic. The coming-to-be it effects will appear as a continuous drift toward some sort of cataclysm.

Now the common pathos of this theoretically constructed art will be rooted in the contemplation, horrifying to a normally placid mind, and the emotional experience of this cataclysm, of the dark and empty abyss that lies between two proximate and unconnected cliffs, in the sensation of the hidden and irreconcilable contradictions of psychical life, the gaps between them permitting a slight glimpse of the mystery of existence which, finding no room within earthly confines, is envisaged by mortal sight as nonexistence. This art must stagger the mind, test it and teach it—by a hallowed terror. Thus we come to the condition most vital to implementing the art we have described, the realization of which is tragedy.

IV

The concept of the dyad presupposes an initial, intrinsic unity, in which an internal opposition is revealed. The art of the dyad is not a merely antagonistic art, that is, one which depicts any antagonism, any conflict of hostile forces. The forces which it represents as warring are conceived of as primordially fused in a single integral existence. From the very start, this existence must harbor a certain duplicity within itself—not as an inner contradiction, but as an inner wholeness. Only as the energy concealed within it grows and is definitely revealed will it assume the masks of division and discord. Into the fray enter those principles basic to it, which by their union substantiate its integrity, much as the opposing supports of two pillars consolidate the stability of an arch.

Therefore the purely superficial clash of opposing powers, which we have not conceived to be primordially united, which are alien to one another or belong to different orders of phenomena (as, for instance, the force of nature and the force of the human soul) cannot serve as matter for the art we describe. Similarly, the portrayal of an individual's inner life, torn between attractions unconnected by a unique law of character, an inner life unintegrated, not self-defined in its heart's core, is alien to this art. The saying "Two souls dwell within this breast" can receive a tragic interpretation only on condition that it refer to the age-old awareness of the discordancy inherent in our psychic nature, between the discrete elements of the multipartite human makeup. If Hamlet were simply a weak man, Shakespeare's tragedy would not seem so inexhaustibly profound; to be more precise, it would not exist at all—as a tragedy. But Hamlet is a kind of temperament; and the enigma of the primal cause that undermines his action turns our thoughts to the primordial and common laws of the spirit.

For the art of tragedy is pre-eminently a human art: a human being does not possess the uniform, unified integrity of beasts or angels; the pale within which he is set in the universe is a tragic boundary; to him alone has fallen the lot of inner struggle, and he is given the possibility to make the decision within time which binds him and his world.

V

Let us compare this *a priori* construct of an art devoted to revealing the dyad (on which account we ought to acknowledge tragedy as the art of Dionysos, if, in accordance with the ancients, few acknowledge the dyad as the principle of Dionysos) with the facts of extant tragedy and historical data about its origin. As to the former, however, they so agree with our *a priori* construct that it would be indistinguishable from a generalization resulting from simple observation. Therefore, we shall confine ourselves to data about the origins of tragedy and its past, forgotten by successive eras, and shall try to track the tragic principle of the dyad back to the very cradle of Dionysian art.

The bifurcation of the original unity into internally warring energies is the intrinsic idea and most profound emotional experience of the Dionysian mysteries. From time immemorial Dionysos was conceived of as a god who inspired the frenzied ones he possessed to turn on him, in order to make him the object of the sacrificial action. He is passive, as a suffering god, in his own persona—and active, as a sacrificial god, in the person of those who carry out his passionate will and fate: thus he is split into antinomic hypostases. Nowhere but in the Dionysian community do all the participants in the ecstatic worship bear the name of their god (the "Bacchae"), that is, they are mysteriously identified with him. So here is the age-old dyad of the religion of Dionysos: he is both the sacrificial victim and the sacrificator.

But in this way the god appears in two different personae: one persona is himself, as a concrete reality of myth or the object of clairvoyant conspection or, finally, as sacrificial animal, mystically transubstantiated into himself through the ritual action; the other persona is that of his votary and officiant, or foe, seized now by inspiration, now by blind dementia (like the Titans who tore the divine infant to pieces), and often imagining himself to be an unchanging hypostasis of the same Dionysos (like the Thracian Lycurgus).[2] For the most part, this second guise—the feminine guise, for the deepest, most intense, richest in religious content of the rites of worship of Dionysos are those of the maenads—appears, by all tokens, also to be the most ancient stratum in the complicated evolution of the Dionysian religion.

Agave,[3] the frenzied priestess and martyr of Dionysos, unconsciously committing a holy filicide, wielding on a sharp-pointed thyrsus the head of her son (who, as the name "Pentheus" itself indicates, is only another guise of the suffering god himself), the head which she takes for the head of Dionysos' lion, this Agave is typical of the primal religious action of the Dionysian dyad, from which artistic tragic action had to develop.

VI

But to make possible the development of this artistic action out of the purely ritual one, the principle of the dyad had to be realized not as two separate exponents but as a single human personality; only then could ritual, after receiving an individually psychological content, put forth the first shoots of art.

It was not a difficult step to take: one need only concentrate on the psychic states of Dionysian man. The bifurcation, which constituted the reason for his temporary delirium, already lay open within him. He was who he was, but he was also different, possessed by an alien will, and this was actually only the awakening of another will of his own, not an alien will that belonged to someone else. The psychic polarity was revealed in him to be a conglomerate of opposing attractions. In the descendants of the Titans who devoured Dionysos the infant (the ancients would have said), the duplex human makeup was uproariously asserting itself: the fiery seed of the Son of Heaven and the chaotic element of dark Earth. The Agave of the original myth and enactment was already a tragic type.

Indeed, by the very nature of the subject under examination, it may be surmised that the revelation of the dyad in personal psychology must be expressed in frenzy, and the art which represents this revelation in action must be reflected not by a state of serene rational consciousness, but by a state which abandons it—mental aberration. And this statement is not contradicted by earlier statements about the immanent dialectic of tragedy or its characteristic propensity for manifest logicality and rational consciousness. An attempt to hold on to formal intellectual faculties and a special adherence to the process of logical cogitation often and for good reason are accompanying signs of the breakdown of mental and psychic equilibrium.

VII

When the dithyramb, the Song of the Axe—that is, a ritual choric song, accompanying the slaughter of an ox by a two-edged pole-axe in honor of the god whose attribute was a double-headed axe, among the Hellenes Dionysos—became appropriated by the "goats" (a circling chorus in goat masks), and the link was lost between ox and axe, at that period the primordial vessels of Dionysian inspiration, the maenads, had long been driven out of the national celebration of the passion of Dionysos by his male votaries. They were left the secret, mystical domain of religion, more important in the cult but only esoterically liturgical—a periodic mystery of mountain rites, closed to men, and other specialized local rituals. Even in the latest period of the Song of the Axe, women take no part in the dithyramb. Such was not the case, apparently, in a more ancient period, when the dithyrambic chorus was a woman's chorus. At least, the double-edged pole-axe remained the traditional weapon of the Thracian maenads and amazons (amazons being only an equivalent avatar of the maenads); and in Cretan illustrations of the cult of the double-edged pole-axe we encounter the ecstatic dances of the priestesses.

The "goats" were Peloponnesian vegetable daemons, subservient to Dionysos and evolving into the throng or *thyas* of his companions. The male religious sects also began to be called "goats," sects whose function it was to praise Bacchus by imitating the doing of his divine deeds, which made it necessary for one of the participants to step into the center of the circle and portray Dionysos himself. But we must not imagine the "goats" as invariably clad in goat-skins and masks, especially since not only the passions of Dionysos, but also the passions of the heroes—his hypostases—began to serve as the subject of the performance: naturally, the chorus had to garb itself in accord with the events depicted.

Thus the circling dithyrambic chorus split into two types, and evolution was carried on in two separate channels. The chorus wearing goat's masks developed the "satyr play" which absorbed into its composition everything that had been disorganized, improvised, unruly and sportive in the original dithyramb. Everything that was heroic, sepulchrally ceremonial and mournfully funereal, superb and portentous, became the property of the other dithyramb—the musical dialogue between the chorus and the hero-protagonist—whence came tragedy.

VIII

And so it would seem that woman was conclusively excluded from influence on the rising art of Dionysos. But since the female type, despite her exclusion from participation in the enactments, remained central to inchoate tragedy, either as heroine of the enactment or in choral roles, how can we fail to perceive in this phenomenon a highly significant allusion to the half-forgotten importance of the maenads in the primordial dithyramb, now fraught with forms of future development? For, no doubt, woman was the first to have an inkling of the psychology of the dyad we spoke of earlier.

We have deemed the female type central to tragedy. And in fact, if one glances over Aeschylus' works, at least, one cannot but take stock of the special significance appertaining to the female type in them. Aeschylus tries to set forth the gigantic visages of male demigods but seems constantly constrained to have recourse to female images. Let us recollect his Clytaemnestra, Cassandra, Antigone; let us conjure up, from the testimony of antiquity, his Niobe, lost to us. In the most ancient and archaic of the tragedies that have come down to us, the leading role belongs to a chorus of the daughters of Danaus.[4] The action of *The Persians* is carried by Atossa; Prometheus bound is contrasted with wandering Io, who is drawn with, possibly, a more enthusiastic imaginative effort (and, of course, by Aeschylus himself, and not by later editors); and just as the captive Prometheus is surrounded by a chorus of Oceanides, so a mixed chorus of Titans and their wives cluster round the freed being.[5]

Woman remained the chief exponent of the most profound idea of tragedy, because from its inception the Dionysian enactment was the concern of woman, a show of her hidden depths and ineffable psychic mysteries. Tragedy is personified in ancient depictions by the maenad Tragedia or the maenad muse Melpomene. Woman, frenzied by her own "woman-crazing" god, brought to religious thought and artistic creativity the revelation of the dyad; and the sages of antiquity were not in error when they perceived in the dyad a female principle.

IX

Tragedy is a maenad, and its protagonist in the most ancient enactment is solely a maenad. The action takes place between a god and a woman he has inspired, who is depicted by a chorus; but the ancient chorus regards itself as one person and speaks of itself in the singular. The god is present invisibly—actively, inasmuch as he controls and possesses his votaries; passively, inasmuch as, having possessed them, he abandons himself to them. The possessed woman, on the contrary, is active; being possessed makes her mighty, prophetic and daring. In her frenzy she finds herself, and this self-discovery in action is the meaning of the tortured and intoxicating psychic spasm. She discovers within herself two souls, two wills, two aspirations. "In my heart dwell two thoughts and two wills: which am I to flee?" sings the amorous Sappho, turning maenadlike.

The maenad loves—and furiously defends herself against love's importunity; she loves—and kills. From the depths of sex, from the dark, primeval past of the battles of the sexes arise this splitting and bifurcating of the female soul, wherein woman first finds the wholeness and primal integrity of her feminine consciousness. So tragedy is born of the female essence's assertion of itself as a dyad.

The emotional experiencing of this inner duality which first renders a woman whole (in contrast to a man, in whom the contradictory duality is a sign of psychic schism and exhaustion), this experiencing contains all the rapture of the Dionysian votaries, the tragic rapture. Here is the conflict of two equal forces, hurtling at one another, striving to absorb one another. But this internal internecine strife is not a principle of self-destruction for women (in contrast to the male tragic type): it is only a rebellion against the monads of masculine light, against Dionysos, insofar as he, having made over, as it were, half of his essence to the dark feminine power gripped by him, now confronts her in the masculine image of the god come down to earth. Who wins in this struggle makes no difference to the maenad with her dual will: she wants simultaneously to conquer and to submit, to be illumined and to put out the light. Either she will experience the most intense intoxication when everything that maddens and harrows her soul begins to subside and die, and—devastated—she will awake and be reborn as someone else—or else she will kill, and in the holy slaying will find her ultimate emancipation, determination, "purification" (catharsis).

Tragedy does not consist in the dyad's wanting to become tragedy, in duality seeking fulfillment and reconciliation in some third party; tragedy does not inhere in the languor of inanition, nor in grief and supplication. On the contrary, it exists wherever something, capable of resolving the conflict, has occurred and exists, but two equal forces, contending, strive to repel and expel it, do not wish an outcome and harmony but blindly want self, nothing but self—to be themselves and in opposition to one another. Therefore the prescribed end for tragedy is ruin, its denouement is homicidal. Thus, by means of the revelation of the age-old duality of the female principle, feminine integrity is asserted in tragedy, and, by means of tragedy's gravitation toward death, woman is reasserted to be the most ancient priestess, the feminine element is reasserted to be the element of Mother-Earth, Earth the Cradle and Earth the Grave.

X

Just as the enthusiastic element was weakened even in the very cradle of tragedy by the replacement of Dionysos, once the sole hero of dithyrambic enactments, by other heroes, stamped with but a reflected glimmer of his divinity, so too the spasmodic experience of the action was weakened by transferring this experience from the female to the male mind.

Because the latter does not find and fortify itself by bifurcation, but loses itself and grows faint, and tragedy has to be fulfilled in a mind replete and not deliquescent, not suffering a paucity of forces but overabundant, then, properly speaking, a male hero, if he is not Dionysos himself, cannot become the hero of tragedy, inasmuch as its nature is comprised of the principle of the dyad. Hence, quests after the revelation of the dyad are not to be found in a unified mind, but in some collective, which constitutes an integral, organic unity. The favorite themes of tragedy turn out to be conflicts between parents and children (Electra, Orestes' matricide, the curse of Oedipus; also relevant here is infanticide, such as the meal of Thyestes, the madness of Heracles, the crime of Medea, the immolation of Iphigenia), between brothers (Eteocles and Polyneices), between spouses (Clytaemnestra and Agamemnon, Heracles and Deianira, the daughters of Danaus).[6] The principle of the dyad is thus preserved as a principle of internecine strife within the natural unity, even when it is collective.

Tragedy is enriched by the motif of the agonist: a male hero is opposed by an antagonist who resembles his own double (Eteocles and Polyneices) or so equal to him in strength that the outcome of the single combat long remains undecided (Prometheus and Zeus).

In exceptional cases the principle of the dyad is revealed in the male hero's fate not through bifurcation but through a kind of replication of his moral essence: blinded by self-sufficiency and by all superficial charms of the eye, Oedipus, on recovering his sight, sees in the mirror of truth the other, original Oedipus.

To the degree that the male type, withdrawing from his Dionysian prototype, began to predominate quantitatively in tragedy (which, by virtue of its religious function, serving the hero's funeral banquet, set itself an artistic task, the interpretation of the whole sacred tradition of the popular epic in the spirit of Dionysos, god-hero and god of heroes), the principle of the dyad created in art a series of superficial techniques for its own revelation, but even in this more superficial interpretation did not forfeit its magical effect on the mind of the spectator. The secret of this fascination lay in the terror, inherited from the depths of the Dionysian cult, at the sight of the doubles, rising up against each other, as they divided Dionysos within themselves (Dionysos and Lycurgus).

We can, to some degree, determine the active power the concrete incarnation of the dyad contained within itself, as a symbol of tragic disruption and schism, by means of a personal aesthetic experiment, if we conjure up in our imagination Aeschylus' tragedy *The Seven against Thebes*, with its twin exchange of blows and its twin division: warrior opposes warrior, fratricidal discord is incessant despite the death of both brothers, and in opposite directions the diverging sisters, Ismene and Antigone, part with their companions.

XI

Tragedy withdrew from its Dionysian prototype; but this withdrawal made it art. When Dionysos reigned supreme, it was not art and could not evolve into artistic forms. The invasion of the primordial action and then its predomination by male characters and participation were a sort of penetration into tragedy of the masculine Apollonian principle. Concomitantly, the original flame of bacchanalian enthusiasm cooled, ecstasis grew tame, proportion and strict portentous structure took over.

It is significant that the first circling chorus, for which most ancient theaters still provided the original, circular *orchestra* [the circular dancing area for the chorus in the ancient Greek theater—tr.], discontinued its arrangement as a choric round. The most ancient outward expression of the dyad—the opposition of the chorus to the god or hero, who stepped into the center of the circle—was replaced by other, more patterned forms commemorating it. The law of the dyad was realized in the action itself, which now demanded a certain number of individual participants and was multiform and complicated; the chorus, too, that primal exponent of dithyrambic animation, no longer a protagonist, took on the responsibility of pacifying and organizing tragic life in the spirit of Apollo.

Once it had become an organ of Apollo in the Dionysian enactment and a kind of interpreter of the Apollonian vision unfolding on stage, the chorus seemed an unnecessary and supererogatory adjunct and was gradually swept aside. One could not sweep aside the spectator, but even he became an unnecessary and supererogatory adjunct to the enactment of Dionysos as a religious enactment: he was now nothing but a spectator, an observer of other men's participation.

Thus art, "advancing to the pearl of creation," subdued and sapped tragedy, which will not and cannot be art and nothing but art to the bitter end. But art could not destroy it, for tragedy comes from life. It was preserved even to our time and will be handed down to future ages by a living principle that lies outside of art, the principle of dying continuously on behalf of a higher existence, the principle of the dyad, as a passionate symbol of sacrificial incarnation and a triumphant symbol of the eternal feminine.

XII

Subsuming the conclusions of our earlier statements about the nature of tragedy and its veritably tragic fate (indeed, it seems itself to have become a victim of the dyad principle revealed in it, a victim of its own division between Dionysos and Apollo), it is appropriate to deduce from our fundamental premises the conditions which prevent the Apollonian element which first introduced tragedy into the sphere of art from paralyzing its Dionysian energy.

The Apollonian element is desirable, first, insofar as it imparts to the stage action formal organization and graceful expressiveness. It is desirable, furthermore, as a kind of supersubtle barrier, protecting the spectator (let us note that the spectator must be not *only* a spectator or observer, but even in the capacity of participant in the action he will not cease to be a looker-on), a magic veil, preserving him from a direct hit by the Dionysian lightning-bolts. But this same Apollonian sheath already, as it were, demagnetizes tragedy if it condenses the rarefied cloud, which resembles the inspiration that occurs in somnolent dreams, into a mass impenetrable by the Dionysian currents, enshrouding what is portrayed on stage in a purely epic alienation from the spectator, now only a spectator.

The inspissation of this protective covering obviously must be, in any case, less important than the isolating or anesthetizing force of that Apollonian obstacle which art creates in the mind of the actor—that enigmatic creature, simultaneously intermingling with his mask and hidden by it, protected in his personal individuality, his private consciousness, from the tragic thunder directed at him as at a lightning-rod. Here is the criterion we propose: tragedy performed by actors must never constitute a psychic event for them, as individuals; the mind of the spectator, on the other hand, must be melted down by tragedy and smelted by it, and therein lies the essence of tragic "purification."

Dionysian energy in tragedy will appear as the emotional experiencing of the dyad. This energy will increase if the dyad is revealed in the most tragic disposition—and will decrease if, due to a disproportionate predominance of the Apollonian element in it, the revelation of the dyad is removed from the depths of psychic life to the plight of the character (the situation). For true tragic quality, the hero's temperament must be tragic by nature; such a temperament will inevitably render a situation tragic.

Therefore the portrayal of female temperament is the most gratifying for the tragic poet. A striking and prominent female personality is naturally tragic. And one may presume that the impending fate of tragedy will be closely connected with the fates and types of the woman of the future. The tragic quality of the male temperament may be measured by the degree to which it has been penetrated by the spirit of Dionysos, by the degree of its resemblance to Dionysos. Such is the internal and historically primordial law of the dyad's art.

Letters on the Theater
by Leonid Andreev

First Letter on the Theater

The modest aim of these pages, brief and fragmentary as they are, is merely to pose a few questions. And if some of my ideas strike you as paradoxical, my alarm excessive and my hopes overstated, blame not me but the breadth of my theme, the complexity of the questions connected with the problem of theater, the newness of certain factors which have only now entered the life of the theater and have neither historical nor literary background . . .

I

Virtually no other invention was ever greeted with such great mistrust and even contempt as was the cinematograph, the living photograph. Although the man in the street and the entire rank-and-file of educated people the world over surrendered enthusiastically and deliriously to the power of "cinema," the upper echelons regarded it coldly and hostilely. It has now become impossible not to notice those countless little vesper lights that ornament the façades of cinemas or to be blind to the variegated mob flocking to its doors—but no one said a word about it, and everyone pretended not to have noticed or sincerely thought it was one of those idle amusements, something along the lines of a skating rink, which every so often and from time to time attract the fickle and vapid man in the street. A few tentative articles in the serious reviews, an excellent but

---

The first of these letters was published in 1912 in Fyodor Kommissarzhevsky's journal *Maski* (*Masks*, III); it was republished in 1914 as a prologue to the second letter in *Literaturno-khudozhestvennye al'manakhi izdatel'stva "Shipovnik"* (*The Wild Briar Almanacs of Literature and Art*), XII. This translation is based on the photostatic facsimile issued by the Prideaux Press (Letchworth, Herts, 1974).

barely appreciated and virtually ignored article by Mr. Chukovsky,[1] vague rumors of some protests in Germany against the cinema's increasing take-over—this is almost the sum total of what, so far, has signaled the emergence of this wonderful guest. A few years ago, when I first began talking to certain writers about the enormous and still unrealized significance of the cinema, the productive role it was destined to play in solving problems of the *theater*, I was merely the occasion for mockery and reproach for my excessive fantasticality.

And the most amazing thing of all was that the theater, which in its very essence has an interest in cinema, and is tied to it by bonds of consanguinity, apparently refuses to acknowledge its rich and vulgar American uncle. It would not acknowledge him even at the moment, so tragic for it, when, under pressure from the cinema, it took to walking the streets, and rented a place next door to the green and red little vesper lights under the name "Theater of Miniatures."[2]

This relationship seems to have changed somewhat, and serious talk about the cinematograph is already being attempted. Why, just the other day we accidentally chanced to hear a whole slew of writers and performers discussing cinema-theater, and I was convinced that by its very nature cinema continues to be the same outlandish alien, free-and-easy and sufficiently offensive to aesthetically and intellectually cultivated persons. An artistic apache, an aesthetic hooligan, an idling and parasitical gearshaft on the wheel of true art—that is how the relationship is defined by most of those who have given thought to the wonderful guest. And such questions have arisen as: Is it seemly for a self-respecting actor to work in the cinema? We have even heard such pathetic exclamations as: No matter how loudly you hymn the praises of cinema, it will no more kill theater than color photography killed painting! *

And not even those who spoke in defense of cinema-theater pointed out the highly feasible eventuality that the cinematograph, at present an aesthetic apache and hooligan, may be the very thing destined to *liberate* the theater from the great burden of things irrelevant, contingent and alien, beneath whose weight the modern stage is perishing and will perish, dramatists are sickening and the mighty word is degenerating and weakening.

*No more than a year has passed since these lines of mine appeared and already what an antiquated mustiness they emit! So impetuously brilliant Cinema completes its history!

II

Does the theater need *action* in its legitimatized form as deeds and movement on stage—a form not only accepted by all theaters but even confessed to be the one necessary and salutary form?

To this heretical question I venture to reply: no. There is no necessity for such action insofar as *life itself*, in its most dramatic and tragic clashes, moves ever further away from external action and probes ever deeper into the innermost soul, into the stillness and inner immobility of intellectual experiences.

Once, rereading the memoirs of Benvenuto Cellini,[3] I was struck by the inordinate number of incidents in the life of this medieval artist and adventurer: all those escapes, murders, surprises, losses and gains, loves and friendships. In truth, our average contemporary does not register as many happenings in his whole life as Cellini encountered on the short walk from his house to the town gate! Nor was Cellini the only one of his kind: so were all who lived then, and so was all life itself in that era with its robbers, dukes, monks, swords, mandolins. For in that period the only man interesting and rich in experience was the one who went places and did things, while the man who sat still was devoid of experience, of life itself—the man who sat still was like a stone in the road, with nothing to be said about it.

But move across a few centuries, and you come upon the life of . . . well, take the life of Nietzsche, the most tragic hero of modern times. Where are incident and action and movement in his life? There is none. During his youth, when Nietzsche still got around and did things in the guise of a Prussian soldier, he was wholly undramatic: drama begins just at the moment when the inaction and silence of the study take over. There lie the excruciating re-evaluation of all values, and the tragic conflict, and the rupture with Wagner, and the alluring Zarathustra. But what has this to do with the stage?

For the stage is impotent and mute. Subservient to the immutable law of action, it will not and *cannot* present the ever so familiar and important and necessary Nietzsche, but in recompense offers in vast quantity the already needless, superannuated, vacuous Cellini with his prop swords. Life has gone inside, while the stage loitered on the threshold. Understand this, and you will understand why, for the last decades, not a single drama has achieved the sublimity of the modern novel or can be compared with it; why Dostoevsky never wrote a play;[4] why Tolstoy, so profound in his novels, is primitive in his plays; why cunning Maeterlinck put pants on his ideas and forced doubt to run around the stage. Follow my idea to its end and you will understand why Ostrovsky, who is grounded in real life, is so marvelously stageworthy (and so no longer necessary) and why Chekhov is so necessary and so "untheatrical."

I do not say that events have come to an end or that nobody *acts* or that history has ground to a halt. No: the calendar of incidents is still rather full, there are still plenty of murders and suicides, complicated swindles, sophisticated and efficient schemes, vital and action-packed struggles, guns in hand, but . . . the dramatic value of all this has diminished. *Life has become more psychological*, if I may use that expression; in line with the primal passions and "eternal" heroes of drama—love and hunger—a new hero has arisen: intellect. Not hunger or love or ambition, but *thought*, human thought, in its suffering, joys and struggle, is the true hero of modern life, and therefore it deserves primacy in the drama. Even bad playwrights and bad audiences in our times have begun to realize that an outward show of conflict, no matter how much blood is spilt on stage, is least meaningful as dramatic conflict. The moment when a worker marches down the street is not dramatic, but the moment when the accents of a new life strike his ear, when his yet timid, powerless and inert thought suddenly rears up on its hind legs, like a raging steed bearing its rider in a single bound to a radiant world of wonders, is dramatic. The moment when, at the factory owner's demand, soldiers arrive and prime their guns is not dramatic, but that moment when, in the stillness of night's meditation, the brooding factory owner wrestles with two truths and neither one can be accepted by his conscience or his overtaxed intelligence is dramatic. The same is even true of modern love—even there, as in every profound phenomenon of life, action has moved from external expression in deeds to the depths and apparent inactivity of inner experience.

An interesting detail. Once upon a time there was a soliloquy for the solitary and paramount thoughts and feelings of the hero, but up-to-date realistic drama has done away even with this last, rather pitiful possibility of plumbing the depths: the soliloquy has been abolished. Odd, what dodges and feints dramatists are driven to, when they feel the need of at least a tiny soliloquy but do not dare openly avail themselves of one: sometimes a deaf old man, sometimes a stove, sometimes a glove are interlocutors, but no one ever talks alone on stage—it's unnatural, unlifelike. But it *is* like life to perform actions without a stop, to babble on incessantly like a deliriously happy parrot and never to think deeply for more than twenty seconds!

Over and over again they paint the same old portrait of life, from models by the masters, not noticing that the likeness has long since vanished and that they are not painting a living face but only *copying an old picture*.

III

And *genius* has gone from the drama—is its mighty scope to be encompassed by this, the stage's dismal narrowness? And when it does contrive to spread its wings a bit wider, it always turns up in a fatal form: the most profound and inspired is the least theatrical.

But not just genius: even mediocre talents are already beginning to find the modern stage constricting, and they have to hunker down and prattle baby-talk so that the results may be *theatrical*. For along with inevitable action, the modern theater wants to put on *spectacle*. And to the question, Must the modern theater put on spectacle? I again venture to answer, Certainly not.

The answer is only logical. Insofar as action is visible and part of the spectacle, they both ought to quit the stage together, to make way for the invisible human soul, its greatest treasure, unseen by corporeal and organic eyes. And here the elegantly dressed vagabond Benvenuto Cellini with all the splendor and magnificence surrounding him makes way for Nietzsche's black frockcoat, the inactivity of somber and monotonous rooms, the stillness and gloom of bedchamber and study. Nowadays the only people who assiduously roam the world over are traveling salesmen, while Lyov Tolstoy with his universal drama has been sitting motionless for a quarter of a century. And now that they have started pelting our prophets and heroes not with stones, but with sheets of written and printed paper: where then is there room for *spectacle* in that? Of course, even there the cunning Maeterlinck keeps searching for ways and means, wishing to say "life" he writes "sea" and thus puts the theater in an impossible bind—for if you paint a picture of the sea for today's stage, it will be taken for the sea . . . Yet everyone knows that it is not the sea, but life. Paint the sea clumsily and it will simply be taken as a bad sea, but it still will not be taken for life, it still won't work!

And, constricted by the modern stage, talented dramatists have recourse to all sorts of shifts! There is Hauptmann's armature of devils in *The Sunken Bell*, and Naidyonov's humble and quite unnecessary *Imatra* and our everlasting samovar[5]—which is at least a samovar and a spectacle too if worst comes to worst. Yet the samovar is action as well: sometimes it's carried in, sometimes it's poured out, sometimes it's taken away—the spectator is diverted and refreshed.

Would it be flogging a dead horse to demonstrate that the modern theater and audience are so devoted to spectacle that more often than not they immolate on the sacrificial altar of that idol of theirs the very meaning of a work and sacrifice its soul for the sake of the unnecessary body? It is ridiculous that, to make room for dancing or to enable the actor to take a few extra steps on stage, they resort to *cutting*, i.e., gently and tenderly amputating the author's tongue, while they insist that the stump will be quite enough to make an impression. Give this some thought, and you will understand the source of that long series of failures which accompanies our most important and interesting productions, and why the worst piece of writing makes a hit, while the best one flops or does not even manage to get on stage; why dramatists sicken again and again; why only the mute do not cry out against the dearth of dramatic literature.

IV

The dearth of dramatic literature . . . You know, of course, that there is a desperate struggle for the stage going on between the symbolists and "wholesome" realism; you know, of course, that, at this very moment, the sorriest one for literature in general, "wholesome" realism has triumphed in Russia. But have you happened to notice that for some reason this triumph has exactly *coincided* with the dearth of dramatic literature and the decline of the theater? Like the nobleman in Shchedrin who, through a misunderstanding, and for the sake of pure air, began to hate his peasants and finally destroyed them, and consequently thereafter fell into a desperate state of starvation and grief,[6] the audience and the theater enthusiastically extirpated symbolism from the stage and suddenly . . . grief, starvation . . . what happened to drama? Ah, how deeply realistic drama breathes in the pure air . . . But where is drama? Where have the dramatists gone? I am ultimately hungry and very bored.

But what exactly was our deceased symbolism, whose demise purified the air but left nothing to eat?

Its name is compromise. Only in a few cases was stage symbolism dictated by the unalterable laws of individual creativity, and for the most part it came across only *as a means* of injecting live thought into the stage, and so played the role of a Jewish smuggler, who, in sheep's clothing, brings Brussels lace across the border. Limited by the demands for "action and spectacle," a dramatist could not embody on stage all the images of the modern *soul*, a subtle and complex soul, irradiated with the light of thought, which has created the value of new inner experiences, which has sought sources of new and profound tragic feeling unknown to the ancients. He could not *embody* it, for the new inner experiences of the soul have no body, and so a long line of smugglers staggers across the stage lugging the heavy burden of contraband goods: stylized figures, barefoot dancing-girls, enigmatic characters without name or patronymic, galvanized (but not resuscitated) Pierrots and Harlequins, the custom-made blind, the custom-made deaf and dumb, the custom-made devils, gnomes, fairies and frogs. The blind bumped into the scenery, the devils did disappearing acts, Harlequin moaned as if alive, the barefoot dancing-girls danced sepulchrally, somebody very fat tried unsuccessfully to turn into a shadow . . . And this whole ingenuous masquerade meant only one thing: thought is gasping for breath on your stage!—the *soul* is expiring on your boards.

Like any compromise, this custom-made, ambiguous smuggler's symbolism was unsatisfactory in every respect and *deserved* to perish. Both author and audience had inherited the bulky, wholly fleshly, three-dimensional figure of an actual, clean-shaven actor. They bent him like a gutta-percha doll, molded him into postures met with only in geometry, forced him to drink vinegar and bile to rattle loose his ability to talk with a lifelike voice and not because real corpses and ghosts talk that way; the actor meekly bowed his neck to the new yoke, but for all his good faith could not turn into steam or air or a real frog. And the audiences sensed the phoniness and departed, whistling in derision, and the author sensed that you cannot capture the bastion of the modern theater by circumventing its laws: either destroy the Bastille or perish in the Bastille!

For a while the theater was spiritually enriched, became inwardly significant and even important, but outwardly took on such a look of blatant absurdity, its nuts and bolts were shaken so loose and it began to creak so, that its continued existence in this compromised form became impossible. And with an unctuously spiteful smirk, that old trull, realistic drama, arrived, readjusted the actor's bones, re-tightened the nuts and bolts, fumigated with Ostrovsky

to chase away the impure odor of Maeterlinck—and there ensued
the dearth of dramatic literature, our own most peculiar kind of
renascence.

V

Not only is our theater perishing, but the audience is perishing as
well. Which is dragging the other into the pit—the theater the audience or vice versa—is hard to say, and of no importance, in any
case. Assume it is mutual.

The important point is that the modern "spectator" (as he is
called), even if he be an inveterate theatergoer, has already grown ri-
diculously unaccustomed to theater and is utterly powerless to cope
and deal with impressions derived from the stage. Unable to linger
long over his extremely interesting psychology, which deserves independent investigation, I will note only a few aspects.

Never before have so many claims been laid against the theater,
never before has it had to satisfy so many *requirements* as now. Suppose I am a lady and I want to learn how to dress: I go to the theater
to find out from actresses and other ladies. Suppose I am pregnant
with an idea and want time to think it out: I go to the theater. Suppose in the drabness of my life no vivid spark of emotion has ever
been engendered: I go to the theater. Suppose my eyes are weary of
the tawdriness of our rooms, the monotony and dreariness of the
street; I ought to travel and feast my eyes on the spectacle of sky, sea,
foreign and eternal beauty, but there is nowhere I can go, for I have
no money: and so I unthinkingly go to the theater and feast my eyes
on beauty and gaiety. Whether I crave laughter or sorrow, excitement
or relaxation—I go to the theater for everything, I demand from the
theater everything, I curse the theater for everything!

And therefore, how absurd is our ordinary auditorium with its
absurdly and wildly mixed components! How many are the divergent and contradictory currents that issue from the audience to the
stage to distract and annoy the actors! No sooner has an intelligent
man begun to pay close attention than twenty fools start yawning
and blowing their noses. The fools are plentiful—the intelligent
man begins to shrivel up in unbearable anguish . . . for there is nothing more anguishing for an intelligent man than the glee of idiots.
Much of the drama aggrieves those looking for rest and "recreation,"
little of the drama aggrieves those who thirst for excitement.

One man knows how to listen, loves to listen, another, a loud-
mouth and chatterbox, is depressed by any coherent speech; one

man understood it all and complains that there's not much to it, no food for thought; another understood absolutely nothing and also complains that it's rubbish!

True, all theaters strive voluntarily, and to a large extent involuntarily, to put together "our own audience," to create a certain congenial, stable and friendly house, but here the insubstantiality of modern serious drama is proclaimed with special force. For the more inferior a theater is in the artistic and conceptual sense, the more no one "gives a damn about it," the more faithful and reliable its chosen audience, and vice versa. The words "our regular audience" take on full meaning at the music hall and operetta; "our regular audience" can be found at Suvorin's dreadful theater and even at Korsh's,[7] but beyond them fluctuation and diversification begin. If there are ten spectators, one of whom prefers to go to the Art Theater, and the rest to the Maly, on a par with them exist thousands and tens of thousands who would just as soon attend two, three, four theaters and set off with just as much interest to see both Hamsun's *Drama of Life*[8] and . . . names are odious.

And the more passionate and agonizing the theater's experimentation—and at present any serious theater is *compelled* to experiment—the less hope it has of its audience and lasting success. Plays varying in spirit and structure contend with one another, enfeebling the actor, hurtling him from extreme realism to extreme symbolism, now rewarding him with flesh and blood, now making off with his very shadow, like poor Peter Schlemihl's.[9] As they undermine the actor, these variegated plays also destabilize the spectator, who, faced with each new production, is turning into a question mark—how is one's own public, a harmonious and cooperative audience, to be put together, when the theater is internally tearing itself to shreds?

A few authors and a few individual plays still create a following, but there is cold comfort in that for the *theater*: look in at a play that has been running for 102 performances, and you will be convinced that far from being the strongest piece of work, it is simply more accessible, and consequently, the most primitive, uncomplicated, unintelligent and vapid work. Very often such plays have the look and taste of very "good" plays, but this is involuntary self-delusion: the actors, insinuating and sympathizing, are well rehearsed and sure of success; the favorably disposed spectators (for they know what they are going to) create that special atmosphere in the theater in which shortcomings are overlooked and the modicum of worth magnified, and, on the whole, everything flourishes.

A small following is created by any play that survives 10 performances, but, to make up for it, what a horror, what an absurdity,
what a merciless condemnation of the whole system of today's theater is an opening night! A few go to the theater fully aware, but the
majority go like a flock of sheep: it's obligatory. And even those who
go for a reason have absolutely no idea, cannot conceive, of what
awaits them; a general promise has been made to amaze them with
something surprising (so-and-so will design the scenery—spectacle;
so-and-so will compose the music, so-and-so will direct . . . and it's
all so-and-so, so-and-so), but whether the reaction will be pleasure
or agony nobody knows. And theaters intentionally enshroud the
mystery even more . . . not realizing that the more enshrouded the
mystification, the more the audience will be composed of an irrelevant and detrimental crowd.

Yet how many serious-minded people have *entirely stopped
going* to the theater?

VI

Now imagine the cinematograph—not as it is now with its corpse-
like, photographically blackened figures, flatly twitching on a flat
white wall, but as it is to be . . . very shortly. Capable technology has
eliminated oscillation, by increasing the film's sensitivity, invested
objects with their true colors and restored true perspective. What
will it be then? It will be a *mirror* as big as a thirty-five-foot wall, but
a mirror which will not reflect you. What is this—technology? No,
for a *mirror* is not technology: a mirror is a *second* reflected life.
Will it be dead? No, for what is reflected in a mirror is neither alive
nor dead; it is a second life, an enigmatic existence, like the existence of a ghost or a hallucination.

There, the curtains are parting—and a fourth wall seems to descend, living pictures of the world spanning thirty-five feet stand as
in a colossal window. Clouds scud across the blue sky, fields of rye
wave and the sultry prospect looms dim in the distance. You can see
everyone and everything, whatever and whomever you choose—the
witch of Endor sells her miracles by the reel. Would you like to see
yourself as a baby or a youth, cover your whole lifetime? Would you
like to see the dear departed?—here they come, at your orders, stare
and smile, and with you—you who have entered through the same
door—they sit down to the table.

But I will not speak here of what a revolution in psychology, in
the very foundations of thought, will be effected by the cinema of

the future. Let us return to the theater. Now imagine that some custom-made stage performance has passed in front of this mirror, that the mirror was set up before the stage of some great and renowned theater with famous actors—why, it will retrieve all of it in entirety, repeat all of it, present all of it and will go on repeating it to infinity. It will retrieve all of it—except the words. And this will be neither "technology" nor dead figures—it will be a second, reflected, enigmatic life.

And then when the cinema has turned into such a wizard, it will calmly relieve the theater of its action and "spectacle." Nor can there be any talk of resistance. If the theater tries to fight back with a painter's hands and creates a particularly marvelous piece of scenery—the cinema will swipe the set in its entirety; but, in recompense, besides scenery, it can also depict the original, which the theater cannot. The cinema is pre-eminent in the field of action too, having at its command the length and breadth of the world, being capable of instant transformations, a sovereign able at any time to call into action thousands of men, automobiles, aeroplanes, mountains and seas—unquestionable and palpable ones. Wherever action occurs, however unusual and varied the forms it assumes, the cinema will overtake it everywhere and capture it on its magic screen.

Moreover: no matter how hard the theater strove for action, it was limited, it could present it only in the most limited ways; no matter how hard it strove for movement, it could present it only within a seventy-foot span, the normal stage allotment. And because we had and have no other *teacher* of action than the theater, we *are unacquainted* with the whole realm of action—acts involving personal participation in some reckless expedition, for instance. Certain novels (say, those of Jack London)[10] are filled with descriptions of such action, but we *have not seen* them, and we do not know them. And the cinematograph is destined to discover this new realm and expand our notion of action to new, unlooked-for limits.

I will fantasize further. There are no limits set on an author's will in creating action, the imagination has been enriched—and so new kinds of cinema-dramatists, talented persons and geniuses still unknown are being born. A Cinematic Shakespeare, having discarded the inhibiting word, will so deepen and widen action and find such new and surprising combinations for it that it will become as expressive as speech and at the same time convincing with that unparalleled cogency inherent only in things visible and tangible. Simultaneously with the Cinematic Shakespeare a few huge and dreadfully luxurious theaters will spring up, in which *new* actors will tread the boards—geniuses of *external* portrayal, mime and plasticity, histrions who have studied and recollected the old prehistoric art of expressing everything by face and gesture. And along with these Cinematic Shakespeares, creators of a new cinematic drama, and those Cinema-Art theaters, brilliant exponents of the new authors' will—through the whole world, in its most obscure and secluded corners, will be scattered millions of stages, modern-day cinema-sarais, requiring as their equipment a few pennies, three men and a valise full of films.

Wondrous Cinema! . . . If the sublime and sacred aim of art is to create a common bond between men and their lonely souls, what an enormous, unimaginable socio-psychological task this artistic apache of modern times is destined to accomplish! Beside it stand aeronautics, the telegraph and the telephone as a guarantee of this. Portable, stowed away in a little box, it will be circulated through the world by mail like an ordinary newspaper. *Lacking a tongue* it will be understood equally well by the savages of Petersburg and the savages of Calcutta—it will truly become the genius of international community, bring together the ends of the earth and the outposts of the soul and switch quivering humanity onto a single current.

Great Cinema!—it will master everything, conquer everything, give everything. Only one thing it will not give—*words*, and there is the limit of its power, the boundary of its might. Poor, great Cinematic-Shakespeare!—he is destined to beget himself a new breed of Tantaluses!

VII

What will be left of modern theater, once it has been relieved of action and spectacle, those very bases of its existence, without which any dramatic substance would seem inconceivable? Will it not perish utterly, incapable of prevailing over the new Cinema-theater, or over itself in the person of its own laws, whose canon has been set since time immemorial?

I hope to address myself to this in the next letter, and at present beg permission to conclude with a joke. Whether the theater will survive or not remains problematical, but that music halls and strip-shows will be preserved inviolably for centuries is a fact. For no spectator at any such establishment will ever be satisfied by a lady who only exists on a screen and cannot go to supper with him.

10 November 1912

Second Letter on the Theater

I

In the relatively short time since my first letter was published, the cinematograph has taken a headlong leap forward. There's speed for you! Unlike other inventions it does not plod along at a decorous pace but flies; it sails through the air, it sweeps ahead irresistibly like a pestilence; and artistic quarantine is no longer capable of halting its invasion.

Yes, people seem by now to have stopped trying and are humbly submitting to the will of the conqueror. Actors have barely had time to put on the shoes in which they frantically flock to the buccaneer Cinema; and already they serve him and their portraits decorate his far-flung billboards. Venerable Varlamov has performed for the cinema, Yureneva and Roshchina-Insarova, Yuriev and many other famous actors have done the same.[1] But an even more striking change has taken place in Germany. About a year ago virtual protest meetings were called against the Cinema, actors who had decided to appear on the screen were declared anathema—and now Albert Bassermann[2] himself can be fleetingly glimpsed on this very screen, famous writers compose scenarios (Hugo von Hofmannsthal)[3] and to set the capstone on these wonders, Max Reinhardt the magus, wizard and highest authority on matters theatrical in Germany has personally composed and mounted for the cinematograph a sumptuous epic based on the lives of gods and men, *The Isle of the Blessed.*[4]

And what is happening to the audience? The theater is merely tolerated, the theater is half deserted, while everyone goes to the Cinema. In Berlin itself the *fashion* is now not for first nights at the theater, but first nights at the cinema—it's ceased to be a laughing matter! However ill-assorted the audience at a first night, it nevertheless creates the climate for a theater; and over the theater storm-clouds are gathering ever more densely.

A few days ago there was a demonstration in Petersburg of Edison's "Kinetophone," a miraculous combination of picture and sound,[5] and it enjoyed a huge success. I would venture to eliminate a syllable and call the gadget "Fon Kinema," Von Cinema, the cinema ennobled, raised to the ranks of the aristocracy, to the realm of the *word.* And many people, after seeing a talking, guffawing Cinema for the first time, panicked: newspapers boomed out in sincerely alarmed tones, forecasting the extinction of "theater." I do not share this anxiety when faced with the talking Cinema: the word is its weakness, not its strength, the word only deflects Cinema from its idiosyncratic artistic path and diverts it to a beaten, rutted and outworn theatrical track; the sluggish word will finally destroy that unparalleled and impetuous rhythm of action which comprises the main allure of madcap Cinema. To bind it with words is almost the same as harnessing an automobile to a horse; it won't improve the horse's stamina and the automobile will break down. Of course, in individual cases the Kinetophone will perform an irreplaceable service to art and life by preserving and enregistering the personality of an actor or musician, certain exceptionally outstanding moments of artistic creativity—but this will be only a *service*: subservient to the word, the Kinetophone will no longer be a master, but merely a servant. For, in the Cinema's general development, the imposition of *the word* onto spectacle and action not only fails to add anything, but, I repeat, simply deflects it away from its true goals.

Render unto Caesar what is Caesar's and unto God what is God's. And our present task is to separate Cinema from theater, to define precisely the basic elements of creativity for each, and likewise to set each on its true path. For it has fallen out that old theater and new Cinema have merged; their kingdom is one: action, spectacle and performance, and young Cinema is devouring his father and will some day sit upon his throne. But there is in the old and nascent theater alike something that the cinema will never take over, and it devolves upon us, the lovers of theater, to identify, define and reinforce this special quality, that it may belong only to the living theater and regenerate it for a new, extensive life.

As I understand it, the *new* theater will be exclusively a theater of *panpsychism*. And in this respect, naturally, I shall try to use the Art Theater as example, having observed its history, both past and present, from a certain point of vantage. By the way, thanks to Gorky's letter about the staging of Dostoevsky and the consequent explanations on the part of the company and V. I. Nemirovich-Danchenko,[6] increased attention is once again being paid to this theater . . . attention which is not, however, devoid of malice.

II

Everyone remembers how clamorously, how extraordinarily the Art Theater entered Russian life: it stunned, blinded, enthused and suddenly forced everyone to shout about its uncommon brand of novelty. Just what, however, this young theater's "novelty" consisted of no one could explain very clearly, although there were dozens of explanations; and even now—although fifteen years have passed and writings about the Art Theater have accumulated by the ton—no one has definitely ascertained the artistic basis of the theater. What's more, I declare with scant modesty that the inspirers of the theater themselves, Stanislavsky and Nemirovich-Danchenko, creators of its strength and novelty, have only the vaguest idea of what they are serving or *exactly* where their strength and novelty lie. Many may regard this as a bad thing, but I consider it a good one: the true artist, like the sinner, ought never to be aware of what he does or else he very quickly turns into a living poetry machine, stamping out verses, like Bryusov,[7] offering up the truth of living creativity on the altar of an often deceptive and mendacious theory. The artist must be a *mystery* to himself, or else he will be robbed of sincerity and, with it, everything else. And if the Art Theater made mistakes because it lacked self-knowledge, that too is a good thing: mistakes are necessary, truth springs from them like ears of grain from dung; and for that reason it was more sincere than any theater sprung from the soil of a ready-made theory or hypothetical brainstorming—we recall the dismal and horribly frigid theater of Meyerhold.[8]

The Art Theater's first sensational production, the one which created its fame for "newness," was Aleksey Tolstoy's *Tsar Fyodor Ioannovich*.[9] The most curious thing about this was that neither the play nor the author was in the slightest degree *new*—what was so novel about the theater using an old play and an old author? True, some did dispute this novelty at the time and mentioned the Meiningen troupe;[10] others, admitting the novelty, at the same time coldbloodedly did it to death as an old-fashioned concept of "naturalism," a kind of historical accuracy—as if such a thing existed and anyone needed it! But something new could undoubtedly be felt, and it was seen chiefly (I venture to pay special attention to this) not in any distinguished performance by the actors, but in the boyars' garments, the inner apartments, the elusive details of everyday customs, and then again, it was not so much historical accuracy that was the attraction—hadn't Ilovaysky[11] taught us about that too?—nor any exceptional splendor, but the fact that the caftans were baggy, the boyars' garments (perhaps even fantasticated) were worn by the actors just as if they had never known any other garb. And it was related with great feeling that even at home the actors walked around in mantles and the actresses in frontlets: and some people laughed, but more were touched, because they were still in love with the theater.

I skip directly from *Tsar Fyodor* to the Chekhov productions: a moment, as people asserted and still assert, of the highest distinction in the theater, from which, as from an eminence,[12] the road could lead only downwards. Chekhov's advent manifested the arrival of a new author and a new form of drama and even a new application of a word to the theater: mood. And with this new word, as with a lock-pick, everything began to break open, Chekhov and all the other plays, for a lock-pick is so much more convenient than a key: for each separate lock has its own key, but a single lock-pick will fit them all. And now it seemed that everyone could guess the riddle of the theater's novelty: it lay in "mood." The Art Theater is the "theater of mood." Apparently the theater itself shared somewhat in the general opinion, and with its new-found lock-pick tried to pry open quite a few unsuitable plays: failures resulted. Chekhovianism turned into Gorkery, and the conviction gained ground that with Chekhov's death there was nothing for the theater to do on God's green earth. But again: *what* precisely was so attractive about the Chekhov productions, what produced the feeling of something wonderfully *new*, no longer extant on the stage?

And there came the same strange answer as with *Tsar Fyodor*, that the actors' performances, though splendid, were not so attractive as the sets, an environment of rooms fit to live in, an engagement ring on the finger and all those other wonderful costumes, military this time, that the actors wore as if they had never known any other clothing. And once more with feeling they told the story about Stanislavsky wearing a military overcoat with shoulder tabs around the house, and once more they laughed and were touched. But even the costumes paled before the striking novelty of the "cricket"[13]—and although, at least out loud, they laughed a great deal at the cricket too, in recompense they were probably even more touched, to the very bottom of their heart: for the cricket was really extraordinary! True, at this point the cold-blooded murderers showed up with their "naturalism" meat-axe, but no particular credence was lent them; a great preference was shown to all-embracing mood. Therefore the cricket was mood, and the rings were required by the mood and over all it was a "theater of mood."

And yet this too was a very good thing, that the word, at least, for the *new* theater was a new one. But it would have been even better and hence more accurate if, instead of a vague concept of "mood," they had used another more precise and narrow term: *panpsychism*. Then there would have been a greater understanding of what comprises the *strength* of the Art Theater; then even the recent staging of Dostoevsky would not seem so startling and matter for absurd protests.

III

As I have already noted in my first letter, every day of our life becomes more *psychological*. And when, almost a century ago, a new psychological novel by Henri Beyle[14] appeared, it only recorded what existed, and concentrated in a single focus the peculiarity of a new phase in life's development—for indeed life has its phases. And although in its pure form the "psychological" novel did not attract a large number of followers and imitators, there is no doubt that it enrolled all literature under the banner of psychology, at times curtailing in very great measure its plot, its action, its adventures. Able to treat this theme only in passing, I cannot show how, in Russian literature, which is generally inclined to the spiritual, this invisible banner of psychology, fluttering over our heads for almost a hundred years, led to severe impoverishment of content, occasionally to virtual thumb-sucking and an obsession with the depressing and monotonous.

It became enough for the narrative to describe some perfectly ordinary man, who did nothing but walk down an ordinary street, thinking the most ordinary things about ordinary shop-signs—and this was in itself a narrative. They had forgotten or never understood that not every psyche is of interest and importance and that psychologists, like jewelers, work only in gold. The masters of psychology (or as I called it, *panpsychism*), Dostoevsky, Tolstoy and Chekhov, conclusively confused the issue: the lawyer, I believe in *Anna Karenina*, who kills a moth during a serious conversation served as progenitor to all those dismal narratives, whose entire point lies in the fact that somebody during a conversation, . . . etc.

Let me return to Chekhov and the Art Theater.

Chekhov's specialty is that he was the most logical of panpsychologists. If in Tolstoy often only a man's body is *animated*, if Dostoevsky is exclusively devoted to the soul itself, Chekhov *animated* everything that meets the eye: his landscape is no less psychological than his characters; his characters are no more psychological than the clouds, stones, chairs, drinking glasses and rooms. All the things in the visible and invisible world take part only as components of one vast soul; and if his stories are only chapters of one vast novel, his things are only *thoughts and sensations* scattered through space, a single soul in action and spectacle. He paints the life of his hero by means of landscapes, relates his past with clouds, portrays his tears with rain, uses a suite of rooms to show that the immortality of the soul does not exist. Chekhov does that in fiction, but he does the very same thing in his plays.

On the stage Chekhov must be performed not only by human beings, but by drinking glasses and chairs and crickets and military overcoats and engagement rings. In *The Cherry Orchard* Chekhov suddenly intrudes a kind of enigmatic sound of "a bucket that fell," a sound that is impossible to reproduce—but it is indispensable, an indispensable part of the soul of the play's protagonists; without it they would not be what they are, without it there would even be no Chekhov. So now it is clear why all the theaters where only persons and not things perform have so far been unable to stage Chekhov; they do not love and understand him. (He is almost never put on in the provinces.) So now we begin to understand not only why the Art Theater is able to perform Chekhov but also what constitutes the Art Theater's strength and novelty and special quality: there, not only human beings but even things perform. It is the theater of psychology. Furthermore—it is the theater of that panpsychism whose purest representative in literature was Anton Chekhov.

So now, turning back to the very beginnings of the Art Theater and my article, we recognize just *what* was so strikingly, staggeringly new about the boyars' mantles and festal garb in *Tsar Fyodor*—it was their psychology. Not precision and not accuracy to an historical era, which we have only the faintest notion of, but vital animation, and therefore a correspondence with the deepest truth of life. One thing only resides in the Prozorov sisters' little garret and Ivanov's study and that cucumber which, overcome with pain and humiliation, Stanislavsky as Shabelsky could not finish eating[15] and the cricket and the rings and military overcoats that the actors wear at home—one thing, and that is: psyche. Things are not so much things as the scattered thoughts and sensations of a single soul.

Chekhov, and the theater with him, created not only things, but *time* itself, not as a watchmaker does, but as a psychologist does; time is only the protagonists' thought and sensation. And where there are no wonderful thought-filled pauses and sensation-filled pauses and where talented persons alone do the acting and time has not yet been taught to act, there is no Chekhov and never will be. Remember how the Germans who knew no Russian wept when the *animation* of time in Chekhov's plays spoke to them from the Art Theater stage in the international language of pauses! And the very fact that the theater knew so well how to render elusive time subservient to its great artistic power makes the theater forever glorious and immortal!

Animated time, animated things, animated persons constitute the secret of the enchantment of Chekhov's plays, which are still in the repertory of the Art Theater. Whether a servant-girl plays a balalaika at the gate, transmitting to the stage the barely audible, almost guessed-at tune "Little Siskin" (*Ivanov*), or tambourines rattle, shouts from a fire are carried on the breeze, Natasha wanders through the dark rooms with a candle, Epikhodov eats an apple,[16] it all contributes to one end, panpsychism, it all comes across not as items from reality or true-to-life sound and its utterance, but as the protagonists' thought and sensations disseminated throughout space. How odd, for instance, that at the end of *Three Sisters*, all the protagonists of the play are *thinking and feeling to the rhythm of the military march* which, as if by chance, is being played in the street by the departing soldiers; and the turmoil in their souls is expressed yet again not by bare, spontaneous remarks, but also by the apparently chance figure of a girl with a harp and her absurd, inappropriate ballad, "Once I loved, once I suffered."

Pay close attention to the dialogue in Chekhov's plays: it is improbable, no one talks that way in real life; it is full of reticences, always an exact continuation of something already spoken; there are none of the sharp cues with which everyone who speaks in any other author's play always chimes in: Chekhov's protagonists never begin their speeches and never end them, they always merely continue them. And as a result, in the reading a Chekhov play is difficult, uninteresting and even unlifelike: and in this respect Tolstoy was right when he deemed a Chekhov play he had read pointless, though it appears he never finished it, out of boredom.[17] But he was also wrong, because he did not visualize Chekhov, he did not visualize Chekhov's things and pauses *as they acted*, nor all the things that the theater so vividly brought to life. Indeed if Chekhov's dialogue always *continues* something, mustn't there be someone or something it continues?—and this enigmatic essence, absent in mere reading, turns out to be precisely the animation of things and time. The dialogue, so to speak, never ceases: it is transferred from persons to things, from things to persons again, and from persons to time, to silence or clamor, to a cricket or shouting at the fire. Everything lives, has a soul and a voice: oh, how remote this theater was from that insufferable naturalism which has been imputed to it and which takes cognizance only of *things*: who needs it?

But now an interesting and very important question arises: who progressed, Chekhov or the theater—who created whom: did Chekhov create the theater or did the theater create Chekhov?—who was the psychologist (panpsychologist) first and who was the later to arrive? May I venture to reply that neither one came first, they moved forward together, simultaneously; but Chekhov had always been like that in every way, whereas the theater became a psychologist gradually—the moment of their encounter only defined and confirmed the fate of both. Possibly, had it not been for the Art Theater, Chekhov would have given up playwriting—laws are writ in vain, if they be not carried out; but without Chekhov the theater might easily have been lured into all sorts of naturalism, realism and symbolism and might never, perhaps, have found its right road.

IV

Naturally, having found itself in Chekhov but without fully understanding how, the Art Theater with the persistence of singleminded artistic willfulness tried to apply the same device of panpsychism, which lay at the very foundation of its artistic organism and had been so brilliantly vindicated in Chekhov, to everything. At this point that series of mistakes and bitter disappointments commenced, those games played to a stalemate, those cold and tiresome victories and equally cold defeats. It was as if something were missing: there were always superb details, the audience applauded the sets in the Turgenev productions and laughed till its belly ached at *The Imaginary Invalid*[18] (and during the intermissions asked, Why did the Art Theater bother to stage this?) and so on and on—but that total achievement and unarguable artistic triumph that Chekhov had won for them put in no further appearances. Along with the splendors there was always a defect, a certain hairline crack down the surface of art, sometimes a blatant and even crude assault on an author whom they did not so much stage as squirm into, did not so much explicate as bone up on in order to rewrite him. In this way they boned up on Gogol and Griboedov and Ostrovsky, for they were not put off by distance. They stuck at nothing. They complained to all the world that in all the world there was no repertory, no plays. Who hasn't heard Nemirovich-Danchenko and Stanislavsky complaining about it?

And of course they were wrong to complain: there are as many good plays in the world as you like, and it isn't Shakespeare's fault that he's a failure at the Art Theater. And of course they were right to complain, a thousand times right: there are many good plays, but not the sort that the soul and will of the *new* theater are thirsting for, none or very few; they must be sought out with great labor and with the great risk that, after all, it will turn out to be a mistake in the end. Apparently the psychological theater has nothing to do and to stage at a time when *the psychological novel already exists and the psychological drama does not,* when up to now comedy of acting and dramas of spectacle and action, an ancient, sumptuous and magnificent fairground booth, have occupied the tottering and worm-eaten throne.

In these unavoidably broad generalizations I may easily have sinned against particulars, but this cannot be helped; only by means of just such broad generalizations can I get to the true meaning, the moment experienced by the theater, without digressing into details, as many have done before me. And, sinning against particulars, I dare affirm: if psychology has not been *totally* missing in drama up to now (there was even some in *Vampuka*),[19] nevertheless (prior to Chekhov), there was no *psychological* drama. There was crudely expressed psychology like the occasional lumps of suet in a pie filling, though the pie itself was baked of a different dough, out of action and spectacle, and *acting* in the straightforward and narrow meaning of the term. Even the greatest and hitherto undisputed psychologist Shakespeare is horribly unpsychological when you approach him with demands for psychic truth as Tolstoy did. Shakespeare is a pose, an actor, *acting in all things,* a brilliant pattern of self-sufficient words, theatrical magnificence; Shakespeare is the richness of Gothic art, Milan cathedral with a thousand spires, a gorgeous spectacle. But to approach Shakespeare with a demand for psychic truth, with its psychic iron logic and simplicity, means killing Shakespeare the way the Art Theater killed him in *Hamlet.*[20]

I said, "acting in all things"—yes, this is the most important, most crucial indication, the border-line between old and new in the theater: acting. But what is "acting," a theater of "acting"? And here I feel most strongly that sense of quasi desperation, when new things have to be discussed in old words whose true meaning has been perverted over the course of their long rambles through the world. First among such words is the aforesaid "acting" in its application to the theater—utterly worn out, applied every which way, it has long ceased to mean anything. If there is "acting" in Shakespeare, is there no "acting" in Chekhov? Did not the very same Kachalov "act" both Hamlet and Ivanov[21]—where is the difference, what does it consist of?

My answer is, first, that Kachalov really does "act" Hamlet

(though he very much wishes not to) yet Kachalov does not act Chekhov but does something entirely different, for which we do not yet possess an exact and generally accepted term. When a novelist or a psychological dramatist invents his heroes, does he "act" them or not? No, he does not, he *experiences*, creates, depicts them—whatever you like, but he does not act. For "acting" is something quite distinct from that artistic process of reconstructing the living persons who form the basis for psychological creativity. Acting is *pretense*, and the subtler, cleverer, more beautiful it is, the better the acting; psychological creation is *truth*, and the more obvious, strict, incorruptible it is, the further it is from pretense and the more sublime and artistic the work. In creating psychological images, the artist must be absolutely sincere, and not merely believe but know for a fact that just such a man with just such a nose and just such a soul as he depicts actually and positively exists; and though he may only show the reader that man's back, he himself ought to know the man's entire life, every pimple on his body, his dreams and his reality. And the writer or dramatist should certainly not be sincere if his task is to provide for acting—God forbid that he seriously believe that the *mask* (a synonym for acting) he wears is his true and authentic face; when acting, one must believe only by halves, like those *acting* dogs, who only bare their teeth at one another but do not bite.

And all of the old theater is theater of *pretense*—in contrast with the new, which is and will be theater of *truth*. So there is no need to bring on stage Harlequin and Pantaloon, pure agents of the *commedia dell'arte*, to see theater of pretense: every play old and modern is permeated with acting, everything is constructed on pretense and the mask, everything is steeped in that happy half-sincerity of author and actors, wherein pain is not truly painful but merely a source of aesthetic delight.* Theatrical tears—the sweat the soul exudes as it strives to detach itself from serious illness and suffering—are just as sweet as laughter, and they justify the indignant words of that most sincere of Russian writers, Veresaev:[22] art stings us with whips, but these whips are intertwined with roses (I

*Note how the *commedia dell'arte* characters Harlequin and Pantaloon, congealed and set once and for all, have found a haven in our ordinary drama, hidden behind such immobile and frozen masks as "romantic lead," "simpleton," "ingenue," "noble father," "raisonneur," etc. Always the same pack of cards, which can be used to play different games—but the king is always king, the knave always knave, and the six of clubs never anything but the six of clubs. All conventional, all based on pretense, all acting!

quote from memory). Quite possibly the whistles and howls with which the audience greets current attempts to make drama psychological are only evidence of its nonhabituation to intense and real suffering, tears that are bitter, not sweet . . . just as the audience's absence at other plays shows its total unwillingness to come to terms any longer with tiresome theatrical pretense.

Truth in art is the slogan of the coming renascence of art, on whose threshold we stand. I steadfastly believe that such a renascence is about to take place here in Russia. But this is by the way.

It is as ridiculous to say of Shalyapin that he "sings" Godunov, although this word is adequate when applied to Lipkovskaya, strenuously singing Violetta,[23] as to apply the term "acting" to the actors in Chekhov's plays on the stage of the Art Theater. And these distinctions, an actor *acts* or an actor *experiences*, have got to be precisely differentiated, even reporters must learn not to mix them up. But an even more precise and stringent distinction must be made between the old theater of acting and the new psychological theater; the highest fire-wall must be erected here, a wall of stone.

The *mask*, which is at the very root of theater of pretense, fatally condemns it to eternal and indissoluble ties with *spectacle and action* in its external manifestations. But some roads lead to truth and others to pretense—and where the way lies so open for acting, it is strait for psychological creativity and artistic truth. Thus, every freedom eventually turns into slavery; thus action and spectacle, which once begot theater have now become its murderers, despots who can be dealt with only by revolution. Revolution has already begun with the advent of Mister Cinema, and the gunshot that does away with old theater, the whistle of an indignant audience and the general strike of dramatists serve as its theme song. For the "dearth of our dramatic literature" is, in the last analysis, only an unwitting and taciturn strike by those who no longer wish to dilute the truth of their literary creations with the still dominant theatrical lie.

V

If *Shakespeare*, falling like an old fortress beneath the mighty onslaught of truth, is seldom psychological, then all those whom the Art Theater continues to stage are even less psychological. So many resources, so much work and talent suddenly becoming powerless in the face of the infeasible task: to find a *soul* where one does not exist, where no one ever meant one to be!

Remember *Brand*.[24] The waves foamed like the real thing, almost as in the cinematograph, and the mountains caved in, and they went to Norway for the costumes; and Kachalov himself, not yet cowed by Hamlet as he probably is now, trying with all the might of his talent to create something . . . and the emptiness, the unbearable tedium, the wooden figures from which they tried fruitlessly to extract at least a smidgeon of psychology. But where were they to find it? Ibsen no more needs psychology than he needs grease for Brand's boots: the image is purely ideal, logical, a kind of Newtonian binomial with its parentheses, equations and questions. And when, yearningly, I beheld this Ibsen, this unstrung Brand, I remembered something Chekhov had said. To a question of mine about Ibsen—something general—Chekhov quite seriously and without the glimmer of a joke replied curtly:

"Ibsen is a fool."

At the time the words hurt me and even made me secretly indignant as an ardent admirer of Ibsen, but, watching *Brand*, I began to think that perhaps Chekhov had been right. From his viewpoint as a panpsychologist, as a quarrier for spiritual truth even in things, Chekhov might have regarded Ibsen much as Tolstoy regarded Shakespeare: as a downright idiot. And the theater, which approached the production of *Brand* with the same demands that it made of Chekhov, was inevitably bound to turn Ibsen into an idiot. And so it did.

Remember too the productions of *Woe from Wit*, *The Inspector* and Ostrovsky—the last only in part, for in some small measure Ostrovsky was nevertheless a psychologist (if only a psychologist of everyday life, as Kommissarzhevsky describes him now).[25] The theater tried with might and main to stuff psychology into exclusively *social* but in no way psychological types like Famusov, Molchalin, Chatsky, Khlestakov, Bobchinsky and Dobchinsky[26]—and the results were Brand all over again. They tried to substantiate Chatsky's declamatory, patently custom-made, forensic sensibility on psychological grounds, and all of Chatsky lost his luster, he simply got lost in the shuffle. His *custom-made* love of Sofiya, as well as Sofiya's *custom-made* love of Molchalin, they strove to stage on a sound foundation of psychology—and suddenly highly intelligent Griboedov started to look like an idiot, incapable of putting two words together psychologically.

There are no things in Gogol's *Inspector*; things do not live or make sounds, Gogol did not require them for his social task—and so, the Art Theater, using Khlestakov's hands, smashed imaginary bedbugs on the wall to no avail: the bedbugs remained imaginary and in no way entered the spectator's soul. And to no avail did that most gifted performer Uralov[27] strive not to act the Mayor but to live on stage, for the Mayor became coarse and unrecognizable; and any actor who ever *acted* the Mayor has provided more than did all the talents in the Art Theater. Even Gogol's fun was lost—and this was supposed to be Gogol!

Nor did Molière himself avoid the common sorry lot. His *Imaginary Invalid*, built entirely on acting and merry pretense, on the most thoroughgoing and enchanting disdain for psychology—enchanting because it is manifest—was weighed down unmercifully, like a fly caught in a web, by a cargo of psychological motivations, a tragic attempt to exact something of psychic substance even from these rollicking boobies. I have no objection to laughter and sometimes I even go to the cinema to watch Max Linder's romantic escapades,[28] as he butts down walls with his head; but if during this jolly story, while smashing down walls with his head, he started to demonstrate and indicate that his love is true love and not for fun's sake, I would simply get bored. And when, in the merry acting of Molière, the imaginary invalid believes, for fun's sake since he exists wholly for fun's sake, that the disguised maid is a real doctor, I can laugh. But when genial Stanislavsky, with a power of creative and psychological talent equal to Shalyapin's, continually demonstrates to me, proving time and time again, that the imaginary invalid is the most alive and real of men, and then suddenly believes in the disguised maid, I get bored, embarrassed, and want to leave the theater as soon as possible. And the more the talented designer Aleksandr Benois[29] tried to present the *truth* of things, the less there was left of truth and Molière; and so, limping on both his acting foot and his psychological foot, the imaginary invalid hobbled to his splendid conclusion, when the colossal clysters triumphantly ended this ridiculous struggle between truth and pretense.

I am very fond of Alexandre Dumas and think him a brilliant writer; but if I came to him with a demand for psychologizing he would instantly turn into a fool. Do the strength and great charm in *Three Musketeers* consist of psychologizing? And this was the recurrent error of the unfortunate, Sisyphian labor of the Art Theater: it solemnly cremated a comedy of acting in the purifying fire of psychology and got nothing out of it but smoke . . . not even the smoke of incense. And yet even in this case the theater was misunderstood both by its friends and its foes; some rebuked it yet again for superfluous naturalism, others reproved it for its penchant for the everyday and its inability to achieve symbols—but mostly it was reviled for its naturalism. How could one possibly mix two such contradictory elements as flat, naked naturalism, true property of the cinema, and panpsychism, true basis for the theater of the future!

To prevent misunderstandings, let me say at once that I am not, in principle, opposed to the comedy of acting, any more than to the prepsychological novel: what's good is good. And I rank a good old comedy of acting much higher than most modern Russian drama, which sedulously strives to be psychological as it mournfully meanders through the wilderness of the sucked thumb. Although the revolution has begun, we are, all of us, still half under the sway of the old despotic theater, who, if we will repudiate *truth*, will gladly grant us amusing theatricality and skillful histrionics. The life of truth is still new and difficult, and there are times when the soul needs a rest: then the novels of Dumas are good, as are the jovial and talented performances of an actor. Which would all be very fine, except for the problem that good acting plays are no longer being written and are not staged either: before it had finished its purification, psychology hastened to poison acting, the way Christianity poisoned the pagan Venus without quite killing her off. But luckily the art of truth and the life of truth raise their stern voices ever more absolutely: even in art people are starting to seek out the difficult for themselves and to avoid frivolous amusements and superficial pleasures. Beautiful were the pagan gods, but on this earth one can no longer return to them—great Pan is dead! Beautiful were the lies of old art, but they are already falling before the most beautiful truth of the rigorous and stringent days of renovation.

And it already means that the end has come for the comedy of acting, if the best and most serious theater in the world, the Art Theater, in each of its new productions, deals a blow to acting even as it acts, devalues *action*, reduces spectacle to a triumphant *no*. Great is the wisdom of the Lord: even when the prophet who wants to bless utters curses, he is a true prophet, and his lips murmur truth itself! And through its mistakes the theater proved two things: first, that it is a theater of incredible force and a *new* theater; second, that there is no *new* drama* and until there is, the theater needs must dwell in the wilderness of the sucked thumb.

But no one can dwell in a wilderness, which is even worse than "living by revolt"; for one cannot spend all one's time cursing and destroying while wishing to bless and create—and so the Art The-

---

*I repeat, I am not concerned with particulars and gladly sin against them. Yet I cannot help but state, in a desire to be honest, that I consider *my* drama *Katerina Ivanovna*, with all the vicissitudes of its fate, a *new* drama. But this is a particular.

ater unexpectedly and abruptly turned to . . . the novels of Dostoevsky and mounted the *novels* of Dostoevsky on its stage. Yet, abrupt as the turning was, it was not properly noted or, for that matter, appreciated: there was more talk about whether or not it was seemly to adapt novels into plays and what the general result was from the literary standpoint; and quite recently, if not quite unexpectedly, Gorky has come out with his "optimistic" censorship, as a certain columnist wittily put it. But it is worth noting that the turning was made on the very edge of an abyss, by the firm hand of the brilliant Helmsman of that glorious vessel. True, people wrote with feeling that the success of the Dostoevsky productions was and is great, but they have not forgotten Chekhov; although belatedly, they aggrandize it as Chekhov's theater (not without malice) at the very time when the theater has already risen to a most sublime new peak called "Dostoevsky."

Yes. Quietly, almost unnoticed, the fateful confrontation took place between the passionately thirsting psychological theater and Dostoevsky, the genius of psychism. Very likely the meeting of Dante and Beatrice took place on the banks of the Arno just as quietly and imperceptibly: who, walking down the street, heard the beating of their hearts?

VI

"Any questions about Dostoevsky's value to us conduce to the primary question: what value has he for the actor?

"I believe that actors truly create only out of their own national literature. With the rarest exceptions, our theater avoids French and Spanish plays. Why? Because the Russian actor with his inherent tempo can act/*demonstrate* plays of the foreign repertory, but cannot *create* them" (*Footlights and Life*).

So says Nemirovich-Danchenko, to whose brilliant instinct the theater is indebted for its new renascence: he staged Dostoevsky. Further on he says:

"Russian drama is, first of all, founded on psychology, and the Russian actor seeks in his roles, first of all, a living and authentic psychology." "Gratifying stage 'situations' alone, which greatly alleviate the actor's task and fully satisfy him with experimentation, technical mastery and stereotyped gimmicks, can no longer enliven the actor's work with that inner excitement which is his greatest delight."

And finally:

"And who knows, maybe the stage adaptations of Dostoevsky promise us new dramatists?" . . .

Consider these words of Nemirovich-Danchenko and see how truth and untruth are wrestling in them, and how the wonderful insight of an artist whose mighty hand set the theater on the road to revival timidly bickers with the old ways of thinking! It is just about to attain its own truth, just about to speak its ultimate decisive word about *new* drama—but no: it recollects old arguments about the actor, wags an admonitory finger at the spectre of Gorky and once again, instead of truth, verisimilitude prevails: which is most dangerous because truth can be irretrievably submerged in verisimilitude. Where is the logic on this: on the one hand our actors are psychologists, on the other the actor's true creativity lies only in national literature. But can *psychology* be *national*? Was not Dostoevsky, for whom the Art Theater actors had so profound a feeling, no less profoundly appreciated by the German Nietzsche and a great many others? . . . And does it not seem ludicrous to have hidebound nationalism injected into psychology by the very theater that knew how to *animate* things and time?

Furthermore, on the one hand "Russian drama is, first of all, founded on psychology," and on the other, "gratifying stage 'situations' alone cannot enliven the actor's work"; and on a third, "who knows, maybe the stage adaptations of Dostoevsky promise us new dramatists?"

How confused truth and untruth are here! If Russian drama is indeed founded on psychology, what is the sense of it, where do we get those wretched "stage situations" which cannot enliven anything? And whence comes that yearning for *new* drama and even the promise that new dramatists will emerge, when as a rule "Russian drama is founded on psychology"?—therefore acting should simply be acting and not adapting *novels* into *dramas* for some reason!

This is how a great artist, how the creator of the first *new* theater in the world, skirts the truth, unable or unwilling to pronounce the ultimate, awful, boat-burning statement: there are *no dramas* for our theater as it wishes to be and can only be. What does this mean? It means taking all dramatic literature from the first play written to the latest of Averchenko's vaudevilles[30] and, in one fell swoop, tossing them overboard from *our ship*. It means that all drama that ever existed before this moment is not psychological and is unsuited to our new *psychological* theater: everything as it stands, from Sophocles to Maeterlinck, Tolstoy and the rest of our contemporaries. It means either concocting one's own plays by dramatizing the *psychological* novel or else staging old stuff and hanging in the lobby, instead of a "Sold Out" notice, "Here is another of our mistakes." It's really dreadful.

But what the Art Theater dares not or will not go so far as to say, I boldly state: I share less responsibility, I do not steer a ship, but simply watch the ship from the coastal ridges and trace its course. And I shall state that in actuality all dramatic literature from Adam to our own time is old literature, doomed to perish, for the *new* theater, the theater of the future, is already moving, will move beyond it. And its besetting sin, I repeat, is its serving, humbly serving, action and spectacle, as the pre-psychological novel did, at a time when the novel and all life as well have moved into psychology, have ceased to be a wonder-filled fairy-tale narrative about the adventures, the duels and love affairs of Benvenuto Cellini. In the last analysis we have grown too intelligent for sincere enjoyment of carefree acting in everything; we love the beauty of silk and velvet, are not averse to feasting our eyes on and rejoicing in gorgeous colors, we also like to laugh—but our greater love is *truth*, which has been taught us by the novel, and which we do not yet find in the theater of good old tragedy and drama.

Now I shall drop the Art Theater for a bit and move on to the most long-range basis for my view of old and new drama, old and new theater. But I anticipate regretfully that even at long range, I shall teeter on the brink of overgeneralization: for a detailed and fully documented investigation of the question requires much too much space and time and work—I am hardly a specialist. And my task does not entail winning over opponents if any exist and put in an appearance, but simply collecting friends—if any are to be found. Friends are not so exigent and will take for granted what others must have proved by whole pages of quotations and an arsenal of documentation.

VII

All contemporary playwrights, critics, audiences and theaters dream about a new drama. When I say *all*, I am referring only to the highest level, for in the lower regions the old drama of action, like the old novel of adventure, still continues to persist, may even, possibly, be only just beginning. But that is quite another, truly awful problem of our times, which I have already glanced at in passing when I spoke of the mixed character and antipodean demands of the modern audience. Incidentally, here's a piece of curious information: in glamorous France, Anatole France and other world-renowned celebrities

are practically unknown, have difficulty finding a publisher, and
their readers are numbered in the thousands, while some thirty mil-
lion Frenchmen daily read boulevard sensation novels and prostrate
themselves at the name of the great Arsène Lupin.[31] In France, "unfortunately, everyone is literate," as Béranger[32] said with misgiving,
not knowing that there is something even more unfortunate: to be
illiterate, as in Russia.

But as they dream about *new* drama, all playwrights, directors,
and theaters for some reason invariably proceed from *form*: all
qualities derive therefrom! They forget that like a *new* man, a *new*
drama will inevitably have the same two arms and one head and all
the rest in place as before; they think that all it needs is a new nose.
Of course, there are Roman noses and Russian ones; but in the last
analysis a nose is a nose; and I have encountered many quite superb
Roman noses on Nevsky Prospect, even though a Roman in our Sen-
ate is something unheard of. Form was and is only the *boundary-
line of content*, those planes which delimit it externally as they
trace the twists and turns of the content, the laws and whims of the
subject matter. And just as a Roman nose is ineffectual in turning a
Petersburgher into a Brutus, so the very finest tragic form for plays,
even with a chorus or a certain highly popular Fate, will never revive
Greek tragedy whose time is past. And conversely, when Reinhardt
in collaboration with von Hofmannsthal stuck an up-to-date, wholly German nose on Oedipus,[33] the result wasn't half bad and rather
Grecian—or so everybody thought.

Dramatists and directors seek new *form* in various ways, and
hope thereby to find a new drama. Incapable of creating a new form
of drama by themselves, directors strenuously demolish the old
drama's form and devise the most unbelievable balderdash, which
Evreinov wittily ridiculed in his *Inspector*.[34] It is hard to believe the
amount of creative energy squandered on simple displacement:
whether light should come from here or there, whether the spectator should be put on stage and the actors seated in the auditorium,
whether sight-lines should be on one side or even from behind,
whether the curtain is to be let down or parted, whether the actors
are to move on stage like mannequins or statues for the most part:
the list is endless. And now, finally, new theaters have to be built—
Here we truly have a mixture of form and content! Structure and
function!—and in the meantime we must go to the circus, even the
woods, even the mountains of the Caucasus. Indeed there were even
Caucasian bandits who sang *The Demon*[35] on real rocks, and the
whole Caucasian sky blushed for shame:

And this is what was so curious: as they cracked the form of the old, these cruel bonesetters did not sense that life itself was oozing out with the blood, they did not see the life's blood on the fractures or hear the heart of mutilated drama cease to beat. See here, I am not satisfied with the orangutan's *form*, I should like to have it turned into a man with all possible haste; but does this mean that I ought to shave it from head to foot? Having shaved it and broken its arms and legs, will I have a man or only a maimed corpse, or at best the man-beast whom H. G. Wells conjures up so horribly? [36] And this is what they did; they refused to recognize that drama is something organic and that its form and essence are united and bound to *life*— not to be torn away or separated one from the other!

The dramatists who sought new forms their own way—as new dramas—were more humane. They had nothing to break (more accurately, they had to begin with breakage, but they did not know it); they themselves began afresh by creating an organism and they did the deed without resorting to murder. But in creating, they too sought only forms bewitched by directors, they poured old sour wine into a few new bottles. It was Grillparzer,[37] I believe, who said that art has the same relationship to life as wine has to the vine— and yet they forgot about new wine and paid all their attention to the bottle, while the liquid remained the same: action and spectacle with pathetic hunks of psychological suet, the same old warmed-over pie. True, in these quests of theirs, as they sought the Indies they didn't fail to discover America: they evolved and perfected a form of symbolist drama (Blok's *The Little Showbooth*);[38] by a smuggler's route—as I've already written in my first letter—they expanded the subject matter of the stage and at times came very close to truth itself, but always by pure chance. So blind men, groping about for *form*, sometimes come upon the face of a loved one but instantly lose it in the unseen and clamorous crowd.

Perhaps Maeterlinck was a psychologist, but the symbolist form is more suitable for ideas, to which it provides unprecedented scope, but is dangerous for psychology; there can be no psychological truth where there is no firm foundation or motivation, where the very *basis* of spiritual actions is symbolic, ambiguous, equivocal. A symbolist does not bring his heroes to tears, he *forces* them to weep: he presents as assumption that which has yet to be proven—psychologically, of course. In *The Death of Tintagiles*, one of Maeterlinck's more powerful pieces, a feeling of terror may be elaborated with amazing accuracy, but it is not sufficiently motivated, is not graduated, is lent credence from the very start: and if I personally fear death, I will willingly, rapidly be terrified; otherwise, I will remain unmoved. More than mathematics, psychology insists: Prove it! You may start yawning if you watch another man yawning, or start weeping if you watch another man weep, or get frightened at seeing another man's terror—the mob is well aware of this—but it is little more than physiological: only *proof* of tears can move us to the point of true grief and elicit a profound spiritual reaction. Maeterlinck does not prove, he merely commands—and his commands cannot be obeyed. I am told that logic is only for the select few, commands are for the masses; which is no doubt true, but only in relation to ideas: the logic of the psyche is universal, no one is bidden or unbidden to it.

Watching Maeterlinck is exactly the same as going cold sober to a nameday party where everyone else has long been drunk, and not only is drunk, but has drunk up all the wine: it is hard to get tipsy from a few alcoholic kisses alone! And this Maeterlinckian failing is, *I believe*, a peculiarity of the symbolist form itself: issuing from something invariably *assumed* but concealed from us, capable of being revealed only after the drama is over, commanding but leaving off proof till tomorrow, and not fully at that—the symbolist drank up all the wine before we got there. It's a lucky thing if I'm drunk with the same booze, and ache with the same hangover as he, for then I share his merrymaking; but otherwise he and I remain isolated, each on his own. But I said, "I believe," for I do not venture to state categorically that the very form of symbolism is exactly like that and that no new symbolist will emerge who, once he understands the meaning of psychology for the new theater, will know how to provide his symbols with a principle of proof and not a doubtful command. For in the last analysis, even symbolism is only a form like realism, and the point is not form, but content.*

What is the content of the *new* drama of the future, and will a *new* theater spring from it?

VIII

However, first let me say a few words about which is to *renew* which: will the theater renew the drama or the drama the theater? In es-

---

*I have only now finished reading Aleksandr Blok's beautiful drama *Rose and Cross*; for all its symbolism, the drama is splendidly based on psychology and gives an impression of living and stirring truth.

sence the answer has already been supplied by what has gone before and I will only emphasize it: of course, only a new drama can renew the theater. Like any school, any practical show of strength, any arrow shot from the bow, the theater has an inherent impulse to inertia, a need to preserve a direction once taken. It can jerk backwards, but it cannot surge forward; and were the Art Theater not its own dramatist—after all, it created dramas out of Dostoevsky—it could not be deflected from the broad highway of old drama and its own habits. And although theater in general (even the Art Theater) may moan and demand new drama, for a long time to come it will not acknowledge the bridegroom who awaits it and will stone many timid prophets until some vulgar and mediocre Arabazhin or Yartsev[39] shows up—the latest immigration inspectors in these matters—and they stamp a visa on the passport. For that would mean that now everyone understands—it may be staged.

The renewal of the theater, however burdened by old ways, is unthinkable without the renewal of the drama, of that basic theatrically dramatic fabric that writers weave in the stillness of their studies. And in the fight between cinema and theater the latter is powerless to win a victory if a new weapon is not forged for it by some glorious dramatist-to-be. He is sure to come, this dramatist of a nascent theater, and his motto will be: Psychology!

Evreinov in his extraordinarily interesting inquiry *Theater as Such*[40] says, among other things, that only persons quite close to the theater, actors or directors, can be good dramatists: only they understand and have a feeling for theater. But this is absolutely false! There is no merit in knowing the *old* theater, slated for demolition from floor to roof; and even less need to live in it, involuntarily saturating one's spirit in putrescence and acid. No, let us have no born dramatists and masters of theatrical affairs, but literary men, once abhorred by the theater, literary men with their blessed ignorance of spotlights and wing-and-border pieces must create the new drama. Indeed the misfortune is not that there is too much literature in the theater nowadays, as many people think, but rather that there is none at all!

Until now contemporaries conceived the theater and literature to be two disparate elements, and the difference between a dramatist and a man of letters was like that between, for instance, a fish and a bird: both had to be born that way. And since a dramatist is not supposed to write novels, it is regarded as even less seemly for a man of letters to write drama: except, at the very most, like a seagull which can glide on the water but cannot actually dive in, oh no! But some fifteen or twenty years ago (in Russia, really not until Chekhov), this biological division between dramatist and writer began to be effaced, though it was far from disappearing. Although acknowledged by the theater, the literary man is, as before, a clandestine foe to it and the actor, and his invasion of the theater always takes on the aspect of that grievous battle when "the deadly pike is wielded and the cossack's head is off"—the present-day man of letters and the present-day theater confront one another not for delight but for mutual woe. It would seem to be something simpler: the literary man is not needed, and that's that, but no!—with gnashing of teeth the theater drags in the literary man, and if he won't come himself, the theater seizes upon his novels, stories, something written with no thought of the theater, and *adapts* it, adapts it! And in so doing the theater says, screams, complains that it has been neglected, that it wants intensely to share literature's lofty position, that it can no longer remain a kind of special element, once an ocean, now merely a swamp. And observe how few born dramatists are left, how pitifully they have degenerated: not whales, but tadpoles!

But why is there no joy at the reunion of the estranged lovers, theater and writer? There is no joy because, while appealing to the literary man, at the same time the theater invariably wants to mash him following its own old recipe, dress him in its worn-out livery, hand-me-downs from servants it had sacked before. The literary man, so talented and audacious so long as he sits in the auditorium and curses, immediately confesses his guilt as soon as he sits down to write a drama, and meekly inquires of the director about those mysterious spotlights—how can you do without spotlights? And when he submits a drama, he fears most of all that he will be rebuked for being literary—he, a writer, for heaven's sake! He, summoned to make new laws for an enfeebled theater, humbly accepts its pettiest regulation, confounds himself, destroys his talent, gets down on all fours and prattles with the voice of a two-week-old baby . . . who needs him in that state?

The theater summons Vikings to be legislators and rulers,[41] but a defendant arrives in a frockcoat and seeks out the prisoner's dock for himself; back home, during the preliminary investigation, he had made a confession, and now he is interested only in the question: hard labor or, God willing, only exile?

And inasmuch as the *new* theater will be a theater of psychology and the *word* (as I mentioned earlier), and must rise to the high level of modern literature, its first place must go to the literary man, who now seldom attends the theater and has not the slightest intention of writing for it: his organic rejection and ignorance of the old theater are a guarantee of brilliant victories in the theater of the future. But only so long as he does not fear the director and the ingenious spotlights!

IX

Of course, to be a good playwright in the old theater, one had to know its special organization, the *language of its conventions*—in this respect Evreinov is absolutely right. We are no longer dealing with spotlights but with something far more complicated. As I eliminate various conventions of scenery, makeup, lighting of one kind or another, act- and scene-divisions and so forth, I pause only at the matter that most concerns me: conventional theatrical psychology.

When I say that the old drama knows no psychology, you must understand me to mean that the old drama knew and still knows nothing but conventional psychology, which is quite distinct from both the psychology of life and that of literature. I shall not discuss the former, for it is only the grapevine from which we must yet press the wine of art; but in the best specimens of literature we meet with such a power of psychological elaboration that perhaps for the very first time the truth of the soul may be discerned in it. The darkness in which the human *soul* has been submerged since ancient times is gradually being dispelled. Just as the sea, which was a smooth surface to the ancients, is now gradually revealing the secrets hidden in its depths, so the plummet of psychology has already revealed many of the soul's innermost secrets; in places—as in Dostoevsky—it has groped the very bottom, slimy and dreadful, black and turbid beneath the mass of limpid waters. Even now the psychological novelist is analyzing *dreams* in that mysterious realm governed by very special laws. Recall old literature where people never seemed to sleep, they had so few dreams! (The matter of *dreams* is dwelt with curiously at the talented Crooked Mirror Theater; Geier's *Dream*,[42] for instance. At the same time do not forget that this theater is *not considered* a serious one!)

In his quest for spiritual truth, refusing to truckle to theatrical laws of "action and spectacle" (not to mention the ruthless law of unity of time, place and action, fortunately long since abolished), the psychological novelist calmly posed and solved his problems, unhurriedly investigating the soul as such. His strength was comprised of freedom from action and spectacle, from theatrical convention. And it may very well be that even Dostoevsky, whose novels are now so neatly fitted up for the stage, would himself have seemed a very second-rate dramatist, had he decided to write for the theater of his time. He would have lost all his strength in the fight with spotlights and director. Freely moving from dialogue to a monologue protracted over the space of ten pages (Nagel in Hamsun's *Mysteries*),[43] rejecting external for internal, beginning whole chapters with the words "He thought . . ." (Tolstoy), the novelist plumbed to infinity the souls of his heroes, brought them near our own and near to the truth of the soul taken in the abstract. His techniques are few: he simply starts to talk about himself, to explicate, to surmise. Sometimes he views things from within, sometimes he stares from the sidelines—he changes the point of view, and seeks and finds in any way he can.

What I am saying is far from new, but it becomes new and interesting if you now endeavor to draw a parallel between this psychology of the novel and its methods, and the conventional, foreshortened body, ragged to the point of nakedness, the beggarly psychology of dramatic action.

The ballet, as everyone knows, has its own language of physical movements and mime: something like this—running on tiptoe for a long while is to express complete spiritual innocence, and at the same time fear or love. Clowns, too, have their own language: e.g., a slap as an expression of anger, turning the toes in as a characteristic of stupidity and imbecility. But few persons seem to realize that the most serious drama also uses exactly the same sort of language, which is precisely adapted to express a thing's most important aspect, its psychology. In *Vampuka*, some gentleman comes in and proclaims, "I have subjugated you!"—and everyone instantly assumes a pose of subjugation and repeats with the most profound assurance, "He has subjugated us." But this takes place not only in *Vampuka*; the drama also lives by such idiotically simple devices. This is convention, plain and simple.

The first necessity for this is a credulous spectator, and if you have that, it's all very simple and easy. If you have to express great sorrow, you would start to weep; sorrow abated, you would lay your head on the table. Putting a finger to your lips apparently without meaning to or watching the door after someone makes an exit signifies: a wife is cheating on her husband, something fishy is going on. Clutching your head, dealing out a slap, running, not walking, into a room, laughing for joy and sobbing for despair, pursing the lips, knitting the brow, putting dark patches under the eyes and so forth are all part of the conventional *language* of the drama, every bit as generally accepted as the conventional Morse code of the telegraph. Aren't we talking about a telegraph here too! Look at the conventional pendulum of a conventional clock: with what intolerable speed it ticks off the conventional seconds!

But this is only *language* and therefore of secondary importance: even the Bible can be translated into Morse code . . . perhaps the psychological content is unaffected?

Unfortunately, in this case the language entirely corresponds to the content transmitted. Telegraphic communication first requires speed—and you can see in modern drama how all the psychological processes and inner experiences are ruthlessly speeded up: love, envy, anger, contempt, illness, (psychological) death, like an actor hurriedly running up a staircase where all the stairs are askew and the steeple itself is only a couple of steps away. To get a better idea of the harsh falsehood of such speed, imagine that a film at a cinema is showing a funeral procession, but the projectionist is drunk and has run the reel at three times the normal speed: the widow sprints, the relations jump and the corpse himself behaves with the celerity of a racehorse—what happened to the funeral? And this is the fundamental, primary lie of conventional theatrical psychology which begets any number of little lies.

If I am watching a comedy of acting and am openly asked to believe in it, I can do so if I wish: just as a child when he chooses to play can believe that this chair, say, is a horse. But even a child at play knows perfectly well that it is still only a chair; and when he is sick and tired of playing, no power on earth can convince him that a chair is a horse: he's tired of playing! He is serious and now wants to look at pictures—one step upward! And when in a serious drama, and not while playing, we are asked as before to believe that a kiss is proof positive of love, I refuse to believe it and demand verification. Such verifications—psychological ones, of course—are almost never provided by our drama, it knows them not. And in this respect, all modern drama with its conventional language and psychology is no less symbolic than Maeterlinck, who commands but does not prove. The only difference is that its symbols are extremely elementary, like a horsey-chair, but it is based on the same thing: faith rather than conviction, commands rather than proof.

Faith was always a slippery and desperate foothold, and nowadays with improvement in toys it has great difficulty holding even a child: the chair is becoming a chair once and for all. On the other hand, a demand for proof is growing daily: the heart, as well as the head, has grown wiser. And the modern drama is daily becoming ever more unbearable with its unsubstantiated, unproven psychology, rapid-fire Morse-code language and naive and childish allegory (for "symbols," in the last analysis, is too important a word to describe ordinary playing with dolls!).

Let that brilliant immigrant from the lower ranks, refulgent Cinema, have all of this for his own. It was made for him: the naive naturalism of things, the impetuous action and impetuous pseudo-psychology, so reminiscent of the headlong funeral; the Morse-code psychological language, the knit brows, the passionate kiss, the tip-toeing to express innocence and love. He will never get far in psychology—he dreams about it and likewise plays host to literary men solely out of youthful ardor and superabundant strength, but he elaborates action to perfection and excavates brilliant new diamonds from that still untapped mine. However, this separation of powers should take place as soon as possible: church from state, and theater from cinema.

X

The *new* theater will be a psychological theater. The *new* drama will have as its exclusive subject the psyche.

No doubt not everyone will agree with my definition of subject, and some may say that psychological elaboration is only a method which still has nothing to do with *content* itself. I venture to reply, somewhat paradoxically, that method is itself content: the whole world changes its essence (which actually abides in immutability) depending on which method of research is used. And if that same good old world and humanity are left as the *matter* of new drama, then the *soul* of the world and humanity will become the *content*, not its body, which—whether we like it or not—belongs, in the last analysis, to powerful Cinema. I strongly emphasize the difference between matter and content: matter is changeless, the same for all eternity, content is fluctuating and changing eternally, with no end to its transformations.

Once he has established *soul* as his content, the new dramatist will suddenly see a brand-new world before his eyes, a world quite untouched by anyone else. It can be perused like a new book, from cover to cover. And suddenly it becomes clear that even after *Romeo and Juliet* one can write about love as if the stage had never once heard the word; that after the millions of faithless wives presented by the theater, a faithless wife can be presented so that the spectator will see her *for the first time,* and the critic, that strict guardian of canon and stereotypes, that sleepy watchman at the tomb of dead truth, will be at a loss. And the new dramatist will present man himself as if the stage had never yet seen a man: no, it has seen man, but never yet noticed his soul. And everything that the new dramatist looks upon with new eyes will become the content for genuine new drama: and serious-minded people will not brush aside the theater as a long-standing but boring and tiresome amusement; for there's really just no way to ask professors to play horsey, entreating the recalcitrant to be as little children!

Now we already have our first *new* theater, the Art Theater. Observe it closely. By staging Dostoevsky's *novels,* it has shown that the old, time-honored dramatic structure is quite secondary. It admitted a *reader,* who explicates. It allowed a single performance *to be extended over two evenings.* It created twenty tableaux instead of five to seven.

"Ultimately, after working on Dostoevsky," says Nemirovich-Danchenko, "you see that an atmosphere has been effected in the theater, which vitiates and etiolates not only theoretical discussions of what is admissible in stage adaptations but even those questions about a production's consistency and harmony . . . Never mind if a production's technical aspects are both lopsided and awkward, the most important thing in the theater is the phenomenon of creativity, not technical expertise."

This is a remarkable statement which ushers in the start of an epoch in the history of the new theater!

Cannot what has been done for Dostoevsky be done for us, the new dramatists? True, Dostoevsky is in good repute: Gorky's letter provided something like a questionnaire about Dostoevsky, and to a man they called him a genius, all the "leaflets" used that expression—but the theater has not worked for a reputation, but for those special artistic values which it called "psychology." And as you work for the new theater, forget about time and the number of acts and the spotlights and form—think only about psychic truth, achieve it in every way you can, insert readers if you cannot manage it otherwise, supply endless monologues, consider neither the spectator nor the critic nor, in the last analysis, theater itself! Your psychic truth will triumph over spectators and theater—and even the critic Aikhenvald,[44] famous for his "thoughtfulness," will grant the theater the right to exist, which he now so frivolously denies it. Be "lopsided and awkward," remember that the theater is sacrificing nothing valuable for your sake except the "technique" which it has long abandoned; all it sacrifices is the rope that was strangling it!

Literature was never intended as an after-dinner amusement, but once it became that, in an unfortunate moment, it perished. Once the theater ceases to be an amusement, it will be hard work for those who wish to work hard, a teacher and friend for truth-seekers and the lonely.

But even the most beautiful wishes and advice are a long way from fulfillment, and so I come back down to earth . . . yet, not entirely to earth: I shall take the well-disposed reader to the Art Theater and, to the best of my ability, will relate how the new psychological content is worked out there. I do not think my eyewitness exposures of the theater's backstage work are indiscreet, for it is work that should be shown on the screen, like Doyen's operations,[45] people learn from such work.

I shall not speak of the amicable preparatory work on the play, the discussions of its meaning and significance, explanations of general principles, but shall begin at the moment when the role is in the actor's hands and he begins to act. The actor suddenly puts down the script, or else tosses it away, and says:

"Vladimir Ivanych, I don't know what I am to live on."

This does not mean that the actor has no money, but that there is something missing in his role that keeps it from coming to life. And the actor goes on to explain rather in this fashion:

"Here it says that *he* smiles, but he has no reason to smile. He's just been beaten up and thrown out, and he's smiling—the idiot! Generally speaking I can't see anything in it to live on; everything is kind of fortuitous."

This means: I accept nothing on faith, I demand proof for both laughter and tears, I demand the strictest proof for every step I take on stage. Nothing is accidental in either psychology or art. And now the most minute psychological analysis begins: psychiatric specialists and experts do not examine each move of a murder suspect as attentively as these "actors" scrutinize the genesis and stasis, past and present of a hero, certify his passport, collate his wrinkles— right down to a dactyloscopic investigation. What a dreadful examination for an author to undergo! What a disgrace when, amid living words, they suddenly discover the venomously tapping Morse-code apparatus, abbreviating psychology to suit spectators of tender age!

And so on for each role and each actor. And occasionally whole rehearsals stop short to deal with a smile that nobody can understand. Occasionally an actor forgets that he must live and search from within, and then he works from external visual impressions—which is a bad thing. One must never forget that such visual impressions can be derived only from the theater and memories of the theater: in life a husband almost never quarrels with his wife in public, and the actor never saw such a thing any more than he saw lovers kiss or lonely people's tears, nor was he invited to be present at murders and betrayals. Like the writer, who similarly has never been by personally to observe kisses and banter between lovers or been a guest at murder and suicide, or an eyewitness to treachery, or watched a safe broken open or lain under the bed and eavesdropped on the conversation of two prostitutes, but spun it all *out of himself,* out of his own psychological experiences, out of the mysterious capacity to put himself in any place and any situation—so the actor can elicit psychic truth only out of himself, and not out of visual impressions, external theatricality. As he finds truth within himself, he also finds the correspondingly correct gesture and mime—not clutching his head and sarcastically screwing up his lips Morse-code style. And this is what is called acting through inner experiences. And so they do not let the actor budge from his place until he has found *something to live on,* and the theatrical gesture is exchanged for the correct and true one.

Now you understand how that wonderful animation of things comes about, as in Chekhov: each thing has to *prove* its necessity, and once this is done, it becomes animate, an indispensable part of the protagonists' common soul. And if the author *himself did not see the things* as he wrote them, did not draw them into the psychological circle, did not make them a part of the common soul, then it has no existence for the actor either: this is what the Art Theater did not understand when it so painstakingly and so pointlessly animated the superfluous things in *The Inspector* and *Woe from Wit* and Shakespeare. In this respect even the most capable theater cannot see farther than the author, and the theater's farsightedness may easily turn into its myopia.

Along this difficult route of psychological proofs and indispensable motives the theater moves to create its own values. And the new dramatist must travel this road too, if he wishes a new serious drama. One must write on inner experiences, I should say, to use the terminology of the Art Theater.

Need I make the proviso that *inaction* is not at all obligatory for new drama? Our task is to liberate the stage from its old mendacious "laws," which are as specialized as is the theatrical censorship, even now so distinct from the general, and to subject it to a general law of literature. And if the dramatist-writer happens to need spectacle and action, so be it; however, he need not invent action where none exists or can exist, he need not be slavishly subservient to stage conventions that have outlived their meaning.

XI

I once attended a masquerade party in Moscow thrown by some artists. This was quite a while ago, some six or seven years, and many who were there are no longer with us: V. A. Serov, Ilya Sats.*[46] Serov was costumed as "Someone in Gray" from *The Life of Man* and stood in a corner with a candle or else would creep up to people and whisper earnestly behind their back:

"You sit here now and know not that thieves have already entered your chambers and are stealing your clothes from their pegs."[47]

But for the most part it was rather boring, almost excruciatingly so—as all our masquerades and merrymaking usually are. And then Sats, who was turning green with ennui, proposed in a terrified whisper to me and some actors from the Art Theater—that we absquatulate.

"Let's go to my place," he whispered, "It's not far from here, we'll find something to do and have a good time! I can't stand this!"

We left. But then something very strange occurred: his room was empty, enormous and horribly cold, and evidently had been unheated that day; there was a total absence of anything cheering: not only did wine, which many had counted on as the only way of escaping their sober and deadly yearning, fail to put in an appearance, but there was not even hot tea, it was too late to get a bit of a warm! Sats was embarrassed, muttered something, poked about in corners and suddenly cheered up: he had found somewhere some small wax Christmas-tree candles and with our help stuck them all over the place—on windowsills, tables, the grand piano. It began to look most peculiar—and rather jolly. And then, on top of this, something quite special and charming began to happen, something I can recall with delight even now: we all started *acting*. There were only a few

---

*Although much has been written about Sats after his death, by no means everything has yet been said about the meaning of this composer's work for the Art Theater. As a *psychological* composer, Sats was, in my view, not only a talented and valuable colleague: he was one of the *creators* of the contemporary theater in its striving for truth and psychic depth. Sats' music penetrated the very soul of men and things.

of us—Knipper, Moskvin, Kachalov, Zvantsev, Leonidov, Sats and I[48]—and we all acted: for ourselves, for there was no audience. There was only a general outline, we were to portray something that would be Spanish to the *n*th degree; and while Sats improvised music, Zvantsev composed a corresponding script in verse and the rest of us entered into it, each with his own contribution. It was hilarious, ridiculous, like *Vampuka* (which did not exist at the time) and remarkably talented: I already had a high opinion of those actors, but now I was struck by the force, clarity and freshness of their talent, the sparkle of their acting. At first I didn't want to act: it was awkward, I was unskilled, but imperceptibly I got carried away by it and began to act, something which made even me laugh. Everyone laughed at himself and the others, the music was punctuated by laughter, and everyone acted: we sang, piled up incidents, gave ourselves direction, latched onto an allusion in mid-flight and kept the dialogue going; some had come from the masquerade in costume. *And there was no audience—they were acting alone.*

And now, many years later, when I write about the theater of psychology and so definitely repudiate the theater of acting, I involuntarily recall that wonderful night of wonderful acting—yes, acting is indispensable! Everyone needs it: dogs and children and professors! And I can still recall so many occasions, weird evenings, days of a special moodiness, when suddenly and unendurably I felt like acting, either in a team or by myself like a kitten. To make a different face, to don fancy dress, a Spanish cape, a crown of gilt cardboard, to act out something, to speak in verse and sing—to act in anything at all.

And I recalled those weeping children, who either were forbidden by their parents or are boycotted by their friends: they are left out of games and watch enviously and tearfully from the sidelines! And it occurs to me: when we go to the theater of "acting" and from our bitter orchestra-seats watch the actors playing, are we not those same forlorn children, segregated by our parents' wishes from the general merriment, absurd and unnecessary witnesses of other people's joy . . . an audience! One must playact oneself and not merely observe—*that is the meaning of playacting* and the indictment of a theater which takes our money and acts superbly for itself and has confined us in the orchestra-seats to envy and impotent, peripheral, sterile laughter.

The theater of acting is unthinkable without the spectator's participation in the acting, for otherwise it becomes mockery and humiliation. And hence all those theoretical and practical attempts to bring the spectator closer to the stage and include him in the chorus: hence Reinhardt's circus,[49] where the spectators ostensibly were to mingle with the actors who moved in their midst; hence all those new cabarets where they not very wittily make jokes at the spectator's expense, trying to involve him in the performance; all those "brilliant" directorial gimmicks which suddenly thrust the stage out into the middle of the audience so that the most remote spectators may become actors of a kind.

And the innumerable mock trials of the heroines of "sensation" dramas?[50] Of course, this is indeed a public moment, but beyond that these trials bespeak a demand to participate in the performance oneself, not to be a mere spectator on the sidelines, a theatrical piece of meat, but to act. And how very significant that in these trials the author and his play appear only as prologue to the creation of a special kind of drama, raw material for a new collective creation, a congregational performance.

In the theater of the future there will be no spectators: that is the first and essential requirement of the new theater, as vitally necessary as the obliteration of *those who dine* and *those who only watch them dine* is in social life—everyone to the table! And the obliteration of the "spectator" will occur in two ways, I believe, inevitably and logically.

The spectators in the theater will disappear because the theater of acting will itself gradually be obliterated, dissolve and be absorbed into life itself, not become a special building with constables at its entrance but enter common private domestic life, as one of its joyous elements. People will act for themselves, without audiences and actors, by themselves. All these rhythmic gymnastics and dances, mock trials, ridiculous futurists with painted faces and masquerade costumes on Tver Street,[51] all this and much else that the reader will kindly recall for himself means only one thing: life has been robbed, it has been deprived of acting, acting has been scooped out like cream from a jug, leaving people nothing but skimmed milk: life insists that acting return to life's ancestral home, like the prodigal son from his wanderings as a bondsman. How this is to be realized in fact, of course, I don't know, nor am I much concerned: life is evolving and growing in such a way that any miracle will become conceivable. For after all, this is already a miracle: to become creators and artists, writers and musicians for ourselves—not just to look and listen, but to create something by oneself for one's own delight! After all, the trouble is not that there are few talented people, but that there are few garden plots and the seeds capable of nurturing life are rotting in damp storehouses. Before the aeroplane, who knew that life held so many extraordinarily daring and determined people, so physically and spiritually perfect! People complain about degeneracy—and then, surprise! Even this has ceased to be a miracle: yesterday *he* was a peasant, jolting on the splashboard of a cart, sleepy and gelatinous, quite hopelessly dim-witted, and today *he* drives an automobile, that diabolical machine that demands such superhuman concentration and vigilance and the quickest kind of thinking.

Of course there will always be people incapable of acting and there will always be people exceptionally capable and fond of acting—and the former will watch if they care to, while the latter act with special skill. But this will not be theater with its invariable division between actor and spectator, any more than it is theater now when old men watch children at play and laugh and sigh! Another foothold for such nontheatrical acting is also promised by a fully evolved social life: there will be processes in which the masses will act; perhaps mystery plays will develop on new principles, but with their inveterate proviso for universal participation in the performance. In this respect the future promises so much that is new that it would be labor in vain to seek an answer in the old and obsolete. For example, we are still not acquainted with societal drama: it was impossible under the conditions of old-fashioned life and an old-fashioned stage: we are still unacquainted with plays whose heroes would be the *people*, the *masses*, and not one individual against a background of a score of supernumeraries. The emergence of the masses into the arena of history—which will characterize our century for centuries to come—will lead the theater of acting from its narrow niche to the open expanses of streets and squares; and who knows?—scenarios (I am not sure what to call them) may be written for such performances, in which the multimillion inhabitants of a city will appear as participants. What can we know of this, we who are subject to the law governing "mobs" and liable to be dispersed by someone in no time if we gather in groups of four.

And already half-despoiled by the cinematograph (I still refer to the future), the theater of acting will replace the cream in the milk and will dissolve into life, after enriching it by its custom-made experiment—and that will spell an end to the spectator, that wretched Lazarus, stealthily stealing crumbs from the banquet of the rich man, his brother. It will be, if I may use the phrase, an *explicit* elimination of the "spectator," like the demolition of an old military depot. But in a different, quite different way will the "spectator" disappear from the auditorium of the new psychological theater. If, in the earlier case, the theater of acting, the *theater itself* is dissolved into the spectator like a lump of sugar in hot tea, so in the psychological theater the opposite will occur: the "spectator" will be dissolved into the psychological drama, cease to be a spectator and become as active as the performers.

The chief and dominant property of any great psychological work seems to be that what is portrayed wholly absorbs anyone who perceives it, and performs a virtual miracle of physics, the absorption of one "ego" by another—by the personality of the author and his characters. The body of the reader or spectator or listener may be situated wherever and however it pleases: in bed, in a theater seat, by a half-illumined window that casts the last rays of daylight onto the pages of a book—his soul has already entered the book or music, becomes its sound and word. Externally, by his appearance and position, he is only a spectator and reader, but in actual fact he is the hero of what is taking place. Is one the "spectator" of one's own dreams?

And that notorious reader who "does a little reading," completely analogous to the spectator who "takes a little look," is never anything more than a victim of the author or theater who are self-sufficient in their acting; he is summoned but not selected, invited merely to pick crumbs from the author's or actor's table. They do the acting and suffering and it has absolutely nothing to do with him: why did they summon him, after all? Whereas psychological drama, the *new* theater's drama which has been provided with models by Chekhov and Dostoevsky, each in his own way, has already eliminated the "spectator." It may be the audience of the Art Theater, which resembles a great many other audiences, but there are no spectators in it. That body in a suitcoat, as docile as a sleeper's, sitting in a seat or on a bench, is only a facsimile which is not asked to mix with the real "spectator." I shall go further: in many plays besides Chekhov's and Dostoevsky's there can be found individually powerful and veracious passages in which true psychism already manifests all its infectious power; and whenever the action reaches such a passage, the *spectators* in a theater disappear, the audience vanishes, nothing is left except a single soul suffering or rejoicing. If you are able to preserve your calm and ordinary powers of observation even at such a moment, then hearken to the hushed auditorium: how immensely significant and even awesome is its silence. I have experimented a few times by observing from backstage the auditorium, invisible in its customary half-light, and each time I noticed the same thing: as it were, a kind of return from life to death, from death to life. Sometimes the spectator appears, sometimes he vanishes, sometimes he is present, other times he is not—at those moments how simply and even ingenuously the "difficult" problem of the spectator who, through some sort of displacement, his body transported from one spot to another, must be reintegrated as the choric element was solved for me!

XII

Just as there is a growing demand to transfer *acting* to life itself and not be woefully amused by it in the theater, so the demand for psychological drama grows daily. The walls of the old theater are quaking, the stage of Alexandre Dumas is splitting at the seams, and even now opera itself and ballet are to some degree wickedly channeled into the parlous straits of psychologizing and "music drama." New theaters are born, because they feel they must be born—but they do not understand the purpose of their life and are orphaned in the wilderness. The "audience" also knows that something new must be born, the time has come and no doubt about it; and promptly it already invests a sort of vague hope in the infant—and is bitterly disappointed. The banner of psychology, once upraised above the novel, is already fluttering over our theater, but still the hands holding it up are not steady and not everyone notices it. The theater senses it fluttering, and with terrific exertions, fighting not only for theory but for its very life and existence, it tries to pour sour old wine into a brand spanking new bottle. On this footing, a great deal that is strange, funny and at times overwhelmingly absurd takes place. Old friends are not recognized in the deceptive mirages of the new, psychism is replaced by curtailed and absolutely counter-artistic naturalism, and arms and legs of the old drama and *old opera* are dislocated.

As to music—as a layman in this field I merely intend to make a few conjectures: for, to the extent that every opera is, for the most part, also literature (*Boris Godunov* belongs both to Mussorgsky and Pushkin), even the very weakest libretto is nonetheless born of a literary matrix. And to the extent that Mussorgsky did not set his own guidelines, but called upon Pushkin, and Pushkin did set guidelines and *bound* the composer, my general statements about the new psychological and literary theater directly involve opera as well. And this is what occurs to me:

As psychism's most direct and sharpest weapon, music is more suitable than anything else for artistically psychological purposes. This in part explains why the current new theater, now entering a new phase of psychism, has increasing recourse to music as an omnipotent resource: it tries to use music to compensate for the shortage of psychologizing which fails to provide the actor and spectator as well "something to live on." Is the wholly unpsychologized *Peer Gynt* possible without music? Besides, dramatic authors are perfectly well aware of the value of music: wedded to that confounded need for action, they strive imperceptibly to dribble in at least ten drops of psychology by means of an itinerant orchestra which suddenly appears out of nowhere or abruptly ignites a craving in the heroine to play "Song without Words." And if, in Chekhov the panpsychologist, the result is integral, natural and necessary, in other cases music sounds like the most discordant of inventions and merely testifies to the poverty of both author and theater. As a *proven* necessity in the new theater, music has a very great and important place, but as a dismal "Song without Words," it will disappear along with action, spectacle and abbreviated Morse-code psychology.

People like to think that opera is something hopelessly artificial—and so it is from the standpoint of blind and deaf naturalism; in reality there is no more artifice in opera than in any old-fashioned drama. It is simply laid on more thickly in opera, as are action and spectacle and their eternal attributes: Morse-code language, knitted brows, the abbreviated psychology of *Vampuka*. The music too is as unpsychological as a good old-fashioned script. We are fed up with Verdi, not because his music is vapid, trivial, hurdy-gurdy stuff, but because it is not psychologized, like the novels of genial Dumas; everything is in the realm of acting with sounds—which is why people love it the same way they love Dumas. And Wagner, a genius of the new music-drama, is dear to the modern heart not so much for his purely musical accomplishments as for his profound psychism. Note too that Mussorgsky's triumph and glory coincided exactly with the birth of the new psychological drama: unluckily for him, Mussorgsky is more psychological than Pushkin was, his wings no sooner fledged than clipped. I do not think it an especially brazen layman's fantasy if I say that *nowadays* Mussorgsky would have written opera to an unrhymed text of Dostoevsky.

But the composer faces one more great vicissitude: he is not autonomous, not sole monarch in the kingdom of opera: he shares his powers with the writer-dramatist. Wagner himself became Wagner only because he was not only sound but word: he created solely and exactly what he wanted to create. He is his own poet and his own psychologist: and does not this lamentable necessity to share one's power with a man of letters and virtually submit to him help explain why the more *masterful* of modern composers do not write operas?

Hesitant to weary the reader's attention by repeating my statements about new drama, I will say briefly that new opera, too, will and must be psychological. Just as professors do not want to go to an up-to-date children's theater and play horsey, so, too, contemporary serious musicians and music-lovers have already stopped going to the opera; and if they do go, it is only on account of those rich gifts of great heartfelt feeling relayed by brilliant Shalyapin, who learned, as only a genius can, how to remain a psychologist in a veritable wilderness. When, as a few days ago, ten thousand people stood in line for tickets to see Shalyapin, and a military squadron had to be called out to disperse them, in the good old Russian way; when suicides—I know this for a fact—are ready to postpone their suicide if someone gives them a ticket to Shalyapin—is this the result of voice and music alone? No. People are swayed this way only by prophets, warriors and brilliant psychologists, who can bring the soul of each of us near to the soul of all humanity, all the world.

But the goal and meaning of human progress lie in what is first accessible to *one man* becoming accessible even to the *multitude*: and what is accessible to the *multitude* becomes the property of all. Aircraft is of little use to us, so long as only aerial geniuses can fly it; and a modern opera is no good if only Shalyapin can rise to sublimity in it. Besides, does he really rise to true sublimity in it? Are there not greater heights which he fails to recognize, as do we, dwellers in a transitional period in art?

Let me say but a few words about the theater of "music-drama" in Petersburg,[52] now that it has earned a position as a kind of "new" theater. Many talented people work in it and it enjoys success at the moment, but its fate is foredoomed and foretold by the fate of the Art Theater which broke the bones of *The Inspector*. Dissatisfied with mere operatic "acting," striving for a truth whose name it knows not, the theater of music-drama displays so many inner contradictions that it is beginning to look like a bristling hedgehog. Sometimes it acts clearly and lucidly, sometimes, as in *Carmen*, it creates through dance a psychological basis and produces irresistible effects—sometimes it runs headfirst into murderous and mendacious naturalism. It degraded its toreador and reduced him to the level of the most ordinary of tedious, vulgar Spaniards from a Spanish slum—a revolting spectacle. But it was thoroughly unbearable in the last scene, the bullfight, when the theater made a whole infirmary mill about the stage: in case of a possible accident, you see! And of course, it thought it was portraying *truth*, but it portrayed the greatest lie, because psychologically death and casualty were absent from this picture of excitement, virility, acting and frenzied animation.

Therefore, in striving urgently to extract the most wished-for psychic truth from both the opera of acting and the drama of acting, they failed to achieve truth, because there was none there, and they butchered acting, transformed sparkling wine into a flat Bavarian near-beer, plain water, in fact . . . this was no longer a wedding, but a funeral, in Cana of Galilee. But by the very urgency of their striving, even by their mistakes and blunders, the theater stressed once more the fact that

> the theater of pretense has passed away!
> The *theater of truth* is on its way!

XIII

For all my desire to be brief, I have protracted my second letter inexcusably . . . and even so did not say even a hundredth part of what I meant to say. Every sphere of life is caught up in the question of the theater, and I have even neglected many very interesting, important and meaningful phenomena in these fugitive lines.

So I shall leave to my next letter the open question of the new *theater of the word*, which, I am deeply convinced, will turn out to be the ultimate stage of the psychological theater and will absorb it in its still unprecedented breadth and depth.

21 October 1913

Notes

Introduction

1. An English version of these accounts, based on German and Italian translations, is in Orville K. Larson, "Bishop Abraham of Souzdal's Description of *sacre rappresentazioni*," *Educational Theatre Journal*, vol. 9, no. 3 (October 1957): 208–213.
2. "K nemyslennym rifmotvortsam" ["To redeless rhymsters"], *Sochineniya*, 2nd ed., 10 vols. (Moscow, 1787), IX, 277.
3. Quoted in V. N. Vsevolodsky-Gerngross, *Russkiy teatr vtoroy poloviny XVIII veka* (Moscow, 1960), 329, by far the best account of Plavilshchikov's work.
4. Leonid Grossman, *Pushkin v teatral'nykh kreslakh* (St. Petersburg, 1926), 48.
5. Ibid.
6. "Literaturnye mechtaniya" ["Literary reveries"], *Polnoe sobranie sochineniy* (Moscow, 1953), I, 23.
7. See L. Senelick, "Rachel in Russia: The Shchepkin-Annenkov Correspondence," *Theatre Research International* (February 1978): 93–114.
8. To N. N. Raevsky, Jr. (c. 19 July 1825), in A. S. Pushkin, *Polnoe sobranie sochineniy*, 10 vols. (Moscow, 1966), X, 162.
9. "O narodnosti v literature" ["On *narodnost'* in literature"], in ibid., VII, 39.
10. See Daniel Gerould, "Russian Formalist Theories of Melodrama," *Journal of American Culture*, vol. 1, no. 1 (Spring 1978): 151–168.
11. To N. Ya. Prokopovich (27/15 July 1842), in N. V. Gogol, *Sobranie sochineniy*, 7 vols. (Moscow, 1967), VII, 233.
12. N. V. Gogol, *Polnoe sobranie sochineniy*, 14 vols. (Moscow, 1937–1952), VIII, 477.
13. Ibid., VIII, 446–447.
14. Ibid., VIII, 270.
15. Ibid., VIII, 396–397.
16. Belinsky, "Literaturnye mechtaniya," I, 79.
17. Ibid.
18. Quoted in *A. N. Ostrovskiy v vospominaniyakh sovremennikov* (Moscow, 1966), 19.
19. Unfortunately, this article is too long to appear in the present collection,

but it can be found with its sequel in an English translation in *Selected Philosophical Essays of Dobrolyubov*, issued by the Foreign Languages Publishing House in Moscow, 1948.

20. Turgenev himself was a contributor to the *Contemporary* and had published therein a critique of Ostrovsky's *The Poor Bride* in 1852, intended to counter the praise lavished on the play by the Slavophiles and Grigoriev in particular. While granting the author's talent, Turgenev deplored his addiction to petty details in drawing characters.

21. The so-called "aesthetic school" had done its best not to encase Ostrovsky in a social straitjacket. Druzhinin, whose essay "The Criticism of Russian Literature in the Gogolian Period and Our Relation to It" (1856) had exempted artists from having to deal in moral absolutes, in his article on Ostrovsky (1859) deemed the demand for protest illegitimate and limited himself to appraising characterization, plot and dialogue. The sophisticated Annenkov, who viewed art as the imperceptible raising of spiritual consciousness, replied to a critic who denounced Ostrovsky's *Storm* for "dragging art back to the fairground booth": "the only means of remedying the ill and recalling Russian theater to real life is to remove it from its decorous lodgings back to the fairground booth" (1850). This was an assertion that Evreinov and Meyerhold were to reiterate loudly fifty years afterwards.

22. Dobrolyubov, *Izbrannoe* (Moscow, 1976), 369.

23. *My Past and Thoughts* ("Second Thoughts on the Woman Question"), part II, ed. Dwight Macdonald and tr. Constance Garnett (New York, 1974), 436.

24. Quoted in A. Anikst, *Teoriya dramy v Rossii ot Pushkina do Chekhova* (Moscow, 1972), 415.

25. (7 November 1888; 20 December 1888) in *Polnoe sobranie sochineniy i pis'em*, 30 vols. (Moscow, 1976), *Pis'ma* III, 69, 94.

26. See L. Senelick, "The Lakeshore of Bohemia: *The Seagull*'s Theatrical Context," *Educational Theatre Journal*, vol. 29, no. 2 (May 1977): 199–213.

27. Letter to Suvorin (2 November 1895); see also 12 November 1897: *Polnoe sobranie sochineniy i pis'em*, 30 vols. (Moscow, 1978), *Pis'ma* VI, 89.

28. Letter to Suvorin (20 June 1896), ibid., 157.

29. A. A. Sanin to Chekhov (12 March 1900), quoted in *Literaturnoe nasledstvo*, no. 68 (1960): 873.

30. See A. B. Goldenveiser, *Vblizi Tolstogo*, 2 vols. (Moscow, 1922), I, 90.

31. *Complete works*, tr. A. M. Ludovic, 18 vols. (New York, 1910), XV, 417.

32. It followed that the finest, most representative Russian actress of the turn of the century was the hypersensitive, other-worldly Vera Kommissarzhevskaya. See L. Senelick, "Vera Kommissarzhevskaya: The Actress as Symbolist Eidolon," *Theatre Journal* (Winter 1980): 475–487.

33. "Le Tragique quotidien," in *Le Trésor des humbles* (Paris, 1896).

34. S. Beckett, *Proust* (London, 1931), 8.

35. V. E. Meyerhold, *Perepiska 1896–1939* (Moscow, 1976), 45.
36. The essay's title is a pun: *Na dne* literally means "At the Bottom," and so "Drama na dne" means both "The Play *At the Bottom*" and "Drama at the Bottom."
37. Blok, *Sobranie sochineniy*, 8 vols. (Moscow, 1971), VIII, 2.
38. On the relationship between the two, see Zoya Yurieff, "*Pridshedshy*: A. Bely and A. Chekhov," in *Andrey Bely, A Cultural Review*, ed. G. Janechek (Lexington, Ky., 1978), 44–55.
39. *Arabeski* (Moscow, 1911), 166.
40. Meyerhold's important essay "Theater: Toward a History and a Technique" was reprinted in his book *On the Theater* (Petersburg, 1913); it can be found excerpted in English in Edward Braun's *Meyerhold on Theatre* (London, 1968). In it he promoted Maeterlinck as the ideal author for a new "static" theater in which the inner experiences would be depicted by "movement as plastic music," an "inner dialogue" overheard through pauses and silences. Agreeing with Bryusov on the whole, he revised the poet's creed, "the sole objective of the theater is to help the actor to reveal his soul to the spectator," so that it read, "the theater must employ every means to help the actor to blend his soul with that of the dramatist and reveal it through the soul of the director." The alteration is vital in its displacement of responsibility and pre-eminence. It was further explicated by a diagram, a triangle with the director at its apex: the spectator will receive the efforts of author and actor through the medium of the director.
41. *Utverzhdenie teatra* (Petrograd, ?1923), 15.
42. Prince Mirsky refers to Aikhenvald's style as "a dense layer of treacle beneath which it is impossible to distinguish between Turgenev and the vulgarest of lyrical journalists": *Contemporary Russian Literature 1881–1925* (London, 1926), 327.
43. For a discussion of the relationship of this production to the intellectual *Zeitgeist*, see L. Senelick, "Moscow and Monodrama: The Meaning of the Craig/Stanislavsky *Hamlet*," *Theatre Research International* (Fall 1981).
44. "Burn, Theater, burn, reduce to ashes! I buss thy very ashes, because from them, like the Phoenix, thou shalt be reborn, each time more and more beautiful!" "Ob otritsanii teatra. Polemika serdtsa," *Strelets*, II (1914): 51.
45. *Sobranie sochineniy v shesti tomakh* (Moscow, 1971), V, 392.

Pushkin: My Remarks on the Russian Theater

1. Pushkin is referring to the anonymous and pseudonymous reviews in journals of the time. "The Luzhniki Hermit" or "Luzhniki Elder," a cognomen that frequently appeared in the *Messenger of Europe* (*Vestnik Evropy*), was believed by Pushkin to conceal the identity of its editor,

M. T. Kachenovsky, who in 1819 had written a five-part article against Karamzin's *History of the Russian State.*

2. In 1816, in *Son of the Fatherland* (*Syn otechestva*), N. P. Gnedich published an article "On the Free Translation of Bürger's 'Lenore,'" in which he compared Zhukovsky's "Lyudmila" and Katenin's "Olga," both transpositions into Russian of Bürger's poem. He concealed his name behind three asterisks and the postmark "SPB guberniya Tentelev village."

3. In *Son of the Fatherland* (29 December 1819) there appeared a letter to the editor from R. Zotov, though bearing the signature V. Kl—nov, praising the French acting troupe in St. Petersburg and abusing the Russian actors. It made the disclaimer, "To stress my impartiality, let me state that I am writing this letter with my left hand, for the right was left behind on the field of Borodino, and I look at the paper with only my right eye, for the left was lost forever on the heights of Montmartre!"

4. Stately Ekaterina Semyonovna Semyonova (1786–1849) was Pushkin's favorite actress; she excelled in neoclassical tragedy and was noted for her rich contralto voice. Her performances were said to combine inspired enthusiasm with disciplined technique. Elena Yakovlevna Sosnitskaya (1799–1855), a lesser member of the Bolshoy company in St. Petersburg, later created the role of the bride in Gogol's *Getting Married.* Evgeniya Ivanovna Kolosova (1780–1869), a sprightly dancer as well as an actress, was one of the first to abandon cumbersome court dress for the Greek chiton in ballet; her home was much frequented by young men of society, for both her own sake and that of her daughter, Aleksandra. Pushkin immortalized Avdotya Ilinichna Istomina (1799–1848), a ballerina of exceptional grace and skill, by a stanza (XX) in chapter 1 of *Evgeny Onegin.*

5. Adrien Boïeldieu (1775–1834), French comic-opera composer, was the musical director of the French opera troupe in St. Petersburg from 1804 to 1811, where his most successful piece was *The Invisible Lady* (1808). The most popular light operas of the French composer Pierre Antoine Dominique della Maria (1769–1800) on the Russian stage were *The Prisoner* (1798) and *The Comic Opera* (1798).

6. Literally, "The Great Stone Theater," the first permanent playhouse in Petersburg (built 1783; remodeled 1802–1804).

7. Readers of Tolstoy's *War and Peace* may recall Mlle. George delivering a recitation from *Phèdre* at Hélène Bezukhova's home (part 8, ch. 13). The temperamental French tragedienne, whose real name was Marguerite-Josephine Weymer (1787–1867), toured Russia with a French company between 1808 and 1812 in a repertory similar to Semyonova's and was instrumental in propagating her own drawling and singsong style of declamation. Nikolay Ivanovich Gnedich (1784–1833), impressed by George and somewhat influenced by his own translation of Homer into Russian hexameters, trained Semyonova note by note to follow the French crooning delivery.

8. Vladislav Aleksandrovich Ozerov (1769–1816) tried in his tragedies to

copy faithfully the school of Racine and instill patriotism in his audiences. His most successful attempts were *Oedipus in Athens* (1804); *Fingal* (1805; from Macpherson's *Ossian*); and *Dmitry of the Don* (1807).

9. Antigone is a character in Ozerov's *Oedipus in Athens*; Moina appears in *Fingal*.

10. Mikhail Evstafievich Lobanov (1787–1845), translator of Racine's *Iphigénie en Aulide* (1815), in which Semyonova appeared as Clytemnestre, is most memorable for having written a neoclassic verse tragedy, *Boris Godunov*, which appeared in the same year as Pushkin's homonymic masterpiece.

11. Cherubic in appearance and razor-sharp in intellect, Pavel Aleksandrovich Katenin (1792–1853) was a close associate of Pushkin who appreciated his translations of Racine, Corneille and Marivaux. To him Pushkin wrote, "I came to you like Diogenes to Antisthenes: 'Thrash me but teach me.'" Katenin took on the acting training of Aleksandra Kolosova and her husband V. A. Karatygin, his method involving the submergence of the actor in the poetic ethos of a play.

12. Voltaire's *Zaïre* had been translated into Russian by a team of five writers (1809); Corneille's *Horace* by four (1817); and Longpierre's *Médée* (1819) by five.

13. Mariya Ivanovna Valberkhova (1788–1867) had begun as a tragic actress and been puffed by Prince A. Shakhovskoy as a rival of Semyonova. She retired from the stage in 1812, but returned as a comedienne in 1815. Of the plays Pushkin mentions, *Dido* is a tragedy by Knyazhnin; *The Jealous Wife*, a comedy by Desforge; *The Misanthrope*, Molière's famous comedy (with Célimène renamed Prelestina [Superba]); *The Accidental Wager*, a comedy by Sedaine; and *Mr. and Mrs. Emptyhouse*, a comedy by Shakhovskoy.

14. Aleksandra Mikhailovna Kolosova (1802–1880) made her stage debut as Antigone in Ozerov's *Oedipus in Athens* (16 December 1818) followed on 30 December by Moina in Ozerov's *Fingal*. The benefit Pushkin refers to took place on 8 December 1819: the bill was made up of Voltaire's *Zaïre* followed by the opera-vaudeville *The Mock Banditti* and an afterpiece danced by Kolosova mother and daughter. Pushkin was for a while infatuated with her and wrote a dithyrambic poem about her to Katenin.

15. An inaccurate citation of *O mater pulchra filia pulchrior* from Horace (book 1, ode xvi).

16. Aleksandra Dmitrievna Karatygina (1777–1859) frequently partnered A. S. Yakovlev and was later the mother-in-law of Aleksandra Kolosova.

17. Anna Lvovna Yablochkina owes all her fame to this mention by Pushkin.

18. Aleksey Semyonovich Yakovlev (1773–1817), a pupil of the "Russian Garrick" Dmitrevsky, made a huge success in 1794 at his debut. Ozerov's heroes became his specialty, and as a tragedian he was noted for his good looks and emotionalism. François Joseph Talma (1766–1825), Napoleon's favorite tragedian, perpetuated neoclassic acting styles but

infused them with a new emotional honesty and introduced historical accuracy in costuming. Yakov Grigorevich Bryansky (*né* Grigoriev, 1791–1853) made his debut in 1811 in the title role of Yazykov's *Shakespeare in Love*; his original emploi had been as first lover in comedy, but after Yakovlev's death he succeeded to the tragic roles.

19. A paraphrase of the moral of Ivan Krylov's fable "The Musicians" (I, iii, 1808), in which a gentleman excuses the discordancy of his village band by pointing out that all the members are teetotalers.

20. A. G. Shchenikov (1784–1859), Aleksandr Glukharev (1786–1820) and Z. F. Kamenogorsky (1781–1832) were actors of no more distinction than Pushkin grants them. Pavel Ivanovich Tolchenov (1787–1862) specialized in the roles of old men and villains, and prided himself on impeccable diction.

21. Ivan Petrovich Boretsky (1795–1842) had begun his career as an officer in the Lithuanian regiment, but entered the roll of actors at the Bolshoy in 1818, making his debut as Ozerov's Oedipus, an impersonation he replicated throughout his career, no matter what his role.

Pushkin: On National-Popular Drama and the Play *Martha the Seneschal's Wife* [Rough Draft]

1. Pushkin seems to mean that Corneille drew many of his plots from the Spanish repertoire. *Le Cid*, for instance, was based on Guillen de Castro's *Las Mocedades del Cid*.

2. Prince Pyotr Andreevich Vyazemsky (1792–1878), one of Pushkin's oldest and closest friends, had been a member of the Green Lamp society for which Pushkin had intended "My Remarks on the Russian Theater." He was, in his early years, an ardent proponent of romanticism.

3. Martha, the wife of Isaak Andreevich Boretsky, seneschal or *posadnik* of the independent city of Novgorod, assumed her husband's functions after his death, and led the city in the fight for its liberty against Ioann III, grand duke of Moscow, until he overcame it and abolished its charters in 1475. The chroniclers are vague about her personal traits, but beginning with Nikolay Karamzin and his novella "Martha the Seneschal's Wife or the Fall of Novgorod" (1808) she took on a heroic and libertarian aura. Kseniya, her daughter, is presented by Karamzin as a typical sentimental ingenue.

Pushkin: On National-Popular Drama and the Play *Martha the Seneschal's Wife* [Final Version]

1. Johann Christoph Gottsched (1700–1766), arbiter of German letters, introduced Boileau's version of the neoclassic rules to Germany and pre-

scribed exact formulas for the composition of tragedy and comedy in his *Versuch einer critischen Dichtkunst für die Deutschen* (1730), which one historian has called "a literary cookbook." Reinterpreting Horace, he emphasized the *utile* in art over the *dulce*. Gotthold Ephraim Lessing (1729–1781) attacked Gottsched and neoclassic French drama and endorsed Shakespeare as a model in his *Hamburgische Dramaturgie* (1764–1768). As to the philosopher Immanuel Kant (1724–1804), his emphasis on subjectivity and the creative power of an organizing intelligence was congenial to early romanticism.

2. Lictors appear in Shakespeare's *Coriolanus*, but Coriolano is the hero of Calderón's historical drama *The Arms of Beauty* (*Las Armas de la hermosura*). Hippolyte is to be found in Racine's *Phèdre*. But there is no Clytemnestre in Corneille; Pushkin must be thinking of her appearance in act 5 of Racine's *Iphigénie en Aulide*.

3. Nero's line is spoken in act 2, scene 3, of *Britannicus*; Agamemnon's opens *Iphigénie en Aulide*.

4. Dmitry Tuptalo, metropolitan of Rostov (1651–1709), was the author of several mystery plays, including a famed *Nativity*, written on the model of Jesuit school dramas; they were produced at the Mohila Academy in Kiev. Princess Sophia Alexeevna (1657–1704), sister and regent of Peter the Great, was alleged to be the author of a number of plays, among them the verse drama *St. Catherine the Great Martyr* (though it is now attributed to her sister Nataliya).

5. Aleksandr Petrovich Sumarokov (1717–1777), one of the founders of the first professional Russian theater and the first Russian tragic dramatist. His five-act, highly decorous tragedies in rhymed verse include *Khorev* (1747), a version of *Hamlet* (1748) based on French adaptations and *Dimitry the Pretender* (1771). His comedies were equally popular in their time.

6. *Dmitry of the Don*, Ozerov's tragedy (1807), was a patriotic appeal in the wake of the defeat at Austerlitz; *Pozharsky*, a tragedy by M. V. Kryukovsky (1807), uses the historical expulsion of the Poles to mirror current events. Despite the Russian content, in form and style both plays are severely neoclassic.

7. Written in 1818 and not staged until 1827.

8. A frequently revived tragedy by A. S. Khomyakov (1829).

9. To wit, Fonvizin's *The Minor* and Griboedov's *Woe from Wit*.

10. Actually Mikhail Petrovich Pogodin (1800–1875), professor of history at Moscow University, editor of the *Muscovite* (*Moskvityanin*), and fervent Slavophile. Pushkin is disingenuous in claiming ignorance of the author's identity. In May 1830 Pogodin had read act 1 aloud to him, and he read the rest of the manuscript that autumn at Boldino. Hopeful of its publication, Pushkin championed the play to Chief of Gendarmes Benckendorff and wrote this essay to herald its public appearance, but it was not passed by the censorship until 1832.

Gogol: Petersburg Notes for 1836

1. Between 1828 and 1837 the Petersburg stage was almost monopolized by the melodramas of Alexandre Dumas *père* (1802–1870) and Victor Ducange (1783–1833). In particular, Dumas' *Anthony, Richard D'Arlington, L'Italienne ou L'Enfer et le poignard, Kean ou Génie et Désordre*, and Ducange's *30 ans ou La Vie d'un joueur* and *16 ans ou Les Incendiaires* were favorites.

2. *Fenella ou La Muette de Portici* (also known as *Masaniello*) by Daniel Auber (1828), first heard in St. Petersburg in German in 1834; *Robert-le-Diable* (1831) by Giacomo Meyerbeer, first heard in St. Petersburg in Russian in 1834; and Gioacchino Rossini's *Semiramide* (1823), first sung in St. Petersburg in Italian (1829) and in Russian translation (January 1836).

3. *A Life for the Tsar* (known in Soviet times as *Ivan Susanin*; 1834–1836) by Mikhail Glinka (1804–1857), usually considered to be the first Russian grand opera in its use of local color, folk tunes and nationalistic sentiment.

4. *Norma*, Bellini's opera (1831), concerning Druids and Romans in ancient Gaul, heard in St. Petersburg in German in 1835 and in Russian in 1837.

5. Alexander I (1777–1825). St. Petersburg was considerably embellished during his reign.

Gogol: A Theater Lets Out after the Performance of a New Comedy

1. This comment appears to echo the opinion of the time-serving Faddey Bulgarin in the *Northern Bee* (*Severnaya Pchyola*, 1 May 1836): "We need contrast and intrigue, verisimilitude and nature, but they are not to be found in *The Inspector*."

2. Although August Friedrich Kotzebue (1761–1819), the German dramatist, is best remembered for his lachrymose plays of sentiment, he wrote a great many comedies and farces, including *Die deutschen Kleinstädter* (1803), *Der Wirrwarr* (1803) and *Fanchon das Leiermädchen* (1805).

3. Civil service titles from Peter the Great's table of ranks. Actual state councillor, the fourth on the list, is equal to the military rank of general and carries with it hereditary nobility, whereas a titular councillor is only ninth and the equivalent of a staff captain.

4. Decorations usually given for civil service achievements: the St. Vladimir, the most exalted and most coveted, the St. Anna, directly below it, and the St. Stanislas, the lowest order bestowed on civilians.

5. Another echo of Bulgarin's criticism; he opined that the action could take place only, "why, point for point, on the Sandwich Islands with Captain Cook!" Chukhotsky Island in St. Petersburg was noted for its bawdyhouses.

6. This echoes a comment of Count N. I. Panin after a reading of Fonvizin's *The Brigadier* in 1766: "we each have a near relation like the Brigadier's Lady: no one could disclaim having a granny or an auntie or a distant cousin like Akulina Timofeevna."

7. According to Gogol's friend Sergey Aksakov, Count Fyodor I. Tolstoy (known as "Tolstoy the American" because of his sojourn in the Aleutians) made a similar remark. "I myself heard how the famous Count Tolstoy the American addressed a numerous assemblage at the home of the Perfilievs, who were fervent admirers of Gogol, saying that he was 'an enemy of Russia who ought to be sent to Siberia in leg-irons'" ("My Acquaintance with Gogol," 1902).

Belinsky: Dramatic Poesy

1. In chapter 12, Conachar the young chieftain of Clan Quhele says to Simon Glover, "Look, my father—the light grows short and pale, a few minutes will extinguish it—but before it expires the hideous tale will be told.—Father, I am—a COWARD!—It is said at last, and the secret of my disgrace is in the keeping of another!"

2. Either Belinsky's memory is faulty or he is referring to a piece of contemporary stage business. In the play, Desdemona's handkerchief is abstracted by Emilia when she forgets it.

3. The *Filippo* of Vittorio Alfieri (1749–1803), whose dramatic works run to twenty-two volumes, was published in 1776.

4. Nestor Vasilievich Kukolnik (1809–1868), whose monotonous and declamatory chauvinistic play *The Hand of the Almighty Has Saved the Fatherland* (1834) was such a phenomenal success that it condemned him to a lifetime of writing patriotic tripe. Russian dictionaries of quotations immortalize him for his remark "If the sovereign ordered it, tomorrow I'd become a male midwife."

5. Mrs. Ann Radcliffe (1764–1823) was a prime exponent of the Gothic novel, her best-known being *The Mysteries of Udolpho* (1794) and *The Italian* (1797), full of gloomy castles and ebon-eyed villains. The Gothic school was popularized in France by François Guillaume Ducray-Duminil (1761–1819), whose *romans noirs* and melodramas have caused him to be called the father of *bas romantisme*. August Heinrich Julius Lafontaine (1759–1831), canon of Magdeburg Cathedral, under several pseudonyms wrote over two hundred volumes of fiction, chiefly concerning middle-class life.

6. *Gonzalvo of Cordova or The Liberation of Granada*, G. Shipovsky's translation of a romance (1791) by Jean-Pierre-Clarisse Florian (1755–1794), French poet and fabulist; *Cadmus and Harmonia* (1786) is a novel by Mikhail Matveevich Kheraskov (1733–1807).

7. The contrast here is between *mysl'*, a generative idea natural to a true artist, and *soobrazhenie*, "consideration," the design aforethought to

create a work of literature. At this stage in his thought, Belinsky distinguished between the true poet inspired by an intuitive idea and the false poet, consciously striving to produce a work of art.

Sleptsov: A Type of the Current Drama

1. Sleptsov is quoting from memory the remarks made by Mikhail Vasilievich Lomonosov (?1711–1765), polymath and so-called "legislator of Russian literature," on A. L. Shletser's *Russian Grammar*: "One can only conclude from this what abominable filth was churned up in Russian antiquarianism by the beasts allowed therein."
2. The influx consisted of *Dmitry the Pretender* by N. A. Chaev (1865) and *Dmitry the Pretender and Vasily Shuisky* by A. N. Ostrovsky (1866). The Ivan plays were *Prince Serebryany* by S. Dobrov (1866), adapted from the novel by A. K. Tolstoy; *The Death of Ioann the Terrible* by A. K. Tolstoy (1866), the first part of his trilogy of historical dramas; *The Oprichnik* by I. I. Lazechnikov (1867), later made into an opera by N. Chaikovsky; and *Vasilisa Melentieva* by A. N. Ostrovsky (1862).
3. L. A. Mey's *The Maid of Pskov* (1860) was retarded not by his death but by the censorship, which objected to the portrayal of Ioann.
4. Aleksandr Aleksandrovich Nilsky (*né* Nilus, 1840–1899) had become a member of the Alexandra company in 1860 and graduated to such juvenile lead roles as Hamlet, Karl Moor, Chatsky and Khlestakov, as well as creating the role of Boris Godunov in Tolstoy's *Death of Ioann the Terrible*.
5. Pavel Vasilievich Vasiliev II (1832–1879) created the title role in *The Death of Ioann*, but proved to be so unsatisfactory that he was replaced by Vasily Vasilievich Samoilov (1812–1887), who also failed in it.
6. G. N. Zhulev (1836–1876), comic poet, minor actor and contributor to the magazine the *Spark* (*Iskra*).
7. Dmitry Timofeevich Lensky (1805–1860), less important as an actor than as the author of sprightly and effervescent vaudevilles, the most famous being *Lyov Gurych Sinichkin*, a hilarious comedy about a provincial barnstormer. In many occasional pieces he appeared as himself.
8. A four-act drama by A. A. Sokolov (1866).
9. The allusions are to V. A. Dyachenko's *Screens of Society* (1866) and *Family Thresholds* (1867), A. N. Ostrovsky's *The Abyss* (1865) and Leskov/Stebnitsky's *The Profligate* (1867).
10. A five-act comedy by A. A. Potekhin (1867). Sleptsov's quotations are snatches of dialogue from this play.
11. Nikolay Semyonovich Leskov (1831–1895) had issued this, his only play, under the pseudonym of M. Stebnitsky.
12. *Krechinsky's Wedding*, the first part of the comic trilogy of Aleksandr Vasilievich Sukhovo-Kobylin (1817–1903), was staged at the Alexandra in 1856; the character Krechinsky is a suave confidence-man, his sidekick Raspluev an absurd and somehow pathetic gambler.

13. Mikhail Ilich Bocharov (?1831–1895) was the principal scene designer for the imperial state theaters from 1864 until his death; he was responsible for the sets for the 1867 premier of *The Death of Ioann the
Terrible.*

Chekhov: More about Sarah Bernhardt

1. *Adrienne Lecouvreur*, a melodrama about the eighteenth-century actress by Eugène Scribe and Ernest Legouvé, had been created by the tragedienne Rachel in 1849. Sarah Bernhardt began playing it in 1880 and
kept it in her repertoire until 1905, when she replaced it by a six-act version refurbished by herself.
2. In 1880 Albert Salamonsky (1839–1913) opened his circus on Tsvetny
Boulevard in Moscow; it still exists as the Moscow State Circus.
3. Lina Munte (d. 1909), a popular Parisian actress who specialized in
femmes fatales, had come to St. Petersburg in a fit of pique and was a
member of the French acting company there till 1893. I have been unable to trace Mme. Sidney.
4. The Russian equivalents of the *Illustrated London News* or *Harper's
Weekly.*
5. To the average Russian, such names conjured up Paris. Charles Paul de
Kock (1793–1871) was an immensely prolific author of mildly racy novels very popular in Russia and elsewhere—the favorite clandestine reading of Verkhovensky in Dostoevsky's *The Devils* and Bloom in Joyce's
Ulysses. Alphonse Daudet (1840–1897) and Emile Zola (1840–1902)
would be best known abroad for *Tatarin de Tarascon* (1872) and *L'As-
sommoir* (1877), respectively. In Turgenev's novel *A Nest of Gentry*
(1859), Varvara Pavlovna Lavretskaya, who has lived in Paris, is taken to
be an authority on all things French: "George Sand drove her to desperation, Balzac she esteemed, though he was tiresome, Sue and Scribe, she
deemed, had a profound knowledge of the human heart, and Dumas and
Féval she adored; at bottom however she preferred Paul de Kock to the
lot of them, but did not so much as mention his name."
6. Fashionable art-dealers in Moscow.
7. Glikeriya Nikolaevna Fyodotova (1846–1925) was the *grande dame* of
the Moscow stage, a Russian Ristori. One of the last pupils of the great
actor Shchepkin, she was acclaimed for her emotional veracity in such
roles as Lady Macbeth, Medea, Volumnia and Queen Elizabeth. Zoya
Rasumnikova Kochetova (1857–1892), a coloratura soprano with a voice
of silvery timbre, was admired for her Antonida in *A Life for the Tsar*,
Lyudmila in *Ruslan and Lyudmila* and Marguerite in *Faust*, before she
retired in 1888.
8. Nikolay Ignatievich Muzil (1839–1906), a member of the Maly company, who specialized in the roles of simpletons in vaudevilles, operettas
and the plays of Ostrovsky.
9. Aleksandr Pavlovich Lensky (*né* Vervitsiotti, 1847–1908), a character

actor noted for his attention to detail in gesture and makeup; he insisted that the theater should be realistic in order to reveal man's inner world. Mitrofan Trofimovich Ivanov-Kozyolsky (1850–1898), a somewhat flamboyant actor, halfway between the old romantic style and a newer naturalism, was best known for his Hamlet and Shylock. Chekhov devoted an essay to his Hamlet, saying, in essence, better this Hamlet than none at all.

10. Tanti-Bedini (d. 1908), Italian "white" clown and animal-trainer, whom Stanislavsky called "almost the only exponent of the true grotesque." He and his learned pig received favorable mention in Chekhov's newspaper pieces.

11. Vasily Ignatievich Zhivokini (1805–1874), a comic character actor appreciated for his simplicity and naturalness, as well as his tendency to improvise in low comedy. Prov Mikhailovich Sadovsky (*né* Ermilov, 1818–1872), character actor of great psychological accuracy, excelling in the Ostrovsky repertoire; he founded a dynasty of actors. Ivan Vasilievich Samarin (1817–1885), although admittedly unable to be anyone other than himself in any role, still affected audiences by his grace, noble elocution and intelligence. Sergey Vasilievich Shumsky (*né* Chesnokov, 1821–1878), another student of Shchepkin, played elegant young men in modern melodramas and social plays and tempestuous roles in the classic repertoire with a close attention to transitional passages between emotions.

12. Baron Georges Cuvier (1769–1832), French naturalist and comparative anatomist.

13. Vladimir Aleksandrovich Maksheev (1843–1901), a comic character actor specializing in dolts and eccentrics; Nikolay Evstafevich Vilday (*né* Karl Gustav Wilde, 1832–1896), a dry and rhetorical interpreter of "romantic leads," who was more impressive as *raisonneurs*. Both were members of the Maly troupe.

Bely: *The Cherry Orchard*

1. In *Les Aveugles* (1890), Maeterlinck frequently uses the old and blind, cut off from the turmoil of life, to sense death and other intimations from the beyond.

2. In act 2 of *The Cherry Orchard*, as the characters are sitting beside the road, dreamily watching the sun go down, "suddenly a distant sound is heard, as if from the sky, the sound of a snapped string, dying away, mournfully." The merchant Lopakhin offers the suggestion that a bucket dropped in a mine shaft, but the characters remain uneasy until a tramp enters and creates a welcome diversion by his begging.

Annensky: Drama at the Lower Depths

1. *The Lower Depths* was first performed by the Moscow Art Theater on 18 December 1902, with Stanislavsky as Satin and Kachalov as the Baron, and proved to be one of the biggest successes in its history, not least because the audience of intelligentsia could vicariously poke about in human degradation.
2. Aleksey Feofilaktovich Pisemsky (1820–1881), who might be called a "sardonic realist," wrote the peasant drama *A Hard Lot* (1859), which some consider to be the first real Russian tragedy.
3. Pécuchet is one of a pair of pedantic autodidacts in *Bouvard et Pécuchet* (1881), and Charles Bovary is the dull but well-meaning husband of *Madame Bovary* (1856/7), both by Gustave Flaubert. Zakhar is the disrespectful, devious manservant of *Oblomov* (1859) by Ivan Goncharov. Becky Sharp connives her way through William Makepeace Thackeray's *Vanity Fair* (1847/8).
4. Oblomov, the slothful non-agonist of Goncharov's novel; Kalinovich, the disillusioned hero of Pisemsky's *One Thousand Souls* (1858); Lyovin, Tolstoy's *alter ego* in *Anna Karenina* (1873–1877); Pozdnyshev, the embittered husband of Tolstoy's *Kreutzer Sonata* (1889); and Ivan Karamazov, the bedeviled intellectual of Dostoevsky's *Brothers Karamazov* (1879–1880).
5. *Byvshie lyudi*, the title of an early story by Gorky (1897), more pretentiously translated into English as "Creatures That Once Were Men." The title indicates life's rejects, who have no hope of rehabilitation.
6. The pseudonym of Aleksandr Aleksandrovich Bestuzhev (1797–1837), a Decembrist, novelist and poet, whose heroes are too often bargain-basement Byron.
7. Vladimir Galaktionovich Korolenko (1853–1921), whose short stories are Dickensian in their sentimental humor and benevolence. The story "Not So Scary" (1903) relates a tragedy that results from the most humdrum causes.
8. Artyom is a strapping stevedore bursting with health and vigor who protects a puny Jew in the story "Cain and Artyom" (1898). Nil, in the play *The Lower Middle Class* (1901), is a railway worker, a one-dimensional depiction of the new "man with a calm belief in his strength, and in his right to reconstruct according to his own judgment." Foma Gordeev, the protagonist of the novel of that name (1899), is a pure-minded idealist lost in a corrupt mercantile milieu.
9. Yudushka or "Little Judas" is the repulsive, cant-spouting parasitic Pecksniff in *The Golovlyov Family* (1876) by Mikhail Evgrafovich Saltykov-Shchedrin.
10. In part 3, chapter 4, of Dostoevsky's *Crime and Punishment* (1866), Raskolnikov visits the saintly prostitute Sonya in her barn-like quarters and asks her to read to him the biblical account of the raising of Lazarus.

Blok: On Drama

1. Gerhart Hauptmann (1862–1946), a German; Gabriele D'Annunzio (1863–1938), an Italian; Maurice Maeterlinck (1862–1949), a Belgian; Hugo von Hofmannsthal (1874–1929), an Austrian; Stanisław Przybyszewski (1868–1927), a Pole; and Arthur Schnitzler (1863–1931), another Austrian, were the leading European dramatists of the time. (The only important name Blok omits is that of Strindberg.) And significantly they were all working in forms removed from naturalism.

2. Rémy de Gourmont (1858–1915), French critic, whose articles in the *Mercure de France* helped to popularize the "decadents"; his *Livre des masques* (1896, 1898) is a series of brief sketches of notable writers.

3. Henrietta Roland-Holst van der Schalk (1869–1952), Dutch journalist and member of the Social-Democratic Workers Party, who was a prolific proponent of "Christian Socialism."

4. Alexandre Dumas *fils* (1824–1895) attempted to instill into the format of the well-made play didactic discussions of social questions; the play which most clearly answers to Blok's notion is *La Femme de Claude* (1873), in which adultery and social breakdown are equated.

5. Georgy Ivanovich Chulkov (1879–1939), an adherent of Vyacheslav Ivanov, founded the journal the *Golden Fleece* (1905–1907), in which he elaborated his doctrine of spiritual freethinking, "mystical anarchism," a result of the abortive 1905 revolution. Evgeny Nikolaevich Chirikov (1864–1932) had begun as a short-story writer published by Znanie, and turned to the stage only in 1902; he excelled at descriptions of provincial intellectuals and stifling middle-class milieux.

6. *Earth* (1904) is the best-known play of the symbolist poet Valery Yakovlevich Bryusov (1873–1924); subtitled "scenes of the future," it shows humanity dwelling underground in hermetically sealed, mechanically maintained chambers. As the sun is let in, humanity perishes but the Earth lives on. *Tantalus* (1904) by the philosophic poet Vyacheslav Ivanov (1866–1949) is a conscious imitation of the tragedies of Aeschylus.

7. Aleksandr Vasilievich Sukhovo-Kobylin (1817–1903), nobleman, whose trilogy is one of the more unexpected phenomena in Russian literature. *Krechinsky's Wedding* (1855) is social comedy with a bitter tinge; *The Case* (1869) is savage satire with tragic implications; and *Tarelkin's Death* (1869) is grotesque farce that foreshadows "absurd theater."

8. "On Shakespeare and the Drama," which appeared in *Russian Word* (*Russkoe slovo*, 1906) was Tolstoy's last published assault in the campaign he had long waged against Shakespeare. Devoted primarily to a demolition of *King Lear*, it finds Shakespeare deficient in subject matter, artistic technique and emotional sincerity and founded on a corrupt moral base.

9. Sergey Aleksandrovich Naidyonov (*né* Alekseev, 1868–1922) made a hit when his Ostrovskyan first play *Vanyushin's Children* (1901) had its debut at Korsh's Theater in Moscow; his later plays *The Prodigal Son*

(1905) and *Walls* (1907) received productions at the Moscow Art Theater. *Vanyushin's Children* concerns a war of the generations, as does
Gorky's *The Lower Middle Class*, which had its premiere at the MAT in
1901.

10. Znanie ("Knowledge"), Gorky's own publishing house, was devoted to
fostering neo-realist writers and combating "art for art's sake": however,
certain of its authors like Blok and Andreev crossed the artistic bound-
ary-lines.

11. *Foma Gordeev* (1899) concerns the misfit, idealistic scion of a Volga
merchant clan. *The Trio* (1901) is a novel centered around a murderer
and is vaguely reminiscent of Dostoevsky. *Summer People* (1904) is a
rambling, Chekhovian play about idle gentry summering at their villas.
Of the other works Blok mentions later, the plays *Barbarians* (1905),
Children of the Sun (1905) and *Enemies* (1905) grow increasingly vo-
ciferous about class hostility and social injustice. *Mother* (1907), a
novel, explores the growth of political consciousness in a working-class
woman in an industrial town.

12. Pavel Vlasov is the revolutionary worker in *Mother* whose trial and im-
prisonment spur his mother to carry on his work.

13. Semyon Solomonovich Yushkevich (1868–1927) wrote his three major
plays between 1906 and 1907. *In Town* premiered at Kommissarzhevskaya's theater; *The King* was forbidden by the censorship but played
the provinces in 1907. Dramas of Jewish life, they are not very original
but steeped in a rich humor.

14. *Peasants* (1905) was banned by the censorship, but *Ivan Mironych* was
produced at the MAT the same year. Neither play was as successful as
Jews (1903), a drama about the Kishinyov pogrom. *Red Flames* (1907) is
a clumsy attempt to write a symbolic drama about slaves forging fetters
into swords and mysterious red lights showing the way to freedom.

15. Osip Isidorovich Dymov (*né* Perelman, 1878–?1955) had his first play
Hear O Israel! (1907) produced at the Contemporary Theater in Petersburg the same year.

16. Sholom Asch (1880–1957) did his best work in Yiddish; *On the Road to
Zion* (1908) was an ill-advised attempt to capture a Russian audience.

17. Sergey Lvovich Rafalovich (1875–1943) had first made a stir in 1905
with the symbolist play *The River Flows*, written especially for the First
Traveling Dramatic Theater. His other works include *L'Une et l'autre*
(1900) and *The Temple of Melpomene* (1902).

18. Zinaida Afanasievna Vengerova (b. 1867), critic and translator.

19. The only Gidoni I have been able to trace is Grigory Iosifovich, a figure
on the fringes of the art world and an expert on bookplates.

20. Mikhail Alekseevich Kuzmin (1875–1936), like many *fin-de-siècle*
aesthetes, turned to the classical decadence of Alexandria for inspiration. *The Comedy of Eudoxia* is one of three miracle-plays of saints'
lives he wrote in a lightly ironic mode in 1908.

21. The schism in the Russian church that occurred in the mid-seventeenth

century caused a considerable eastward migration of Dissenters: some fled across the Volga to preserve their primordial religion in the depths of forests and wilderness; others, like the Archpriest Avvakum and his followers, were deported to remote outposts.

22. *What Is to Be Done?* (1864), a novel written in prison by the utilitarian critic Nikolay Gavrilovich Chernyshevsky (1828–1889), was meant as a tendentious and didactic reply to *Fathers and Children*. With its vague but appealing portrait of an abstemious revolutionary socialist, it became the Bible of radical youth. Kuzmin's *Wings* (1907), on the other hand, is an equally vague but suggestive paean to homosexuality, and middle-class critics feared it would win young converts to its banner as the earlier novel had.

23. The character named Fanfreluche (i.e., Baubles) appears in the earlier version of Aubrey Beardsley's (1872–1898) elegantly pornographic novel *Under the Hill*, with an illustration depicting him, entitled "L'Abbé."

24. Leonid Nikolaevich Andreev (1871–1919) had rapidly risen to fame with his sensational stories and was taken under the wing of Znanie. His first plays, such as *To the Stars* (1906), were realistic and mildly Chekhovian; but he soon moved to a more enigmatic and symbolic style, exemplified by *The Life of Man* (1907). Appositely, his favorite writer was Edgar Allan Poe.

25. Celestina is an ancient, ugly, life-loving bawd, the motive factor in the early Spanish drama *La Tragicomedia de Calisto y Melibea* (first published 1499). Lepestina (the name translates as something like Pox-abella) is probably a similar decrepit go-between in a play of the Spanish Golden Age.

26. The heroine of *What Is to Be Done?*, Vera Pavlovna, a type of the New Woman, marries the medical student Lopukhov to escape her family; when he realizes that she loves Doctor Kirsanov, he fakes a suicide and goes to America, where he becomes a journalist, under the name Beaumont.

27. Meyerhold's staging of *The Life of Man* at Vera Kommissarzhevskaya's theater in St. Petersburg (1907) was based on the stage direction "Everything takes place as if in a dream." The stage was draped in gray cloth and the props and set-pieces were larger than life-size.

28. In act 1 of Chekhov's *Seagull*, Nina Zarechnaya in the character of the Universal Will performs a symbolist drama by Konstantin Treplyov on an outdoor stage at the estate of his mother, the actress Arkadina. At a climactic moment, the red eyes of the devil, created by flares, appear in the mist. Arkadina laughs at the "special effects," which infuriates Treplyov, who stops the performance.

29. "James Lynch" was Andreev's journalistic pseudonym. He was closely allied to the Moscow Art Theater, which produced a number of his symbolic plays.

30. V. F. Botsyanovsky, a popular critic; *L. Andreev: Critico-biographical Etude* is a 64-page pamphlet (1903).

Sologub: The Theater of a Single Will

1. Erich Christian Wiesener (1798–1861), German preacher (*Das Gotteshaus*), poet (*Sundine*) and writer of tales in the style of E. T. A. Hoffmann.
2. Aisa, the Greek goddess of fate; the word also came to mean a divinely decreed destiny. Anankē is the force of necessity.
3. The great basso Fyodor Shalyapin (or Chaliapin) was known for his elaborate character makeups and assiduous attention to detail in the creation of individual characters.
4. The challenge is offered by Man to the impassive Fate figure "Someone in Gray" in Leonid Andreev's play *The Life of Man*.
5. The princely boyars Shuisky and Vorotynsky appear together in the first scene of Pushkin's *Boris Godunov*, as well as in A. K. Tolstoy's historical trilogy and numerous other Russian plays. Sologub prefers their depiction in Karamzin's history of the Russian state.
6. In the last phase of his short, mad reign, Ludwig II of Bavaria (1845–1886) often had performances staged for himself alone in his various dream castles.
7. Goethe's *Die Leiden des jungen Werthers* (1774) climaxed with the suicide of its hyperemotional hero, due to unrequited love; it excited a rash of adolescent suicides throughout Europe. Sologub compares it with the suicide of pubescent Melchior in Frank Wedekind's *Frühlingserwachen (Spring's Awakening)* (see note 10).
8. Isadora Duncan (1878–1927) brought her barefoot, Greek-inspired dancing to Russia first in 1905, and then on several occasions between 1907 and 1913, when she made a vivid impression on Stanislavsky and many other Russian artists.
9. A reference to Sologub's play of the Laodamia legend, *The Gift of the Wise Bees*.
10. A quotation from the last scene of Frank Wedekind's "tragedy of sex" *Frühlingserwachen* (1891), in which society's repression of natural urges during puberty has disastrous consequences.

Bely: Theater and Modern Drama

1. Καθαρσισ (catharsis) refers to Aristotle's notion that, in some way, tragedy purges pity and fear. ἀναγκη (anankē), or the force of necessity, is often taken to be the tragic impulse.
2. Nietzsche, in his early career, believed Richard Wagner to be the artist most capable of preparing the mind of humanity for the coming civilization, and they became firm friends. But Wagner's francophobia, anti-Semitism and mystical Germanism increasingly disgusted Nietzsche, who lost his faith in Wagner, concurrently losing his faith in art as the redemption of the future. Edouard Schuré (1841–1929), French author of works on musical history, mysticism (*La Vie mystique*, 1903; *L'Ame*

des temps nouveaux, 1909) and dramas (*Les Enfants de Lucifer*, 1900). His *Théâtre de l'âme* was Gordon Craig's bedtime reading while in Russia in 1912.

3. Nietzsche's *Die Geburt der Tragödie* (1872) defined tragedy as a juxtaposition of Apollonian form on Dionysian content; he asserted that it suffered a decline in the Socratic age because of an emphasis on rationalism. Siegfried, traditionally played by a *Heldentenor* with boar-spear, hunting horn and bear-pelt, is the noble if obtuse hero of Wagner's *Siegfried* (1876) and *Götterdämmerung* (1876). Zarathustra, an avatar of Nietzsche's Superman (*Also Sprach Zarathustra*, 1883–1892) leaves the mountains for a town, but abandons preaching to the people in the marketplace when he finds them more attracted by a rope-dancer.

4. Schiller's *Die Braut von Messina* (1803), a neoclassical tragedy, attempts to rehabilitate the dignity of the chorus and devotes an important preface to this matter.

5. Robber chieftains were common heroes of early Russian folk drama and the plays put on in fairground showbooths. N. I. Pastukhov's novel *The Bandit Churkin* had appeared between 1882 and 1885.

6. Vyacheslav Ivanov's plays *Tantalus* and *Prometheus* were imitations of Aeschylus not only in their mythological subject matter and classical format, but in the obscurity and archaism of their language.

7. Solness is the title character of *The Master Builder* (1892), who overcomes his inhibitions and ascends a church spire from which he plunges to his death. Rubek, the demonic sculptor of *When We the Dead Awaken* (1899), similarly meets his end on the heights, in an avalanche. John Gabriel Borkman, a ruined banker, in the play of that name (1896) leaves his sequestration to encounter death in the snow. Ellida (Bely mistakenly calls her Hilda) is *The Lady from the Sea* (1888), who finds freedom in the responsibility of choice. Little Eyolf, the crippled child in the play of that name (1894), drowns after the first act, becoming the symbolic cause of guilt in his father. All these are Ibsen's last plays except for *Brand* (1866), where the hero's motto "All or Nothing" leads him, too, to death by avalanche.

8. At the end of Ibsen's *Ghosts* (1881), Oswald Alving, victim of his father's sin, begins his decline into syphilitic idiocy and blindness calling, "Mother, mother, give me the sun!"

9. Stanislavsky's production of Ibsen's *Wild Duck* at the MAT in 1901 had been an undistinguished failure.

10. The mysteries at Eleusis were a widely attended annual event in ancient Greece, centered around the mother-earth goddess Demeter as paramount divinity. The Epopteia was a vigil held by the *epoptai*, or initiates into the greater mysteries.

11. Christian August Lobeck (1781–1860), German classical scholar and historian of Greek religion. His masterpiece *Aglaophamus* (1829) maintained that the Greek mysteries were a national and indigenous religion that promulgated no esoteric doctrines.

12. The Mystai, or catechumens, after undergoing purification, would make

a procession to Eleusis, where they celebrated a midnight revel under the stars.

Bryusov: Realism and Convention on the Stage

1. The historical detail and naturalistic crowd formation in the productions of Georg II, duke of Saxe-Meiningen, made a strong impression on André Antoine and on Konstantin Stanislavsky when his company toured to France and Russia between 1874 and 1890. The Théâtre Libre and the Moscow Art Theater were founded to promote to some degree the kind of stage realism and ensemble acting found in the Meiningen troupe.
2. Johann Immanuel Volkelt (1848–1930), German philosopher, whose works include studies of Kant and the "problem of individualism."
3. Zeuxis, a Greek painter (fl. 420–390 B.C.), who is reputed to have painted a bunch of grapes so realistically that birds flew at it to peck it.
4. Clearly a reference to the finale of the Moscow Art Theater's production of Ibsen's *Brand* (1907), at the moment when Brand and the madwoman Gerd are swallowed up by an avalanche.
5. The Théâtre de l'Oeuvre in Paris was founded in 1892, as a development from Paul Fort's Théâtre de l'Art, by the actor Aurélien-Marie Lugné-Poë (1869–1940); although the theater was never programmatically symbolist, it did stage many of the plays of Maeterlinck and the late "symbolic" dramas of Ibsen, Strindberg and Björnson. At the period of Bryusov's essay, Max Reinhardt (*né* Goldmann, 1873–1943) managed a number of Berlin theaters, but it was at the Kammerspiele that he mounted works of Maeterlinck, von Hofmannsthal, Wedekind, Osip Dymov and Takedo Izumo and Strindberg's chamber plays. Vsevolod Meyerhold took over the artistic direction of Vera Kommissarzhevskaya's theater in St. Petersburg in 1906, staging controversial experimental productions of *Hedda Gabler*, Maeterlinck's *Soeur Béatrice*, Blok's *The Little Showbooth*, Andreev's *Life of Man*, Wedekind's *Spring's Awakening*, and Przybyszewski's *Eternal Legend*. Between 1907 and 1909, the Moscow Art Theater made several sorties away from naturalism with productions of *Brand*, Hamsun's *Drama of Life*, *At the Gates of the Kingdom* and *In the Claws of Life*, Maeterlinck's *Blue Bird* and Andreev's *Life of Man* and *Anathema*.
6. Aleksandr Afansievich Potebnya (1835–1891), Ukrainian philologist and ethnographer, who developed a theory of the relation of thought to language and a linguistic poetics. His ideas were popularized by Dmitry Nikolaevich Ovsyaniko-Kulikovsky (1853–1920) in a monograph on Potebynya (1893); he himself is best known for his *History of the Russian Intelligentsia* (1906/7). Karl Groos (1861–1946), German philosopher, whose writings on aesthetics and psychology include *Der aesthetische Genuss* (1902) and *Einleitung in die Aesthetik* (1892).
7. Isaak Ilich Levitan (1861–1900), Russian artist of Jewish antecedents

and one of the greatest of landscape painters; his works comprise a panorama of the Russian countryside.

8. Kālidāsa (fl. 400 A.D.), the Indian poet, may have been in Bryusov's consciousness because a production of his play *Vasantasena* had been performed at Suvorin's Theater in St. Petersburg in 1898. Similarly, Frank Wedekind's *Spring's Awakening* had been staged by Meyerhold for Vera Kommissarzhevskaya in 1907.

9. Dante Gabriel Rossetti (1828–1882), English pre-Raphaelite painter and poet, painted several versions of a portrait of a russet-haired, square-jawed maiden under the title *Beata Beatrix*; the earliest version, now in the National Gallery, London, Ford Madox Ford called "the setting in paint of a mood."

10. Open-air stages in France were a byproduct of the movement for *théâtre populaire*. Maurice Pottecher (1867–1960) mounted several open-air productions in the town of Bussang in the Vosges; in 1898 the Arènes de Béziers opened, and in 1903 the actor-manager Firmin-Gémier (1865–1933) began staging open-air pageants of enormous size.

Evreinov: Introduction to Monodrama

1. Karl Borinski (1861–1922), German philologist and academic, whose dissertation had been *Über poetische Vision und Imagination* (1897). In 1899 he published *Das Theater, seine Geschichte, seine Meister*, which appeared in a Russian translation in 1902.

2. Karl Groos (1861–1946), German philosopher and writer on aesthetics and psychology; his *Die Spiele der Menschen* (1899) goes into questions of illusion and play in art.

3. Gustav Theodor Fechner (1801–1897), German psychologist, began an experimental inquiry into the aesthetics of pleasing forms and the golden section in his *Zur experimentalen Aesthetik* and *Vorschule der Aesthetik* (1876).

4. Leopoldo Fregoli (1867–1936), Italian quick-change artist, who appeared in music halls all over Europe in sketches singlehandedly playing half a dozen characters in split-second transformations.

5. Stanisław Przybyszewski (1868–1927), Polish naturalist writer and expressionist playwright, a follower of Strindberg. His play *Snieg* (*Snow*, 1903) was very popular in Russia.

6. Aleksandr Rafailovich Kugel (1864–1928), who wrote under the name Homo Novus, was editor of the influential magazine *Theater and Art* (*Teatr i iskusstvo*, 1897–1918) and co-founder of the Crooked Mirror, where much of Evreinov's comic work was performed. Kugel warmly endorsed improvements in performance techniques, but was a staunch opponent of decadent playwriting and directorial excesses.

7. Charles Aubert (b. 1851), author of *Nouvelles amoureuses* and the mildly scabrous *Pantomimes modernes* (1897), in some of which Colette performed.

8. Quintus Roscius (?126–?62 B.C.), regarded as the greatest of Roman comic actors and honored with equestrian rank by Sulla, had been the occasion for Cicero's oration *Pro Roscio Comoedo*. Flavius Magnus Aurelius Cassiodorus, Roman statesman and writer who retired c. 540 A.D., was an antiquarian of some repute.

9. Tsarevokokhaisk was a district in the Kazan gubernia. Evreinov means any out-of-date provincial theater.

10. In Gerhard Hauptmann's *Hanneles Himmelfahrt* (1893) a peasant girl experiences a vision of her own death and heavenly apparitions just before she dies. Maurice Maeterlinck's *L'Oiseau bleu* (1909) concerns the quest of two children for the Blue Bird of Happiness, which they find back home on Christmas morning. Leonid Andreev's *Black Masks* (1907) is an allegory in which the central character is assailed by his own thoughts and fears disguised as masks.

11. "Eternal recurrence" is enunciated by Nietzsche in *Also Sprach Zarathustra* (1883), as the perennial recurrence of any moment in human existence through infinite time. Similar ideas appeared earlier in *L'Eternité par les astres* (1872), an astronomical work by Louis August Blanqui (1805–1881), and in *L'Homme et les sociétés* (1881) by the sociologist Gustave Le Bon (1841–1931).

12. Daltonists were followers of the English chemist John Dalton (1766–1844), who gave the first detailed description of color blindness, from which he and his brother suffered.

13. Friedrich Theodor Vischer (1807–1887), German philosopher, whose *Aesthetik* (1846–1854) tries without much success to apply Hegelian dialectic to art; one of his primary concerns is the distinction between object and subject.

14. Johann Peter Hebel (1760–1826), Swiss-born German poet, whose dialect poems *Allemannische Gedichte* (1803) were greeted favorably by Goethe.

15. Wolfram von Eschenbach (?1170–?1220), Middle High German poet and minnesinger, renowned for his metrical romance of the Holy Grail, *Parzival*.

16. Hermann Siebeck (1842–1920), German philosopher. *Das Wesen* (1875) is a psychological study of the theory of beauty and art.

17. The references are to Oscar Wilde's *Salomé* (1891), which Evreinov had directed for Vera Kommissarzhevskaya in 1909, although the production was forbidden to open by the Holy Synod. The moon is present and appealed to throughout the play; Salomé first sees it as an undefiled virgin, her page sees it as a dead woman's hand, while Narraboth, the Syrian in love with Salomé, views it as a little princess. For Herod, it is a naked woman, mad and drunken, and for Herodias "the moon is like the moon, that is all."

18. Théodule Armand Ribot (1839–1916), French experimental psychologist, whose investigations of mental suggestion influenced Strindberg and whose discussion of affective memory influenced Stanislavsky.

19. The novel was written in German as *Die Totenmesse* (1895).

Meyerhold: Russian Dramatists

1. The king of Poland sent to the coronation of Anna Ioannovna in 1730 a few Italian singers who had recourse to pantomime because the empress knew no Italian. The first troupe of Italian comedians appeared in Russia in 1733 and 1734/5. Pietro Miro, who played Petrillo, was made to function as the empress' court jester.
2. Yakov Borisovich Knyazhnin (1742–1791), son-in-law and successor to Sumarokov, was so notorious for plagiarizing the set-pieces and complicated plots of European tragic authors that he was satirized on stage as Rifmokradov (Robrhyme).
3. Bartolomé de Torres Naharro (?1480–?1524), a Spanish humanist who experimented with popular dramatic forms; his realistic farces and *comedias* anticipate the "cloak and sword" comedies of the *siglo d'oro*.
4. Dmitry Vasilievich Averkiev (1836–1905), an associate of Apollon Grigoriev and a minor dramatist, founded the magazine *Writer's Journal* (*Dnevnik pisatelya*, 1885/6) solely to publish his own writings on the theater. His book *On Drama* (1893) is the first Russian work to treat dramatic theory from Aristotle to Lessing.
5. The heroine of *Evgeny Onegin*, Tatyana, can be seen to "overcome passion" in her dutiful marriage and in her polite coldness to an older, wiser Onegin.
6. *El Castigo sin verganza* (1631) by Lope Felix de Vega Carpio (1562–1635) is an intense and sanguinary tragedy of incest and revenge. The theological drama *El Condenado por desconfiado*, putatively by Tirso de Molina (pseudonym of Gabriel Tellez, ?1580–1648) and believed to be a companion piece to his Don Juan drama, *El Burlador de Sevilla*, depicts a hermit damned for his lack of faith in God's mercy.
7. The eight prose *entremeses* or one-act farces (1615) by Miguel de Cervantes Saavedra (1547–1616) combine a shrewd observation of real life with poetic idealism.
8. Meyerhold sees the first Russian revolution of 1905 as an end to intellectual as well as political torpor. Ironically, his production of *Hedda Gabler* in 1906 was attacked by the socialist critic Lunacharsky as perverse and unfaithful to the play's satire on bourgeois life.
9. Viktor Aleksandrovich Krylov (1838–1906), immensely popular dramatic hack, who wrote everything from tragedies of modern life to operetta librettos, stealing indiscriminately from foreign authors and sensational news items. After Chekhov's *Ivanov* had opened (1887), Krylov offered to make a few improvements and split the royalties fifty-fifty; Chekhov delicately refused the offer.
10. Konstantin Dmitrievich Balmont (1867–1943), decadent poet of lush symbolism, whose *Three Blooms*, a pallid pastoral, was a resounding flop when produced at the avant-garde Theater of Dionysos in 1905. Valery Yakovlevich Bryusov (1873–1924) attempted to oppose theatrical naturalism not only in his theoretical writings but by his symbolist plays; *Earth* (1904), which depicts the birth of humanity and its destruc-

tion by the forces of future technology, appealed to Meyerhold, but
it was not in fact staged until 1922. N. Minsky was the pseudonym
of Nikolay Maksimovich Vilenkin (1855–1937), a Jew who may be
credited with the first symbolist drama in Russian, *Alma* (1900); the
humorless tale of a nymphomaniac, it was written to show that the purpose of life is the pursuit of the unattainable. Lidiya Dmitrievna Zinovieva-Annibal (1866–1907), the wife of Vyacheslav Ivanov, was noted
for the eroticism of her writing; *Rings* (published 1909), to quote George
Calderon, "is the story of two twin souls, husband and wife, torn asunder by volcanic passions of irrelevant people, and converging at last on
the Meon of love, through suffering, in death. All the characters suffer
from acute neurasthenia, and, in this country [England], would be con-
signed to Parkhurst or Bedlam." Zinaida Nikolaevna Gippius (1869–
1945), the foremost poetess of the Russian *fin de siècle*, shared with her
husband Dmitry Merezhkovsky a taste for mystical metaphysics. This
affects the political views which pervade her plays. Georgy Ivanovich
Chulkov (1879–1939), a disciple of Vyacheslav Ivanov and his creed of
mystical anarchism, looked ahead in his play *Taiga* (1907) to a new race
of apparently Aryan supermen to free the world; the doctor's wife, who
is the heroine, symbolizes the desolate Asian steppe. Leonid Nikolaevich Andreev (1871–1919) had begun his career under the aegis of
Gorky, and fluctuated between socially conscious realism and a cos-
mically fatalistic symbolism in his playwriting. *The Days of Our Life*
(1908), an autobiographical play that was published, significantly, by
Znanie, is a lively drama of student life, quite unlike the obscure allegory *Black Masks* (1907), which Evreinov hailed as close to monodrama.
11. Vyacheslav Vasilievich Ivanov (1866–1949) carried out his poetical theories of the Dionysian origins of tragedy in plays based on Greek myth
or reconstructed on fragments of lost tragedies. *Tantalus* (1904) is typical in its consciously fabricated pseudo-archaic language.
12. Aleksandr Aleksandrovich Blok (1880–1921) is not only one of the
greatest of Russian poets but also one of the most successful of its symbolist dramatists. His *Lyrical Dramas* include *The Little Showbooth*
(1906/7), an ironical farce in the style of the *commedia*, which Meyerhold mounted with great *éclat*; *The King in the Square* (1907); and *The
Incognita* (1907/8), in which his favorite eidolon The Beautiful Lady
slums in a boozy tavern. It is the "romantic irony" of these plays which
recalls to Meyerhold the names of Novalis (pseudonym of Friedrich von
Hardenberg, 1772–1801), the German poet whose allegorical works are
filled with the notion of a musically poetic apocalypse ushering in the
Golden Age, and Ludwig Tieck (1773–1853), whose plays *Der gestie-
felte Kater* (1797) and *Die verkehrte Welt* are charming, anarchic satires
directed against critical canons of taste.
13. A frequenter of Zinaida Gippius' *Green Lamp* salon, Aleksey Mikhailovich Remizov (1877–1957) extended his experiments in devising fairy
tales and imitating ancient Greek romances to the theater. His synthetic
mystery plays, *The Play of the Devil, George the Dragon-Killer* and *Of*

Judas, Prince of Iscariot, culminated in 1918 with a full-scale revision of the folk play *Tsar Maximilian.*

14. Mikhail Alekseevich Kuzmin (1875–1936), perhaps the most cosmopolitan and crepuscular of the Russian decadents, is reminiscent of Anatole France in his reworkings of medieval miracle plays: *The Comedy of Eudoxia of Heliopolis, The Comedy of Martinian* and *The Comedy of Alexis.* His other plays, like *The Chimes of Love,* for which he composed the music, are often set in an idyllic eighteenth century *à la* Watteau or Longhi.

15. Andrey Bely (pseudonym of Boris Nikolaevich Bugaev, 1880–1934), like his colleagues, dabbled in revitalizing the mystery play, using music as the bridge between audience and actor. The fragments of his *Anti-Christ, He That Is Come* (1903) and *The Jaws of Night* (1907) proclaim a millennium of doom and despair.

16. Thanks to Meyerhold, *The Triumph of Death,* a legend of Bertha of the Big Foot by Fyodor Sologub (pseudonym of Fyodor Kuzmich Teternikov, 1863–1927), was one of the few Russian symbolist plays to be well received in the theater. On the other hand, his production of *Vanka the Steward and the Page Jehan,* a scene-by-scene comparison of lovemaking in Villon's France and medieval Russia, was booed by the gallery of the Alexandra Theater. *The Gift of the Wise Bees,* a retelling of the tale of Laodamia and Protesilaus, is imbued with a classic serenity and lyricism.

17. According, once more, to George Calderon, in *The Singing Ass* (1907), "the crystalline innocence of Shakespeare's poetry is stained with garish orgiastic purple. 'On croit voir / Glisser sur une fleur une longue limace.'"

18. Evgeny Aleksandrovich Znosko-Borovsky (1884–1954), secretary of the literary revue *Apollo (Apollon),* set the action of *The Transformed Prince* in a mythical "Spanish" duchy. Meyerhold's production of it in 1910, with music by Mikhail Kuzmin, took full advantage of the fantasy element to create an exuberant, highly colored quasi cabaret.

19. Vladimir Nikolaevich Solovyov (1887–1941) was a young director who wrote a number of pantomimes on *commedia dell'arte* themes to enable Meyerhold to experiment with traditional stage types. *Harlequin Marriage Broker* was produced by Meyerhold in 1911; one performance, given at the home of Fyodor Sologub, was played in tuxedos and evening gowns, thus getting the drop on Vakhtangov's *Princess Turandot* by one year.

Ivanov: The Essence of Tragedy

1. Friedrich Nietzsche's *Die Geburt der Tragödie aus dem Geiste der Musik* (1872) is characterized by its division of the artistic impulse into an Apollonian and a Dionysian experience. The Apollonian is formal,

contained and scrupulously coterminous with the actual world; the Dionysian is uncontrolled and ecstatic and coalesces with the divine and animal worlds. Dionysian experience provides the material which the Apollonian shapes into art.

2. According to one legend, Lycurgus was maddened by Dionysos as punishment for a threat and cut off his own son's limbs, in the delusion that he was pruning a vine-stock. That his death might deliver the land of the Thracian Edoni from barrenness, he was led to Mt. Pangaeus, where Dionysos caused him to be torn to pieces by horses.

3. Agave, mother of Pentheus, king of Thebes, and daughter of Cadmus, is among the first to follow the god Dionysos and during the mountain revels mistakes her spying son for a lion and joins in his dismemberment. Her entrance with his head spiked on her thyrsus and her gradual awakening to consciousness are among the most powerful moments in Euripides' *The Bacchae*. The name "Pentheus" means grief.

4. Clytaemnestra and Cassandra appear in Aeschylus' *Agamemnon*; Antigone, in his *Seven against Thebes*; Niobe, in a lost play of that name cited by Plato; and the daughters of Danaus, traditionally fifty in number, make up the chorus in *The Suppliant Women*.

5. Atossa, in *The Persians*, is the daughter of Darius and the mother of Xerxes; Io, metamorphosed into a cow by a jealous Hera, in her goaded wanderings comes across *Prometheus Bound*, surrounded by a chorus of sea-nymphs, the daughters of Oceanus; *Prometheus Unbound* is another lost work, though its outline has survived.

6. Electra appears in *The Libation Bearers* of Aeschylus, the *Electra* and *Orestes* of Euripides and the *Electra* of Sophocles. Orestes' murder of his mother Clytaemnestra is touched on in a number of plays, particularly Aeschylus' *Libation Bearers* and *Eumenides*, and Euripides' *Orestes*. The curse on the house of Labdacus which compels Oedipus to commit incest and parricide is worked out most fully in Sophocles' *Oedipus the King*. Although the only full-scale extant play devoted to Thyestes' feeding on a banquet of his own children served up by his brother Atreus is that of Seneca, the anthropophagic repast brings down the curse on the House of Atreus. Heracles' madness in which he slays his wife and children had a whole play devoted to it in the *Raving Heracles* of Euripides. Medea's murder of her children was treated in the *Medea* of Euripides. The immolation of Iphigenia at the behest of her father Agamemnon was another theme for Euripides in *Iphigenia at Aulis* and *Iphigenia in Tauris*, as well as being a motive factor for Aeschylus' *Oresteia*. The fraternal quarrels of Eteocles and Polyneices appear in both Aeschylus' *Seven against Thebes* and Euripides' *Phoenician Women*, and provide the background for Sophocles' *Antigone*. Clytaemnestra butchers her husband Agamemnon in the play that bears his name by Aeschylus. Deianira is inadvertently the cause of her husband Heracles' death in Sophocles' *Women of Trachis*. The Danaides, who slew their husbands on their wedding-night at their father's command, not only appear as

chorus in Aeschylus' *Suppliant Women* but are believed to have dominated the two lost plays in that trilogy, *The Egyptians* and *The Danaides*.

Andreev: First Letter on the Theater

1. Korney Chukovsky (pseudonym of N. I. Korneichuk, 1882–1969) published a witty though subjective essay on cinema, "Nat Pinkerton and Contemporary Literature," in 1910. It discussed the work of Méliès and put forth a plea for a dramatic literature written especially for the film.
2. At the end of the nineteenth century a number of theaters devoted to staging one-act plays were found in the larger Russian cities. Some, like the Crooked Mirror in Petersburg, specialized in parody and satire; others, like the Flitter-Mouse in Moscow, came closer to revue. Some, like the Stray Dog, were out-and-out cabarets.
3. The Florentine goldsmith Benvenuto Cellini (1500–1571) dictated his picaresque *Vita* in 1558, but it remained unpublished until 1728. It is a rollicking gallimaufry of anecdote and adventure.
4. Dostoevsky once told the editor Suvorin, "Belinsky said that dramatic talent developed on its own, in youth. So I thought if I started with novels and was good at them, I must be no dramatist" (Suvorin's *Diary*, 17 September 1899).
5. Gerhardt Hauptmann's *Die versunkene Glocke* (1896), an avowed "fairy play," features elves, trolls, dwarfs, a wood-sprite, an elemental spirit and the maiden Rautendelein, "an elfin creature." The Imatra is a picturesque waterfall on the Wuoksi River, Finland, with an enormous rock-face in its center. But I have been unable to locate a reference to it in any of Naidyonov's published plays. As to the samovar, it was such an omnipresent element in plays of Russian life that Meyerhold's omission of it in his production of Yushkevich's *In Town* was cause for critical comment.
6. One of the satiric *Fables* (1884/5) of Mikhail Evgrafovich Saltykov (pseudonym Shchedrin, 1826–1889).
7. The powerful editor of *New Times* (*Novaya vremya*), Aleksey Sergeevich Suvorin (1834–1912), ran the Theater of the Literary-Artistic Society in Petersburg; although it began as an operation dedicated to modern literary drama and did stage works of Chekhov and Tolstoy, it grew increasingly commercial and trite, especially during the regime of the *prima donna* Lidiya Yavorskaya. Fyodor Abramovich Korsh (1852–1923), a former ticket-broker, opened the Russian Dramatic Theater in 1882, the first private theater in Russia; it too subsisted on such popular hits as Sardou's *Madame Sans-Gêne*, but its repertoire included many masterpieces and it instituted Friday matinees to promote new Russian drama. Despite Andreev's scorn, both theaters helped create audiences drawn from previously untapped ranks of society and paved the way for the Moscow Art Theater.

8. Knut Hamsun's *The Drama of Life* (a mistranslation of *Livets Spill* [*The Game of Life*], 1896) received a notable production by the MAT in 1907.

9. *Peter Schlemihls Wunderbare Geschichte* (1814) by Adelbert von Chamisso (1781–1838) is the tale of a man who sells his shadow to the devil in return for worldly prosperity.

10. The crude but exciting Darwinian stories and novels of the American Jack London (1876–1916) gained early popularity in Russia but kept it, not least because his soapbox socialism made him acceptable to the Soviet censorship.

Andreev: Second Letter on the Theater

1. The elephantine Konstantin Aleksandrovich Varlamov (1848–1915) and dapper Yury Mikhailovich Yuriev (1872–1948) were stars of the Alexandra (they had played together as Sganarelle and his master in Meyerhold's production of *Dom Juan* in 1910) when they condescended to appear in the Tanagra films made in the Berlin Bioscope studios by Georg Jacobi. Varlamov also appeared in a series of crude Russian one-reel comedies in 1913. Vera Leonidovna Yureneva (1876–1962) was the leading lady of Nezlobin's Theater when she made her film debut in 1913 in *The Precipice*. Ekaterina Nikolaevna Roschina-Insarova (*née* Pashennaya, 1883–1970) entered the Maly company and cinema almost simultaneously in 1911 and was featured in the films *Old Days in Kashir* (based on Averkiev's play about seventeenth-century merchant life), and Andreev's own *Anfisa* (1912).

2. Albert Bassermann (1867–1952), who had worked in the Meiningen company, in Ibsen plays under Otto Brahm and in Shakespeare with Max Reinhardt, first appeared in a film as Dr. Hallers in *Der Andere* (1913), a Jekyll-and-Hyde story about a lawyer.

3. In 1911 Max Reinhardt and Hugo von Hofmannsthal were initiated into film by the film producer Paul Davidson. Hofmannsthal wrote a "dreamplay" scenario, *Das Fremde Mädchen* (1913).

4. *Die Insel der Seligen* (1913), filmed in Florence. Reinhardt's only other film ventures were a recording of the stage version of *Sumurun*; a lavish *Venezianische Liebesnächte*; and (in Hollywood) a garish misrendering of *A Midsummer Night's Dream*.

5. The Edison Kinetophone was first demonstrated at the Hermitage Amusement Park in Moscow in May 1896, when it inspired the music critic Vladimir Stasov and the composer Glazunov to shout "Vivat Edison!"

6. Vladimir Nemirovich-Danchenko and the best actors of the Moscow Art Theater developed through studio work a stage adaptation of *The Brothers Karamazov* in twenty episodes spread over two nights. It premiered on 12 and 13 October 1910; some monologues lasted as long as twenty-eight minutes and one scene ran to an hour and twenty minutes. In 1912, Nemirovich-Danchenko announced an adaptation of *The Dev-*

ils in fourteen episodes; in private correspondence Gorky objected and withdrew his own play *The Zykovs* from the theater. On 22 September 1913 his open letter "On Karamazovism" appeared in the *Russian Word* (*Russkoe slovo*) with an appeal to all literary men to protest a further fraying of society's edgy nerves by public performances of morbidity and sadism; he referred to Dostoevsky as a black spot "on the bright background of Russian literature." The letter, which Nemirovich referred to as a "bombshell," evoked a spate of meetings, debates and counter-letters from such pundits as Aleksandr Benois, Fyodor Sologub and Dmitry Merezhkovsky. Gorky's supporters included Lenin. Gorky riposted with "More on Karamazovism" (27 October 1913), pointing out that his objections were not to Dostoevsky but to stage adaptations of his novels which sensationalize the characters.

7. Valery Bryusov's provocative arrogance (he called his first collection of poems *Chefs d'oeuvre*), his patent careerism and his sheer output annoyed many of his contemporaries, who were fond of pointing out his merchant ancestry as cause for his import trade in European culture.

8. It is unclear whether Andreev is referring to Meyerhold's experiments in decorative stylization at Vera Kommissarzhevskaya's theater (1906/7) or to his more recent studio work on *commedia dell'arte* techniques at Interlude House (1910–1915).

9. A. K. Tolstoy's *Tsar Fyodor Ioannovich* (1870), the second part of his blank-verse historical trilogy, was the unexciting choice to open the Moscow Art Theater on 14 October 1898; it was a success due chiefly to the archaeological precision of the costumes, the picturesqueness of the groupings and Ivan Moskvin in the title role.

10. The acting company of the duke of Saxe-Meiningen, celebrated for its historical authenticity of costumes and props and the picturesque grouping of its extras, visited Moscow in 1885. Ostrovsky was moderate in his praise, admiring the company's discipline but objecting to the obviousness of the director's manipulation. Young Stanislavsky was inspired by it and for a time became a stage-despot in imitation of the Saxe-Meiningen *régisseur* Cronegk.

11. Dmitry Ivanovich Ilovaysky (1832–1920), historian and journalist, author of textbooks on world and Russian history, much used in primary and secondary schools before the Revolution.

12. A pun on *gorki* ("low eminences") and Gorky (Maksim).

13. Veristic details characteristic of the Moscow Art Theater. For *Three Sisters*, in which many of the characters are officers, Chekhov insisted that a colonel be on hand at rehearsals to teach the actors proper deportment and the correct way to wear a uniform.

14. Presumably one of the masterpieces of Stendhal (1783–1842), *Le Rouge et le noir* (1830) or *La Chartreuse de Parme* (1839), in which a multidimensional reality is composed of a great many precise observations.

15. In act 3 of *Three Sisters*, the Prozorov sisters have taken refuge in Olga's attic room during the conflagration; the study is the locale of act 3 of

Ivanov, and Stanislavsky, who played Count Shabelsky, devised the cucumber business, which is not in the script.

16. Tambourines accompany the Shrovetide mummers in act 2 of *Three Sisters,* which opened in the MAT production with Natasha crossing the darkened stage holding a candle "like Lady Macbeth." Epikhodov's apple-eating was a piece of business in *The Cherry Orchard* added by Ivan Moskvin.

17. P. P. Gnedich wrote to his wife in 1903, "I can understand your being unable to sit through *Three Sisters,* for Tolstoy could not even finish reading it. Remember when he told me something very astute: 'If a drunken doctor lies on a sofa and rain pours down outside the window, that, for Chekhov, makes a play, and, for Stanislavsky, makes a mood; but for me it's god-awful boredom, and lying on a sofa won't help you come up with dramatic action. . . .'"

18. In 1912 the MAT staged three of Turgenev's shorter plays, *The Charity Case, Thin Ice* and *The Provincial Lady,* with pastel-toned scenery by M. V. Dobuzhinsky. Molière's *Imaginary Invalid* followed in 1913, with colorful setting and *mise-en-scène* by Aleksandr Benois.

19. *Vampuka or The Bride of Africa, A High-Class Opera in Every Respect,* with music by V. D. Erenburg, was a screamingly funny parody of grand opera (especially *Aïda* and *L'Africaine*) put on at the Crooked Mirror Theater in Petersburg (1909). It was so enormously popular that words like "vampukicize" were added to the language. The author of the libretto, Prince M. N. Volkonsky, got the title from an anecdote: some young gentlewomen of the Smolny Institute accosted a benefactor singing *Vam puk, Vam puk, Vam puk tsvetov podnosim* (loosely, "You smell, you smell, you smell the flowers we bring").

20. Between 1909 and 1912, the Moscow Art Theater worked with Gordon Craig on a production of *Hamlet;* the finished product, falling halfway between his monodramatic, expressionistic concept and Stanislavsky's psychological realism, was a qualified failure.

21. Vasily Ivanovich Kachalov (*né* Shverubovich, 1875–1948) joined the MAT in 1900 and soon became its most popular leading man; besides Hamlet and Ivanov, he played Chatsky, Brand, the Baron in *Lower Depths,* Julius Caesar and Ivan Karamazov.

22. The *nom de plume* of Dr. Vikenty V. Smidowicz (1867–1945), who, like a Russian Fulton Oursler, became a best-seller in 1901 with his *A Doctor's Casebook;* like Andreev, he was published by Znanie.

23. Fyodor Ivanovich Shalyapin (or Chaliapin, 1876–1938), the great basso, first played Mussorgsky's Boris Godunov in Mamontov's private opera company at Nizhegorod Fair (1898); it became his greatest achievement. Lidiya Yakovlevna Lipovskaya-Marschner (1882–1958) was a coloratura soprano soloist at the Mariinsky Theater (1906–1908, 1911–1913) in the roles of Violetta in *La Traviata,* Gilda in *Rigoletto,* Rosina in *Il Barbiere di Siviglia* and Micaëla in *Carmen.*

24. *Brand* had been staged at the MAT in 1906 by Nemirovich-Danchenko

with Kachalov in the title role. It was not well received.

25. Fyodor Fyodorovich Kommissarzhevsky (1882–1954) had directed an idiosyncratic production of Ostrovsky's *Feast or Famine* (or more literally, *Before Not a Farthing and Now a Whole Shilling*) at Nezlobin's Theater in 1910; he published his correlative interpretation of Ostrovsky in his *Theatrical Preludes* (1916).

26. Famusov, Molchalin, Chatsky and Sofiya are the central characters of Griboedov's *Woe from Wit*; Khlestakov, Dobchinsky and Bobchinsky appear in Gogol's *Inspector*.

27. Ilya Matveevich Uralov (1872–1920), who had risen to fame playing Ibsen roles in Vera Kommissarzhevskaya's company, joined the MAT in 1907 to play the Mayor in *The Inspector*; he found the experience unsatisfactory and left in 1911.

28. Max Linder (*né* Gabriel Levielle, 1883–1925), a French silent film comedian who began his screen career in 1906, is often thought of as Charlie Chaplin's inspiration.

29. Aleksandr Nikolaevich Benois (or Benua, 1870–1960), best known in the West for his designs for the Ballets Russes, was a leading member of the "World of Art" circle. He was invited to the Moscow Art Theater to design and direct Molière's *Marriage on Compulsion* and *The Imaginary Invalid* (1913), Pushkin's *Mozart and Salieri* and *The Feast in Plague-Time* (1915) and Goldoni's *Mistress of the Inn* (1914).

30. Arkady Timofeevich Averchenko (1881–1925), editor of the satirical journal *New Satyricon* (*Novy satirikon*) and celebrated for his short comic skits and vaudevilles, wrote a parody of Tolstoy's *Power of Darkness* for the Crooked Mirror.

31. Arsène Lupin was a combination jewel-thief and detective who appeared in a series of novels by Maurice Leblanc (1864–1941).

32. Pierre Jean de Béranger (1780–1857), French poet whose politically libertarian ballads and *chansons* had been popular with Russian liberals from the middle of the nineteenth century.

33. Von Hofmannsthal's *Ödipus und die Sphinx* (1905), a Freudian version of the tragedy, written for Max Reinhardt, gave rise to the joke that *Neuromantik* should be read *Neuro-mantik*.

34. One of the greatest successes of the Crooked Mirror was Nikolay Evreinov's *The Inspector* (1914), which purported to show excerpts from Gogol's comedy as staged in five different ways: the traditional stock-company manner, the Moscow Art school of naturalism, Max Reinhardt's Munich Secession charade style, Gordon Craig's mystico-allegorical approach and silent film slapstick.

35. Anton Rubinstein's opera *The Demon* (1875), from Lermontov's poem, is set high in the mountains of the Caucasus.

36. H. G. Wells' *The Island of Dr. Moreau* (1896) concerns a fanatical scientist who creates humanoids by vivesectional grafts onto savage beasts.

37. Franz Grillparzer (1791–1872), Austrian dramatist, some of whose plays attempt to combine mythic spirituality with humdrum reality.

38. Aleksandr Blok's lyrical ironical farce *The Little Showbooth* was produced by Meyerhold in 1906 and again in 1914, the latter production serving as a proof of his theories of "theatrical theater."
39. Konstantin Ivanovich Arabazhin (b. 1866), literary critic who had published a study of Andreev in 1910. Pyotr Mikhailovich Yartsev (d. 1930) was the dramaturge of Vera Kommissarzhevskaya's theater (1906/7), where he directed Przybyszewski's *Eternal Legend*, Yushkevich's *In Town* and Andreev's *The Life of Man*, before joining the MAT.
40. Nikolay Evreinov's *Theater as Such* (1912) is a series of loosely knit *causeries*, parables and aphorisms, arguing the elemental theatricality of the theater.
41. This alludes to a well-known line from the Nestorian Chronicles which states that the Russians had summoned the Vikings (or Varangers) to be their legislators and rulers.
42. Boris Fyodorovich Geier (1876–1916) wrote a number of monodramatic pieces staged at the Crooked Mirror Theater in Petersburg, including *In the Gloaming of Dawning* (1907); *Memories*, versions of the same events as remembered by different characters; *What They Say, What They Think* (a forerunner of Eugene O'Neill's *Strange Interlude*); and *Snout and Love*, a parody of the MAT's productions of Andreev's plays.
43. Knut Hamsun (*né* Pedersen, 1859–1952), the Norwegian novelist, wrote *Mysteries* (1892) as an experiment in creating fiction dealing not with man in society but with the "unconscious life of the mind." In it, the "outsider of existence" Nagel is referred to as "God's obsession."
44. For Aikhenvald's views, see the Introduction.
45. Eugène Louis Doyen, French surgeon, who devised new techniques of heart surgery and bullet removal.
46. Valentin Aleksandrovich Serov (1865–1911), painter and son of the composer A. N. Serov, did much work for Diaghilev, including the poster of Pavlova and the 1911 curtain for *Scheherazade*. Ilya Aleksandrovich Sats (1875–1912) composed the music for the MAT productions of *The Bluebird*, Hamsun's *Drama of Life*, *Hamlet* and Andreev's own *Life of Man* and *Anathema*. "His music," said Stanislavsky, "was always an indispensable and inalienable part of the total production." "Someone in Gray" is the mysterious Fate figure in *The Life of Man*.
47. A parody of the lines "And ye who have come hither for mirth, ye who are doomed to die, look and listen," spoken by "Someone in Gray."
48. Olga Leonardovna Knipper (1868–1959), Chekhov's widow, had been a charter member of the MAT acting company; her leading roles at the time of this essay included the Queen in *Hamlet* and Béline in *The Imaginary Invalid*. Ivan Mikhailovich Moskvin (1874–1946), another charter member and a superb character actor with wonderful comic gifts, had created, among other roles, Epikhodov in *The Cherry Orchard*, Snegiryov in *Brothers Karamazov* and Fedya Protasov in Tolstoy's *Living Corpse*. Leonid Mironovich Leonidov (*né* Volfenzon, 1873–1941) had joined the MAT in 1903, going on to play Lopakhin in

The Cherry Orchard, Man in *The Life of Man*, Dmitry Karamazov and Peer Gynt; his massive physique and turbulent emotionalism marked him out for "heavies." N. N. Zvantsev was a minor MAT player who advanced from such roles as the Sixth Blind Man in *The Blind* and Oak in *The Blue Bird* to the Narrator in *The Brothers Karamazov*.

49. The most famous of these was Alexandre Bisson's three-act drama *Madame X* (1908), whose final act is the fully staged murder trial of an errant wife.

50. In 1910 Max Reinhardt produced *Oedipus Rex* in Berlin in the Zirkus Schumann, which sat 5,000 persons. He did away with the proscenium arch and sent crowds spilling into the audience.

51. In response to Filippo Marinetti's futurist manifestos, a group of young Russian poets including Vladimir Mayakovsky, David Burlyuk, Vasily Kamensky and Viktor Khlebnikov organized their own "Slap in the Face of Public Taste." The painter Mikhail Larionov issued the manifesto "Why Do We Paint Ourselves?" to justify a group sortie to Kuznets Bridge, faces painted with aeroplanes and dogs.

52. The Theater of Musical Drama opened in Petrograd in 1912, under the directorship of I. M. Lapitsky, with the intention of extirpating operatic conventions and instituting the artistic principles of the MAT in opera; their *Carmen* was produced in 1913. For the most part, the productions were well received and lasted until 1919; but Evreinov made devastating fun of their naturalistic excesses in his play *The Fourth Wall*.

Selected Bibliography

An attempt at a complete bibliography would require another volume, for each author represented has spawned his own library of critical works, and the separate topics of Criticism and Theater entail an even vaster array of books. I have therefore limited myself to citing for the Russian reader a few of the basic sources of information and for the English reader some aids to further study.

I. IN RUSSIAN

Aixenval'd, Julij. *Slova o slovax: kritičeskie stat'i.* Petrograd: Knigoizd. byvš. M. V. Popova [?1923].

Alt'shuller, A. Ja., ed. *Očerki istorii russkoj teatral'noj kritiki: Konec XVIII–pervaja polovina XIX veka.* Leningrad: Iskusstvo, 1975.

———. *Očerki istorii russkoj teatral'noj kritiki: Vtoraja polovina XIX veka.* Leningrad: Iskusstvo, 1976.

Andreev, Leonid. *Pis'ma o teatre.* Letchworth, Herts: Prideaux Press, 1974.

Anikst, A. *Teorija dramy v Rossii ot Puškina do Čexova.* Moscow: Nauka, 1972.

Annenskij, Innokentij. *Knigi otrazenij.* Munich: Wilhelm Fink Verlag, 1969.

Belinskij, Vissarion. *Belinskij o drame i teatre. Izbrannye stat'i i vyskazyvanija.* Ed. A. M. Lavretskij. Moscow-Leningrad: Iskusstvo, 1948.

Belyj, Andrej. *Arabeski* (1911). Munich: Wilhelm Fink Verlag, 1963.

Blok, Aleksandr. *Sobranie sočinenij v šesti tomax.* Moscow: Pravda, Ogonëk, 1971.

Brjusov, Valerij. *Sobranie sočinenij.* Moscow: Xudožestvennaja literatura, 1975.

Brodskaja, G. Ju. "Brjusov i teatr," *Literaturnoe nasledstvo,* 85 (1976): 167–199.

Čexov i teatr. Pis'ma, fel'etony, sovremenniki o Čexove-dramaturge. Comp. E. D. Surkov. Moscow: Iskusstvo, 1961.

Dobroljubov, Nikolaj. *Izbrannoe.* Ed. M. F. Ovsjannikov. Moscow: Iskusstvo, 1975.

Dukor, I. "Problemy dramaturgii simvolizma," *Literaturnoe nasledstvo,* 27–28 (1937): 106–166.

Emel'janov, B. "Ostrovskij i Dobroljubov," in *A. N. Ostrovskij. Sbornik statej i materialov*. Moscow: Vserossiskoe teatral'noe obščestvo, 1962.

Evrejnov, Nikolaj N. "Ob otricanii teatra. Polemika serdca," *Strelec*, II (1914): 36–51.

———. *Teatr kak takovoj*. Moscow: Vremja, 1923.

Fëdorov, A. V. *Teatr A. Bloka i dramaturgija ego vremeni*. Leningrad: Izd. Leningradskogo Universiteta, 1972.

Garanina, N. S. *Stil' russkoj teatral'noj kritiki: Učebno-metodičeskoe posobie* . . . Moscow: Izd. Moskovskogo Universiteta, 1970.

Gerasimov, Ju. K. "Krizis modernistskoj teatral'noj mysli v Rossii (1907–1917)," *Teatr i dramaturgija*. *Trudy Leningradskogo gosudarstvennogo instituta teatra, muzyki i kinematografii*. Part 4 (1974): 202–244.

———. "V. Ja. Brjusov i uslovnyj teatr," *Teatr i dramaturgija*. *Trudy Leningradskogo gosudarstvennogo instituta teatra, muzyki i kinematografii*. Part 2 (1967): 253–273.

Glagolin, Boris. *Teatral'nye epizody*. St. Petersburg: Sirius, 1911.

Gogol' i teatr. Ed. N. L. Stepanov. Moscow: Iskusstvo, 1952.

Grigor'ev, Apollon. *Sobranie sočinenij pod redakciej V. F. Savodnika*. Moscow: I. N. Kušnerëv, 1915.

Grossman, Leonid. *Puškin v teatral'nyx kreslax: Kartiny russkoj sceny 1817–1820 godov*. St. Petersburg: Brokgauz-Efron, 1926.

Istorija russkogo dramatičeskogo teatra v semi tomax. Ed. E. G. Xolodov. Moscow: Iskusstvo, 1977– (in progress).

Istorija russkoj kritiki. 2 vols. Moscow-Leningrad: Izd. Akademija Nauka SSSR, 1958.

Ivanov, Vjačeslav. *Borozdy i meži*. Letchworth, Herts: Bradda Books, 1971.

Kalašnikov, Ju. S. *Estetičeskij ideal K. S. Stanislavskogo*. Moscow: Nauka, 1965.

Kommissarževskij, Fëdor. *Teatral'nye preljudii*. Moscow: n.p., 1916.

Kugel', A. P. *Utverždenie teatra*. Petersburg: Teatr i iskusstvo, [1923].

Lapkina, G. A. *Istorija russkoj teatral'noj kritiki*. Part 1. Leningrad: Ministerstvo kul'tury RSFSR, 1975.

———, and N. V. Koroleva. *Istorija russkoj teatral'noj kritiki*. Part 2. Leningrad: Ministerstvo kul'tury RSFSR, 1976.

Litvinenko, N. *Puškin i teatr: Formirovanie teatral'nyx vozzrenij*. Moscow: Iskusstvo, 1974.

Lunačarskij, A. V., and P. I. Lebedev-Poljanskij, eds. *Očerki po istorii russkoj kritiki*. 2 vols. Moscow-Leningrad: Gos. izd. xudožestvennoj literatury, 1931.

Mejerxol'd, V. E. *Stat'i, reči, pis'ma, besedy*. 2 vols. Moscow: Iskusstvo, 1968.

———. *Perepiska 1896–1939*. Moscow: Iskusstvo, 1976.

Nikolaev, N. I. *Efemeridy. Stat'i po voprosam iskusstva, teatra i literatury, kritičeskie etjudy, literaturnye očerki, nabroski, vpečatlenija*. Kiev: Izd. Kievskago obščestva iskusstva i literatury, 1912.

Puškin i teatr. Dramatičeskie proizvedenija, stat'i, zametki, dnevniki, pis'ma. Ed. B. P. Gorodeckij. Moscow: Iskusstvo, 1953.

Red'ko, A. E. *Teatr i evoljucija teatral'nyx form*. Leningrad: Izd. M. i S.

Sabašnikovyx, 1926. Reprint ed. Letchworth, Herts: Prideaux Press, 1977.

Remizov, Aleksej. "Tovariščestvo novoj dramy," *Vesy*, 4 (April 1904): 36–39.

Rodina, T. M. *Aleksandr Blok i russkij teatr načala XX veka.* Moscow: Nauka, 1972.

Russkaja teatral'naja parodija XIX–načala XX veka. Ed. M. Ja. Poljakov. Moscow: Iskusstvo, 1976.

Šax-Azizova, Tatjana. *Čexov i zapadno-evropejskaja drama ego vremeni.* Moscow: Nauka, 1966.

Sobolev, P. "Kategorija tragičeskogo v russkoj estetike 1800–1840-x godov," *Teatr i dramaturgija. Trudy Leningradskogo gosudarstvennogo instituta teatra, muzyki i kinematografii.* Part 3 (1971): 14–58.

"Teatr," kniga o novom teatre. Sbornik statej A. Lunačarskogo, E. Aničkova, A. Gornfel'da, Aleksandra Benua, Vs. Mejerxol'da, Fëdora Sologuba, Georgija Čulkova, S. Rafaloviča, Valerija Brjusova i Andreja Belogo. St. Petersburg: Šipovnik, 1908.

Turgenev i teatr. Ed. G. P. Berdnikov. Moscow: Iskusstvo, 1953.

Vsevolodskij (Gerngross), V. *Istorija russkogo teatra v dvux tomax.* Ed. A. V. Lunačarskij. Leningrad-Moscow: Tea-kino-pečat', 1929.

Znosko-Borovskij, E. A. *Russkij teatr načala XX veka.* Prague: Plamja, 1925.

II. IN ENGLISH

Dobrolyubov, N. A. *Selected Philosophical Essays,* tr. J. Fineberg. Moscow: Foreign Languages Publishing House, 1948.

Donchin, Georgette. *The Influence of French Symbolism on Russian Poetry.* The Hague: Mouton, 1958.

Evreinov, Nikolay. *The Theatre in Life.* New York: Brentano, 1926.

Gerould, Daniel C. "Andrei Bely: Russian Symbolist," *Performing Arts Journal*, III, 2 (Fall 1978): 25–29.

———. "Valerii Briusov: Russian Symbolist," *Performing Arts Journal*, III, 3 (Winter 1979): 85–99.

Gibian, George. *Tolstoj and Shakespeare.* The Hague: Mouton, 1957.

Ivanov, Vyacheslav. "The Theatre of the Future," tr. Stephen Graham, *English Review*, X (March 1912): 634–650.

Janecek, Gerald, ed. *Andrey Bely, a Critical Review.* Lexington: University Press of Kentucky, 1978.

Malnick, Bertha. "The Theory and Practice of Russian Drama in the Early 19th Century," *Slavonic Review*, XXXIV, 82 (December 1955): 10–33.

Matlaw, Ralph, ed. *Belinsky, Chernyshevsky and Dobrolyubov: Selected Criticism.* New York: E. P. Dutton, 1962.

Meyerhold, V. E. *Meyerhold on Theatre.* Tr. and ed. Edward Braun. London: Methuen, 1968.

Proffer, Carl, ed. *The Critical Prose of Alexander Pushkin.* Bloomington: Indiana University Press, 1969.

Rosenthal, Bernice Glatzer. "Theatre as Church: The Vision of the Mystical Anarchists," *Russian History*, IV, 2 (1977): 122–141.
————. "The Transmutation of the Symbolist Ethos: Mystical Anarchism and the Revolution of 1905," *Slavic Review*, XXXVI, 4 (December 1977): 608–627.
Senelick, Laurence. "Chekhov's Drama, Maeterlinck and the Russian Symbolists," in *Chekhov's Great Plays*, ed. J.-P. Barricelli. New York: New York University Press, 1981.
Stacy, R. H. *Russian Literary Criticism, A Short History.* Syracuse, N.Y.: Syracuse University Press, 1974.
Terras, Victor. *Belinskij and Russian Literary Criticism. The Heritage of Organic Aesthetics.* Madison: University of Wisconsin Press, 1974.
Tolstoy, Leo. *What Is Art?* Tr. Aylmer Maude. London: Walter Scott, n.d.
Wellek, René. *A History of Modern Criticism: 1750–1950.* New Haven: Yale University Press, 1955–1965.
West, James. *Russian Symbolism: A Study of Vyacheslav Ivanov and the Russian Symbolist Aesthetic.* London: Methuen, 1970.
Woehrlin, William. *Chernyshevsky.* Cambridge, Mass.: Harvard University Press, 1971.
Wolff, Tatiana A., tr. and ed. *Pushkin on Literature.* London: Methuen, 1971.
Woodward, J. B. "From Brjusov to Ajkhenval'd: Attitudes to the Russian Theatre 1902–1914," *Canadian Slavonic Papers*, VII (1965): 173–188.

General Index

Index of Fictional and Mythological Characters

H1